ROAMING THROUGH SEDUCTIVE GARDENS

VERHANDELINGEN
VAN HET KONINKLIJK INSTITUUT
VOOR TAAL-, LAND- EN VOLKENKUNDE

167

G.L. KOSTER

ROAMING THROUGH SEDUCTIVE GARDENS

READINGS IN MALAY NARRATIVE

1997
KITLV Press
Leiden

Published by:
KITLV Press
Koninklijk Instituut voor Taal-, Land- en Volkenkunde
(Royal Institute of Linguistics and Anthropology)
P.O. Box 9515
2300 RA Leiden
The Netherlands

Cover: Youetta de Jager and Rita DeCoursey
ISBN 90 6718 084 X

© 1997 Koninklijk Instituut voor Taal-, Land- en Volkenkunde

No part of this publication may be reproduced or transmitted in any form or by any means, electronic or mechanical, including photocopy, recording, or any information storage and retrieval system, without permission from the copyright owner.

Printed in the Netherlands

Contents

Preface		vii
Introduction		1

Part 1 Conventions of Malay narrative

I A medicine of sweetmeats; On the modes of reception of Malay narrative 15

   1 The Malay state and its oral-aural mode of communication 15
   2 A predominantly profitable narrative: the Sejarah Melayu 23
   3 A predominantly soothing narrative: the Syair Ken Tambuhan 29

II Variation within identity; Formulaic devices for the construction of narrative 35

   1 The principle of variation within identity and the Syair Ken Tambuhan 35
   2 The verse form syair 36
   3 Formulaic devices for the construction of narrative in the SKT 43
   4 A sung performance of the SKT 48

III Dalang or dagang; Narrator, authority and poetics 53

   1 Narratorial roles 53
   2 The narrator as dalang 55
   3 The narrator in the role of dagang 64
   4 Commemoration and the Idea of the Book 76
   5 The place of fiction within the Books of Malay culture 86

Part 2 Readings in heroic epic, Panji romance and parodies

IV The Kerajaan at war; The Syair Perang Mengkasar as heroic epic 97

   1 Genre as a tool for interpretation 97
   2 The SPMR as a heroic epic 105
   3 The heroic epic and modern historiography 122

Contents

V   Lest we become indifferent; Commemoration in the Syair
    Perang Siak   127
    1 Narrativity, legality and the SPS 127
    2 Comedies of memory 131
    3 Dramas of forgetfulness 137
    4 A revenge tragedy 141
    5 A tragedy of divine nemesis 146
    6 A Divina Commedia 149
    7 Mediation and tragedy 152

VI A signifier-errant in exile; The Syair Ken Tambuhan as a
    Panji romance   161
    1 The Syair Ken Tambuhan and the study of the Panji romance 161
    2 The SKT as a marriage story 166
    3 Exile and return, signification and interpretation: the SKT as
       a romance 173
    4 Divine couples: another plot of exile and return? 183
    5 Mediation as the function of the Panji romance 190
    6 The SKT and the generic plot of the Panji romance 194

VII A fishy story; Exercises in reading the Syair Ikan Terubuk   199
    1 Scholarly lore about the SIT and intertextuality 199
    2 Confirmations and frustrations: heroic epic or romance? 202
    3 Historiography and other intertexts of reality 208

VIII The soothing works of the seducer and their dubious fruits;
     Interpreting the Sair Buah-Buahan   217
    1 Muhammad Bakir and his Sair Buah-Buahan 217
    2 A didactic fruit-fable 224
    3 A referential reading 226
    4 Parodied romance 227
    5 Reading from the Book of the Devil 235
    6 The seductive garden of literature 239
    7 Irony, writing, Origin and authority 241

Bibliography   253
Index   267

Preface

In the making of this book a number of people and institutions have played a role. First and foremost are my parents, who have always given me their full support, financial and otherwise, even though the path of my development as a pupil in school and later as a scholar must often have seemed to them to be a tortuous and erratic one. I hope this book may make up for some of the patience they have shown towards me. I hereby thank them for everything.

I also wish to thank the Programme of Indonesian Studies (PRIS) for granting me ample research time. Without the amount of research time given to me I would not have had the advantage of sufficient leisure to sit back and think, so that my ideas could ripen. If the decision of the Dutch government to abolish the PRIS is not followed by the creation of a new programme for cooperation in Indonesian Studies, Dutch scholarship in this field, in which the Netherlands have traditionally excelled, will certainly lose an important source of support.

As the teacher who initiated me into traditional Malay literature and taught me how to enjoy it I owe an immeasurable debt to Muhammad Bakir, owner of a manuscript lending library in Batavia at the end of the 19th century. It was with his *Sair Buah-Buahan* (Poem of the Fruits) that he taught me the fundamentals of Malay poetics and provided me with ideas for how I could emplot my study.

If the English in this book has any quality, it is in a large measure due to Rosemary Robson-McKillop. She not only frequently succeeded in helping me to expressions from literary English that could convey some of the beauty of the Malay texts, but also acted as an insightful and critical reader, who did not spare the rod when necessary.

I wish to thank the staff of the library of the Koninklijk Instituut voor Taal-, Land- en Volkenkunde and the staff of the Section Oriental Manuscripts of the Leiden University Library for the efficient and kind assistance they have always provided. Hopefully this book will not remain my only one, so that I may again profit from their services.

Writing this book has proved to be a lonely job. The confrontation with my own self and the daunting task of transcending my own doubts and weaknesses did at times drive me to despair. I owe it to a small circle of friends that I did not give up. Of these friends I can here only mention one person, Kuniko Ukai.

For more than a year she cooked my meals, so that I could devote all my time to writing, and took in her stride the often grumpy mood in which I attended dinner. More importantly, she provided me with insightful criticism of my writings, talked courage into me at moments of self-doubt, and took me to concerts to help me forget things for a while and relax. I am sure that later, when I look back on this period, I will feel the same nostalgia once expressed in a *tanka* by the Buddhist Priest Saigyo (1118-1190) (*Shinkokinshu* 1676):

> Shigeki no o iku hitomura ni wakenashite
> sara ni mukashi o shinobikaesamu.

Introduction

> *Uns verwirrt es, die wir seiend heißen*
> *immer so zu leben: nur von Bildern;*
> *und wir möchten manchesmal mit wildern*
> *Griffen Wirklichkeiten in uns reißen, Stücke,*
> *Abzufühlendes, ein Sein.*
> Rainer Maria Rilke
> August 1907

'Malay literature is dead, faded away, since the glory of the Malay kingdoms has been eclipsed' (Die malaiische Literatur ist tot, dahingewelkt seit der Glanz der malaiischen Reiche verging). In 1925, when the German Malayist Hans Overbeck spoke this lapidary obituary, there were good reasons – at least for an observer in a colonial city such as Singapore – to consider the Malay textual heritage a thing of the past, dead and gone, without relevance for the ongoing discussion that was shaping Malay culture. What was taking place in the urban centres in Overbeck's day was the transmutation of traditional Malay oral-aural culture into a modern print-culture (Sweeney 1987:34).

Attracted by the cheap, easily readable printed and lithographed books and impressed by the challenging new Islamic and European forms of knowledge they contained, the Malays in the urban centres became increasingly critical of the knowledge offered by the stories of oral storytellers and the manuscripts.

Experiencing their oral-aural formulaic style as a hindrance to the new modes of thinking, they stopped visiting the oral performances and laid aside the manuscripts. The spoken word and the manuscript, excluded from contributing to Malay culture, began to lose their authority (Maier 1988:101-28).

If they were not simply left to moulder and decay in the tropical climate, the manuscripts with their tales, which had once provided amusement or guidance to Malay audiences, ended up in the museums of the colonial rulers as objects of scholarly curiosity rather than living components of culture. Those of their stories which fared worst were thenceforth only accessible in the desiccated and mummified form of summaries in manuscript catalogues. The luckier ones were published in school editions, abridged and shorn as much as possible of formulaic repetitions. Only few were deemed to merit a complete scholarly edition. Fewer still were considered to bear translating.

Those texts that were published generated little enthusiasm among their readers. The Malay intellectuals, who had only recently stepped out of their oral-aural tradition and were now only interested in Western and Islamic literate forms of knowledge, found them still too close to that against which they had reacted. European readers, who had never tried to become insiders, found them too far removed from their own textual experiences to take more than an academic interest in them.

Separated from its potential readers by an ever more formidable barrier of historical and cultural distance, the Malay textual tradition became increasingly inaccessible, as the oral-aural experience and the network of rules which had implicitly or explicitly circumscribed and prescribed its production and reception sank more and more into oblivion. For the educated Malays their textual tradition was indeed to all practical purposes dead.

Since Overbeck spoke his obituary the Malay textual tradition has by and large remained what he declared it to be: a corpus of texts without an interested public, dead because no efforts are made to enter into a dialogue with it. As is the case with, for instance, Middle Dutch literature in the Netherlands – another relic from a defunct oral-aural manuscript culture – for the modern Malaysian or Indonesian to read its texts is either a chore performed in the name of academic learning, or it is a duty performed as part of the obligatory school curriculum. In spite of all efforts, both in Malaysia and Indonesia, as part of their respective cultural policies, to try and recycle the Malay textual heritage into their modern cultures by making an ever increasing number of its texts available in easily readable and cheap transcribed editions, a genuinely interested readership has thus far failed to develop (Sulastin 1986:126-7).

In this book a sustained effort is made to show how one may fruitfully enter into a dialogue with the Malay textual heritage, notably with that part of it that consists of narrative, so that its texts may shake off the torpor of their long deathlike sleep and may awaken to a new lease of life and a new relevance, radiant once again with their own peculiar beauty. The central part of this book therefore consists of a series of readings of narrative works, which may hopefully be instructive for other readers in their attempts to come to terms with Malay stories.

A dialogue implies the sharing of a common system of rules regulating our utterances and understanding. Therefore in Part II of this book, preceding the readings, a systematic description is given of the system of conventions that may be usefully presupposed as having once governed the production of meaning in Malay narrative (Culler 1981:100-18). It is hoped that this presentation will help the readers of this book to follow the way the dialogue is carried on in the readings.

Dialogue is a matter of give and take. Although dialogic communication requires us to use a certain amount of commonly understood language, it necessarily also entails the use of terms that are entirely our own. In fact, there can be no dialogue where only the voice of the other is heard. The language in which this book speaks with and about Malay narratives is therefore ineluctably a hybrid form, in which now the voice of the one discussant, now that of the other may be heard to speak loudest (Bakhtin in Todorov 1984:104-12).

For a model showing how one may define the field of Malay narrativity in terms of the conventions that may once have regulated the production of meaning within it, this book owes a great debt to an article on the system of narrative genres of the German High Middle Ages by Jauss (1977). In this article Jauss makes use of four coordinates to circumscribe the field of narrativity: 1. the mode of narration, that is, the way a narrator manifests himself in the act of story-telling; 2. the formal mode of representation, that is, the devices used for the construction of the story; 3. the contentual mode of representation, that is, the type of plot, type of protagonist and sort of universe represented; and, finally, 4. the mode of reception and social function (Jauss 1977:114-8).

Adapting the model of Jauss, in this book the description of the general conventions of Malay narrative has conveniently been ordered according to the following three points of view: 1. Mode of reception (Chapter I); 2. Mode of formal representation (Chapter II); 3. Mode of narration (Chapter III).

The discussion of the contentual mode of representation – the type of plot imposed on the narrative, the type of protagonist and type of universe represented – is postponed to the readings, where the different genres of narrative are characterized.

In Chapter I it is shown that in Malay oral-aural culture stories were expected to be either predominantly 'profitable' or principally 'soothing'. 'Profitable' stories were those which were felt to be concerned directly with upholding the Malay religious, political or social order. Stories were considered primarily 'soothing' if they were above all enjoyed for their beauty, rhetorical power and fantasy, which afforded momentary relief from the unpleasant realities of life. As an example of 'profitable' narrative a passage from the *Sejarah Melayu* (Genealogy of the Malay Rulers) is discussed. As examples of 'soothing' narrative some passages from the Panji romance *Syair Ken Tambuhan* (Poem of Lady-in-Waiting Tambuhan) are analysed.

In Chapter II the use of formulaic elements for the construction of narrative is examined in the *Syair Ken Tambuhan*. A distinction is made between verbatim repetitions (formulae), varied repetitions (formulaic expressions) and stock patterns of action and schemes for ornamental description (type-scenes). These units are shown to be used in a perpetual process of variation within identity. The principle of variation within identity is also shown to operate in the prosody of the verse form *syair*, of which a characterization is given. Finally, the sung performance of *syair* is discussed on the basis of a recording of a singing of part of the *Syair Ken Tambuhan*.

All narrative presupposes a story-teller. Matching the distinction between primarily 'soothing' and predominantly 'profitable' narrative, in Chapter III two types of narratorial roles are discerned, that are respectively dubbed *dalang* (puppeteer) and *dagang* (stranger/trader far from home) after the terms they most often use in self-characterization. The *dalang* appears in the epic *wayang*-stories and the Panji romances, whereas the sphere of the *dagang* is less clearly limited to a literary genre. Whereas the *dalang* is an embodiment of the force of orality, the *dagang* is a manifestation of that of literacy.

In different ways both narrators are expression of the commemorative nature of Malay poetics in that they are both agreed that for man in all his acts, reading and writing included, wisdom and divine guidance are indispensable. The *dagang* is a figure associated with remembrance of God and edification. Within the perspective of Islam the *dalang* as commemorator of a fallen religious order has come to be viewed as merely the purveyor of soothing, seductive beauty, and is associated with forgetfulness and illusions.

It is shown that the two conflicting forces of orality and literacy are pressed into coherence by what may be called the Idea of the Book: the notion that all production of meaning, if it is to be valid, must emphatically claim to point back to and to have been authorized by an already codified, unassailable truth or Origin. Consequently Malay poetics is one of repetition, recall, representation and copying. Finally it is shown that the place of fiction within the Books of Malay culture is a problematic one, because there is a strong tendency to equate it with feigned representation, with lying.

In all Malay narrative, no matter whether it is of the fictional or of the factual kind, there is a tension between the demand for the recall of what is and must be (*mengingat*) and the desire to give in to forgetfulness and dreams of how one would like things to be (*mengenangkan*), between representation of the proper (*mematutkan*) and giving in to the pleasures of amplification (*memanjangkan*). If a narrative is not seen to properly represent the culturally accepted orders (*mengadakan*) it is prone to come under the suspicion that it merely mimics truth (*mengada-ada*) or leads away from it by its improprieties, fantasies and illusions. What connects the readings offered in Part 2 of this book is that in each text the conflict between the law and desire, recall and forgetfulness, representation and illusion is shown to be fought out in a different way, with the use of patterns of plot, such as those of comedy, romance and tragedy (Frye 1973, 1976).

Within the traditional Malay textual system there was a certain scope for forgetfulness, play and criticism. Even parody and stable forms of irony, persiflage and satire had their place in it as devices serving to point out the dynamic side of myth and preserve order from becoming rigid. But all disturbance or suspension of the mythical order by improprieties, by disjunctions between signifier and signified, were to be only temporary; in the end the order of the Books of Malay culture had to be reaffirmed.

Malay textuality was traditional so long as it remained tied to the repetition and confirmation of Origin and so long as the encyclopaedia of oral tradition and Islamic codified knowledge reigned over it alone and unchallenged. Change came in the last quarter of the nineteenth century, concomitant with the disintegration of the political order of the Malay *kerajaan* and the intrusion of new forms of knowledge, rivalling the old.

To question the authority of the Books is to challenge the priority of speech over writing, presence over absence, the Origin over that which merely repeats, reduplicates or inscribes the Origin. It also means to question the idea of a proper good writing – a stable permanent message – the meaning of which can be contained within bounds by the presence and intention of an author, unaffected by the aesthetic play of variation, amplification and stylistic ornament. Where it is permanently questioned, it entails a destabilization of signification, in which the authority for making sense is located not in the pages of the past, but in the hands of the reader.

Where the Idea of the Book is challenged, the notion that writing and reading are a matter of commemorating, reproducing, or copying is displaced by another notion which no longer validates meaning in an old book, a hallowed sequence of events or the voice of the speaker. A movement occurs from mirror to method: away from the reproduction of meaning by imitation to its production by interpretation (Gellrich 1985:224-7). It is this movement which is traced in the course of the readings in Part 2 of this book.

These readings are concerned with the two central and mutually complementary (Boon 1977:6-7) genres of narrative of the traditional Malay textual system, namely the heroic epic and the Panji romance, and with parodies of these two genres. The texts selected for interpretation are all written in the verse form *syair*. The advantage of *syair* is that they tend to have a covert narrator, whose comments provide useful clues.

As is shown in Chapters IV and V, the heroic epic is pre-eminently a discourse of the *patut*, as direct as possible a commemoration and confirmation of the order of the authoritative Books of Malay culture. Characteristically the heroic epic has a *dagang* as narrator. Its typical plot – its hallowed sequence of events – is that of comedy: it has to tell a success story about the courage of fighters for a just cause duly rewarded. As is argued in Chapter IV, its central motivation is provided by the heroic oath (*cakap*) sworn by both warring parties: the words of courage to be uttered by loyal vassals in the presence of their lord.

These oaths were a cornerstone of the *kerajaan* order. By uttering them one was honour-bound to perform what one had sworn to do, as much as if one had signed a written contract. The implicit assumption is that the validity of their meaning is guarantied by the voice of the speaker. They are an invocation, a formulaic recall, of noble origin and thus of identity, an effort at representation (*mengadakan*). A lasting disjunction between oath and action, signifier and signified was unacceptable; where it occurred it had to be set right in one way or another by poetic justice: the narrative punishment of cowards and traitors. The *kerajaan* order had to be maintained.

In such a mode of discourse a narrative ending in defeat forms a major problem; it amounts to a defeat of memory in the war against oblivion. The *Syair Perang Mengkasar* (Poem of the Macassar War), treating the war between Macassar and the VOC fought from December 1666 to July 1669, largely limits its efforts to solve this problem to obstinately trying to ignore it. Almost to the end it sticks as much as possible to an account of a 'frischer, fröhlicher Krieg' (a vigorous, merry war).

The problem of telling a heroic epic ending in defeat is solved in a rhetorically much more effective way by the *Syair Perang Siak* (Poem of the Siak War, SPS) (Chapter V). The poem tells of the war fought in 1761 by Raja Alam, in alliance with the Dutch, against his nephew, Sultan Ismail of Siak, and ends with the latter's defeat and flight into exile. The poem was written – presumably in the last quarter of the 18th century – as a last-ditch attempt to bring about a reconciliation between the descendants in the two rival lines of Raja Alam and Raja Muhammad, lines who had opposed each other in the Siak War.

A reading of the SPS against the foil of inimical Malay and Dutch works of historiography makes clear that one reason why the *syair* must indeed have succeeded as a narrative of reconciliation is that it adroitly selects what it commemorates in order to keep all the skeletons of the dynasty's history in the family closet. The representation of improprieties transgressing the Book of the Malay *Kerajaan* Order is avoided as much as possible; decorum is deftly maintained.

But no amount of selection can transform defeat into victory and for this problem the *syair* has to offer another solution, which it finds in a clever juggling with plots. Against the failing plot of comedy in the heroic epic – the central story of the SPS – it pits the plot of tragedy and thus exonerates Ismail for his defeat. This tragedy is prepared for in the course of the long genealogical chronicle with which the SPS begins. To fall low one must first rise high. The genealogical chronicle first tells – in the form of a comedy, a story of ambitions effectively realized – of the glorious rise of the dynasty of Siak under its founder, Raja Kecik. It then dwells extensively on the stories of the tragic strife that broke out between his sons, Raja Alam and Raja Muhammad, a strife which ended in Alam being humiliatingly ousted by Ismail's father Muhammad.

On one level this tragedy may be seen as a revenge-tragedy: Ismail is shown as the innocent victim of another law from the Book of the Malay *Kerajaan* Order which contradicts that of family loyalty. This law is the rule of *talio*, that had descended upon him because his late father, Muhammad, had disgraced his uncle by ousting him from Siak. In this way the narrative does much to restore the *kerajaan* order. Yet the question of the impropriety of representing brother fighting brother and of Raja Kecik not doing very much to patch up their quarrel still remains.

These problems may be seen to be solved on another level of reading, which sees the tragedy as an Epiphany of yet another Law, one from the Book of God's Writing. This higher law is God's Will, overruling all human ambitions, the Book of the Malay *Kerajaan* Order included. It overturns and exiles great rulers and thwarts all their earthly ambitions to remind them of their human lot as powerless *dagang* in exile in this transitory world.

If one reads a work as tragedy, one does not stop at reading it as a cautionary tale, reminding weak and powerless man of the powers-that-be. It also means allowing oneself to feel torn between two conflicting attitudes: to affirm the law or to give in to one's desires; to accept the inevitable reality of catastrophe or to dream away in the vision of a lost paradise; to be resigned or to protest. Then there is not just the certainty of the Epiphany of law, there is also the doubt and the questioning. There is always the urge to interpret: what have we done wrong to deserve this fate?

This attitude is exemplified by the *dagang*-narrator of the SPS, who fluctuates between two forms of commemoration: *mengingat* (to mind, be heedful) and *mengenangkan* (to dwell on something in a mood of elegy or nostalgia). Here, and in its setting off of one plot against another, the SPS can be seen to solve its problems by mediation, a highly unusual procedure in the heroic epic.

Within the order of the Books, tragedy, too, is ultimately inadmissible as improper. Tragedy leaves us, like the sad *dagang*, gaping in a world of traces, which we must try to decipher; lost in exile among the opaque signifiers, unable to regress beyond their inertness to signified Truth. From the confirmation of the order of the Books, tragedy leads to its disintegration in uncertain interpretation.

In an effort to restore mimesis, confirm the order of the Book of God's Writing and escape from uncertain interpretation, the narrator ends his narrative in prayer, suggesting that the story of the Siak War, instead of being a tragedy, was really a Divine Comedy – the successful working of God's Will in the world – for which man must render thanks unto Him. The SPS, thus, only just manages to reconfirm the traditional order.

Whereas mediation is a highly unusual phenomenon in the heroic epic, it is an essential characteristic of the Panji romance. In Chapter VI in a reading of the *Syair Ken Tambuhan* as a marriage story it is shown that this story of the love between Raden Inu and Lady-In-Waiting Tambuhan mediates between the demands of individual happiness vs the laws of social hierarchy; sexual desire vs social obligation; love for love's sake vs love for the sake of status, power and property. On the one hand the aristocratic model of marriage is asserted and the belief is endorsed that worth and birth are synonymous. On the other it is suggested that, although a commoner, one may perhaps marry into the aristocracy after all, provided one can prove one's worth.

On a deeper level the poem is read as a drama of signification, that is patterned on the generic plot of all romance. This plot mediates between remembrance and forgetfulness, the law and desire, identity and interpretation. The main protagonist is temporarily exiled from a state of clear fixed identity, which is a matter of commemoration by formulaic repetition, into a state of alienation, forgetfulness and opacity. Origin, royal identity and the Book of the Malay *Kerajaan* Order are temporarily suspended, forgotten, as the *dalang* – typically the type of narrator prescribed for romance – spins out a narrative fraught with uncertain meaning and desire.

From a sign properly coinciding with meaning the main protagonist by a change in fortune and loss of memory is turned into a signifier-errant, whose meaning has been set adrift and is a matter for interpretation and conjecture. Thus proper (*mematut*) representation (*mengadakan*) is temporarily disrupted by a proliferation of meaning (*memanjangkan*) in a play of semblance (*mengada-ada*) and reality (*mengadakan*). The main protagonist connects these two orders of signification by making a circular movement of exile and return.

After a temporary carnivalesque suspension of the serious monological Voice of Accepted Truth the poem restores the identity of the main protagonist and returns to the proper order prescribed by the Book of the Malay *Kerajaan* Order. Thus the poem both confirms and denies the feasibility of invoking and commemorating noble origin and both confirms and denies the power of language to represent, another instance of its mediatory character.

The *kerajaan* order seems to be lastingly disturbed in the *Syair Ikan Terubuk* (Poem of the Terubuk-fish), of which I offer a reading in Chapter VII). This *syair* may well have been written in the second quarter or the middle of the 19th century. Its story is told by a *dagang*, a sign that it is to remain within the Books of Malay tradition. The poem, which parodies the genres of the heroic epic and the Panji romance, may be primarily regarded as a questioning of the Book of the Malay *Kerajaan* Order as it is expressed in the heroic epic.

In my reading of the *Syair Ikan Terubuk* a prominent thread is to see it as a comical satire on the Siak War of 1761 between Raja Alam and Sultan Ismail. This satire is dressed in the guise of an animal-fable with fishes as protagonists: the story of the unrequited love of Prince Terubuk (Prince Shad) for Princess Puyu-Puyu (Princess Climbing Perch) and his unsuccessful efforts to make her his by military might. An important manifestation of its satirical purport is the incongruous, parodical description of the heroic oaths sworn by both parties.

In the *syair* the disjunction between these oaths and their meaning is thematized in a narrative which conspicuously parodies the heroic epic. Almost to the exclusion of all other action its text is almost entirely taken up by two disproportionally protracted councils of war, the first called by Prince Terubuk and the second by Princess Puyu-Puyu. In these councils, continually disturbed by incongruous references to motifs taken from romance, one fish after another declares his willingness to offer battle. However, the story fails to implement the pattern of the success story – a story about rewarded heroic courage – but ends in an utter anti-climax: not a single blow is struck.

The warning of the Sebahan-fish to Princess Puyu-Puyu not to believe the oaths of her courtiers because *sekaliannya cakap tiada berguna* (all their oaths have no use) and *sekaliannya itu mengada-ada* (all just pretend) are proven true. At first sight poetic justice seems to have its way: the perjurious fish-heroes, and with them the historical figures for whom they stand, are ridiculed. The disjunctions and improprieties seem to have been solved. Ultimately, however, the Book of the Malay *Kerajaan* Order is not reconfirmed, in that no party in the conflict is proved right: comical laughter is aimed at both parties.

Another playful questioning of the Idea of the Book – this time one by parody and the ironic foregrounding of fictionality – which does not resolve the disjunctions between sign and meaning and does not reconfirm the Books of Malay culture, is found in the writings of Muhammad Bakir, who ran a manuscript lending library in Batavia in the late 19th century. His works may be seen both as looking back to traditional Malay literature and as preparing the way for modern Indonesian literature. A case in point is his *Sair Buah-Buahan* (Poem of the Fruits), a chain of stories, the first and longest of which is about fruits falling in love with each other.

As is shown in the reading of this *syair* in Chapter VIII, it is ostensibly a work of subservient fiction – a serious didactic fruit-fable warning the young in *dagang*-style against giving in to one's desires and against reading the romances of the paper-*dalang* because these come from the Book of the Devil. On closer reading, however, it unfolds a playful narrative about reading and writing, authority and authorship. This narrative jestingly exceeds the limits of the Books of the Malay tradition without returning within them. Disturbing their mythical sacrality by its humorousness and unresolved improprieties, it asserts the rights of fictional writing.

One way in which the work betrays a non-serious intent is by its persistent parodying of the very genre the narrator ostensibly warns against. The other is that it pits an ironical unreliable writer/narrator (*pengarang*) against the truth-seeking *dagang*. This writer is clearly an avatar of the *dalang*. By the jocular comments of the narrator about the presumed *asal* (origin), *sebab* (cause) and *mula* (beginning) of the narrative and its events, all unquestioning assumptions of Origin and Truth are problematized. As one story follows another as 'proof' of the truth of its predecessor, the question about locating the authority of meaning in an origin or an authoritative text is postponed indefinitely.

The rise to new dignity of the amplifying *dalang* and his rebirth in the transformation of the fictionalizing *pengarang* is signalled when the narrator as the Origin of his story indicates: *Sebab pengarang mau panjangkan* (Because the writer wants to spin out his story). The writer is the Origin of the story and reigns over it like a god: *Dengan takdir orang yang mengarang* (By the will of the person who writes). Ultimately, however, this Origin, too, is spirited away: at the end of the last story in the chain, its hero the Green Beetle – obviously a portrait of the seductive writing author – is nowhere to be found. Authority is ultimately located where autonomous fiction lays it: in the hands of the reader.

> Maka adalah diumpamakan fakir hikayat ini seperti suatu taman, yang amat permai lagi dengan indah-indah perbuatan-nya. Maka adalah dalamnya itu beberapa pohon buah-buahan yang amat lazat citrarasanya dan beberapa bunga-bungaan, yang amat harum baunya. (Abdullah 1919:5.)

> (Now this beggar likens this *hikayat* to a garden which is exceedingly beautiful and has been laid out with great allure. In it there are several trees with fruits which are exceedingly delicious to the taste, and several kinds of flowers, the scents of which are exceedingly fragrant.)

Malay authors occasionally compare their work to a garden. They may do so by means of the title, as we see, for instance, in titles such as *Bustan us-Salatin* (Garden of the Rulers) or *Bustan ul-Katibin* (Garden of the Writers). Another way in which they may do so is by having their narrator make such a comparison in the prologue, as we see in the above example, which has been taken from the prologue of Abdullah ibn Abdulkadir al-Munsyi's *Hikayat Panja Tanderan*.

In both East and West gardens have always been fraught with symbolism. In Malay romance the garden, with its voluptuous princesses bathing in a pool, surrounded by the lush scenery of trees laden with fruit and shrubs full of flowers in bloom, has always been the locus of refreshment, amusement, forgetfulness, soothing one's longing for the beloved and erotic wish-fulfilment.

In Sufi allegory the garden is understood in a spiritual sense, as a tiny microcosmic reflection of the macrocosmic uncreated Heavenly Garden of Paradise mentioned in the Koran (*Jannat al-Naim*, see e.g. Sura 18.107) (Schimmel 1980:82-3). In the microcosmic garden man's longing for the Beloved, the Great Gardener, may temporarily be soothed because the splendours with which He has endowed His created garden, through their veil, grant a fleeting glimpse of His radiant beauty. Thus, in the *Hikayat Gul Bakawali*, that may be read both as a worldly and as a spiritual romance and tells of the quest by a prince for the Rose of Bakawali – significantly a flower that restores the faculty of sight – the narrator draws our attention to his story in the following words:

> Bahwasanya dapatlah hikayat ini dinamakan Taman Penglipur Lara bagi sekalian mereka yang berdendam birahi (Siti Hawa Salleh 1986:1).
>
> (Verily, this *hikayat* may be called the Garden that Soothes all Cares for those who are filled with longing.)

In these examples of the romantic and the spiritual vision of the garden in the Malay textual tradition attention is in different ways drawn to the garden's sensuous beauty, that is, to the garden as a signifier.

What the use of garden imagery shows is that the Malays were very much aware that language is ever an instrument of seduction. It is from a growing awareness of how Malay narratives, as do all texts, try to seduce us, either by their beauty or by the apparent self-explanatoriness of their claims to truth, that this book was born.

The free play of signifiers is understandably feared and mistrusted. It can not be stopped, except by the power of our own will, which in turn is very much determined by the power of the community, the culture and the tradition to which we belong. In the Malay textual tradition this decision to end the play of the signifiers and return to representation is figured as the plucking of the fruits by the wise man, who does not abandon himself to the forgetfulness induced by the sensuous beauty of the garden (Abdullah 1919:6).

This book is a quest for the Flower of Malay narrative, that has long been thought to have forever faded away and died. On its way it roams through many gardens, one even more seductive than the other. No doubt the road that it follows is not always a straight one. Attracted by the lush beauty of fruits and flowers it often goes astray. Whether it succeeds in plucking the Flower of Malay narrative and obtaining a glimpse of beauty and truth, it is for others to say.

PART 1

CONVENTIONS OF MALAY NARRATIVE

CHAPTER I

A medicine of sweetmeats
On the modes of reception of Malay narrative

1. The Malay state and its oral-aural mode of communication

In the 18th century, the coastal areas around the Straits of Malacca and the South China Sea presented the picture of a motley variety of petty states constantly engaged in struggles for power, wealth or survival in ever changing configurations and alliances. In spite of this heterogeneity, however, a unifying bond continued to provide a certain cohesion: Malayness. Similar political notions and concepts, similar customs and rituals, the same religion, Islam, the same language, and the same textual tradition provided the Malays, dispersed over this vast area, with a common identity. Both in this area as a whole as well as in its constituent parts, the *negeri* (kingdoms), it was this Malayness which served as a common bond and permanent cohesive factor.

In this chapter[1] I will focus on one component of the Malay textual tradition, notably narrative texts, to propose a model of the traditional Malay modes of reception of narrative. As I will argue, the Malays expected the stories they listened to to be either predominantly 'profitable (*berfaedah, bermanfaat*)' or principally 'soothing' (*menghiburkan, melipurkan lara*). Those narratives which managed to blend profit with delight, giving instruction by their exemplariness and providing pleasure by their playful rhetoric at the same time, were apt the more readily to win appreciation. In different degrees all stories were exemplary. This exemplariness, I will argue, allowed them to express and confirm the Malay identity and strengthen the cohesion of Malay life and society. The power of the texts is an ambiguous one: they may not only be regarded as providing examples for imitation, but can also – albeit not without risks – be read as reflections of Malay reality.

In contrast to the Malay world as a whole, the *negeri* possessed an extra

---

[1] This chapter is a revised version of Koster and Maier (1985). For a critical reaction by the late G.W.J. Drewes I refer to his short article 'Reality? Or delusion?' (1987). Where this seemed called for I have tried to profit from his remarks.

unifying factor, namely the figure of the *raja* (ruler), who was the apex of its political system. The *raja* lived in an *istana* (palace). This was a spacious wooden dwelling on piles that was surrounded by a fenced compound in which a number of other buildings – housing members of the royal household, its entourage and its servants – were erected. The royal compound used to be situated near the estuary of some river. It formed the centre of a cluster of a few hundred huts and houses, with an occasional mosque and prayer house, where lived the *rakyat*: traders, artisans and other commoners.

The palace compound – and in particular the *balai* (audience hall) – was the focus of public life. Here affairs of state were discussed and settled, and here ceremonies affecting the life of the *negeri* were enacted. In the *balai*, on a dais, stood the royal throne, draped in yellow cloth, on which the *yang dipertuan* ('he who is acknowledged as lord'), as the linchpin of the *negeri*, would be seated while performing his ceremonial functions. There, in impassive majesty, he would give audience, surrounded by servants holding the regalia: the royal lance, the sword of state, the silver *sirih* box and other sacred heirlooms of the dynasty. Also on the dais, to the left and to the right, the ruler's dignitaries of state would be seated, in an order carefully graded according to each grandee's position in the court hierarchy. These audiences took place according to strict rules prescribing proper behaviour and fitting speech, and for good reasons: these conventions and rules of decorum were vital in formally preserving the power of the *raja* and the cohesion of the *negeri*.

The Malay state was not a political unit in the modern sense – based on abstract legal principles, circumscribed by well-defined territorial boundaries and supported by the mechanism of a bureaucratic apparatus. The cohesion of the *negeri* was a matter of subtle diplomacy and of networks of personal relations. The essential precondition of power, both for the ruler at the centre and for the district officials in the outlying regions of the *negeri* upstream, was personal loyalty. The commoner was expected to be loyal to his local chief, the local chief was bound by loyalty to the person of the ruler. The unity of the *negeri* was founded on the mutual self-interest of the ruler and the ruled. The ruler bestowed honour, prestige and power on his district officers and dignitaries. Conversely the ruler was paid tribute and homage and was even – at least in theory – attributed divine power (*daulat*). In practice the ruler was very much a primus inter pares: he performed the same role as the local chief in that, by his justice and munificence (*adil dan murah*), he, too, provided his direct subjects, the *rakyat* who lived in the immediate vicinity of the royal compound, with the necessary income, protection and focus of loyalty.

Seated in his estuary like a spider in its web, the ruler was motivated by a twofold concern. On the one hand he had to maintain sufficient control over his district officials in the interior to be sure of continuing to receive his share, in the form of taxes or goods, of the products from the interior. On the other hand, he had to see to it that he received his share of the profit from the foreign trade passing the river mouth either on its way to the interior or in transit. Only thus could he increase his wealth and secure the basis of his power and his position as the linchpin of the *negeri*.

The district official acted as the focus of loyalty at the local level. Functioning as a petty ruler in his own area, he derived his power in an important measure from his ability to secure a share in the taxes or produce supplied by the local population which he was appointed by the *raja* to rule. In return for these goods and taxes he was expected to afford the population in his district the necessary income and protection. In return for his appointment he would pay the ruler the necessary tribute and homage and provide him with soldiers in times of war, while leaving foreign affairs to him.

It will be obvious that the balance of power within the *negeri* was a delicate one: it called for the constant diplomatic manoeuvering by both the *raja* and the district officials, as well as the regular ceremonial confirmation of established ties of loyalty. The prime locus of such confirmation were the ceremonies performed during the audiences in the ruler's hall. On specific occasions the district officials would come to the centre and present tribute and pay homage to the ruler. In return the *raja* would bestow symbolic gifts of clothes (*persalinan*) and titles (*gelar*) on them. In this way, on the one hand, their prestige was strengthened, enabling them to act more successfully as patron in the interior. And, on the other hand, their loyalty to the centre was confirmed, enabling the ruler to play his role better.[2]

In the *negeri*, comprising as it did a cluster of small political units each based on personal loyalties, a developed bureaucracy was not necessary. Usually problems were solved through personal contact with the authority concerned, whether this was the district chief or the *raja* himself and his direct representatives, the ministers of state (*menteri*). Reading and writing were skills mastered by only a small number of people in the *negeri*.

Scattered over the area, occasionally in the service of some nobleman or the ruler, were the Muslim dignitaries who dedicated themselves to the painstaking study, transmission and exegesis of religious tracts and treatises

---

[2] It should be noted that I have only given a typical sketch of the Malay body politic, without going into the many differences of detail that might on closer inspection be indicated between the states of the Malay world. The best description of Malay political institutions is still provided by Gullick (1958). In Reid and Castles (1975:1-43) the nature and concept of the state in 17th and 19th century Johor, 18th century Perak and 18th and 19th century Kedah are discussed by Leonard Andaya, Virginia Matheson, Barbara Watson Andaya and Dianne Lewis. Milner (1982) has greatly stressed – and in my view overstressed – the pivotal importance of the figure of the *raja*. For a critical review of Milner (1982), see Gullick (1982).

and of the Koran, the main spring of literacy. These people were held in high esteem as moral teachers and formed a small circle of initiates. In addition there were the clerks at the court, frequently foreigners who enjoyed the confidence of the ruler. They would compose or copy religious works, works on the history of the state or works for entertainment, as well as writing letters on the ruler's behalf. Sometimes noblemen or rulers, too, were active literati and would try their hand at writing literary works. But this was the exception rather than the rule. Both within the *negeri* as well as at the court communication was predominantly oral-aural.[3]

Naturally, in an oral-aural culture like that of the Malays, a high premium was placed not only on behaving in a gentle, restrained, oblique and diplomatic manner, upholding the codes of proper conduct, but also on displaying verbal and rhetorical skill. On official occasions the courtier had to have a sufficient mastery of suitable sayings and appropriate parables, examples and comparisons (*kias dan ibarat*), in order to be able to please his audience and plead his case successfully, or extricate himself from a knotty situation by witty repartee.

The same rhetorical skill and playfulness were also valued highly on other occasions, by courtiers and commoners alike. People in all walks of life would try to outdo each other. For these verbal battles they needed a large variety of weapons. In love the young man had to be able to improvise gentle and coaxing addresses and croon sweet love-songs to his lady. At village meetings speakers needed a knowledge of proverbs and rhymed sayings in order to be able to persuade their opponents in deliberation. Religious teachers, too, would not shun the devices of rhetoric and would admonish their flock about the Day of Judgement in resounding prose and memorable verse. Story-tellers would avail themselves of the phrases and examples of the days of yore to impart beauty and relevance to the tales they had to tell.

This is not to say that writing was not part of the way in which Malay culture was codified and preserved. There were manuscripts. And the same rhetorical weapons that stood the Malay in good stead in verbal exchanges were also required in written documents, for instance, in exchanges of letters. These, too, had to be witty and elegant. Their effect was all the greater if they lent themselves to being read out aloud in a sweet mellifluous voice, pleasing to the ruler and to the courtly audience. The formal features of most Malay manuscripts bespeak the fact that they served mainly as a prop to memory and were not meant to be read silently, but were supposed to be

---

[3] On the basically oral-aural nature of communication in the Malay world, see Sweeney (1980:13-6) and Sweeney (1987). About the task of the copyist at court see Skinner (1963:27) and Gullick (1958:53).

read out aloud or sung to a listening audience. They are teeming with repetitions: formulas, parallelisms, rhythm and rhymes.

The main group of texts which do not share in these oral-aural features was formed by those that were intimately connected with the Written Book par excellence, the Koran. Most religious treatises and exegetical works were not intended to be read out to a large audience, but to be discussed by a small gathering of scholars: their strongly Arabized diction, their unfamiliar syntax and complex turns of thought and argumentation made them difficult to understand for anyone but the initiated scholar. Legal texts as well, in view of the specialized knowledge they required, must have been less fit for public recitation.[4]

In all predominantly oral-aural textual traditions the attitude of reception the public may take, schematically speaking, oscillates between two poles: the demand that the text be profitable and the requirement that it provide soothing pleasure. In the Malay context the interplay between the devices of the text and the situation in which it was presented determined which of the two functions would be given dominance.[5]

Profitable texts were those texts which were felt to be concerned directly with the upholding of the religious, political and social order of the *negeri* and in a wider sense of the Malay world. If these texts were expected to be primarily profitable, this did not mean that they were not supposed to be pleasing as well. An elegant style could only enhance the effect of those texts that were considered useful in underpinning the *negeri*. By their exemplary reference to reality they confirmed the position of those groups which together possessed religious and political authority. It will be obvious that these texts were taken very seriously, both directing and reflecting as they did the (re)cognitive experience of the Malay public.

Soothing texts were those which were primarily enjoyed for their playful rhetoric and beauty: for their play on sounds, rhythm and rhyme, for the elegance of their comparisons, and for their amplifications and elaborations. Some would transport the audience to a never-never land of far-away kingdoms by way of romantic adventures of princes and princesses. Others would warn about the Eternal Life hereafter and point the way there by a path made pleasant by all the devices of rhetoric. Although here emotional experience prevailed over intellectual experience, predominantly soothing texts were also in a sense exemplary, in that they, too, offered models, albeit more implicitly, of behaviour according to the Malay way of life.[6]

---

[4] For a discussion of the respective patterns of thought and expression of predominantly oral and predominantly literate cultures, see Havelock (1963) and Ong (1982).
[5] See Havelock (1963:105, 108-9), on the dual function of the Homeric Greek oral poet as the useful instructor of the tribe and as a teller of pleasing and seductive tales.
[6] This distinction follows Jauss (1984), who in the receptive aesthetic experience of the

Of course especially profitable texts, those texts that served directly to uphold the legal and political order, were found worthy of being recorded and preserved in writing. Legal texts, state histories and religious texts, fixed in writing, would by their physical existence legitimate the exertion of secular and religious authority (if one may make this un-Malay distinction), provide standards of conduct and function as sources of relevant knowledge.

The comparatively small number of predominantly soothing texts that have been preserved in manuscript may be seen as an indication that most texts of this type circulated in oral form in the Malay world.

Another dichotomy that can be made within the corpus of the Malay textual heritage is one on the basis of considerations of form. On the one hand there are narrative texts, on the other hand non-narrative ones.

I consider as narrative those texts in which temporal and – implicitly or explicitly – causal relationships prevail, or in other words, texts in which the structure of a sequence of events dominates over whatever other structures there may be perceptible and is considered to be of paramount importance by the listener or reader. An example of a minimal narrative may be the following fragment from the *Hikayat Indraputra*:

> Alkisah peri mengatakan tatkala Indraputra diterbangkan merak emas dan peri mengatakan Indraputra jatuh kepada kebun nenek kebayan maka diambil oleh nenek kebayan, dan peri mengatakan Indraputra diangkat anak oleh perdana menteri, dan peri mengatakan Indraputra ada dengki hati oleh menteri Raja Syahsyian (Mulyadi 1983:51).
>
> (This story is concerned with telling about when Indraputra was snatched away by the Golden Peacock and with telling about when Indraputra fell down into the garden of the old woman and was taken in by the old woman and with telling about when Indraputra was adopted as his son by the Prime Minister and with telling about when Indraputra incurred the jealousy of the ministers of Raja Syahsyian.)

Non-narrative texts are those in which the thematic elements are contemporaneous or in which there is some shift of theme without an internal exposition of the causal connections. In this category one could place those texts in which the sequence of events is not considered to be the dominant structuring force (as in lyrical poetry, expository prose and so forth.).[7]

An example of such a non-narrative text may, for instance, be the Malay *pantun*, like the following one concluding the *Syair Nuri* by Sultan Badaruddin of Palembang:

---

reader distinguishes (re)cognitive aisthesis and emotive catharsis. Jauss (1984:34-5) stresses the role of catharsis in shaping social norms.

[7] My criteria for distinguishing between narrative and non-narrative texts are derived from Tomashevsky (1965:66) and Rimmon-Kenan (1983:14-5).

Ke Siam pergi membeli kici / orang bercamat dalam perahu / dilihat diam dikatakan benci / dendam gelomat siapakan tahu (*Antologi* 1980:233).

(To Siam I went to buy me a boat. / The sailors were hauling the sheets. / Does she love me, I wonder, with glances remote? / A heart is distraught when passion it meets.) (Overbeck 1934:127.)

On the basis of the two dichotomies made above, a taxonomy of the Malay textual system comprising four classes may be made.[8]

	Profitable	Soothing
non-narrative	*Undang-Undang Melaka* (Melaka Digests)	*Pantun*
narrative	*Sejarah Melayu* (Genealogy of the Malay Rulers)	*Hikayat Raja Muda* (Story of Raja Muda)

The Malay textual system was fundamentally encyclopaedic and citational: every word, phrase and sentence in one way or another referred to, and was a variation on, similar words, phrases and sentences in other texts. Every text was a play on previous texts, was an imitation in ever changing ways of existing and already accepted phrases and fragments, and presented already sanctioned notions and codes of behaviour. In short, every text was in some sense exemplary, deriving much of its authority from its appeal to hallowed tradition.[9]

This exemplariness was a quality shared by both profitable and soothing texts, a characteristic of both serious and playful works. The Malay textual heritage, in describing what the world looked like, simultaneously prescribed what it had to be like. It is this very exemplariness from which it derived its power to function as a source of standards of appropriate conduct and a touchstone of relevance, so that it could fulfil its role as a factor in support of the cohesion of the *negeri* and Malay life in general.

Some non-narrative texts, such as Malay legal texts or religious tracts, which were close to the centre of the textual tradition, required a specialized training, a certain amount of learning, to be understood. It will be clear that for us modern readers, who have not been raised in traditional Malay society and therefore not only lack familiarity with the countless unspoken assumptions of its culture but also often do not, or only partially, share its

---

[8] Taxonomies, as mere classifications for the sake of convenience made on the basis of observed similarities, should not be confused with genres, groups of conventions or devices that are related and motivated in a particular way, and are allowed to guide the production and interpretation of texts. For an elaboration of the notion of genre I refer to Chapter IV, part IV.

[9] See Havelock (1963:36-60) about the Homeric poems as the encyclopaedia of culture of the archaic Greek world. On the principle of variation within identity in the Homeric poems, see Havelock (1963:92). For a demonstration of this principle in the *Syair Ken Tambuhan* I refer to the next chapter.

values and concepts, it will be even more difficult to understand and appreciate such texts. Among the non-narrative texts of the Malay tradition there were, however, also some that were of a more popular nature, because they did not require their audiences to possess a special education in order to be able to understand and enjoy them. A good example is the *pantun* I quoted above.[10]

Narrative texts, too, generally did not require their audiences to possess specialized learning. Although their understanding and interpretation may pose difficulties to us which the Malay audiences did not experience, to us, too, these texts will generally speaking be more readily accessible and have a more direct appeal. We may of course enjoy these texts as more or less direct evocations of the historical reality of their times, but we may also choose to let ourselves be drawn into the intricate network woven by the narrative and try to unravel its complexities. I shall limit my examples of how literary works by their exemplariness confirm the Malay style of life and uphold the *negeri* to narrative texts, both profitable and soothing.

I will illustrate the intricate interrelation of these different features, both in form and reception, by discussing fragments taken from two major works of the Malay literary heritage, the *Sejarah Melayu* (Genealogy of the Malay Rulers, henceforth SM), and the *Syair Ken Tambuhan* (Poem of Lady-in-Waiting Ken Tambuhan, henceforth SKT). I will argue in favour of a reading in which the former work may be treated as a predominantly profitable (*berfaedah*) text, whereas the latter may be read as a primarily soothing (*penglipur lara*) text.[11]

Perhaps the best characterization of how exemplary narrative works in an oral-aural textual tradition is to be found in Sir Philip Sidney's famous essay *A Defence of Poetry* (1595). Distinguishing the 'poet' (the writer) from the moral philosopher and the historian and extolling him above them on account of his capacity to stimulate his listeners more forcefully to virtue, he remarks:

> 'Now therein of all sciences [...] is our poet the monarch. For he does not only show the way, but giveth so sweet a prospect into the way, as will entice any man to enter into it. Nay, he doth, as if your journey should lie through a fair vineyard, at the first give you a cluster of grapes, that full of taste, you may long to pass further. He beginneth not with obscure definitions, which must blur the margin with interpretations, and load the memory with doubtfulness; but he cometh to you with words set in delightful proportion, either accompanied with, or prepared for, the well enchanting skill of music; and with a tale forsooth he comes unto you, with a tale which holdeth children from play, and old men from the chimney corner. [G]lad

---

[10] For a demonstration of how to read *pantun* see Muhammad Haji Salleh (1980), Thomas (1980) and Thomas (1984). For a critical review of Thomas (1986), see Koster (1988).
[11] The editions I use are Situmorang and Teeuw (1952) and Teeuw (1966), which for the sake of convenience will henceforth be referred to as SM and SKT.

they will be to hear the tales of Hercules, Achilles, Cyrus, Aeneas; and hearing them, must needs hear the right description of wisdom, valour, and justice; which, if they had been barely, that is to say philosophically, set out, they would swear they be brought to school again.' (Sidney 1971:39-40.)

Literature, Sir Philip pointedly says, instils wisdom and virtue like a 'medicine of cherries' (Sidney 1971:41). Since cherries do not grow in the tropics, and I would not want to risk discussing Malay narrative in terms that are alien to it, I have adapted his words and spoken of a 'medicine of sweetmeats' in the title of this chapter.[12]

2. A predominantly profitable narrative: the Sejarah Melayu

A major theme in the SM, a genealogical chronicle treating the history of the Sultanate of Melaka, is the relationship between the ruler and his dignitaries, as exemplified in the story of the contract concluded by Lebar Daun, the ruler of Palembang, and his dignitaries with Sang Suparba, descendant of Iskandar Zulkarnain and founder of the royal line of Melaka. In this story the ruler is clearly presented as primus inter pares, the ideal status for a ruler in the body politic according to Malay political theory.

In the preface to the variant of the SM I base myself on (hence for the sake of convenience called 'the' *Sejarah Melayu*) we are told how the narrator, who identifies himself as Tun Seri Lanang, with the title of Bendahara, is commissioned by the ruler to revise a 'story about the Malays that was brought from Goa' (*hikayat Melayu dibawa oleh orang dari Goa*) and to compose a tale (*hikayat*) 'about the fortunes and genealogies of the Malay rulers as well as their court ceremonials, so that our grandchildren who will come after us will know about them, will remember them and will subsequently profit from them' *(peri peristiwa dan peraturan segala raja-raja Melayu dengan istiadatnya sekali, supaya diketahui oleh segala anak cucu kita yang kemudian daripada kita, diingatkannya oleh mereka itu, syahdan beroleh faedahlah daripadanya)*. The narrator then tells us that he has called the text composed by him *Sulalat as-Salatin*, the Genealogy of the Sultans and characterizes the work as 'the pearls of all stories and the lustre of all examples' (*mutia segala cetera dan cahaya segala peri umpamaan*) (SM 0.2-0.3). In other words, the SM is presented as a text that is both profitable and soothing, but in that order.

To illustrate my point I will discuss two anecdotes that occur at the beginning of the 34th story, when a Frankish fleet under the command of Alfongso Zalberkerki (historians will point out that this must be identified

---

[12] For a spirited critique of an undue emphasis on the 'Oriental Otherness' of Malay literature, see Umar Junus (1984:169-70).

with the Portuguese fleet under Alfonso d'Albuquerque) has appeared in the roads of Melaka and is ready to attack the town. It is the climactic moment of the narrative of the SM, when the decadence at court has reached its zenith.

Then and now, the fall of Melaka has always been seen by Malays as a fatal turning-point in their fortunes. Perhaps the finest testimony, not only to its deep emotional importance for them as a past event, but also to its relevance as a lesson in the present Malay condition, is the bitter poem that this episode has prompted one of the outstanding poets of Malaysia, Muhammad Haji Salleh, to write. The narrative power with which the episode is endowed is evidenced by the fascination it has had for so many scholars who have been tempted into efforts to pin-point what it was all about.[13] By its presentation of a series of captivating scenes that show the rapidly increasing moral and social disintegration of the *negeri*, the 33rd story has carefully set the stage for this crucial turn in the narrative. The Prime Minister, we are told, contrary to custom, fails to show his beautiful daughter to the Sultan before giving her in marriage to another man, thus causing estrangement between the Sultan and his prime dignitary.

The Prime Minister's sons, together with the jeunesse dorée of Melaka, after an unsuccessful hunting party shoot the buffaloes in their father's own pen. The ruler lends his ear without due enquiry to rumours that the Prime Minister is plotting to assassinate him, and has him executed without a formal trial. The new Prime Minister he then appoints is a lame, toothless, mumbling old man. The new Prime Minister's son publicly ridicules his aged father with impunity. The sultan, Mahmud, marries the daughter of the executed Prime Minister, who is so sad about her father's death that she could never smile again. The rueful sultan abdicates and is succeeded by his son, Ahmad, who takes more pleasure in the company of the frivolous young nobles of the court than in that of the military officers and state dignitaries. The conclusion is inevitable: Melaka is about to fall. And the Franks will merely be the instrument which happens to bring about this fall:

> Maka berperanglah Feringgi dengan orang Melaka, maka dibedilnya dari kapal, seperti hujan datangnya dan bunyinya seperti guruh dilangit; rupa kilat apinya seperti kilat diudara, bunyi istinggarnya seperti kacang direndang. Maka segala orang Melaka tiada boleh berdiri dipantai daripada kesangatan bedil Feringgi itu. Maka ghalai dan fusta dilanggarkannya kepantai, maka Feringgipun naik; maka dikeluari oleh orang Melaka, lalu perang terlalu ramai. Maka sultan Ahmadpun keluar naik gajah, Jinakji namanya, Seri Awadani dikepala gajah, Tun Ali Hati

---

[13] See Wilkinson (1907:16), Brakel (1975:9-11), Yusoff Iskandar and Abdul Rahman Kaeh (1978:193-5), Milner (1983:40-1) and Umar Yunus (1984:56-8). Umar Junus (1984) presents the first full-scale inquiry into the textual forces structuring the Malay Annals, making a daring break with the hallowed tradition of reading this work only in a referential mode. For the poem, see Muhammad Haji Salleh (1981:87-8).

dibuntut gajah. Maka makhdum dibawa baginda bertimbal rengga, karena baginda berguru kepada makhdum ilmu tauhid. Maka sultan Ahmad pergilah kejambatan mendapatkan Feringgi, terlalu banyak hulubalang mengiringkan baginda. Maka oleh sultan Ahmad ditempuh baginda dengan gajah dan segala hulubalang Feringgipun pecah berhamburan, lalu keair; maka sekaliannyapun undurlah turun keperahunya. Maka dibedilnya dari kapal dengan meriam yang besar, seperti halilintar bunyinya. Maka baginda terdiri diatas gajah baginda dihujung jambatan, khabarpun baginda tiada akan bedil yang seperti hujan itu. Maka makhdum berpegang dua-dua tangannya pada kiri kanan rengga gajah. Maka kata makhdum:'Hai sultan, disini bukannya tempat tauhid; mari kita kembali'. Maka sultan Ahmadpun tersenyum, maka bagindapun kembali keistana baginda. Maka Feringgi berseru-seru dari kapal, katanya: 'Hai orang Melaka, ingat-ingat kamu sekalian, demi dewasa, esok kita naik kedarat'. Maka sahut orang Melaka: 'Baiklah!' Maka sultan Ahmadpun menghimpunkan orang dan disuruh berhadir senjata. Maka haripun malamlah; maka segala hulubalang dan segala anak tuan-tuan itu semuanya bertunggu dibalairung. Maka kata segala anak tuan-tuan itu: 'Apa kita buat bertunggu dibalairung diam sahaja, baik kita membaca hikayat perang, supaya kita beroleh faedah daripadanya'. Maka kata Tun Muhammad Unta: 'Benar kata tuan-tuan itu; baiklah Tun Indera Segara pergi memohonkan Hikayat Muhammad Hanafiyyah; sembahkan mudah-mudahan dapat patik-patik itu mengambil faedah daripadanya, karena akan melanggar esok hari'. Maka Tun Indera Segarapun masuk menghadap sultan Ahmad. Maka segala sembah orang itu semuanya dipersembahkannya kebawah duli sultan Ahmad. Maka oleh sultan Ahmad dianugerahi Hikayat Amir Hamzah. Maka titah sultan Ahmad pada Tun Indera Segara: 'Katakan kepada segala anak tuan-tuan itu, hendakpun kita anugerahkan Hikayat Muhammad Hanafiyyah, takut tiada akan berani segala tuan-tuan itu seperti Muhammad Hanafiyyah, hanya jikalau dapat seperti Amir Hamzahpun padalah; maka kita beri Hikayat Hamzah'. Maka Tun Indera Segarapun keluarlah membawa Hikayat Hamzah, maka segala titah sultan Ahmad itu semuanya disampaikannya pada segala anak tuan-tuan itu; maka semuanya diam tiada menyahut. Maka kata Tun Isap pada Tun Indera Segara: 'Persembahkan kebawah duli Yang Dipertuan, salah titah baginda itu. Hendaknya Yang Dipertuan seperti Muhammad Hanafiyyah, patik-patik itu adalah seperti hulubalang Baniar'. Maka oleh Tun Indera Segara segala kata Tun Isap itu semuanya dipersembahkannya kepada sultan Ahmad. Maka bagindapun tersenyum, maka titah sultan Ahmad: 'Benar katanya itu'. Maka dianugerahi pula Hikayat Muhammad Hanafiyyah. (SM 34.1-34.4.)

(And the Franks engaged the men of Melaka in battle, and they fired their cannon from their ships so that the cannon balls came down like rain. And the noise of the cannon was like the noise of thunder in the heavens; the flashes of fire from their guns were like flashes of lightning in the sky; the noise of their matchlocks was like that of groundnuts popping in a frying pan. And the men of Melaka could no longer hold out on the shore, so heavy was the gunfire of the Franks. Then they bore down upon the shore with their galleys and foysts, and the Franks landed; and the men of Melaka sallied forth, and thereupon they engaged in battle in great numbers. And Sultan Ahmad came forth mounted on his elephant, named Jinakji, with the Seri Awadani on its head and Tun Ali Hati on its croup. And, to balance him on the saddle, His Majesty took with him the Reverend Master (Sadar Johan), because His Majesty was studying theology with the Reverend Master. And Sultan Ahmad went to the bridge to meet the Franks, and his officers accompanied His Majesty in very great numbers. And Sultan Ahmad attacked with his elephant, and the Frankish officers broke ranks and scattered, and thereupon proceeded to the water; and they all withdrew and boarded their ships. And they fired from their ships with the great cannon, whose noise was as when lightning flashes. And His Majesty stood on his elephant at the end of the bridge and His Majesty paid no attention to the cannonballs that fell like rain. And the Reverend Master clasped the elephant's pannier to the left and right with both hands. And the Reverend Master cried out: 'Sultan, this is no place for the study of theology; let us go home!' And Sultan Ahmad smiled, and His Majesty returned to His Majesty's palace. And the Franks shouted from their ships, saying: 'Take warning, you men of Melaka, by the gods, tomorrow we will come ashore!' And the men of Melaka answered: 'Very well!' And Sultan Ahmad then assembled his men and ordered them to get their weapons ready. And evening fell; and the military officers and the young nobles were all waiting in the audience hall. And the young nobles said: 'Why are we sitting here in silence? It would be well for us to read out a tale of war, so that we may profit from it.' And Tun Muhammad Unta said: 'That is well spoken, sirs. Let Tun Indera Segara go and ask the sultan for the Story of Muhammad Hanafiyyah, submitting that hopefully his humble servants may obtain profit from it, because they are launching an attack tomorrow.' And Tun Indera Segara then went into the palace and presented himself to Sultan Ahmad. And he submitted to Sultan Ahmad all that they had said. And Sultan Ahmad gave him the Story of Amir Hamzah. And Sultan Ahmad said to Tun Indera Segara: 'Tell the young nobles that we would give them the Story of Muhammad Hanafiyyah did we not fear that the bravery of these gentlemen may fall short of the bravery of Muhammad Hanafiyyah; but if only they could be as brave as Amir Hamzah, that already would suffice. That is why we are giving the Story of Amir Hamzah.' Tun Indera Segara then left the palace bearing the Story of Hamzah, and he reported to the young nobles all that Sultan Ahmad had said; and they were all silent and did not respond. And Tun Isap said to Tun Indera Segara: 'Submit to the ruler that His Majesty has spoken wrongly. If the ruler will only be like Muhammad Hanafiyyah, his humble servants will be like his military officers at Baniar.' And Tun Indera Segara submitted all that Tun Isap had said to Sultan Ahmad. And His Majesty smiled, and Sultan Ahmad said: 'That is well spoken!' And he gave them the Story of Muhammad Hanafiyyah.)

The above fragment consists of two anecdotes that are seemingly unconnected, but which, on closer inspection, prove to be related in form and therefore in meaning: both anecdotes have the result of making Sultan Ahmad smile (*senyum*).

In the first fragment we are told how the sultan in the company of his religious teacher, Sadar Johan, rides forth into the thick of the battle on his elephant, in the firm conviction that the presence of this holy man has made him invulnerable.[14]

To his embarrassment, but, it may be thought, perhaps also to his amusement, his revered teacher suddenly shows an unbecoming fear of the Frankish bullets and an unexpected desire to save his 'phenomenal self' when they are in the midst of the battle. He begs his master to return to the safety of the palace as a more suitable place for theological study. And Sultan

---

[14] See Milner (1983:39-41) on the magic power (*keramat*) that the Sufi mystic was popularly believed to acquire.

Ahmad smiles – an ambiguous reaction. Is he amused? Or embarrassed? Does he smile because the situation is so comical? Or does he smile because his teacher causes him to lose face? One lesson this anecdote teaches may be that although the ruler shows a praiseworthy courage in battle, his courage is an ill-founded one, based as it is on a mere superstitious belief in his invulnerability.

In the second fragment we are told how the officers and young nobles are sitting together in the ruler's audience hall. They are sitting there, each man wrapped in his own thoughts, isolated, in an uneasy silence, awaiting the imminent battle with the Franks. To prepare themselves for this trial by profitable examples and to break the oppressive silence and create an atmosphere of solidarity through the sound of a recitation, they ask Sultan Ahmad for the *Hikayat Muhammad Hanafiyyah*, the story about that Shiite paragon of martial virtue and heroism for the cause of the True Faith, Muhammad Hanafiyyah. This pious legendary story tells how Muhammad Hanafiyyah, the son of Caliph Ali by a Hanafite woman, fights the Ummayads, who have usurped the caliphate and at whose hands his two half-brothers and the Prophet's grandsons, Hasan and Husain, have suffered a martyr's death.

It would therefore seem that the young nobles are really preparing themselves seriously, and it is precisely this that the sultan does not believe. Instead of giving them the more profitable *Hikayat Muhammad Hanafiyyah*, he fobs them off with the predominantly soothing *Hikayat Amir Hamzah*. This *hikayat* tells about the exploits of the great warrior and champion of early Islam, Hamzah Ibn Abd al-Mutallib, a nephew of the Prophet, many of whose exploits are in fact derived from the biography of another Hamzah, namely Hamzah Ibn Abdullah, a Persian warrior who became famous as a leader of holy wars against the Hindus in India. Although without any doubt also concerned with a Muslim hero, it is full of amorous adventures and gallant quests in far-away lands.[15]

No wonder the frustrated nobles feel greatly offended by this slight inflicted by the ruler. But then they find a way of extricating themselves from this humiliating situation and, by witty repartee, turn the tables on His Majesty. His Majesty was mistaken in improperly comparing mere courtiers with a great Islamic leader. In fact, they point out, it would be more apt if the ruler should compare his own person to Muhammad Hanafiyyah and model himself on this hero. Then he would be a true leader who – instead of slighting his men – would inspire them by his example to behave like

---

[15] For the Story of Amir Hamzah, see Van Ronkel (1895), for the Story of Muhammad Hanafiyyah, see Brakel (1975) and for the Malay Islamic romances in general, see Ismail Hamid (1983a, 1983b).

proper officers, like Muhammad Hanafiyyah's officers fighting in his capital, Baniar.

And the ruler once more smiles – again an ambiguous reaction. Is he amused? Or rather, embarrassed? Does he smile because he is pleased at the seriousness with which they are preparing themselves for the decisive battle, and at the signs of their skill in a battle of words as well? Or is he hiding his discomfort at being outdone in erudition and wit and being lectured to by his own courtiers, usually his companions in more frivolous pastimes? One lesson this anecdote may be seen to contain is related to that major theme of the SM: only in harmony with his nobles may the ruler preserve the realm. And to maintain this harmony, an effort is required from both sides.

As has already been indicated, the smile of the sultan is a trait d'union linking the two anecdotes. The Malays have a saying *senyum raja*, meaning literally 'smile of a ruler', but often used in the sense of 'a forced or hypocritical smile' (Wilkinson 1943, II:441). This formal correspondence puts us on the trail of another line of interpretation: the possibility of reading the two anecdotes as being in some sense mutually complementary. The second anecdote, it then transpires, provides an alternative to the first which implies the rejection of the concentration on religious study – primarily concerned as it is with personal salvation – as an example for an Islamic ruler who has to provide leadership for his *negeri*. As opposed to this negative example for a ruler who should be concerned with the well-being of his community, the second anecdote presents a positive one, that of Muhammad Hanafiyyah, who by his good leadership inspired his men to solidarity and courage in defence of the common cause.

It will be clear that this fragment of the SM confirms the claim made in the preface: it must have impressed the Malay public as being highly profitable indeed in that it provided an example buttressing the coherence of the Malay *negeri*. But it also confirms the second claim of the preface: it truly shines forth like a resplendent gem that is soothing to behold. The narrative is presented in a rhythmic and elegant manner. It is composed of short, well-balanced sentences, strung together paratactically and frequently punctuated by the word *maka*, and presented in a formulaic type of diction. Comparisons and elaborations ornament the skeleton of the narrative, which proceeds in an orderly and balanced manner. Its soothing effect is enhanced by the subtle wit pervading the fragment, which must have caused the Malays to react like Sultan Ahmad and smile, as we smile now on reading it.

3. A predominantly soothing narrative: the Syair Ken Tambuhan

The SKT is a Panji romance (see Chapter VI). This genre enjoyed great popularity in the Malay world, and with considerable variations in the names of the protagonists, has been practised in frequently very lengthy, but sometimes also short, narratives, both in prose and in verse form. It has even been adapted for the stage in a Malay type of drama, the *bangsawan*.

The story of the SKT may be summarized as follows: Prince Kertapati (Inu Kertapati) of Kuripan is about to be engaged by his parents to marry a princess of Banjarkulon. However, when out hunting in the pleasure garden of his father, he meets the princess of Daha, who under the name of Lady-in-Waiting Tambuhan, is detained at his father's court as a captive and is weaving the betrothal gift for the princess of Banjarkulon with the other princesses kept as hostages in Kuripan. He immediately falls in love with her, and to the great anger of his mother makes her his wife. By a ruse the queen of Kuripan manages to separate the two *karma*-bound lovers: she sends the prince away to hunt deer for her and in his absence has Lady-in-Waiting Tambuhan killed by the executioner in a lonely spot in the forest. Finding her body, the prince commits suicide. Thanks to the intercession of the gods the two are brought back to life again, and, with the consent of their respective parents they are solemnly married and become king and queen of Kuripan.

Whereas the SM, as we have seen, gives priority to an intellectual mode of reading (*faedah*) in its preface, the reverse is the case with the SKT. Here clearly the recommended attitude of reception is the emotional one, as is intimated in the *syair's* prologue.

> Dengarkan tuan suatu riwayat / orang dahulu empunya hikayat / madahnya tidak banyak ibarat / sekedar kisah juga disurat // inilah ceritera Ken Tambuhan / puteranya ratu jadi tawanan / jikalau sungguh khabar demikian / segala yang mendengar belas dan kasihan. (SKT I, 1-2.)

> (Listen, gentlefolks, to a story, / a tale which people of old already possessed. / Its words do not offer much edification. / I have merely written a story. // This is the story of Lady-in-Waiting Tambuhan, / the daughter of a king who had become a captive. / If what is told did really once happen, / all those who listen will feel sympathy and commiseration.)

An example of how a text may invite one to let oneself be carried away by a soothing emotional experience is provided by the following passage, a variant of a type-scene that is widespread in Malay narrative, namely that in which the dress of the hero or heroine is described.

> Ken Tambuhan sudah berhias / berkampuh rangdi jingga pengaras / berkemban kesumba diantelas / ditulisnya dengan bayu emas // berkamar ikatan Melayu / bersubang lontar perbuatan bayu / indahnya tidak dapat dipayu / segala yang

memandang berhati sayu // bergelang kana dua sebelah / ditatah dengan permata merah / bibirnya merah terlalu cerah / giginya laksana delima merkah // bercincin emas permata pudi / intan ditatah lazuwardi / diikatnya dengan permata baiduri / bersambutan dengan canggai kiri // bersunting bunga cempaka digubah / berpatutan dengan malai yang indah / tubuhnya halus sederhana rendah / mengorak senyum manis bertambah // setelah sudah puteri memakai / ditentang indah terlalu permai / didalam dunia tiada berbagai / segala yang memandang heran terlalai // parasnya laksana gambar wayang / bagaikan lenyap di mata orang / cahaya durjanya gilang-gemilang / segala yang memandang suka dan sayang. (SKT I, 28-34.)

(When Lady-in-Waiting Tambuhan had finished dressing, / she wore a silken robe that was crimson as the sky at sunset. / Around her breast she had wrapped a saffron-coloured cloth of Indian satin, / on which patterns had been drawn in gold leaf. // The sash she was wearing was a Malay cloth. / Her ear-studs were shaped like palm-leaves and were the work of slaves. / To buy such priceless beauty no treasure could suffice; / all who beheld it felt wistful. // On each arm she wore two kana-bracelets / inlaid with red gems. / The colour of her lips was a fiery red / and her teeth were like the bursting pomegranate. // She wore gold rings studded with tiny gems, / diamonds mounted in lapis lazuli, and inlaid with costly and beautiful opals / that enhanced golden nail-protectors. // In her hair she wore a garland of *cempaka* flowers / that matched her beautiful hairpins perfectly. / She was slenderly built, neither tall nor short, / even sweeter when her face unfolded into a smile. // When the princess had finished dressing, / she presented a lovely sight, most beautiful to behold. / She was without a peer in all the world; / all who beheld her were spellbound with amazement. // She looked like a puppet in the *wayang*, / the shadow of which may at any moment fade. / Her face was of a resplendent beauty; / all who beheld it felt affection and love.)

Passages like the above, describing the appearance and manners of royal persons, are to be found in ever-varying amplifications and elaborations in a great many Malay narratives. They must have instilled gentle feelings of affectionate sympathy, of protective tenderness and of courtly erotic love, similar to those depicted in these stories in the hearts of the Malay listeners. The refrain-like repetition of formulaic lines like 'All who beheld it felt affection and love', 'She presented a beautiful sight', and so on, invite the public to identify with the protagonists in the narrative.

Exemplary scenes are presented that prefigure proper, refined manners, feelings and emotions, which therefore invite imitation by all members of the *negeri*. Thus the listener is allowed to get a taste of a world that is more ideal and elevated than that of his own everyday, often boring and humdrum existence. The abundance of pleasant-sounding rhymes, polished rhythms and pleasingly familiar formulas – to which my translation hardly does justice – gives one a sensation of beholding a radiant jewel from ever-changing facets. The comparison of Lady-in-Waiting Tambuhan's appearance to that of a *wayang*-puppet underlines the elusive ideal nature of beauty, which is always threatening to vanish. The soothing experience of beauty evokes the emotional experience of a tender sadness: 'All who beheld it felt sad at heart'.[16]

Viewed from an another angle, the impact of the passage, as of the entire *syair*, is like that of a fairy-tale. Stories that are predominantly oriented towards a soothing effect (*penglipur lara*) tend to be set in some never-never land: in far-away Java, in the exotic, unfamiliar Near East or in the impenetrable jungles of the Malay world itself.

The *penglipur* aspect is also evident in the following passage, which presents a state wedding – that of Lady-in-Waiting Tambuhan and Inu Kertapati:

> Sang nata keluar lalu ke paseban / menyuruh memalu bunyi-bunyian / ramailah menteri punggawa sekalian / tandanya negeri beroleh kesukaan // sesaklah lebu pekan dan pasara / segala rakyat isi negara / berhimpunlah sekalian dengan segera / hendak mengadap Raden putera // ramai diluar ramai didalam / segala bunyi-bunyian tidaklah diam / segala permainan berbagai ragam / hingga jenis negeri Kemboja dan Siam // joget dan tandak wayang sekalian / orang menonton laki-laki perempuan / ada setengah mabuk dan edan / tidaklah sedar minum dan makan // titah sang nata disuruh berjaga / paseban didalam ramaikan juga / segala kedayan terlalu suka / riuhlah dengan gurau jenaka // berhimpunlah segala yang muda-muda / seorang pun tidak ada yang berida // empatpuluh hari titah baginda / hendak mengerjakan paduka anakanda / disuruh perbuat panca persada / tempat memandikan anakanda baginda / serba jenis permata ada / disuruh kenakan pada panca persada // setelah sudah sekaliannya dikerjakan / ditepi laut sebelah wetan / segala alat sudah dikenakan / diarak Inu dengan Ken Tambuhan // setelah sampai ke panca persada / segala bini menteri punggawa ada / dengan dayang-dayang tua dan muda / serta sekalian anak biduanda // ramailah siti mendara mengilir / ada berbedak ada berlangir / berbagai-bagai kidung tembang dengan syair / sambil mandi kedalam air. (SKT IX, 102-11.)

(His Majesty stepped outside onto the veranda, / and ordered that the musical instruments be played. / The ministers and district officials thronged together, / a sign that an entertainment was to take place. // Dense clouds of dust hung over the shop-streets and markets. / All the commoners, the entire community, / all quickly gathered, wanting to wait upon the ruler's son. // It was crowded outside and crowded inside. / The musical instruments never stopped playing. / All sorts of plays were performed, / even types hailing form Cambodia and Siam. // There was *joget* and *tandak*, there was *wayang* as well. / The crowd of onlookers included men as well as women. / Some of them were almost drunk with amorous passion, / and had no thought for food and drink. // His Majesty's orders were that there should be celebrating day and night. / On the palace veranda, too, there was to be feasting. / The royal retainers enjoyed themselves greatly. / Their jesting and joking made a great din. // All who were young were gathered together. / Not one was there among them who was old. / Forty days of feasting had the ruler prescribed, / to celebrate the wedding of His Highness, his son. // He ordered a tiered bathing-pavilion to be built, / where his royal son might be ceremonially bathed. / All sorts of precious gems were there, / set into the pavilion on his orders. // When all the preparations were finished on the seashore away to the east, / and when all the accoutrements

---

[16] On the 'beautiful' in Malay poetics, see Braginsky (1979).

had been fitted, / the prince and Lady-in-Waiting Tambuhan were carried there in solemn procession. / When the procession arrived at the bathing-pavilion / the wives of the ministers and district officers were already awaiting it there, / escorted by their maids, both the yong ones and the old, / as well as by their pages. // In throngs the ladies and maidens came down the river, / some powdered their faces, others washed their hair. / All sorts of *kidung, tembang* and *syair* were sung / as they bathed in the water.)

Here again we have the same abundance of ever-varying elaborations and amplifications, and again the beautiful sounds and rhythms noted above – again a passage that is resplendent like a multi-faceted gem and soothes the weary heart. The recitation of the SKT itself would have been quite fitting on an occasion like the one presented in it, in which the unity of the *negeri* finds expression in the shared celebration by all its members of a royal marriage. In describing such an important ritual, the *syair* at the same time demonstrates how the *negeri* could be held together, and what a proper Malay state and its rituals should be like.

At the centre of the action is the ruler: he is the figure who controls the scene and he sets each new development of the narrative in motion by his commands. Inside, the court is celebrating, and the ruler, his dignitaries and the district officials are 'jesting and joking', while outside the commoners are making merry, 'drunk with amorous passion'. The entire passage is pervaded with references to all sorts of art forms, some more vulgar ones like *joget* and *tandak*, others more refined ones like *kidung, tembang* and *syair*. These arts join the different sections of the community together, while they also give coherence to the *negeri* as a whole: the *wayang*, visible from both sides of the screen, and the resounding boom of the *gamelan* join court and commoner alike in shared revelry, conjuring up and confirming the state's coherence.

As a final sample of exemplariness in the SKT I would quote the following passage:

Dalam banyak para puteri / anak ratu di Tanjungpuri / parasnya seperti bidadari / sukar didapat mahal dicari // namanya Raden Puspakencana / lakunya arif bijaksana / akal bicaranya sangatlah sempurna / sifatnya lengkap tujuh laksana // zaman itu sukar dicari / manisnya seperti Mandudari / dikasihi sang nata dan permaisuri / dilebihkan daripada segala para puteri // empatbelas tahun umurnya tuan / dinamai ratu Ken Tambuhan / cantik manis barang kelakuan / memberi hati bimbang dan rawan // sekaliannya heran memandang parasnya / kasih dan sayang rasa citanya / baik sekali budi bahasanya / patutlah dengan tegur sapanya. (SKT I, 13-7.)

(Among these many princesses / there was also the daughter of the ruler of Tanjungpuri. / She looked like a nymph descended from heaven, / but rarely met and seldom found. // Her name was Raden Puspakencana. / Her demeanour was wise and sensible. / Cleverness and wit she had. / Her appearance encompassed all the feminine charms. // At that time anyone who was her equal would have been hard to find. / Her beauty was like that of Mandudari. / She was loved by the king and by the queen, / and was favoured above all the other princesses. // Fourteen years of age was the maiden. / The king had named her Lady-in-Waiting Tambuhan. / Lovely and sweet was her every action, / filling one's heart with longing and tenderness. // All who beheld her appearance were amazed; / affection and love were felt by all. / Excellent were her breeding and manners, / befitting her courteous speech.)

Apart from undeniable soothing qualities, this description of Lady-in-Waiting Tambuhan also clearly has intellectual potential: she is presented as the embodiment of all those qualities that a genuine Malay princess should have, of the way a lady of high birth, and a refined lady in general, was supposed to look, speak and act. The *syair* subtly interweaves example with example: Lady-in-Waiting Tambuhan is compared to Princess Mandudari of the *Hikayat Seri Rama*, a woman known to the Malay as the very epitome of feminine beauty, cleverness and loyalty.

Every Malay will immediately have been reminded by this reference of the story how Mandudari managed by a ruse to avoid being given away by her hapless husband, King Dasarata, to the evil demon-king Rawana, who, overwhelmed by her beauty, demanded her as his wife. From the exudations of her own skin (*daki*) she fashioned a princess, Mandudaki, who was her exact image, tricking the unsuspecting Rawana into accepting this copy as his bride. Thus Lady-in-Waiting Tambuhan, herself a mirror of Malay femininity, is given her own model in this exemplary character.[17]

Above I also suggested that both the SM and the SKT were pervaded by exemplariness. This could with equal right be said of texts of the Malay heritage in general. For all situations in life, both formal and informal, this heritage offered an abundance of examples. Proper behaviour, appropriate sentiments, fitting demeanour and good government all had their precedent and example, which were necessary for maintaining the coherence of the *negeri* and the character of the Malay style of life.

I have suggested that soothing texts may also be read referentially, if we decide to accept their invitation to do so, and the SKT may well serve to illustrate this. Soothing and fairy-talelike though it may be, it does afford some good glimpses of Malay life and the workings of the Malay state. The modern historian of the Malay world tends to divide the Malay textual heritage sharply into the large bulk of useless and irrelevant fanciful tales on the one hand, and the small number of texts from which 'facts' may reliably be derived. Would it not be more feasible, one wonders, for him to shift his attention to what may well be an unexplored field of referential information?

But what about those allegedly referential texts, of which the SM is

---

[17] For the story of how Mandudari tricked Rawana, see Achadiati Ikram (1980:fol. 155-8).

perhaps the one most cherished by the historian? Are those seemingly realistic glimpses of Malay life the SM has always been so highly praised for, really as reliable as the historian likes to believe, or is he the victim of the 'reality effect' of a grand narrative tradition? Did d'Albuquerque really appear before Melaka in 1511? His opponent, Sultan Ahmad, may well never have existed.[18]

---

[18] About 'reality effect' in narrative, see Barthes (1982). For an argumentation for the non-existence of Sultan Ahmad, see McRoberts (1984:26). After the first publication of this chapter as an article in 1985 I received a personal communication from Dr. Russell Jones who brought to my attention numismatic evidence in favour of accepting the existence of Sultan Ahmad. As he wrote to me, Hanitsch (1903) mentions some coins found near the Melaka River in about 1900, which were presented to the Raffles Museum in Singapore. Two of these bore the name of Ahmad bin Mahmud, with the epithet of Sultan al-'Adil. Dr. Jones surmised that it was possibly one of these coins which Dakers (1939) mentions. Dakers gives the inscription as 'Ahmad bin Mahmud Shah', but according to Dr. Jones the coin illustrated seems to read 'Ahmad bin Mahmud'. Dr. Jones also mentioned the existence of a coin in the British Museum thought to be from Melaka, but the inscription on that appeared to him to be 'Ahmad *Abu* Mahmud Shah' (Ahmad, father of Mahmud Shah), which he found puzzling. This suggests that perhaps Sultan Ahmad did exist after all, but that the question what is counterfeited history, and what reality, may by no means be so clearly answerable yet.

CHAPTER II

Variation within identity
Formulaic devices for the construction of narrative

1. The principle of variation within identity and the Syair Ken Tambuhan

Anyone who first hears or reads a Malay story, no matter whether in prose (*hikayat*) or in verse (*syair*) will, as the narrative proceeds, note the repetition of words, phrases, lines and whole passages. He may stop at this first impression of all-pervading identity and repetition, and remain satisfied with the conclusion that Malay stories are bad literature. Or he may consider that they cannot have been esteemed and enjoyed as literature by the Malay world without having some sort of literary qualities, in which case he will seriously try and find out what the Malays may have enjoyed in them.

He will then read them more carefully and will gradually find himself developing a sense of expectancy for the next word, the next phrase or line that may be used, for the next turn and form the narrative may take. Against this background of a pleasingly familiar, almost incantational repetition of identical words, phrases, sentences and passages, he will gradually begin to notice a subtle play of small differences, continuous variations, that are all the more effective against the background of marked similarities. He will then have discovered that these stories are constructed by means of an ever varied repetition of fixed formulaic schemes, and that the art of Malay storytelling is one of variation within identity. These features are characteristic of oral-aural narrative (see Introduction).

Having mastered the principle of variation within identity in one story, that is, intratextually, he will then find out that this play of varied repetition is also carried on between that story and other stories, that is, intertextually. It will become apparent that the words, phrases, sentences and passages of his story turn up in identical or varied ways in other variants of it, in thematically or generically similar stories, or in traditional Malay stories in general. As his experience with these stories deepens, his competence as a reader will develop and he will acquire a sensibility that gives him access to an aesthetic experience of Malay narrative.

In this chapter[1] the use of formulaic devices in the construction of narrative and the principle of variation within identity (Lotman 1977:290-1) will not be examined in their complex intertextual dimension, although much of all this can only be understood by way of that text's intertextuality. Instead I will concentrate my analysis on one text only, examining these phenomena in the limited scope of its intratextuality. As will be shown, even within this limited scope they can be clearly perceived. The text I have chosen is a story in the verse-form, *syair*, namely the *Syair Ken Tambuhan* (henceforth SKT) or Poem of Lady-in-Waiting Tambuhan, as published in the edition by Teeuw (1966). This work appears to have enjoyed great popularity in the Malay world and is relatively old, its oldest known manuscript, a copy made at Bangkahulu, dating from 1791 (Teeuw 1966:230-6). The choice of a narrative in the verse form, *syair*, gives me the opportunity to examine the use of formulaic devices within the constraints of verse.

In my demonstration of the use of formulaic devices and the principle of variation within identity in the SKT, first the dominating identities and tendencies towards schematism will be established at different levels; then, against this background, the possibilities for variation will be indicated. Since the first three chapters of Teeuw's edition have already been carefully studied from the point of view of prosody, and since I also have a tape-recorded spoken and sung performance of the first two chapters available (for a transcript of the melody used in the sung performance and an ethno-musicological analysis of its structure and function I refer to part 4 of this chapter) I will take my examples at the level of half-line, line, couplet, and quatrain mainly from these first two chapters.

2. The verse form syair

The *syair*, that besides being read out aloud may also be performed in song, may be characterized as a more or less long chain of quatrains rhyming *a a a a*. The *syair*-quatrain shows a striking symmetry: four lines falling into two couplets, each couplet dividing into two lines, and finally each line being split up into two half-lines by a strong caesura.

The dominant prosodic requirement in the *syair*-line is that four stresses must be produced, two on either side of the caesura. Lines with only three

---

[1] This chapter is a revised version of Koster and Maier (1982). Jauss (1977:16) has pointed out that in order to enjoy texts of this type, such as the modern detective story or the Old French *chansons de geste* (heroic epics), 'the reader first has to deny the individual character of the individual text to enjoy the enchantment of a game already started, a game with known rules and as yet unknown surprises'. Jauss calls this reader's attitude the reception structure of the *plurale tantum* (plural only).

stresses do occur, but are extremely rare. The majority of the *syair*-lines contain four words, in the sense of minimal free forms (rootwords), to which may or may not have been added bound forms such as prefixes (*ber-, di-, ke-, ku-, men-, per-, se-, ter-*) and/or suffixes (*-an, -i, -kan, -lah, -nya*). The predominance of lines of four words in the technical sense indicated here is understandable in the light of the rules concerning stress in Malay: all forms, whether only consisting of a two- or three-syllable minimal free form or of a two- or three-syllable minimal free form plus prefixes and/or suffixes, take one stress. The position of this stress differs according to the number of syllables of the form and the presence or absence of a *pepet* (mute e), as appears from the following rules:

1. Stress is always on the penultimate syllable, unless that syllable contains a *pepet*, in which case stress usually falls on the last syllable. Examples: *lári, ítu, kelapáran, tentára* but *menáng, tegúh, berenáng, beledú*.
2. Monosyllabic forms, generally being bound forms, as a rule do not take any stress.

In order to meet the requirement of producing a verse line with two stresses on either side of the caesura the poet observes the following two rules:

1. Minimal free forms of two or three syllables and forms made up of a two-syllable free form and a monosyllabic prefix or suffix have one stress.
2. Forms that consist of a. one minimal free form of two or three syllables plus affixes and/or suffixes, b. two minimal free forms and are foreign loan-words, c. two identical minimal free forms with or without an affix and are duplications, d. two minimal free forms and are compounds, all, if they have a total of four or more syllables, may be given either one or two stresses, as the balance of the line requires.[2]

---

[2] Examples of rule 1:
  I.   15a   záman / ítu // súkar / dicári;
  II.   11d   lálu / bertítah // rátu / yang ánom.
Examples of rule 2:
a. I.   3c   tákhta / kerajáan // yang ámat / besár;
    IX.   97b   kárar / diátas // kérajáan;
    I.   3b   bagínda / bangsáwan // yáng muktábar;
    I.   4a   beberápa / rátu // yang bérmakóta;
    III.   118   lálu / kembáli // ké / istána;
    III.   56b   didukúngnya / másuk // ke péradúan;
    III.   112   lálu / didúkung // másuk / ke peradúan.
b. I.   12c   disurúhkan / rátu // pérmaisúri;
    II.   9a   permaisúri / tersenyúm // seráya / katánya;
    III.   9a   Wiradandáni / menyembáh // lálu / pergí;
    III.   11a   Wiradandáni // berdátang / sembáh;
c. I.   23d   bangúnlah / sekalían // dáyang-dáyang;
    VI.   3b   segála / dayang-dáyang // menyelámpai / tetámpan;
    VII.   8d   màsing-másing // dengán / perángai;

In a simplified way the rules can be formulated thus:
1. A form of two or three syllables takes one stress.
2. A form of four or more syllables takes one stress or two, as the balance of the line, that is, the necessity to have two stresses on either side of the caesura, requires.

Rule 2 is a convention by which lines with three and five words can be made to have the required number of stresses. This is apparent in the frequent cases where monosyllables like *yang, di,* and *ke* may receive stress *metri causa,* and in those cases where unstressed bound forms in polysyllabic forms may receive a stress. Both phenomena are observable in the spoken performance recorded for me. Here I give one example of each phenomenon:

SKT I, 3.b   bagínda / bangsáwan // yáng / muktábar;
SKT I, 4.a   beberápa / rátu // yang bérmakóta.

Clearly, as constructive principles of the line, word and stress have different hierarchical positions. As the Russian formalist Jurij Tynyanov has pointed out: 'A system does not mean coexistence of components on the basis of equality; it presupposes the preeminence of one group of elements and the resulting deformation of other elements' (Ehrlich 1980:199). The constructive principle of having four stresses per line, two on either side of the caesura, together with the rhyme *a a a a,* forms the pre-eminent group of components or, as Tynyanov would have termed it, the *dominanta* of the *syair*.[3] Especially these two characteristics guarantee the perceptibility of the lines as *syair*-lines and as literature. The tendency of the *syair*-line to have four words, strong as it may be, must be considered a secondary phenomenon.[4]

This must also be said of two other tendencies in *syair*-prosody: that towards the use of certain line lengths and that towards intralinear isosyllabicity. From my examination of the number and distribution of syllables in the first 896 lines of the *syair*, that is, in its first three chapters (see table on p. 40),

	I.	6a	masing-másing / hendák // berbúat / bákti;
	VII.	36b	diaráknya / dengán // búnyi-bunyían;
	II.	6a	segála / bunyi-bunyían // teláh berbúnyi.
d.	III.	69	kálau / ayah bundánya // tiáda / berkenán;
	V.	146c	tersedárlah / ákan // áyah bundánya;
	V.	41d	tinggállah / ráden // dúa / laki ísteri;
	III.	114a	beradúlah / ráden // láki / ísteri;
	I.	113a	didálam / bányak // pára púteri;
	I.	15d	dilebíhkan / daripáda // segála / para púteri.

[3] The concept of *dominanta* was propounded by Tynyanov in his 1927 essay 'On literary evolution'. For a full translation of the essay I refer to Striedter (1971).
[4] It will be clear that my theory differs from that advocated by Situmorang and Teeuw (1952:10) and Thomas (1979:53), according to which *syair*-prosody is based on a system of four wordclusters per line.

it appears that there is a strong preference for lines of 10 or 11 syllables. It seems reasonable to ascribe this to the prevailing occurrence of *syair*-lines that accommodate four minimal free forms of two or three syllables plus some affixes necessary to bring them into syntactical order. The intralinear isosyllabicity is often perfect, but even more often only approximate in nature.

These phenomena show that a syllabic principle, too, plays a role in *syair*-prosody, which is also apparent in the simplified formulation of its rules. Clearly, syllabic length is important for the question whether and where a form may be stressed, but it is subordinate to the necessity to produce a line with two stresses on either side of the caesura. This necessity may lead to the stressing of the usually unstressed monosyllables and decides whether a four or more syllable form, that normally will receive only one stress, may be given two. Apparently intralinear isosyllabicity is the concomitant result of the tendency to produce the necessary two stresses on either side of the caesura by producing two words on either side.

The *syair*-line forms a complete syntactic and semantic unit, being either a sentence or a clause. The half-lines also often form syntactic and semantic units. Very frequently, however, lines occur in which the caesura does not respect the syntactic units. Thus the poet prevents his verse from becoming a droning see-saw, varying half-lines that coincide with syntactic units with half-lines that do not.

Examples of half-lines that do not coincide with syntactic-semantic units are:

SKT I, 14.a	namánya / Ráden // Púspakencána;
SKT I, 15.d	dilebíhkan / daripáda // segála / para púteri;
SKT I, 17.d	patútlah / dengán // tegúr / sapánya;
SKT III, 23.d	Seórang pun / jángan // diberí / kesítu.
SKT I, 14.a	her name was Princess Puspakencana;
SKT I, 15.d	and she was their favourite among the princesses;
SKT I, 17.d	befitting her courteous speech;
SKT III, 23.d	he was to allow no one to enter.

It would be interesting to know how much scope for syntactic variation the *syair*-poet does enjoy within the line, and whether certain syntactic constructions are intensively used by him. It may well be that a preference for an intensive use of a limited number of syntactic constructions together with a narrowly circumscribed poetical vocabulary are largely responsible for the verbal formulaicness that is characteristic of the *syair*. Since linguistic research on the syntax of the *syair* - and unfortunately not only of the *syair* – has yet to begin, I cannot discuss this matter any further.

Summing up, it may be said that, on the level of the line, the recurrence of four stresses, two on either side of the caesura, is the stable anchor of

Isosyllabicity in first 896 lines of SKT

Line length	Syllable-distribution	Total	%	Total	%
8	4 + 4	2	0.2		
	5 + 3	0	0.0	3	0.3
	3 + 5	1	0.1		
9	5 + 4	63	7.0		
	4 + 5	42	4.7	108	12.1
	6 + 3	1	0.1		
	3 + 6	2	0.2		
10	5 + 5	328	36.6		
	6 + 4	55	6.1	393	43.9
	4 + 6	10	1.1		
11	6 + 5	136	15.2		
	5 + 6	95	10.6	244	27.2
	7 + 4	9	1.0		
	4 + 7	4	0.4		
12	6 + 6	49	5.5		
	7 + 5	32	3.6		
	5 + 7	15	1.7	101	11.3
	8 + 4	4	0.4		
	4 + 8	1	0.1		
13	7 + 6	15	1.7		
	6 + 7	10	1.1	40	4.5
	8 + 5	11	1.2		
	5 + 8	4	0.4		
14	7 + 7	1	0.1		
	8 + 6	0	0.0	4	0.4
	6 + 8	3	0.3		
15	8 + 7	0	0.0		
	7 + 8	1	0.1	2	0.2
	9 + 6	1	0.1		
	6 + 9	0	0.0		
16	8 + 8	1	0.1	1	0.1
Total		896	99.7	896	100.0

Fractions of 0.05 and over have been counted as a whole number, the rest has been disregarded.

identity.⁵ Besides this, a number of concomitant tendencies are observable: four words per line, two per half-line, a preference for lines of 10 or 11 syllables, more or less perfect intralinear isosyllabicity, a tendency of lines and half-lines to coincide with a syntactic-semantic unit.

Against this background the poet creates, and the reader perceives and enjoys, a play of variation and continuous shifts in meaning. Thus a lively verse is constructed, of which I offer the following example, quatrain SKT I, 21 (compare with SKT II, 23):

a. adápun / ákan // Kén Tambúhan   9: 5 (3+2) + 4 (1+3)
b. bermímpi / búlan // játuh / ke ribáan   11: 5 (3+2) + 6 (2+4)
c. cahayánya / límpah // sekalían / bádan 12: 6 (4+2) + 6 (4+2)
d. pínggang / dibelít // nága / gentáran   10: 5 (2+3) + 5 (2+3)

(As for Lady-in-Waiting Tambuhan, / she dreamed that the moon fell into her lap. / Its radiance flooded her entire body. / A snake was coiling around her waist.)

The next level at which identity is found is that of the couplet, of which two types can be distinguished:

A. The couplet that forms a finished syntactic unit.

B. The couplet that consists of two closed syntactic units that prompt a certain semantic relationship.

In the above example the first couplet exemplifies A, the second couplet exemplifies B. An example of a couplet entirely consisting of B is the following:

Raden Menteri sudah memakai / eloknya tidak dapat dinilai / patutlah diadap diseri balai / segala yang memandang heran terlalai (SKT X, 53).

(When the prince had finished dressing, / he was the nonpareil of beauty. / He was worthy to receive homage in the royal audience hall; / all who beheld him were spellbound with amazement.)

---

⁵ A theory which evidently clashes with mine and poses some tough questions to it but unfortunately came to my notice in an accessible language at too late a moment to be properly taken into account has been proposed by Braginsky. In Chapter I (pp. 10-39) of his book in Russian about the evolution of classical Malay verse, as summarized at the end of that book in English (Braginsky 1975a:201), Braginsky argues that 'the phonetic structure of Malay is highly conducive to the realization in Malay poetry of a syllabic metre. This is evidenced by the weakness and the phonological irrelevance of the word stress, the important role of the sentence stress, tied to ends of the syntagms, the almost equal sound values of the vowels in the stressed and unstressed positions, the minor qualitative reduction of the vowels.' Braginsky discerns two metre-forming principles coexisting over the whole history of Malay verse: the syntactic-intonational and the syllabic. According to him, the role of the syntactical principle has constantly diminished in importance, whereas that of the syllabic principle has become more and more prominent. *Syair* of the 'post-Hamzah' period (2nd half 17th century - beginning 20th century) have a metre that is based on a syllabic-syntactic principle (Braginsky 1975a:206). A recent publication in which he has further pursued this line of research is Braginsky (1991).

In dialogues, too, the couplet structure is respected as may be seen in the following example:

> Berdatang sembah sekalian kaka / mengapakah tuanku berupa duka // patik memandang selaku bercinta / apakah disugulkan emas juita / Ken Tambuhan mengecap seraya berkata / kaka wai ngelu kepala beta // marilah kakang kita nin mandi / karena sudah tinggi hari / orang bekerja dari tadi / aku nin juga yang belum pergi // lalulah mandi Ken Tambuhan. (SKT I, 24.c-27.a)

> (Bowing respectfully her nurses spoke to her: / 'My lady, why do you look so sad? // From your looks your servants think you must be dejected. / Is there something which ails you, my precious gold?' / Lady-in-Waiting Tambuhan answered with a sigh: / 'Older sisters, oh, how my head aches. // Let us take our bath, older sisters, / because it is already broad daylight. / The others are already at work. / Only I have not yet gone there.' // Then Lady-in-Waiting Tambuhan took her bath.)

If the *syair* ultimately cannot be defined as a chain of couplets, this is due to the rhyme that welds the couplets into the larger unit of the quatrain. In the rhyme the background of identity is that the last syllable of each of the four lines shares an identical vowel preceded and/or followed by an identical consonant. An example of rhyme sharing CV is SKT I, 6: *bakti, pati, henti, kati;* of rhyme sharing CVC, SKT I, 21: *Tambuhan, ribaan, badan, gentaran;* of rhyme sharing SVC, SKT I, 18: *silam, pualam, malam, tilam*. Against this background of identity may be constructed minimal rhymes sharing one identical vowel, as in SKT I, 20: *beradu, bertunggu, bercumbu, berilmu*. Or rhyme may be expanded as in SKT I, 44: *tempatnya, peranginannya, tenunannya, perbuatannya*. A tendency also exists to construct couplet-wise rhyme extending beyond the rhyme shared by all lines of the quatrain, as in SKT I, 31: *pudi, lazuardi, baiduri, kiri*.

It will be obvious that certain rhymes can be matched with words less easily than others. Thus for example the use of the word *tertawa* necessarily entails *jua, dua, Jawa, bawa* (see SKT III, 36, 121, 124; IV, 64, etc.). Part of the formulaicness of the *syair* is to be explained by this constraint.

This group of rhyme words in fact forms a 'rhyme-formula', a device helping the poet to construct his verse.[6] Conversely there are rhymes that match more easily with words. One of the ways by which the poet can bring diversity into the words he may use in rhyming position is by rhyming on *-an* (see SKT I, 2, 16, 21, 27, etc.).

Besides rhyme, the second feature ensuring the coherence of the quatrain is its syntactical closure.

---

[6] Rhyme-formulas can also be found in the Malay *pantun*. As Overbeck (1922:18) has pointed out, 'any adept in *pantun* has at his command a large number of rhyme-equivalents which will enable him to construct at a moment's notice the first couplet that gives the rhyme for the second'. For more details, see Koster (1988:208).

3. Formulaic devices for the construction of narrative in the SKT

The text of the SKT as a whole is structured by the creation and perception of correspondences as it unfolds to the listener or reader. This is achieved by the operation of a number of devices that can be loosely subsumed under the term formulaicness. The following devices can be discerned[7]:

a. Lexical repetition: the formula. This device serves for the construction of the verse line. The formula was defined by Parry as 'a group of words which is regularly employed under the same metrical conditions to express a given essential idea' (Lord 1960:30). The basic unit of the formula is the half-line. Formulas with the length of a line are made by accumulating verbal repetitions of the length of a halfline. In his fieldwork among the Yugoslav singers of orally improvised heroic epics Lord (1960:63) noticed that, although these singers shared a common formulaic language, each could be seen to handle it in his own individual manner; accordingly, he counted a group of words as a formula when he found it repeated verbatim at least twice within the course of a single poem. Following Duggan (1973:108-9) one may usefully distinguish between formulas furnishing essential actions in the narrative and descriptive formulas. The verse lines of prologues, narratorial comments and epilogues, too, are constructed with the help of particular formulas.

b. Syntactical repetition with some lexical repetition: the formulaic expression. This, too, is a device for the construction of the verse line. Here, too, the basic unit is the half-line. Formulaic expressions of the length of a line are created by combining half-line length formulaic expressions. Formulas are not sacrosanct, immutable fixed expressions. Rather, for the poet they are a pattern-making device by means of which by lexical substitution he may generate a whole series of derivative forms, the formulaic expressions (Lord 1960:35-45). For a half-line or line to be considered a formulaic expression it must be seen to follow not only the same basic patterns of rhythm and syntax as other half-lines or lines but also to have at least one word in the same position in common (Lord 1960:47).

c. Semantic repetition on a frame of some lexical repetition: type scenes and topical schemes for constructing the role of the narrator. Type scenes are stock patterns of action and habitual schemes of ornamental description used for the construction of the story. Lord, who less fortunately calls them 'themes', has characterized them as 'a traditional grouping of ideas used for the construction of narrative' (Lord 1960:68-9). Besides type scenes the poet

---

[7] My discussion of the devices of formulaicness serving for the construction of narrative is based on the concepts formula, formulaic system, and theme developed by Lord (1960). These are, however, modified to fit the specific literary tradition investigated. I do not assume that the *syair* has been orally composed in the specific Lordian sense.

avails himself of topical schemes to construct the role of the storyteller speaking his prologue and/or epilogue and commenting on his story in asides to the audience (for examples, see Chapter III). The scope of these two devices varies from a line to a passage of several quatrains, as the artistic purpose of the poet requires.

All formulaicness in the SKT is created and perceived against the background of both intertextuality and intratextuality. Intertextually the poet had a command of the literary conventions that he put to use for his own artistic purposes. These conventions have to be mastered by the reader in order to be able fully to enjoy the play of variation within identity in the words, phrases, lines and passages of the SKT. Even in reading this one *syair*, the reader finds himself developing a sense of expectancy of what may come next and perceives a coherence in its parts and in its whole. The explicit repetition of lexical, syntactical and semantic patterns draws his attention to the constructional nature of the SKT. Against this background variations that produce semantic shifts become perceptible.

As examples of the three types of formulaicness used for the construction of narrative I will discuss variants of two type scenes that I have respectively dubbed *berjalan* (to set off) and *memakai/berhias* (to dress/to adorn) after the keyword signalling the beginning of these passages. In my examples each expression that appears to be a formula according to the concordance I have made of the SKT[8] will be marked as such by being underlined with a continuous line. If the formula has the length of a line the entire line will be underlined with a continuous line. If one or both half-lines can be found as a separate formula, the verbatim repeated component is marked with the sign x. Formulaic expressions will be indicated by a dotted line. The keywords of the type scenes will be marked by an asterisk. For the sake of simplicity I have not indicated the countless ways in which formulas, next to being verbal repetitions, simultaneously form part of intricate networks of formulaic expressions. By means of my presentation I hope to give an impression of the operation of formulaicness in the composition of the story told in SKT. It should, however, be borne in mind that this impression can only be an approximate one; the ever-dynamic process of formulaic composition cannot really be adequately fixed in a static written presentation. The first example I offer is a *berjalan*-scene:

puteri pun turun* / lalu berjalan*
diiringkan* oleh / pengasuh yang andalan
Ken Penglipur / menatang puan
membawa kendi / Ken Tadahan (SKT I, 39)

---

[8] For all programming and technical assistance in making the concordance of the SKT I am grateful to Professor C.H.A. Koster and M. Gruis.

II Variation within identity 45

(The princess descended and set off, / accompanied by her devoted nurses./ Lady-in-Waiting Penglipur carried her betel box. / Her water-pitcher was brought along by Lady-in-Waiting Tadahan.)

This *berjalan*-scene is closed by the signal *setelah sampai ia ke balai* (when she had arrived at the hall) in SKT I, 40 and the *datang* (coming) of the princess being noted by the other princesses in SKT I, 41.

The poet may expand the *berjalan*-scene in all sorts of ways, as his narrative requires. In the following example of *berjalan* he amplifies the scene by fleshing out his description with details and by introducing direct speech:

raden pun turun* / lalu berjalan*
didapatnya hadhir x / segala kedayan x
marilah kita / kakang sekalian
masuk ke balai / pengadapan

raden pun naik / keatas kuda
berpayung kertas / tulis perada
diiringkan* kedayan / yang muda-muda
langsung mengadap / paduka ayakanda (SKT IV, 79-80)

(The prince descended and set off. / He found his retainers waiting for him in readiness. / 'Older brothers, let us go / to the royal audience hall to present ourselves.')

Here the scene is closed by the line *ratu sedang diadap orang* (the king was holding court) in SKT, IV.81, and the word *datang* in the line *dilihatnya Inu barulah datang* (he saw that Inu had just arrived) (SKT IV, 81d) signals that a *datang*-scene is beginning. The keywords of the *datang*-scene are *naik* (to ascend), *duduk* (to sit down), and usually *menyembah* (make an obeisance). Examples of this *berjalan-datang* pattern can also be found in SKT IV, 90-4, 109-11, 122-V, 11, 102-22; VI, 4-8, 19, 47-75. Other *berjalan*-scenes are SKT II, 37-50; X, 9-17, 73-5; XI, 19-23. In this way variation is constructed on the basis of identity.

An interesting variation on the *berjalan*-scene is the following quatrain in which the poet tells how the news of Inu's suicide is received by the king:

Setelah sang nata / <u>khabarkan diri</u>
baginda menangis / <u>tiada terperi</u>
<u>segera turun</u>* / <u>lalu berlari</u>
diiringkan* oleh / isi negeri (SKT VII, 82)

(When the king had regained consciousness / His Majesty burst out weeping. / Immediately he descended and set off at a run, / accompanied by the entire populace.)

This scene acquires much of its effect from the expectation that the *berjalan* of royalty takes place in a leisurely, elegant and dignified manner, whereas servants always *berlari* (run) when they *berjalan*, as in SKT VI, 35, 153-4; VII, 68-74. For a similar twist of the conventions see the undignified *berjalan* of the angry queen in SKT VI, 4-8, contrasted in SKT VI, 19 with the gracefulness of Lady-in-Waiting Tambuhan's *berjalan*.

Perhaps the most beautiful expansion of a *berjalan*-scene is SKT VI, 47-75, which is amplified by a description of the feelings of the bystanders seeing Lady-in-Waiting Tambuhan pass, by the description of her beauty like the moon rendering the viewer the more helpless the longer he gazes at it, by the description of comments attributed to the bystanders (*setengah berkata*, some said, SKT VI, 50a), by the description of her sadness, by the description of the calling of the birds of the forest as if welcoming her, and so forth. Interestingly, the scene, that is given its over-all coherence by the continuous repetition of the *berjalan* motif, is closed off by the line *naiklah duduk Ken Tambuhan* (Lady-in-Waiting Tambuhan ascended and sat down) in SKT VI, 75a when she sits down on a stone, wearied by the journey. For a similar method of expansion see SKT IV, 22-V, 11.

The second type scene to be discussed is *memakai/berhias* (to dress/to adorn). It can be exemplified in a short form by SKT X, 53, quoted above in the discussion of the couplet, a passage that epitomizes much of the Malay concept of the beautiful as characterized by Braginsky.[9] A fine example of an expansion of a *memakai/berhias* type scene is the following passage:

Ken Tambuhan / sudah berhias*
berkampuh rangdi / jingga pengaras
berkemban kesumba / diantelas
ditulisnya dengan / banyu emas

berkamar / ikatan Melayu
bersubang lontar / perbuatan bayu
indahnya tidak / dapat dipayu
segala yang memandang / berhati sayu

bergalang kana / dua sebelah
ditatah dengan / permata merah
bibirnya merah / terlalu cerah
giginya laksana / delima merkah

bercincin emas / permata pudi
intan ditatah / lazuwardi
diikatnya dengan / permata baiduri
bersambutan dengan / canggai kiri

bersunting bunga x / cempaka digubah
berpatutan dengan / malai yang indah

---

[9] See especially Braginsky (1979) about the emotion of *heran* provoked in the beholder by the diversity in which beauty manifests itself according to Malay aesthetics.

II Variation within identity

tubuhnya halus / sederhana rendah
mengorak senyum / manis bertambah

setelah sudah / puteri memakai*
ditentang indah / terlalu permai
didalam dunia / tiada berbagai
segala yang memandang x / heran terlalai x

parasnya laksana / gambar wayang
bagaikan lenyap / di mata orang
cahaya durjanya / gilang-gemilang
segala yang memandang suka dan sayang (SKT I, 28-34)

(When Lady-in-Waiting Tambuhan had finished dressing, / she wore a silken robe that was crimson as the sky at sunset. / Around her breast she had wrapped a saffron-coloured cloth of Indian satin, / on which patterns had been drawn in gold leaf. // The sash she was wearing was a Malay cloth. / Her ear-studs were shaped like palm-leaves and were the work of slaves. / To buy such priceless beauty no treasure could suffice; / all who beheld it felt wistful. // On each arm she wore two *kana*-bracelets / inlaid with gems. / The colour of her lips was a fiery red / and her mouth was like the bursting pomegranate // She wore gold rings studded with tiny gems, / diamonds mounted in *lapis lazuli*, / and inlaid with costly and beautiful opals / that enhanced her golden nailprotectors. // In her hair she wore a garland of *cempaka* flowers / that matched her beautiful hairpins perfectly. / She was slenderly built, neither tall nor short, / and looked even sweeter when her face unfolded into a smile. // When the princess had finished dressing, / she presented a lovely sight, most comely to behold. / She was without peer in all the world; / all who beheld her were spellbound with amazement. // She looked like a puppet in the *wayang*, / the shadow of which may at any moment fade. / Her face was of a resplendent beauty; / all who beheld it felt affection and love.)

Here the poet can be seen to amplify the same pattern that underlines SKT X, 53 in a constant play of variation in identity.

In this description the emphasis is laid on the beauty of Lady-in-Waiting Tambuhan's dress. Other *memakai*-scenes describe both dress and physical beauty. See for example SKT IV, 49-65, in which Inu dresses in 49-54 and adorns Lady-in-Waiting Tambuhan in 55-65, and also SKT V, 78-86, which is similarly structured, although the dressing-scene of Lady-in-Waiting Tambuhan clearly hurriedly passes over the obligatory details of the clothes she puts on (*memakai serba rupa pakaian*, she wore all sorts of finery, SKT 83c) to dwell somewhat longer on her physical beauty. In the description of both dress and physical beauty there is a more or less stable order that the poet follows, in itself another example of a helpful scheme for compostion.

An interesting variant of the *memakai*-scene is SKT VI, 20-25, which occurs just after Lady-in-Waiting Tambuhan has been told by a maidservant that the angry queen orders her to hurry to court. First the poet tells us:

tiada memakai sekedar bersahaja / berkampuh lusuh bunga seroja (SKT VI, 20).

(She did not dress for the occasion, / but wore a threadbare *kain* in lotus motif.)

subsequently to launch into a laudatory description of her physical beauty which, even under these adverse circumstances, is still able to *menghabisi seisi desa* (cause the entire populace to turn out, SKT VI, 24a). Other type scenes could be discerned: *santap/sirih* (to take a repast/to chew a betelquid) (SKT I, 37; II, 32-3; III, 88-93, 92-3,118-27; IV, 66-75; V, 88-90; VI, 3-4; IX, 125-7), *mandi* (to have a bath) (SKT I, 26-7; III, 112, 115-7; IV, 47-8; V, 77; VII, 14-5). The sequence of *bangun* (to rise), *mandi*, *memakai*, *santap/sirih*, and *berjalan*, not surprisingly, can be found occurring three times in the *syair* (SKT I, 23-41; II, 26-50; IV, 47-81); SKT III, 115-23 has the sequence *mandi*, *memakai*, *santap/sirih* but not *berjalan*; SKT IV, 47-81 omits *mandi*.

4. A sung performance of the SKT

Last but not least I would like to make some remarks concerning the structure and function of melody in the performance of *syair*. These remarks are tentative since they are based on the analysis of a single sample of a *syair* performed in song.[10] This sample was sung and recorded for me in 1981 in Holland under studio conditions by Dr. Nafron Hasyim, a staff-member of the Pusat Pembinaan dan Pengembangan Bahasa, Jakarta, who hails from Tebing Abang, South Sumatra. According to his information traditional *syair*, which also circulate in manuscripts, are still sung in the region around Palembang, although no new ones are being composed. A transcription of the melodies used in the singing recorded for me, has been included in this chapter.[11]

The melodies to which *syair* are sung are not tied to particular poems. Singing *syair* is usually an amateur activity in which specialization does not play a significant role. In Tebing Abang *syair* are sung only by males, mostly on private occasions, during moments of relaxation in the daytime or in the evening. Occasionally *syairs* are sung at marriage celebrations or at the farewell ceremony when someone is about to leave on a pilgrimage to Mecca. The melody analysed here clearly functions as the vehicle of the text but also adds to its meaning structurally by the correspondences it imposes on it, which create identities against which variations are made perceptible.

---

[10] Unfortunately very little material is available about the singing of *syair*. It seems only reasonable to assume that further research would show the existence of a variety of singing styles. Djaafar et al. quoted in Goudie (1976:6-7), have given a fascinating description of the way the *Syair Perang Siak* was performed at the palaces of Siak and Pelalawan, that indicates a style of singing that differs considerable from 1976 used by my informant. I quote this description at the close of Chapter V.

[11] I thank Dr E. Heins of the Jaap Kunst Ethnomusicological Centre of the University of Amsterdam for his kind permission to incorporate into this chapter the text and musical notations of his note on the structure and function of melody in *syair*-performance, which he wrote on the basis of my recordings of the performance of the SKT (Heins 1982:15-7).

MELODY TYPE II

MELODIC VARIATIONS

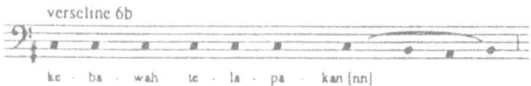

II Variation within identity

The melodic style of the performance is entirely word-oriented and serves to enhance the verbal message, as will become clear in the ensuing analysis.

In the recorded performance two types of melodic shapes can be discerned. As can be seen from the transcription, these melodic shapes coincide with the quatrain of the *syair* and form a closed melodic phrase. The melodic phrase of both type I and type II divides into an antecedent (protasis) and a consequent (apodosis). The antecedent (a + b) and the consequent (c + d) in their turn each coincide with the couplet in the verbal medium. The division is marked by the occurrence of a melisma on one or more final voiced phonemes, followed by a sustained note in the middle of the vocal pitch range, and a breathing pause (V). Type I and type II have a different antecedent, but share an identical consequent.

The antecedent and the consequent are divided into musical subphrases which in the verbal medium coincide with the line. The division here is also marked by a sustained note in the higher range of the melodic ambitus, preferably also embellished with a melisma, but without a breathing pause. Characteristic for the consequent, however, is that both its subphrases end on the same pitch, the note G, the final note of subphrase c anticipating that of d. The overall symmetry is sustained in the subdivision of the subphrases into smaller melodic segments. These are again marked by a sustained last note. This note is never embellished in the subphrases a and c, but slightly in b and d.

The overall scheme given above leaves possibilities for variation, which enhances the pervasive effect of the performance. The interval width is small, the melody moving stepwise as a rule. Throughout the b and c subphrases microtonal intonation occurs, that may be traced back to Koranic recitation, considering the use of the note A sharp. The subphrase d reverts to a pronounced natural A.

Unstressed syllables are preferably sung on short notes. Stresses, accents, pauses, rhythmic patterns are derived from, or identical to, those of spoken language. The overall rhythmic scheme is a *parlando-rubato* close to speech.

The number of syllables per unit does not influence the overall contour of the melody. The number of notes sung is identical to the number of syllables, and one note more or less in the recitation does not bring about any change in the melodic structure (compare for instance the way the same melody accommodates *sekedar kisah* and *segala yang mendengar*). One may regard the sustained notes at the various caesuras as the core notes of the melody.

Type I is the dominant melody. Its melodic shape can be described as arched: the low initial and low final notes have the same pitch, whereas in between the melody rises and then descends again.

Type II is terraced: from an initial high note it cascades down until the lower octave is reached. Type II, used in 27 of the 94 quatrains recorded and investigated, occurs roughly every three or four quatrains. The alternate use of the two types does not seem to be prompted by mimetic-dramatic considerations. The type II melody is used to introduce melodic variation and break up the monotony of the repetition of type I, without however disturbing the overall effect of continuity and the formal coherence of the *syair*.

In the above analysis I have concentrated my discussion of formulaicness in the construction of narrative on a story in the verse form *syair*. I have refrained from trying to give a full survey of all formulaic devices of storytelling, all the way from the surface phenomenon of verbal repetition to the use of deep-structural patterns of type episode and plot. Such a survey would in itself fill a monograph.[12] Nevertheless I hope to have shown how one can learn to read formulaic Malay narrative with understanding and pleasure. Only by mastering its codes can the reader create a setting in which a jewel like the SKT will acquire its glow and lustre.[13]

---

[12] About the generic plots of the heroic epic and the Panji story, see Chapters IV, V and VI.
[13] The intended intertext here is Wilkinson (1913:97): 'When I read Van Hoëvell's magnificent edition of the *Shair Bidasari*, with his translation and notes, I could not help viewing it as a dull stone in a magnificent setting. It seemed a pity that the talent and power there displayed had not been devoted to a worthier literature'. For the many-faceted jewel as the embodiment of the Beautiful in Malay literature, see Braginsky (1979).

CHAPTER III

Dalang or dagang
Narrator, authority and poetics in Malay literature

1. Narratorial roles

In order to be told, a tale obviously needs a storyteller. When a tale is told by word of mouth the storyteller is actually present and visible to his audience. He can address the audience directly to try and capture its interest in what he has to tell. By the inflections and pitch of his voice, by his gestures and his facial expressions, and by his comments he can explain the meaning and purport of his story, and highlight important moments, thereby ensuring a correct interpretation. The writer, however, cannot appear in the presence of his readers and enter into direct contact with them to perform the same function. There is, nonetheless, a device by which he may, in spite of his absence, accomplish the same purposes, namely the projection into the text of a fictional proxy, the narrator, who enacts the situation of the storyteller addressing his audience.

In this chapter[1], I will show that among the multitude of narrators we meet in the manuscripts, we may basically discern two types of narratorial roles. I have emblematically dubbed the one narratorial role that of the *dalang* (the puppeteer of the shadow-play), after the term most often used in self-characterizations by this type of narrator. Other terms by which this narrator may refer to himself are *yang empunya cerita* (the owner of the story), *paramakawi* (expert in Old Javanese poetry) and *bujangga* (scholar, sage). In the same vein I have called the other type of narrator *dagang*. The word *dagang* can simultaneously mean trader and stranger. Other terms domiciled in this field are *gharib* (outsider), *musafir* (passing stranger) and *fakir* (beggar).

The narrator in the role of *dalang* appears in epic *wayang*-stories and Panji romances, both in prose and in *syair*-verse. It is not so easy to delimit the sphere of the narrator in the role of *dagang*. This role cannot be related

---

[1] I published a draft in Dutch of parts 2 and 3 in 1990 (Koster 1990). A summary in English of part 3 appeared in 1992 (Koster 1992).

to a specific genre but occurs both in the serious more playful works. Whereas the self-characterization of the narrator as *fakir* or *gharib* is found in narrative in prose as well as in *syair*-verse, the use of the term *dagang* for the narrator seems to be tied strictly to narrative in *syair*-verse.

These two types of narrators are connected respectively to a Hindu-Javanese and a Muslim – particularly Sufi – strain in Malay culture. To understand them it is therefore helpful to take a look at relevant Javanese and Middle Eastern sources. But this does of course not suffice; in the Malay textual system these borrowed elements have been combined into a coherence which is uniquely Malay. The function and meaning of these two elements ultimately must therefore be understood in their unique interrelation within that system.

The two narratorial roles of *dalang* and *dagang* dramatize the two powers which (see Chapter I) Malay reception could ascribe to the texts in different degrees and in different mixtures; the capacity to soothe the weary heart (*menghiburkan, melipurkan*) and the capacity to edify (*memberi faedah, memberi manfaat*). From the Islamic point of view, the *dalang* is the protagonist of pleasure and soothing, seductive beauty; the *dagang* that of edification. The *dalang* is a figure who takes a certain pleasure in his own creative powers; he stands on the side of forgetfulness through emotional catharsis. The *dagang*, in contrast, denies all creative power and shows himself a reluctant author; he is the protagonist of remembrance through the intellect. Nevertheless, the *dalang* may also indicate a desire to be taken as a figure involved in remembrance, whereas the *dagang* may betray a secret longing to indulge in forgetfulness. The *dagang* represents what was ideologically considered the central task of Malay textuality, whereas the *dalang* embodies its peripheral function.

Besides oral storytelling, both roles thematize writing and the power required for it. Both roles show remarkable agreement about the fundamentals of the poetics of Malay narrative. Whereas they differ in the scope they leave to man to be creator and shaper of his own works and destiny, they are agreed in the belief that in all his acts, writing included, wisdom and divine guidance are indispensable. This shows that in different ways both roles are manifestations of a commemorative epistemics and poetics. These are typical for an oral-aural manuscript culture, such as the Malay one, in which the texts are produced in a complex interplay between the forces of orality and literacy. Whereas the *dalang* is an expression of the force of orality, the *dagang* is a manifestation of that of literacy.

These two conflicting forces are made to converge by what may be called the Idea of the Book. The Idea of the Book – a translation in terms of literate thinking of the mythologizing, totalizing epistemics of oral tradition – is an attempt to control and harness interpretation and signification. It intimates the vital knowledge of a culture as a closed, supernaturally guaranteed and supervised, body of codifications. In traditional Malay culture such Sacred Books are on the one hand the unwritten remembered Books forming the encyclopaedia of oral tradition, such as the Book of the Malay *Kerajaan* Order[2] or the Book of Geomancy, and on the other the written books of Islamic knowledge, such as the Koran, the Book of the Universe written by God, the Book of Memory inscribed by God in the hearts of the wise, the Book of the Pious Traditions, or the Book of the Writings by Holy Men and Divinely Inspired Theologians.

Good writing, that is, writing that is morally justified and will not lead man astray, must be a mirror of these books. Traditional Malay poetics is therefore commemorative, that is, it entails a gesture of remembrance, of return to Origin, by repetition, representation, copying, imitation. Within such a paradigm fiction is at best ideologically admissible if it fulfills the role of a subservient vehiculation of Truth. If fiction is not a direct or indirect representation of Truth, it merely mimics it and is nothing more than a lie.

Within the perspective of Islam the *dalang*, with his stories full of gods and genies, commemorates the Sacred Books of a religion which has been proved false by the message of the Prophet. The only function it assigns to the *dalang* is that of a purveyor of pleasant forgetfulness through the dangerous beauty and seductiveness of mere fictional stories, that really are sinful lies.

2. *The narrator as dalang*

Let us now turn to a consideration of the two narratorial roles, first of all of the *dalang*. As an example of a narrator as *dalang* I offer the prologue of the Panji romance *Hikayat Andaken Penurat* (Story of Prince Andaken Penurat):

> Alkisah inilah suatu hikayat cerita Jawa, dipindahkan kepada bahasa Melayu yang terlalu indah-indah karangannya, dipatut oleh dalang yang arif lagi bijaksana yang amat masyhur ditanah Jawa. Maka barangsiapa membaca dia atau menengarkan dia, jikalau orang itu ada menaruh percintaan sekalipun, maka hilanglah percintaannya, sebab mendengar hikayat inilah yang meliputi dendam dan birahi sekalian, astamewa yang ada menaruh rindu dendam akan kekasihnya. Walakin dendam dimana kan hilang dan birahi dimana kan luput. Perinya juga hamba berkata kepada sekalian tuan-tuan yang membaca ini hikayat dan sekalian yang mendengar akan dia. Maka di dalam pada itu pun terlebih maklumlah tuan-tuan sekalian akan peri hal-ahwal kita orang muda ini, karena hamba pun tahu jua merasai pekerjaan orang muda betapa rasanya. (Robson 1969:21.)

---

[2] My reference here is to the characterization of the traditional Malay socio-political order as *kerajaan*, that is, the condition of having a *raja*, as it has been given by Milner (1982).

(This story is a Javanese tale which has been rendered into beautifully composed Malay, and has been fittingly worded by a wise and discreet puppeteer, who is very famous in the land of Java. Now no matter who reads this work or hears it being read, even if he should be nursing a grief, then his grief will vanish because of hearing this story, which can soothe all feelings of yearning and desire, especially in those who may be longing for a loved one. But how can the yearning vanish and the desire be soothed? Yet this your servant will tell all you who read this story and all who hear it, and in this respect you will all be exceedingly knowledgeable concerning the affairs of us who are young, for your servant, too, knows how it feels to experience the trials of youth.)

This prologue in miniature reveals the interaction between orality and literacy, which is characteristic of most of the Malay textual tradition in general: it thematizes storytelling as well as writing, listening as well as reading (out aloud). Obviously the prologue's function is to argue that the story offered to the public is worth reading or listening to.

To accomplish this purpose the author has his mouthpiece, the narrator in the role of the puppeteer of the shadow-play, make a number of significant claims. First he states that he has derived the tale he has written from an authoritative source, Java, a region which enjoyed considerable cultural prestige in the Malay world. The version he offers is not only beautiful but also authoritative, so he claims, as it has been composed by a wise and discreet puppeteer, whose abilities are widely recognized by the Javanese themselves, witness the fact that his name is famous among them.

One could, of course, assume that this prologue says that the *hikayat* has been composed by a Javanese *dalang* in Java. However, the composition of a Malay literary work by a Javanese *dalang* in Java seems unlikely because of the low prestige Malay has always enjoyed there. It is more likely that, if we may assume that the author of the story was really a *dalang* – and that could of course well be the case – he was a Malay. Clearly, then, the author is less interested in informing his public of his actual individual identity than in claiming a generic identity, a role, which gives him authority as an expert in matters considered Javanese (see Robson 1969:12-4, 1992:35-6).

As the prime effect of his story on its audience or readers the narrator as *dalang* promises that it will soothe all feelings of yearning and desire, especially of those who are in love. He suggests that he is indeed capable of writing a story that has such a power because he himself has also suffered the pangs of love and therefore knows what it means to be young.

Authority is argued in a similar way, and a similar power to soothe feelings of yearning is claimed, in the prologue of another Panji romance, the *Hikayat Kuda Semirang Sira Panji* (Story of Kuda Semirang Sira Panji).

> Alkisah ini adalah cerita orang dahulu kala, hikayatnya terlalu indah, ceteranya dipindahkan daripada bahasa Jawa kepada bahasa Melayu, akan penghibur hati yang masyghul, akan pengulit hati yang dendam. Maka dikarang oleh segala orang

yang bijaksana di tanah Jawa dan dinamainya hikayat ini Kuda Semirang Sira Panji. Maka dicetcrakan oleh dalang yang empunya cetera ini [...]. (Nik Maimunah binti Yahya dan Zaharah Mohd. Khalid 1964:1.)

(This is a tale people told in the days of yore. The story it recounts is very beautiful and was rendered from Javanese into Malay to soothe our feelings of sadness and to lull our feelings of yearning. It was written by the wise men in the land of Java and they named this story that of Kuda Semirang Sira Panji. Now it is told by the puppeteer who owns the story that [...].)

Both prologues are clearly based on the same formulaic pattern, in which the narrator is to refer to the beauty of his tale and its power to soothe feelings of yearning. He is to explain these qualities by referring to the tale as the product of the wisdom and discretion of an author. He may either claim this wisdom and discretion for himself, as happens in the prologue of the *Hikayat Andaken Penurat*, or he may credit them to the source from which he has derived his tale. The prologue of the *Hikayat Panji Kuda Semirang* is an example of the latter.

This formulaic pattern, which manifests itself in the use of certain keywords, underlies all *dalang*-type prologues. It can easily be discerned for instance in the following quotation, the prologue of a version of the *Hikayat Cekel Wanengpati* (Story of Valiant Knight Bachelor), yet another Panji romance.

Bahawa ini cerita orang dahulu kala daripada bahasa Melayu dan Jawa (?), diceriterakan oleh dalang dan bujangga yang paramakawi di tanah Jawa. Dipindahkan dengan bahasa Melayu, maka akan menjadi penghibur rasa yang dendam dilelakonkan. Dalam itu pun masygul dimana kan hilang? Dendam pun tiada terbilang. Akan perinya juga pun dalang katakan akan pemadam hati yang birahi. Maka dalang panjangkan lelakon ini supaya menjadi lanjut tembang dan kidung dan kekawin segala yang arif bijaksana daripada menyatakan asyikin dalam kalbu. Hendak pun dikeluarkannya yang ada di dalam hatinya itu, tiada kan datang kebajikan padanya. Oleh karena itulah maka dikarang hikayat ini bernama Cekel Wanengpati. Itulah yang amat masyhur gagah beraninya dan saktinya lagi dikasihi segala dewa-dewa dengan arif bijaksananya dan pandainya mendam kulah dan amat elok rupanya, tiada terbanding dalam jagat buana tanah Jawa. Ialah yang dibirahikan oleh segala perempuan menjadi tembang kekawin dan rawitan oleh segala perempuannya dan ialah yang menaklukkan segala raja-raja di tanah Jawa sekaliannya dibawah perintahnya. (Winstedt 1977:55.)

(Verily this is a story people told in the days of yore, rendered from Javanese into Malay (?), which is told by a puppeteer and sage, who is an expert in composing poetry in the land of Java. It was rendered into Malay and, in order to become a soother of the feelings of yearning, it was made into a play. But how can sadness disappear? Feelings of yearning, too, cannot be spoken. Yet this the puppeteer speaks about in order to extinguish his feelings of passionate love. And the puppeteer spins out this play in order that the *tembang*, *kidung* and *kakawin* of all those who are knowledgeable and skilled in giving expression to the feelings of passion of the heart may be protracted.. But even if one utters what one feels in the heart, it will bring one no profit. Therefore he wrote this story which is called Valiant Knight

Bachelor. He it was who was renowned for his strength and courage and supernatural power and was loved by all the gods for his wisdom and discretion and cleverness [...], and was handsome to behold, without rival in the entire land of Java. He it was who was desired by all women and was made by them the theme of their *tembang, kakawin* and *wayang*-preludes, and he it was who subjected all the kings in the land of Java to his rule.)

In spite of occasional modest disclaimers of their own abilities, the narrators of *dalang*-type prologues show considerable belief in authorial creative power. They will describe themselves or the author on whose writing they have based their own work as a wise (*arif bijaksana*) storyteller, renowned (*masyhur*) in the land of Java, a scholar (*bujangga*) and an expert in Old Javanese poetry (*paramakawi*), who could compose a beautiful (*indah-indah*) and soothing (*menghiburkan*) work because of these qualities. If the *dalang* indicates that he has derived his story from a previous author, he will refer to the wisdom and renown of his predecessor in the same terms. What is the reason for the fictional *dalang* to have such a firm faith in the capacity of his work to provide its public with beauty and solace?

For an answer it is useful to turn from the paper-*dalang* to the real flesh and blood *dalang* and the poetics of his profession. It then becomes apparent that this faith in the powers of authorship is based on the identification of arcane knowledge and wisdom with power. Through this power the *dalang* can enter into communion with the divine, as seems to be indicated by the present-day poetics of *dalang*-ship on Java as described by Clara van Groenendael (1985:2-3, 24-7) and Keeler (1987:104-40, 202-42). The clue that we must primarily search for an answer in this direction is indicated by the fact that, as we have seen above, paper-*dalang* almost always refer to their work as having been produced in the tradition of Javanese *dalang*-ship.[3]

In the living oral tradition, the Javanese *dalang* of flesh and blood masters his art, the *pedhalangan*, not only through technical ability but also through asceticism, meditation (*tapa*) and spiritual concentration on the divine principle hidden deep in himself beyond the reach of his rational self (*cipta hening*). Through such exercises he accumulates the spiritual strength that gives him power over the invisible forces and thus over events in the

---

[3] The reason I have chosen primarily to try and elucidate the poetics of the paper-*dalang* from what is known about those of the Javanese *dalang* and his literary background rather than from what is known about *dalang*-ship in the Malay world, is because the prologues explicitly point to the Javanese tradition of *dalang*-ship. However, as is shown by Sweeney's monograph on the Wayang Siam – a form of *wayang* concerned with the Rama story, but often combining this with elements of the Panji story – besides significant differences there are many parallels; in the Wayang Siam, too, the *dalang* is very much a magician who derives his power over the spirits and his ability to enthrall his audience from the *ilmu* he has mastered and the secret spells and charms he knows. And he, too, presents himself as a soother of cares (Sweeney 1972:39, 44, 273-9).

life of the community, individual fortune and adversity, as well as over his own success and fame as *dalang*.

As appears from the chapter in Tsuchiya Kenji (1987:1-15) on the Javanese concept of *kebijaksanaan*, the association of wisdom with power is what connects the figure of the *dalang* with that of a sage (*bujangga*) and even that of a king. It is wisdom which provides each of these figures with magical power, gives them access to Divine Guidance, and thus lends them authority.

Obviously, the paper-*dalang*, too, is something like a magician. A prologue showing something of the connection between wisdom and magical power, *dalang*-ship, kingship and authorship is found in the *Hikayat Dewa Mandu* (Story about Prince Dewa Mandu), an Islamized romance which must have been derived from a pre-Islamic Javanese *wayang*-tradition in the opinion of Chambert-Loir (1980:14):

> Wa bihi nasta'inu bi'Llahi 'ala. Ini Hikayat Dewa Mandu yang amat indah-indah karangannya lagi arif bijaksananya serta dengan gagah beraninya bertambah-tambah dengan elok mujelis rupanya, patutlah dengan yang empunya surat ini, karena pada zaman itu tiada siapa samanya, maka termasyhurlah wartanya kepada segala negeri indera dan cendera dewa dan mambang, tiada berlawan sekaliannya itu di dalam hukumnya dan takluk kepada baginda itu, demikianlah diceriterakan oleh orang yang empunya ceritera ini maka dikarang orang arif bijaksana, dipatutnya lelakon yang empunya surat ini bersamaanlah dengan hikayat Dewa Mandu beristerikan puteri Ratna Kumala, anak raja Langka Dura yang menjadi gajah putih disumpahi oleh raja Dewa Raksa Malik. (Chambert-Loir 1980:89.)

> (With this we beseech the help of God Most High. This is the *hikayat* about Dewa Mandu, which has been beautifully composed, and (tells of this prince who was endowed with) knowledge and wisdom, strength and courage, and above all, was divinely handsome and therefore matched the one who owned this text.[4] For at that time there was nobody who could equal him and his fame was spread far and wide, even to those lands where the deities of Indra's heaven and the gods of the moon, the spirits of the air and the spirits of the sunset dwell, and there was not one among them who could resist him, all were completely in his power and were subject unto him. Thus it was told by the one who possessed this story. It was written by a man both knowledgeable and wise. He composed [this version of] the play of the owner of this text so that it was identical with the tale of how Dewa Mandu made Princess Ratna Kumala, the daughter of the king of Langka Dura who became a white elephant by the curse of King Dewa Raksa Malik, his wife.)[5]

---

[4] Because in his view my translation here casts the narrator into a role that is too boastful to fit Malay conventions of modesty, Dr H. Chambert-Loir has suggested as an alternative translation: 'and therefore fits the conception of the hero of the one who owned this text'. I hereby wish to thank him for drawing my attention to some mistakes in my translations and some problems of philology.

[5] My quotations of the prologues of the *Hikayat Cekel Wanengpati* and the *Hikayat Dewa Mandu* could be translated differently. I leave it to the ingenuity of my reader to find out what other translations are possible. As far as I can see, none of them invalidates my thesis that *dalang*-type prologues express a measure of belief in authorial power. The difficulty of

For the Arabic phrase with which the text begins – a formula which seems to be only used in *hikayat* prologues and, as far as is known, does not occur in the same form in Arabic and Persian texts (Ras 1968:612-3) – several different translations have been proposed.[6] Whatever the correct translation may be, it expresses the Islamic belief that for his act of creation man is ultimately dependent on God, the only genuine Creator. In this formula we may perceive a link with the religious beliefs underlying prologues of the *dagang*-type.

The idea that the paper-*dalang* is something of a magician is also suggested by the fact that he may claim to be a *paramakawi*, that is, an expert in Old Javanese poetry. As this self-characterization of the *dalang* indicates, his description of his work as beautiful and its effect as soothing may well – however unwittingly, remotely or confusedly – echo the poetics of Old Javanese literature. These poetics seem to have much in common with those of the *dalang* of flesh and blood of the living Javanese oral tradition. In Old Javanese poetics, too, power, successful authorship and authority are very much a matter which the writer has in his own hands. Old Javanese poetics were a poetics of salvation through a return to the divine principle in oneself. Composing writing was a form of literary magic. The writer was a magician.

According to Old Javanese poetics as characterized by Zoetmulder (1974: 173-86), writing poetry is one of the many means by which the mystic (*yogi*) may seek to reach his goal of the actual realization in an ultimate absolute union of his already existing essential unity with the divine in its immaterial, subtle (*suksma*) state and his release from the snares in which the world keeps man trapped and the cycle of recurrent rebirths. For the poet the divine throughout creation manifests itself in the form of beauty.

The poet, who has acquired the necessary wisdom and power by *yoga*, can see the beauty of the divine shimmer through the veil of the beauty of

---

translating these passages consists in their contextual vagueness and their lack of markers indicating the time aspect of the verbs. One may disagree with my suggestion that *patutlah dengan yang empunya surat ini* must be translated as 'and therefore matched the one who owned this text' by arguing that the Malay words are the product of copyist's error and must originally have been something like *dipatut oleh yang empunya surat ini* ('and has been adapted by the owner of this text', compare the prologue of the *Hikayat Andaken Penurat*), but such an alternative is not supported by the available evidence concerning the manuscripts of the *Hikayat Dewa Mandu*. All the manuscripts used by Chambert-Loir for his edition have the same reading here (Chambert-Loir 1980:89).

[6] Ras has translated the formula as 'His help we invoke; may it excel through God', in which 'it' apparently refers to the story opened by the formula. Djadjuli, who reads the word 'ala' as 'ini hikayat', has rendered it as 'To Him, to God we ask assistance on this *hikayat*'. Jones has suggested rendering it as 'With this we beseech the help of God Most High'. Braginsky has recently advocated translating it as 'To him we resort, because thanks to Allah is all the most sublime (a perfect work of literature)' (Braginsky 1993:218-9; Jones 1985:53, 183; Ras 1968:612-3; Roolvink 1987:592-3).

created nature. Beauty also resides in himself. There, beyond the illusion (*maya*) of the intellect and the senses, the divine resides in its subtle (*suksma*) state, a hidden treasure difficult to reach for the apprentice mystic – of course, the poet modestly reckons himself among them – like a pearl of exquisite beauty. By asceticism and concentration through which he strives to free himself of the consciousness of the self and to become more and more absorbed in the divinity, the poet acquires the power to evoke beauty from the ultimate depths of his being and project it into the material form of a beautiful poem as an object of meditation (*yantra*).

According to Old Javanese poetics by creating a poem, which embodies beauty with words and sounds, or by relishing it after it has been completed, one may be transported into the ecstatic rapture of *langö*. This is a swooning sensation in which all consciousness of the self vanishes in a cathartic experience of oneness with the beauty of the divine, which gives a foretaste of and prepares for the ultimate release in union, when man goes home, once and for all, to the abode of the gods.

The beauty of the poem which entrances the beholder does not do so by its clarity or immediacy, but, quite the contrary, because it seems distant, half hidden and apparently inaccessible, alluring, hinting at as yet unrevealed riches, so that the seeker after beauty is consumed by longing and the desire to reach it, as Zoetmulder points out.

This aesthetics of the suggestive is indeed very much characteristic of the stories which the paper-*dalang* tells, stories many of which do indeed derive from the *kakawin* literature. The theme of beauty just out of reach or threatening to vanish at any moment is a pervasive theme in them, as is that of the all-consuming desire for it. It is such a desire which the *dalang* usually promises to assuage by the beauty of his narrative.

As Braginsky (1986) has indicated, the notions of the enrapturing power of *langö* in Old Javanese literature and the soothing power of *indah* in Malay literature may well be explained by assuming both to be versions of the originally Sanskrit poetics of *rasa* (feeling, sensation, mood).

Rasa, like *langö*, is both the particular quality of an object inducing aesthetic experience and, at the same time, this very aesthetic experience itself. Its source are the stable psychic complexes inherent in the human psyche, such as love, fear, anger and similar emotions, which have been formed as a result of present and former births and preserved in the subconsciousness in the form of impressions. Since a direct description of an affect is unable to impart an aesthetic emotion, this must be effected through a *dhvani* (a sound, an echo) – a hidden sense suggested through descriptions of symptoms, stimulants and transient emotions.

Tasting *rasa* is not only an emotional process but also a special kind of cognition, an immediate intuitive perception of a universalized object (for example, love as such) by a universalized subject, who has renounced his ego. This perception, brought about by a complete identification of the subject-connoisseur with the object, arouses the state of blissful forgetfulness in the beholder. It is a self-cognition of the subject free from the limitations of his ego and illusory distractions, a realization of the absolute self or Brahman (Braginsky 1986:192-4).

It does indeed seem likely that a form of *rasa*-poetics resounds in the prologues of the *dalang*-narrator. In the prologues of the *Hikayat Andaken Penurat* and the *Hikayat Cekel Wanengpati* I quoted above, we find references to the psychotherapeutic ineffectualness of the direct expression of emotions: how can yearning vanish and desire be assuaged? And both prologues claim that only the work of a wise, and therefore accomplished, author has the power to offer consolation and forgetfulness to the weary heart.

As Braginsky (1986:193) has pointed out, a confirmation of the force of such a poetics in the prologues of Panji stories may also be seen in a passage in the epilogue of the Middle Javanese Panji story *Wangbang Wideya*, in which the narrator states: 'For it [my work] serves as the tears of those bowed down under the pain of heart-ache and longing. But how could it give relief? By becoming a *kidung* in the metre Rara Kadiri.' Commenting on this passage Robson underlines the importance in this *kidung* of the descriptions of the internal emotional states of the personages, accomplished through external manifestations (Robson 1971:241).

That Malays indeed very much expected Panji stories to work by the suggestion of *rasa* is confirmed by the remark made by a Minangkabau-Malay copyist to Overbeck that 'a *shaer* [of this genre] was read not so much for the story as for the delight one experiences from witty dialogue and in finding one's own feelings, passions or self-pity well expressed' (Overbeck 1934:111).

It is in this light that we are to understand a promise to the public like the following, made by the *dalang*-narrator in the prologue of the Panji story *Syair Ken Tambuhan*: *Jikalau sungguh khabar demikian / segala yang mendengar belas dan kasihan* (If the story told is really true / all who hear it will feel mercy and compassion) (Teeuw 1966:2c-d). As I show in my reading of this poem (Chapter VI), its soothing power does indeed proceed from the artful way in which in his *lakon* the *dalang* temporarily suspends the commemoration of the Book of the Malay *Kerajaan* Order to spin out a story of the blissful forgetfulness of love, interlarded with and delayed by lyrical passages to such an extent that one comes to feel that the emotions of the lovers are ultimately even more important than the fate that befalls them in the narrative.

As we see, the prologue of the *Syair Ken Tambuhan* unobtrusively hints at the possibility that its story may be fictional: 'If the story told is really true'. And this leads us to another side of the *dalang* as a magician: his role as a conjurer of illusions. The self-confidence of the *paper*-dalang as an author proud of his own powers and abilities may even go so far that he manifests a certain pleasure in his own power as a creator of fiction. This appears, for instance, from the title of the *Hikayat Andaken Penurat*, which I translated as the 'Story of Prince Andaken Penurat'. On the basis of the evidence given in Robson (1969:19), we may also translate this title as: 'The Story of Prince Andaken (the Creature) of the Writer'.[7]

Evidence that this may indeed be an acceptable interpretation of the title of this *hikayat* comes from an episode in the *Hikayat Cekel Wanengpati* in the version studied by Rassers. Here the story tells that in a dream Raden Inu, fallen ill with longing for his beloved Raden Galuh Candra Kirana, sees a beautiful boy, who says that he is his son and promises to bring his parents together again. The boy gives as his name Ki Desti Pengarang, that is, Lord Lovecharm of the Author (Rassers 1922:76).

Obviously, courtly Panji novels were felt to be a form of fiction. This argument could be supported by many more references. To give only one more example, in the *Hikayat Misa Taman Jayeng Kusuma*, we are told about two *kelana* (knights-errant) who go on a spying mission in Tambak Kencana – a town which has been created with the help of a magical ring – in the disguise of two female *gambuh*-dancers. When people ask them whence they hail, they reply: *Beta sekalian datang dari dusun cerita* (We come from the Village of Stories) (Abdul Rahman Kaeh 1976:382-3).

Already in ancient Java the wise censured *wayang* as seductive illusion. This appears from a conversation in the kakawin *Arjunawiwaha* (The Wedding of Arjuna) between Arjuna and Indra, who is in the disguise of an old brahmin. The latter, so Zoetmulder (1974:209-10) tells us, gives an exposition on the true value of power and pleasure. The world, with all that attracts and ensnares the senses is nothing but vain illusion. Pleasure in all its forms, even the pleasure of heaven, belongs to the realm of unreality: 'Blinded by the passions and by the world of the senses, one fails to acquire knowledge of one's self'.

Then, to bring his point home, Indra uses this comparison: 'For it is as with the spectators of a puppet-performance (*ringgit*). They (are carried away,) cry, and are sad (because of what befalls their beloved hero or heroine) in the ignorance of their understanding. And this even though they

---

[7] Robson points out that the use of animal names is typical of Javanese Panji stories and Middle Javanese literature in general and suggests that Andaken is probably a misspelling for the Javanese word *undakan* (horse). He reports that, according to Pigeaud, the name Jaran Penulis occurs in the Javanese *Kidung Arok*. He also mentions that there is a Batak story which features two brothers, Si Aji Panurat and Si Aji Pamasa, the Writer and the Reader.

know that it is merely carved leather that moves and speaks. That is the image of one whose desires are bound to the object of the senses, and who refuses to understand that all appearances are only an illusion and a display of sorcery without any reality.'

As this passage from the *Arjunawiwaha* indicates *dalang*-ship has of old been seen as a profession fraught with ambiguity. On the one hand, the puppeteer may be viewed as a white magician – as a mediator between man and the invincible forces in society (Clara van Groenendael 1985:3) and as a provider of salvation from the distractions of the illusionary self by the unforgetting of and return to real absolute self. On the other hand, he may be seen as black magician, a figure whose craft is 'a display of sorcery without any reality', which only blinds the beholder and makes him forget his true self.[8]

If the *dalang* could already be criticized as a purveyor of illusions by the Hindu Javanese pundit, this could have been all the more the case with the coming of Islam. From the point of view of Islam to deal with the spirit-world was *kafir*, an act of an unbeliever. And the notion that salvation could come from the emotions was equally unacceptable. This only left the *dalang* his role as black magician. Muslims claim that salvation is the sole preserve of Islam, and that leads us to the second type of narratorial role to be discussed, that of the *dagang* who is the embodiment of another poetics of salvation.

3. The narrator in the role of dagang

Like the *dalang*, the *dagang*, too, presents himself in a manner which is clearly formulaically patterned. He characterizes himself as a trader far from home and/or outsider, and/or beggar, who is writing/has written a poem, but is/has been unable to produce a worthwhile work because sorrow about

---

[8] Etymology can be a slippery subject to handle, especially for the non-specialist, but in this context it is interesting to note the etymology Kern has proposed for the word *dalang*. As Kern (1940) has suggested, via the Sundanese word for *dalang, padalang*, the word *dalang* may etymologically be connected to a root word *lalang*, as known in certain languages on the Philippines. From the evidence he presents, derivatives from this root word in a number of these languages take a positive and/or negative meaning. Thus, in Tagalog *paglalang* or *paglalalang* in a positive sense means 'creation, establishing, invention, ability', in a negative sense 'artifice, machination, intrigue'. In one of these languages, in which he finds only positive meanings for the root word *lalang*, it means 'virtue, capability, understanding, wisdom with which one designs, invents or makes something easy, ability, inventiveness'. Kern concludes that *lalang* therefore means 'to create with intelligence, understanding and so forth' and that 'the *padalang* is the man who enacts on stage with intelligence, the man who creates something, a name which also implies a gesture of homage'. It should, however, be noted that Kern's etymological explanation is not the only one proposed; Hazeu connected *dalang* to a root word *langlang*, meaning 'to go the rounds, make a tour, wander about'. According to him the word *dalang* meant 'the man wandering about (to give performances from place to place)' (Clara van Groenendael 1985:4).

his fate robs him/has robbed him of his sense (his reason, his wisdom). He writes/has written the poem only to soothe his own feelings of sadness.

Like the *dalang* the *dagang*, too, thematizes the act of writing alongside that of storytelling. But, whereas the *dalang* is a self-confident author, the *dagang*, in contrast, behaves as what can best be described as a reluctant author. He disclaims all wisdom, power and ability, and denies, or even rejects, all worldly success. For him writing is merely a necessary evil, that cannot, unfortunately, be dispensed with.

To learn to recognize the pattern it is enough to read in succession a series of examples of *dagang*-type narrators one after the other. The first one is the prologue of the *Syair Nyamuk dan Lalat* (Poem of the Mosquito and the Fly). Here the narrator characterizes himself only as a *dagang*.

> Dengarkan tuan suatu rencana/ madah dikarang dagang yang hina / sajaknya janggal banyak tak kena / hati di dalam gundah gulana. (*Antologi* 1980:200.)
>
> (Good sirs, listen to a composition,/ written by an insignificant trader far from home. / Its rhyme limps along and is often lame / because he was sick at heart.)

In the prologue of the *Syair Lampung Karam* (Poem of the Tidal Wave in Lampung) the narrator, besides *dagang*, calls himself at one and the same time *fakir* (beggar) and *musafir* (stranger on a journey):

> Bismillah itu permulaan kata / alhamdulillah puji yang nyata / berkat Muhammad penghulunya kita / fakir mengarang suatu cerita // fakir yang daif dagang yang hina / mengarang syair sebarang guna / sajaknya janggal banyak tak kena / daripada akal tidak sempurna // jikalau ada khilaf dan sesat / janganlah tuan sahaya diumpat / diambil kalam dicecah dakwat / hati mengingatkan tangan menyurat // awal mula hamba berpikir / di Tanjung Karang tempat musafir / menghilangkan dendam sebabnya khawatir / dikarangkan nazam suatu syair. (Lithograph UB 895 D 6.)
>
> (The invocation 'In the name of God' commences these words./ 'Praise be to God' is the laudatory address which opens them./ With the blessing of Muhammad, who is our leader,/ this beggar writes a tale. //This sinful beggar and trader far from home / writes down in his poem whatever seems of use to him./ Its rhyme flows not freely and is often halting,/ because his intellect is far from perfect.// If he commits an error and goes astray, / please do not heap scorn on your servant, good sirs./ He takes up his pen and dips it in the ink. /While his mind recalls, his hand writes down.// At the beginning your servant is deep sunk in thought;/ Tanjung Karang is the place where this stranger sojourns on his journey./ In order to rid himself of his yearning, the source of his worries, / he writes a composition in the form of a *syair*.)

In the following passage, which opens the *Syair Negeri Mekah dan Medina* (Poem of the Cities of Mecca and Medina) the narrator calls himself *fakir* (beggar) and *gharib* (outsider):

> Amabadu inilah nazam / tiadalah fakir perpanjang kalam / hati yang safi menjadi kelam / sebab bercinta siang dan malam // [...] // inilah nazam fakir yang gharib / duka percintaan dibawa nasib. (Lithograph UB 891 F 30.)

(This then is the work that was composed. / The beggar who wrote it did not spin out his tale. / Indeed the clarity of his mind was dimmed / because from dawn of day till the close of eve he was afflicted by despondency. // [...] // This is a composition wrought by a beggar who is an outsider. / Pain and sorrow are the fate he has to bear.)

Finally, in the prologue of the *Syair Sultan Marit* (Poem of Sultan Marit) the narrator characterizes himself as a trader far from home and an outsider:

Dagang menyurat tiada arif / karena hati terlalu gharib (Van Ronkel 1921:74).

(This trader far from home writes without wisdom / because he feels himself an utter stranger.)

The finest example of narratorial musings by a *dagang* is found in the following prologue and epilogue of a version written in 1924 of the *Syair Siti Zubaidah* (Poem of Lady Zubaidah, henceforth SSZ).[9] Irritated by a similar epilogue in *syair*-form – apparently he failed to grasp its point – the great 19th-century philologist Van der Tuuk once grumpily noted: 'There follow 4 pages of drivel in the limping rhyme of the copyist, a native of Java' (Van der Tuuk 1875:1).

Bismi'Llahi'-Rahmani'r-Rahim. Inilah Syair Siti Zubaidah sangatlah indah./ Dengarkan tuan suatu peri / syair dikarang dagang yang ghari(b) / bukan menunjukkan bijak bestari / sekadar menghiburkan hati sendiri // [...] // encik dan tuan muda yang pokta / jangan kiranya fakir dikata / kerana mengarang suatu cerita / hendak melipur hati bercinta // kerana fakir hina dan miskin / tiada menaruh baju dan kain / lagi kerja tiada yang lain / disuratkan syair jadi permain. (Abdul Mutallib 1983:1.)

Tamatlah syair Siti Zubaidah / tiga bulan baharu sudah / Rajab akhir habislah madah / tengah gelorat hendak berpindah // [...] / kerana sajaknya tak boleh ingat / pinggang dan tengkuk seperti lumat // [...] // suratan pun tidak ketahuan rupa / dikarangkan oleh dagang yang papa / dengan orang tidak serupa / tambahan tidak ibu dan bapa // sanak saudaranya sekali / misal umpama akar dan tali / hina miskin keturunan asli / tiadalah orang yang sudi peduli // tiada orang seumpama saya / badan tak sehat hati tak daya / duduk bercinta seumur dunia / seperti orang hilang upaya // sangat bercinta rasanya hati / mengenangkan untung nasibnya pasti / di Singapura tempat berhenti / [...] // [...] / sahabat handai tak boleh saba[r] / mana-mana yang dekat menjadi tuba // rasanya hati terlalu rawan

---

[9] The oldest known version of the SSZ – ms. Klinkert 130 (Van Ronkel 1921:73) – dates from the middle of the 19th century. From a letter by Klinkert to the Executive Committee of the Nederlandsch Bijbelgenootschap, dated Riau, 2 September 1864, we know that he acquired the manuscript, with a number of others, from a *selir* of Tengku Putra, the Yamtuan Muda of Siak, who at the time lived in Riau, exiled there by the Dutch. According to Van Ronkel this poem is entirely identical with the *Syair Abdul Muluk* (v.d. W 257 in Van Ronkel 1909:321-2) which was published with a free translation in Roorda van Eysinga (1847:285-6). Interestingly, the SSZ is also acted on stage (Chambert-Loir 1980:8; Robson 1969:139-42). R. Dumas is writing a dissertation about this Dul Muluk theatre. The version of the SSZ I quote was produced in 1924 and printed in lithograph in Singapore in 1927. The name of the compiler is not known. When it is compared with earlier versions it becomes clear that it is largely the fruit of copying.

/ terkenangkan nasib untungku tuan / menanggung percintaan sangatnya haiwan / fikiran akal tiada ketahuan // [...] // nasib tak boleh dikenangkan lagi / kehendak Allah sudah terbahagi / seperti tampak gunung yang tinggi / tidaklah daya hendak pergi // sakitnya badan tidak beruntung / tiadalah tempat hendak bergantung / [...] // wahai nasib untungku tuan / siang malam berhati rawan / seperti orang mabuk cendawan / oleh mendengar katamu tuan // [...] // jika sampai kuasa dan kudrat / dengan seketika pergi mengerat / entah ke timur entah ke barat / membawa dendam dengan hasrat // [...] // [...] / membaca syair jangan dikata / kerana tulisan terlalu leta // [...] // menyurat pun ini di dalam bercinta / tidak sempurna sajak dan kata / [...] // [...] sudah membaca kisah diingatkan / supaya boleh tuan iktibarkan // [...] / encik dan tuan lebai dan haji / jika tuan berkehendak membeli / syair dan kitab banyak sekali / harganya murah tidak terperi. (Abdul Mutallib 1983:469-75.)

(In the name of God the Merciful and the Compassionate. This is the Poem of Lady Zubaidah, a very beautiful tale. / Hearken, noble sirs and ladies, to this story, / a poem written by a trader far from home. / In it he betrays little wisdom. / He wrote it only to console himself. // [...] / Sirs, noble lords, young gentlemen, / do not, nonetheless, find fault with this beggar. / That he wrote a story was indeed / only because he sought comfort for his heavy heart. // Despised and impoverished as this beggar is,/ he does not even possess a jacket and kain in which to clothe himself. / Moreover, he has nothing else to do. / Therefore he just jotted down a poem for distraction.)

(The story of Lady Zubaidah has drawn to its close. / After three months' travail it is finally finished./ The story was rounded off at the end of the month of Rajab,/ in the midst of sorrow, for here we have no abiding place. // [...] / Because he was not always able to remember to heed the rhyme,/ his limbs and neck, everything ached // [...] // What has been committed to writing has no rhyme or reason, / composed as it was by a destitute trader far from home, / who is not as other men, / yea, is even bereft of both father and mother. // His kinsfolk find him merely an obstacle / as the root of a tree or as a liana in the impenetrable jungle. / Despised and destitute as is the trader far from home, / there is not a single soul who cares what happens to him.// No one suffers as does your humble servant; / his body is ailing, his spirits are exhausted. / Filled with grief he sits out his allotted span of life in this world,/ as a man forlorn. // Deep sorrow overwhelms him/ as he becomes aware of the fate and fortune that are his portion: / Singapore is to be his temporary abode./ [...] // [...] / His friends are unable to bear their fate with patience; / all that was close to him has turned into a stupefying drug. // His heart is filled with deep sadness / as he dwells on his fate and fortune. / Suffering sadness, a prey to his animal passions / he loses his wits completely. // [...] // Fate is not to be pondered about; / it has already been decided by the will of God./ It is as when you spy a high mountain in the far distance;/ you desire to draw nigh but do not have power to do so. // Suffering in body and forsaken by fortune / he has no one to turn to. / [...] // How distressing is the fate and fortune of your servant, / who is assailed by care from early morn till deepest eve. / He is as one intoxicated by eating a hallucinatory fungus, / because he heard your malicious gossip, sirs and ladies ! //[...]// When his power and strength are sufficient,/ after a while he will leave on his journey to Heaven / and – Eastwards or Westwards, who will say whither? – he will bear his desperation and yearning with him. // [...] // [...] / When you read my poem do not revile me / because it has been written so badly. //...// As your servant was writing it he was constantly assailed by grief, / so that both in rhyme and word choice it is far from perfect. / [...] // [...] / When you have read my tale, remember it, / so that you may draw an example from it. // Noble sirs and ladies, mosque attendants and *haji*, / if it chance that you wish to make a purchase, / I have *syair* and religious tracts for sale in abundance, / for a price so low it passes understanding.)

The story of the SSZ tells how the pious and wise Lady Zubaidah, thanks to her faithful trust in God and steadfastness in the face of adversity, after protracted wanderings and many battles during which she performs many feats of magic, succeeds in freeing her husband, Sultan Zainal Abidin of Kembayat, from his captivity under the unbelieving princesses of China. By doing so, she shows that, although she is merely the daughter of an *ulama* (theologian), she is a better spouse than her husband's other wives who are of royal blood. After they have been defeated in war by Lady Zubaidah, disguised as the Sultan of Yunan, the princesses of China, of course, convert to Islam.

In the prologue and epilogue of the SSZ we are confronted with a figure who describes himself as a trader far from home. This trader bewails the fate which has landed him in Singapore and laments that he is forced to live as a beggar in abject poverty and failing health. He complains about the humiliation, the hatred and the slander which he encounters on all sides, not only from those in high places, but even from his friends and close relatives. He suggests that instead of bearing this pain and being driven insane by grief, it would be better for him to move elsewhere.

He denies that his story has any quality. It is of no account, so he says, because he has been unable to concentrate on his writing because of his misery. He claims he wrote his poem in 1924 and did so in an effort to seek solace from his woes. Indeed, as a man without employment he had nothing better to do. After begging his reader not to revile him and to heed the moral of his tale, he finally makes it known that he trades in *syair* and pious literature and urges his public to purchase from him at an advantageous price.

As this summary indicates it is not impossible to take this description that the narrator offers of himself and his circumstances merely as references to the person and life of the anonymous real author who produced this version of the SSZ in 1924. Then we are quite simply dealing with a Malay author and bookseller who uses the prologue and epilogue of his work in order, in the words of his narrator, to give vent to his frustration that the bad business suffered by his bookshop has reduced him to penury, and that he has had to supplement his meagre income by writing. And we may assume that he has seized this opportunity especially to urge his public to buy from him.

But such a reading creates more problems than it solves. If the bookseller is so keen to sell his books, why, so we may wonder, does he denigrate his own work after first having called it beautiful? And why does he snub potential clients by accusing them of having taken part in a slander campaign against him? Yet, if the author allows his narrator to say that he could not concentrate on his writing, is there not a not unintentional kernel of truth lurking in this feigned negative qualification of his own ability? Are we not confronted here with a native who just burbles on without thinking, as Van der Tuuk would no doubt have opined.

When we read the prologue and the epilogue of the SSZ alongside other *dagang*-type prologues and epilogues – I have already cited a few examples of these above – it will quickly become obvious that it follows consistently the now familiar pattern: the narrator presents himself as a merchant from afar (outsider, beggar), who is writing/has written a poem, but is not/has not been very successful because sorrow about his fate robs him/has robbed him of his sense, his reason (*akal*), his wisdom (*bijak bestari*).

There is no reason to deny the possibility that the prologues and epilogues of *dagang*-narrators contain real referential and biographical information. Thus there need be no doubt that the 1924 version of the SSZ was indeed produced by a real bookseller, who actually lived in Singapore. But it is hard to accept that so many Malay authors only wrote *syair* when they were abroad on a business trip, in order to assuage their feelings of homesickness. Rather than assuming that all these traders far from home refer to historical individuals behind the texts – a referential mode of reading – a more fruitful view is to see them as variants of a stereotyped narratorial role. This brings us to another, more meaningful way of reading the prologue and epilogue of the SSZ, a rhetorical one.

A rhetorical mode of reading regards the appearance of the narrator as a trader far from home as an artistic device of the author who wishes to produce a certain effect on the public. If we adopt this rhetorical way of reading we will come to see that the narrator as a sad and unloved outsider longing for home is not an indication of the historical and individual situation of the author, but a metaphor for man's fate in this world. And we will then understand that the narrator in the role of a stranger appears as an incarnate – or rather, impapered – admonition to the public to be aware of its own situation.

Significantly, the prologue of the SSZ opens with the pious formula *bismi'Llahi-Rahmani'r-Rahim* (In the name of God, the Merciful and the Compassionate). By pronouncing this formula the narrator recalls that man is dependent in all his actions on God and implores His help for the creation of his work (Braginsky 1993:218-9). At the same time he admonishes his public to be ever mindful of God.

In fact, we can see the whole of the prologue and the epilogue of the SSZ as the preaching of a sort of sermon by the narrator. In the role of the trader far from home he enacts the yearning for God of the pious man, who, forever on the road, longs to return whence he came. It is a rhetorical device employed by the author to preach that whoever longs to be reunited with God after death will have to renounce the world and all its vanities.

The message of this sermon can be paraphrased as follows:

> 'Remember, O mankind, that you have no permanent abode in this world, and are but as one on a journey, by which eventually you shall return unto God. In His Unfathomable Wisdom God has decided that you shall return unto this world. Accept without complaint this sad fate that He has decreed for you and bear all your trials with patience. However difficult this may be for you, and no matter how sorely you are despised, hated and slandered by those around you, do not be corrupted by the sinful temptations of the world and do not become attached to its so-called pleasures. In this world be like a trader far from home; longing to return, he never settles anywhere permanently but roams throughout the world in order, after he has made rich use of the talents God has bestowed on him, to finally return to his own country when the season is ripe.'

In the metaphorical web which is spun in the SSZ by means of the figure of the narrator, two metaphors take a central place: the image of the pious man as a stranger/trader far from home who must view the world as no more than a temporary abode and has to live in it as an outsider; and the image of the pious man in this world as a beggar, who has to live in poverty, and to patiently bear the fate dealt out to him by God's will in the devout faith that He knows what is best for him. These metaphors have been derived from religous literature, pious traditions and sermons.

Thus, there is a pious Arabic tradition (*hadith*) about the Prophet attributing to him the saying: 'In this world be as if you were a stranger (*gharib*), or one passing along the road'. With the addition of the sentence 'and reckon yourself already among the denizens of the tomb' this saying is to be found in all sorts of Malay collections of traditions about the Prophet (Jones 1985:202, note 78).

In the Malay textual tradition we meet these pious thoughts in different versions of the *Taj us-Salatin* (Crown of the Sultans), an early seventeenth-century mirror for princes, in passages such as the following:

> Lagi pun dunia ini umpama jalan, perhentian juga adanya, tiada dapat tiada lalu juga kita, tiada harus berbuat rumah pada pertengahan jalan itu, karena kita lagi akan lalu juga.
>
> (Furthermore, this world may be likened to a road with halting places; we have perforce to travel this road, [so] we should not build a house along it, since we have to keep on travelling (Jones 1985:205).

> Keadaan dunia itu seperti suatu titi juga pada antara jalan akhirat. Adapun barang siapa yang berbudi tiada berbuat rumah di atas titi itu, hanya lalulah daripada atasnya [...] tetapi orang yang tiada berbudi berbuat juga rumah di atas titi itu dan suka duduk selamanya di situ.

(The world is like a bridge along the road to the next world; now the sensible person does not build a house on that bridge, he merely crosses over it [...] but the person who is not sensible does build a house on that bridge and desires to live there forever (Jones 1985:205).

It is within this field of imagery, that, in the heroic epic *Syair Perang Mengkasar* (for my reading of this work see Chapter IV its presumed author, Encik Amin, can make his narrator – who is, indeed, every inch a narrator in the role of a trader far from home and outsider (Skinner 1963:v. 22a, 26a, 204c, 214b, 525c) – close his narrative with the words:

Fakir yang gharib punya karangan / kalamnya tidak berpanjangan / kertas sekeping bekal tangan / akan penghibur angan-angan. (Skinner 1963:v. 534.)

(This is the composition of a destitute stranger / He shall not spin out his discourse. / A sheet of paper is his provision for the journey / as a soother of his cares.)

In Persian devotional literature and in some of the mystic poets – for instance in al-'Attar (d. 1220) – the metaphor of the one who seeks God, living in the world as a trader in the market-place, is a well-known image; the merits he accumulates in the world, which give him access to the rewards and delights of the life eternal in the Hereafter, are compared to the profits made by the trader at the market. One Malay work in which we can find this metaphor is again the *Taj us-Salatin*, where, in the section *Peri mengenal dunia* (On knowing the world), we find the following passage:

[...] dunia ini itulah pasar negeri akhirat, dan segala manusia berdagang dalamnya itu dengan senentiasa berbeli dan berjual [...].

([...] the world is a market of the world hereafter, and mankind is trading in it, continually buying and selling [...] (Jones 1985:195-6)).

We also find it in the *Hikayat Sultan Ibrahim ibn Adham*, a story based on the life of an 8th-century Sufi saint in Afghanistan. The *hikayat* tells of a sultan who abandons his throne, his riches and even his wife and children to become a Sufi *syaikh* in quest of his true self in order to return to God. It is with the following words that Ibrahim ibn Adham admonishes his wife not to be sad about their parting:

Hai Siti Salihah, jangan kau sangat dukacita sebab perceraian dunia ini, karena bahwa kita dan segala manusia dalam dunia upama dagang juga adanya: apabila datang musim lagi akan kita pulang juga pada negeri kita yang sebenarnya. Demikianlah adanya dunia ini. Apabila datang ajal kita nescaya kembali kita mengadap negeri kita yang baka. (Jones 1985:85).

(Siti Salihah, do not upset yourself on account of partings of this world, for we and all mankind in the world are to be likened to [foreign] merchants: when the appropriate season comes we shall return to our proper land. That is what this world is like. When our alloted span ends certainly we shall return to the eternal land. (Jones 1985:133, 135.)[10]

The metaphor of the trader far from home plays an important role in the work of the Sufi mystic Hamzah Fansuri, who came from Baros in the north-west of Sumatra and wrote homilies on Sufi mysticism in *syair*-form at the end of the 16th century. Hamzah's poems have been much imitated by other writers in works in which this metaphor is equally prominent. The popularity of these homilies in verse must certainly have contributed to the rapid expansion of the importance of the *syair* within the Malay textual system and the enduring fondness of the Malays for the *syair*.

Hamzah, who as a Sufi mystic was concerned with the mystical unity which the individual person can achieve with God even during his lifetime, likes to combine the image of man as a trader far from home with the imagery of the voyage of a ship over the stormy seas of God's will exercised by Him in the world:

Hidup dalam dunia upama dagang / datang musim kita kan pulang / [...]. (Drewes and Brakel 1986:XIII, 6a-b.)

(Live in this world as a trader far from home. At the change of the season we will return.)

Kenali dirimu hai anak dagang / jadikan markab tempat berulang / kemudi tinggal jangan kaugoyang / supaya dapat hampir kaupulang. (Drewes and Brakel 1986:XXIII, 8.)

(Know yourself, o trader far from home. / Turn it into a vessel for your return. / Steer a steady course without wavering / so that your return may be at hand.)

---

[10] In another version of the *Hikayat Sultan Ibrahim ibn Adham*, the sultan first admonishes Siti Salihah by likening this world to a house furnished with beautiful adornments and clothing and good things to eat. The owner of the house being exceedingly hospitable, the house is never without guests; the sensible (*budiman*) and fortunate (*beruntung*) ones of these enjoy the facilities but never lose sight of the fact that they are guests, and so cannot take any of the good things away with them when they leave. Moreover, on their departure they show proper appreciation of the things they have enjoyed, and as they have realized all along that they were only guests (*maka iapun ingat akan tuan rumah itu, lalu ia mengucap beribu-ribu kali syukur*), they are not sorrowful when the time comes to depart. But the foolish (*bebal*) and unfortunate (*celaka*) people who visit the house are delighted by what they find, and imagine that when the time comes to leave they can take things along with them. They forget that they are only guests (*hatta berapa lamanya ia didalam rumah itu dengan sukacitanya, dan lalailah ia akan dirinya itu jamu [...] hatinyapun terikatlah pada segala perhiasan itu. Maka tuan yang empunya rumah itupun murka tersangat akan dia olehnya tiada teringat pada tuannya yang empunya rumah itu*); they neglect to give thanks to the owner of the house for what they have enjoyed, and, when they are thrown out of the house by order of the angry owner, they are filled with sorrow (Jones 1985:223-4). For this metaphor of man in the world as a guest (*anak jamu*), which is closely related to that of man as a trader far from home in the poems of Hamzah Fansuri and his imitators see Drewes and Brakel (1986: XX, 2a, XXVI, 13a) and Doorenbos (1933:23, 34, 84).

Bahr al-Haqq terlalu dalam / ombaknya menjadi 'alam / asalnya tiada bersiang malam / di laut itu 'alam nin karam // Dengarkan hai anak dagang / lautnya tiada bersurut pasang / muaranya tiada bersawang-sawang / banyaklah orang sana terkarang. (Drewes and Brakel 1986:XXX, 1-2.)

(God's Ocean is unfathomable. / Its waves form the world. / Originally there was no alternation of day and night. / In this Ocean the world will founder. // Listen, oh trader far from home. / This Ocean has no tides. / Its estuaries have no horizon. / On the reefs there many people have struck.)

Tark al-dunya akan labanya (Drewes and Brakel 1986:XXXI, 7a).

(The renunciation of the world is the profit he [the Godseeker] makes.)

Imitators of Hamzah have written such works as the *Syair Perahu* (Poem of the Ship) (Braginsky 1975b) and the *Syair Dagang* (Poem of the Trader Far from Home). The first-mentioned of these works presents the voyage of devout man through the life in this world back to God as a perilous sea voyage across the Indian Ocean and up the Red Sea, undertaken by a trader in his ship. In the second work, in a sermon, the preacher admonishes his audience thus:

Amat-amati membuang diri / menjadi dagang segenap negeri / baik-baik engkau pikiri / supaya dapat emas sendiri. (Doorenbos 1933:22.)

(Be mindful to take yourself into exile / and become a trader far from home in all the lands you visit / Ponder upon this well, / that you may earn your own gold.)

Ketahui olehmu hai anak dagang / badanmu itu di rantau orang / pikiri jua malam dan siang / supaya jangan beroleh utang. (Doorenbos 1933:32.)

(Know this, O trader far from home, / that in this earthly life ye find yourself abroad among strangers./ Ponder upon this day and night, / so that you may incur no debts.)

He interlards his sermon with the same complaints about his sorry state, his ailments and his poverty, the calumny of others and his own powerlessness that we came across in the narrator of the SSZ, and to do this he uses the same sorts of formulas. He also says he is writing his poem to console himself in his misery. We may therefore assume that it is above all by homilies like this that the role of the narrator as a trader far from home is inspired.[11]

---

[11] It is interesting to note that even in a certain genre of *pantun* quatrains the 'lyric I' - or is the 'lyric he' perhaps a more suitable term? - can appear in the role of a trader far from home and that the features which this figure can assume in the poem are broadly speaking the same as that of the preacher and of the narrator as a stranger: *Anak engggang di kayu tinggi / patah ranting terbanglah ia / anak dagang lama di sini / sampai musim pulanglah dia* (Zainal Abidin Bakar 1983:pantun 1164) (The hornbill perches in a lofty tree. / When the branch breaks he flies away./The trader far from home has tarried here long. / When the monsoon arrives he will return.)

Now let us turn to the second metaphor, the image of devout man as a beggar, doomed to live in poverty, patiently bearing the blows which fate has dealt him, inflicted on him by God's Will, in the confident knowledge that God knows what is best for him. First of all this metaphor may be connected to the belief in the need of man for God, as this is expressed in the Koran, in Sura 35.16, where it is written:

> O men, you are the ones that have need of God; He is the All-sufficient, the All-laudable (Arberry 1983:446).

Whereas destitute man cannot exist without God, God, rich as He is, is sufficient unto Himself. In the prologue of a Malay religious tract, the *Kitab Mukhtasar* (Compendium for Travellers on the Mystic Path) by Kemas Fakhruddin of Palembang (active in the last quarter of the 18th century), this religious awareness of human poverty is expressed as follows:

> Bismi 'Llahi 'l-Rahmani 'l-Rahim. Qala al-faqir al-da'if al-dhalil ila mawlahu al-ghani al-jalil, Kata pekir yang laip lagi hina kepada Tuhannya yang kaya lagi mahabesar [...]. (Drewes 1977:107.)
>
> (In the name of God, the Merciful, the Compassionate. This feeble and lowly beggar before the Lord rich and exalted says [...].)

Another source from which the imagery of man as a destitute mendicant is fed are the traditions about the Prophet. Thus the Prophet is said to have cried out *Faqri fakhri*, that is, 'Poverty is my pride' (Schimmel 1975:120-1).

There are also numerous anecdotes about the poverty of the Prophet's family. Perhaps the best known story, which is also to be found in Malay texts, is that of the poverty of the Prophet's daughter, Fatima al-Zahra, who was so poor that once, when the Prophet came to visit her with a friend, she felt herself obliged to refuse to receive them because she, just like the narrator of the SSZ, who apparently makes an allusion to this, did not even have something in which to clothe herself decently. Finally she was able to receive her visitors in a garment borrowed from her father and her father comforted her in her distress and advised her to bear her earthly suffering patiently because in the Hereafter a rich reward would be her portion. In the *Hikayat Sultan Ibrahim ibn Adham* this story is told to Siti Saliha by her father to admonish her to be patient for the present (Jones 1985:106-9).

For the Sufi mystic outward poverty is a requisite stage on the road of the seeker after God (Schimmel 1975:120-6). Even more important to him is inner poverty: only those who desire no more for themselves in this world or in the Hereafter can justly be called *fakir*. Because they desire to possess nothing, they are possessed by nothing. They only need God into Whom they desire to be absorbed. Poverty must be borne patiently. Patient suffering means remaining unmoved by the arrows of God's decrees. Absolute patience is to accept everything that comes from God, even the heaviest blows of fate, indeed even to render thanks unto Him for these. The symbol of this devout attitude is the figure of Ayub (Job), about whom Sura 21.83-4 of the Koran says:

> And Job – when he called unto his Lord, 'behold, affliction has visited me, and Thou art the most merciful of the merciful'. So We answered him, and removed the affliction that was upon him, and We gave his people, and the like of them with them, mercy from Us, and a Reminder to those who serve. (Arberry 1983:330.)

And in Sura 38.44 God praises Job for the patience with which he bore his afflictions, saying:

> Surely We found him a steadfast man. How excellent a servant he was! He was a penitent. (Arberry 1983:467.)

The fictional narrator, in the role of the trader far from home, is thus a Job. Just as the much afflicted Job, while tethered to this world he patiently endures all the blows which fate deals him at the command of God, trusting in Divine Providence. Living as an outsider in the world each day he is prepared to set out on his journey home.

In the Persian and the Malay textual tradition the longing for God has found allegorical expression in narratives in which the motif of the quest, familiar from among others the Panji romances (see Chapter VI) is connected with that of the spiritual ascent of the mystic through the several stages of gnosis. A fine Malay example of such a narrative is the *Hikayat Syah Mardan* (Braginsky 1990). The expression of man's longing for God by means of prologues and epilogues spoken by a narrator in the role of a trader far from home seems to be a uniquely Malay invention.[12]

---

[12] In Old Javanese and Balinese *kakawin* literature the quest for spiritual awareness and for the revelation of divine beauty, too, may be symbolized as a journey. For a discussion of this I refer to a study of the Balinese ritual of *kakawin* composition by Rubinstein (1988). This study amongst other points examines the account of the mystical journeys of the Balinese Brahmana priest Nirartha as found in his biography, the *Dwijendratattwa*, for the light it throws on the Balinese view of the process of literary creativity (Rubinstein 1988:128-41). In the Western tradition there are obvious parallels to be found with the Malay metaphor of devout man's life in the world as that of a trader far from home and the use of the figure of Job as the symbol of patient suffering. In the religious literature of Christianity Job has always been the prime example of the virtue of *patientia*, suffering with patience fully trusting in God (Besserman 1979:125). The Christian counterpart of the Malay-Muslim foreign trader is the pilgrim. As well as in sermons and in religious plays performed in the churches, this metaphor has also been expressed in narrative texts in the plot-pattern of the 'spiritual journey' through life which the pilgrim, driven by longing, makes through a land of exile on the way to his heavenly homeland. This plot is to be found in such edifying works as the Old English poems *The Wayfarer* and *The Seafarer*, Dante's *Divina Commedia* and Langland's *Piers Plowman*, as well as in Chaucer's entertaining *Canterbury Tales* (Gardiner 1971:1).

4. Commemoration and the Idea of the Book

As we have seen, besides oral storytelling the *dalang* and the *dagang* both thematize their act of writing and the wisdom and power good writing requires, but do so in a different way. The *dalang* tends to show himself a self-confident narrator, who makes no bones about vaunting his own – or his source's – ability and creative role in the process of composition. By contrast the *dagang* is a painfully selfconscious narrator, who broods over his lack of wisdom and power, his inability to write and the imperfection of whatever he creates in the face of divine perfection.

What both narrators are agreed about is that a writer requires divine inspiration and guidance. To be able to partake of these an author has to possess wisdom. This wisdom is claimed by the *dalang*. It seems to be denied by the *dagang*, but is, of course, claimed by him as the wisdom of knowing oneself to have no wisdom. By their insistence on the importance of wisdom for the creative process both narratorial roles manifest that they are founded on a commemorative episteme, as is typical for an oral-aural manuscript culture. A concomitant manifestation of this episteme is the Idea of the Book.

Commemoration may be defined as 'any gesture, ritualized or not, whose end is to recover, in the name of a collectivity, some being or event either anterior in time or outside of time, to make meaningful a moment in the present' (Vance 1979:374). A commemorative culture will inevitably rationalize its knowledge in the perspective of a metaphysics of signs. Within this episteme Reality or Truth is conceived of as existing in ideal perfection, immanent in the present or anterior to existence itself. Hidden in immanence or transcendentally absent, this Truth will signify itself partially to man in time and space by means of the words and things that constitute this palpable world.

The commemorative impulse – the ontological privileging of some moment or principle of Origin – which dominates in cultures with purely oral communication as well as in oral-aural manuscript cultures – manifests itself in such seemingly diverse phenomena as the cult of the ancestors, precedence and customary law, the ritual of pilgrimages, the centrality of the exemplary, and so forth. Within a commemorative paradigm, any notion of recall – in other words, any notion of representation, mimesis – will ultimately involve some form of return through regression, an erasure of self. The gap between the signifiers that constitute the empirical world and the signified to which they point – an immanent or transcendent Truth standing at the origin of all – is bridged by an act of remembrance, or rather, of unforgetting. Both the *dalang* and the *dagang* acknowledge that the prerequisite for the ability to perform this act of unforgetting is wisdom.[13]

In the poetics of the *dalang* of the oral tradition and those of Old Javanese *kakawin* literature commemoration – the gesture of return through the erasure of self – manifests itself as the forgetting of one's illusory rational self in an emotional state of trance or enthusiasm to become possessed by the spirits or by the divine immanent in oneself. Under the pressure of his Islamic environment, the paper-*dalang* has more or less renounced the *jahil* claim that his writings can point the way to salvation by leading back to true knowledge and the divine. As we have seen, the paper-*dalang* largely contents himself with characterizing his composition as just a venting of his emotions, as just a giving in to desire and forgetfulness, which provides both the writer and his public with solace from their daily cares. Yet the paper-*dalang* has never entirely relinquished his claim to commemorate. This appears from his emphasis on the necessity of wisdom for the creation of a good work. And it is underlined by his conviction that, albeit not primarily, his work not only offers soothing forgetfulness but memorable examples, as witness for instance the way in which the narrator of the *Syair Ken Tambuhan* expresses his belief in the exemplary power of his narrative: *Madahnya tidak banyak ibarat* (Its words do not contain many examples) (Teeuw 1966:v. 1c).

In the poetics of the *dagang* the emphasis lies heavily on commemoration, exemplariness and edification. Man's emotional self, his desires, are seen as mere seductive illusions tying him to the sinful world. They form obstacles preventing him from returning to God, from acquiring True Knowledge. For the *dagang* commemoration is to unforget one's real self by an effort of the intellect (*akal*). His term for this erasure of illusionary self, and return by commemoration to one's real self and, by way of this real self, to the One and Only Reality determining all that was, is and will be, is *meninggat*. For his oblivion of the Real under the pressure of his emotions and wordly desires he has another word, namely *mengenangkan*, which means 'to dwell on something in loving or nostalgic memory'.

Although the *dagang* emphasizes his duty to be ever mindful of God, imposed on him by his longing for salvation and True Knowledge, he can not quite forego human forgetfulness of God and giving in to earthly emotions and desires; all *dagang*-prologues hinge on this conflict. A good example of a dramatization of man's lot to be torn between love of God and love of the world is provided by the narrator of the *Syair Siti Zubaidah*. As we will become aware, we may align other antitheses to the opposition *mengingat* vs *mengenangkan*, such as the following: the spirit or higher self

---

[13] In my characterization of the commemorative paradigm follow an article by Vance (1979), entitled 'Roland and the Poetics of Memory'.

(*ruh*) vs the body or earthly self (*badan*); the spiritual (*ruhani*) vs the merely animal (*haiwani*); rationality (*akal, fikir*) vs the emotions (*hati, mabuk*); bearing in patience the fate God has decreed (*sabar, tawakkal*) vs rebelling against God's will (*ganggu tawakkal*); self-sufficient divine power (*kuasa, kudrat*) vs the inherent frailty and dependency of man (*tak sehat, tak daya, bergantung*); the joy of beholding the Truth face to face vs the sadness of having to grope for understanding in exile in this world (*gelorat, rawan, percintaan*); the all-embracing and perfect writing of God on the Safely Preserved Tablet (*di luh ul-mahfuz suratan terjumlah*) vs the inherently imperfect inscriptions of man (*suratan tidak ketahuan rupa, tulisan terlalu leta*) that may at best lead to only partial knowledge.

The commemorative episteme is invariably linked to an ideology of logocentrism: the privileging of the natural presence in speech over the artificial and therefore dangerous and potentially dissembling, feigning representation in writing; the preference for the living Spirit over the dead Letter, for the signified over the signifier. In Islamic terms: *ruh* is privileged over *badan*, *makna* over *lafaz*. If speech is conceived – as is done not only in Islamic thought but in oral tradition as well – as giving access to truth through its proximity to a self-present consciousness, writing is prone to be suspected of obstructing that access by obtruding its opaque, material inscriptions in the place of an ideal transparency.

From the viewpoint of the mythologizing mode of cognition of oral tradition writing is liable to be viewed as a threat to memory and true knowledge, as an obscuring of presence and as a barrier to the 'true self' of wisdom emanating from the universe, in which the divine is immanently present. Oral tradition's mode of cognition is 'totalizing' in nature; its important knowledge and wisdom form a vast unwritten encyclopaedia. In this encyclopaedia – the *summa* of the culture's accepted knowledge and the embodiment of the eternal present in all things – all items of the universe and all events past and present have been classified into an elaborate system of related meanings, which leaves nothing unexplained. Existing phenomena are read as connected by a pre-existent design and then catalogued and indexed from a seemingly unquestioned sense of the unity and continuity of the universe.

The unwritten encyclopaedia of oral tradition, consisting of the several volumes of knowledge of the culture – its history, religion, physical science and domestic lore – is kept alive by being constantly recalled and recreated in performance with the help of an apparatus of formulas, type-scenes, rhymed sayings and so forth. The ability and authority required to pass it on are acquired in the course of a closely supervised process, in which a wise old man keeps an eye on his pupil, thus preventing him from introducing undesirable high-handed and unauthorized deviations, until he has acquired the wisdom and power qualifying him to act on his own without endangering the tradition.

The descriptions given by Clara van Groenendael (1985:21-30) and Sweeney (1972:41-8) of the training of prospective *dalang* in the traditional *wayang* on Java and in Kelantan confirm this picture of the process of learning in a world of oral communication. Sweeney reports that in Kelantan there are *dalang* who may claim not to have learned their craft from a *guru*. Even these *dalang*, however, cannot do without proper authorization by a higher power. Accordingly, they claim to have received their craft by revelation (*tajalli*). Referring to such a *dalang* an orthodox, properly authorized *dalang* may say that 'a child without a father is usually known as a bastard' (Sweeney 1972:41).

For an oral culture the intrusion of writing not only poses a threat to memory and the stable and proper transmission of myth but also undermines the grip on these processes of proper authority. A writer may pursue his own self-opiniated ideas without any supervision or ratification from an accepted teacher. Making misuse of script he can pretend to possess wisdom. Released from the control of the presence of an audience, he can feign sincerity, concealing himself behind the letters; whether sign and meaning coincide can no longer be immediately checked.

In Islamic Malay oral-aural manuscript culture the opposition between orality and literacy, speech and writing, presence and absence, is resolved by what Gellrich (1985) in his study of European mediaeval notions of textual interpretation has called the Idea of the Book. The Idea of the Book may be seen as a continuation in the world of literacy of 'totalizing', mythologizing thought. By this epistemological model a form of writing can be conceived of that guarantees the continuation of memory and the stable, proper and authorized transmission of the vital values and ideals of a society.

The Idea of the Book may be characterized as the idea of a totality, finite or infinite, of the signifier, conceived as a Book; this totality of the signifier cannot be a totality, unless a totality constituted by the signified, pre-exists it, supervises its inscriptions and signs, and is independent of it in its ideality. The Idea of the Book is a metaphor for a kind of writing held within bounds by the author's sovereign presence, a writing whose integrity of purpose and theme comes from its acceptance of proper, self-regulating limits.

The Idea of the Book admits of a writing that is not semblance but revelation; a writing that does not consist of an arbitrary collection of words, but of special divine words, whose signifying is not truncated from signified truth. This divinely supervised, controlled, authorized writing – 'good writing' in contrast to disruptive, aphoristic, unauthorized 'bad writing' – does not get in the way of truth with artificial inscriptions, but reveals divine wisdom like a brilliant mirror.

As in mythologizing, 'totalizing' thought, the Idea of the Book conceives of the universe and all phenomena in it as consisting of signs forming part of and being informed by a grand design; the universe reads like one vast Book, which refers to the wisdom of its Divine Author and thus enables man to return to True Knowledge and Origin. All signs within this Book are understood as pointing to a system of supernatural truth, and as instructing moral conduct.

By the Idea of the Book – a translation in terms of literate thinking of the mythologizing, totalizing epistemics of oral tradition – the two forces of orality and literacy are made to converge into one poetics. The paper-*dalang*, who echoes the poetics of the real *dalang*, is still very much connected with the world of orality and mythologizing thought. In the voice of this type of narrator – a figure still striking the stance of an untrammelled oral storyteller – we continue to hear the voice of the wise, and therefore powerful and properly authorized, puppeteer unselfconsciously practising his craft in front of his audience for all to hear and see. The *dagang*, on the other hand, is connected with the world of literacy. A writer – albeit a reluctant one – rather than a storyteller, in his quest for authority he reflects with painful self-consciousness on his own act of writing, brooding over his lack of wisdom, and therefore of power and authority in the face of God, the only Real Author.

According to the Idea of the Book, if human writing is to be properly authorized and is to instruct moral conduct, by a gesture of return it is to mirror Divine Revelation as it stands inscribed in the pages of the Koran, the Book of the Universe, the Book of memory of the wise, and the writings of properly authorized, wise religious teachers. Writing, if it is to be properly authorized, is to try and repeat these Books or copy from them. 'Good writing' as well as 'proper reading' are viewed as a form of imitation.

The Idea of the Book is an effort to stabilize and harness signification. It is profoundly alien to the notion of human writing and reading as an uncontrolled, freely creative activity. As mythologizing thought strives to safeguard the correct, properly authorized transmission of oral tradition, so the Idea of the Book endeavours to keep out 'bad writing' and uncontrolled, unauthorized interpretations, which in its opinion are a mere semblance of truth and wisdom and will only lead away from Origin into exile.[14]

In the Islamic version of the Idea of the Book the central place is taken by *al-lawh al-mahfuz*, the Safely Preserved Tablet mentioned in the Koran. According to the authorative commentaries on the Koran this tablet is kept

---

[14] My argument about the Idea of the Book follows Derrida's discussion of writing as poison and cure in Plato as discussed in chapter 3 of Norris (1987:30-96) and the chapter 'The argument of the book: Medieval writing and modern theory' in Gellrich (1985:29-50).

in the Seventh Heaven. God inscribed the decisions of His divine will on it with His Reed (*qalam*), recording the archetypes of all that is to be. The Safely Preserved Tablet is also the Mother of the Book (*umm al-kitab*), being the original copy of the Koran, uncreated and co-eternal with God (*Encyclopaedia of Islam* 1986:698).

This original copy of the Koran was sent down from the Seventh Heaven to the First and revealed to Muhammad as the expression of God's will (*Encyclopaedia of Islam* 1986:698). In a vision the Archangel Gabriel appeared before the Prophet and, holding up a silk cloth on which the Koran was inscribed, commanded him to read it out in the name of his Lord and then communicated to him the first verses of the revelation (Kramers 1985:x).

The Koran thus appeared not as a mere signifier but as the direct revelation of God's will. As the receptacle of the best of all meanings (signifieds) for every Muslim it is the paradigm and fountainhead of all knowledge and a model for all human writing, yet unsurpassable in its perfection, beyond the reach of successful human imitation (see *i'djaz* in the *Encylopaedia of Islam* 1971:1018-20).

Elaborating on the Idea of the Book, Sufi mysticism conceives of creation as the act of writing immediately following the Divine Command 'Be!' (*Kun*). According to 'Abd al-Karim al-Jili's tract *Kitab al-Insan al-Kamil* (The Book of the Perfect Man), the correlation of Divine Being and creation sets in by the play of God's attributes of action, the effects of which show in the variegated pattern of the world. First the Prime Intellect and the Exalted Reed are created, to be followed by the Safely Preserved Tablet, on which the reed imprints the forms of existence (Drewes and Brakel 1986:169).

In Sufi speculation the universe and the wise man are respectively viewed as a macro and microcosmic copy of the Koran, the reading of which may enable the mystic seeker to return to God. An example of a description of the universe as a Koran is the following passage from the poem *Gulshan-i Raz* (The Mystic Rose Garden) by Mahmud ash-Shabistari (d. 1320):

> The Universe is the book of 'The Truth Most High'.
> Accidents are its vowels, and substance its consonants,
> And grades of creatures its verses [*ayat*] and pauses.
> Therein every world is a special chapter [*surah*],
> One the Chapter Fatihah, another Ikhlas (quoted from Braginsky 1993:204).

Because God knew that for weak, imperfect man, the macrocosmic Book of the Universe would be too vast to comprehend in full, in His bounty He created him as a microcosmic copy of the macrocosmos. Thus Aziz Nasafi (early 14th century) in the treatise *Zubdat al-Haqaiq* (The Cream of the Truths) states:

> We [humans] were too small and the Book was too vast, and our sight could not see it in full – its margins and all its pages. The Supreme Teacher, seeing our feebleness, [...] diminished it in size. He called the first the great world and the second the small world; He called the first the great macrocosmic book and the second the small macrocosmic book. Everything that the first book contained He inscribed in the second book, so that anyone who has to read the smaller book could by means of this act read the great one (and could thus know the Lord). (quoted from Braginsky 1993:204.)

Malay Sufis, too, have formulated fine expressions of the Idea of the Book. One is that of the universe as a Tree of Writings leading back to the Reality of Certitude (*Sajarat Haqq al-Yakin*), that is, to the attainment of annihilation in God at the highest stage of gnosis (*fana*), as it is found in the mystical *Hikayat Si Burung Pingai* (Story of the Pure Bird):

> Maka disanalah Si Burung Pingai mendapat sebatang kayu yang bernama Sajarat Haqq al-Yakin maha indah-indah, berbatangkan kalam, berbanyirkan lawh, berkulitkan kertas, bergetahkan da'wat, berbuahkan auraq, berdaunkan baris, berputikkan suatu nokhta. (quoted from Braginsky 1993:212.)

> (And there the Pure Bird found a tree, called the Tree of the Reality of Certitude that was very beautiful to behold. As its stem it had the Pen, as its roots it had the Tablet, as its bark it had the paper, as its sap it had the ink, as its fruits it had the writings, as it leaves it had the lines and as its buds it had the dots.)

A description of man as a scroll, pointing the way to those who long to return to God, is given in a Rencong version of the *Syair Perahu* (Poem of the Boat) (Braginsky 1992:18):

> Dengarkan ibarat, hai segala fa'ilun / insan seperti kayu jawwabun / batangnya lahir pada kun fa-yakun / mencari dia hai raji'un / insan itu terlalu kamilun / ialah pohon sekalian raji'un / muhitnya lengkap pada sekalian bajilun / [...] // sungguh sepohon tiada lenyap / kedua matanya adanya mushaf / [...]. (quoted from Braginsky 1988:282.)

> (Hear the parable, O all ye doers. Man is like unto a tree for travellers / of which the trunk grows from 'Be thou!' – and it becomes', / Seek it, O ye who return. // This man is most perfect. / He is the tree for all who return. / He thoroughly encompasses all who are worthy / [...] // Truly he is the tree unperishable. / There is a scroll in each of his eyes.)[15]

For the Sufis the mystic can be guided to God not only through reading the Koran or observing the signs of the universe but also by reading the signs inscribed in his heart, which remind him of his Lord. The mystic, in his striving to gain the vision of God, has to become empty of self in order to become a clear mirror reflecting His face.

---

[15] When I presented the draft of my argument about the Idea of the Book at the Seminar on Comparative Poetics held at the Leiden Centre for Non-Western Studies in May 1992, Professor Braginsky happened to be among my audience. I learned from him that in a somewhat different manner he, too, had worked out similar ideas in a recent article (Braginsky 1993).

Constant recollection polishes the mirror of the heart to show God's hidden beauty, that 'hidden treasure' that wanted to become manifest (Schimmel 1975:382). Thus it has been said about Bayezid (d. 874) that he was 'for twelve years [...] the blacksmith of his self until he made of himself a pure mirror' (Schimmel 1975:49). And an 18th-century mystic in Delhi, describing the process of meditation, states: 'He [the mystic] sees the blessed figure of the word Allah in the color of light written on the tablet of his heart and the mirror of his imagination' (Schimmel 1975:421). A comparison by Hamzah Fansuri of the mystic to a mirror goes:

> Rupamu zahir kausangka tanah / itulah cermin sudah terasah / jangan kaupandang jauh berpayah / mahbubmu hampir sertamu ramah. (Drewes and Brakel 1986:88.)
>
> (Your outward form you consider as clay, / whereas it is a polished mirror. / Do not strain your eyes by looking into the far distance. / Your Beloved is intimately close to you. (Drewes and Brakel 1986:89.)

The mystic's vision of the Divine can become blurred. From having been transparent the spiritual self of the mystic can become opaque so that his heart no longer mirrors God. This may happen if his earthly body with its carnal desires proves the stronger. Instead of striving to return to God, patiently bearing God's decree to live in this world, he may then be seduced to turn away from Origin and abandon himself to worldly pleasures. Instead of remembering his Lord, he may become a prey to forgetfulness. Meditation (*fiqr*) serves to prevent his spiritual heart from going astray and helps to keep it stilled and turned inward to God (Bakhtiar 1976:15-9).

For Sufi-inspired Malay poetics, like gnosis, good writing and proper reading similarly result from a spiritual ascent to God by an act of unforgetting. Only writing and reading which does not forget God is a work of merit, which brings benefit (*manfaat, faedah*) to man by edifying him. God is the only true creator. In order to receive His divine inspiration man has to remember God as he inscribed himself on the tablet of his heart. Only the wise man who is endowed with an illuminated spiritual heart may mirror the luminous stream of His creative energy and be inspired by it in his reading and writing.

The all-embracing knowledge of God contains the archetypes of all things created. God's Omnipotence (*kudrat*), manifesting itself as the creative energy of his Mercy (*rahmat*), makes these archetypes present in the phenomenal world, making them accessible to the senses, through the agency of the Prophet Muhammad in his form of the pre-eternal *logos (Nur Muhammed)*. Actualized by the creative light mirrored in his heart, the archetypes appear as a complex of ideas in the imagination of man (Braginsky 1993:217).

Man's act of authorized writing and proper interpretation therefore consists of establishing a proper correspondence between the signified (*makna*) mirrored in his imagination as he remembers God and the signifiers by which he tries to render them into speech (*lafaz*). As Braginsky has indicated, the Malay term for this proper mode of commemorative composing, that belongs on the side of *mengingat*, is *mematutkan* (Braginsky 1979:2-4, 1992:24-5). Its opposite is *memanjangkan*, from the Islamic point of view an unwarranted giving in to the seductions of authorship and the forgetting of God in a playful proliferation of the signifiers. *Memanjangkan* therefore belongs on the side of *mengenangkan*. Under the pull of *mengenangkan* the brilliant mirror of the heart may be clouded, so that the writer may complain that *hati yang safi menjadi kelam* (the pure heart is obscured) (*Syair Negeri Mekah dan Medina*).

We have already seen in part 2 of this chapter that the *dalang* characterizes his compositorial activity not only as *memanjangkan* but also as *mematutkan*. Here we have another indication that he does not want to be just a purveyor of soothing pleasure but claims to be something of an edifying remembrancer as well.

An example of the use of the term *mematutkan* for the composition of proper, commemorative writing by a *dagang* is the following passage, that closes the epilogue of the *Syair Sultan Maulana*, a poem about the role of a Kedah fleet as auxiliaries of the Siamese in a war fought in 1810 against the Burmese:

> Patutlah kita sekalian ummat / membaca salawat pohonkan rahmat / diatas fakir[16] yang mencari hemat / mematutkan sair sehingga tammat (Skinner 1985:v. 1102).
>
> (It is proper that we Muslims all / invoke God to grant His blessing and pray to Him to take pity / with this beggar who seeks for a state of watchfulness / in order to compose his poem until it has been finished.)

Typically, the *dagang* will exert himself as best he can to deny that he gives in to *memanjangkan*; he will claim to tell nothing but the truth, nothing more, nothing less. Indeed, not to spin out the story, but to tell exactly what is to be told is the stock promise of *dagang*-type narrators.

In order to write and read properly and reach the truth man is to see it that he is not ensnared by the material signifiers of the text – potentially a veil as well as a revelation, a source of forgetfulness as well as of wisdom. If the text he writes or reads has been grafted onto Divine Revelation and is written or read by him with wisdom and discrimination, its signifiers will not lead him into the exile of uncontrolled interpretation and forgetfulness,

---

[16] Skinner's reading of *fakir* as *fikir* is obviously a misreading.

but will point out to him the way back to the Lord. Yet, that the *dagang*, too, is not averse to the charms of amplification, appears when the *dagang*-narrator of the *Syair Perang Mengkasar* (Poem of the Macassar War) promises his audience: *Tidaklah saya panjangi lagi* (I will not spin out my story any longer) (Skinner 1963:v. 438c).

By putting his narrator in the pose of the *dagang* the writer, although of course very much aware that he writes, demonstrates his reluctance to be an author. He disclaims that he has any power or capability of his own. If he has any wisdom, any knowledge – and of course the *dagang* really considers his attitude a form of wisdom – it is that only God knows. He belittles his creative authorship and retires under the mighty shadow of the Creator. If he can accomplish anything, it is not in his own name, but in the Name of God, the Merciful, the Compassionate. And he argues that his work, although the sinful product of human creation, as an attempt to remember God is a work which strives not to lead the reader into banishment, away from the greatly longed-for reunion with God.

The *dagang*, who represents the central urge in the Islamic system of traditional Malay textuality, rather than being an author is in every respect a scribe, bent on copying from the Books of Holy Scripture, the Universe or Memory, in order to reach out by an act of commemoration to God's writing and revelation. He shows himself painfully aware that his own writing cannot recreate God's writing without errors, and that, flawed by comparison with the divine it tries to mirror with full clarity and transparency, it is at best an unworthy gloss. He therefore sets himself to writing only with reluctance, trying with the patience of a Job to bear God's decree which has sent him into exile in this sinful sickly world of opaque material signs (*badan*), yet too human and too weak not to bemoan his sad condition.

Caught between the need to remember and the desire to forget the *dagang* is something of a tragical figure caught in a situation of aporia. In the *Syair Siti Zubaidah* the narrator aptly expresses his sense of the impossibility of crossing the ontological abyss that separates man from God, signifier from Signified, by a comparison:

> Nasib tak boleh dikenangkan lagi / kehendak Allah sudah terbahagi / seperti tampak gunung yang tinggi / tidaklah daya hendak pergi (Abdul Mutallib Abdul Ghani 1983:470).
>
> (Fate is not to be pondered about; / it has already been decided by the will of God. / It is as when you spy a high mountain in the far distance; / you desire to draw night but do not have the power to do so.)

5. The place of fiction within the Books of Malay culture

As we have seen, the Idea of the Book makes a distinction between 'good writing', and 'bad writing'. It considers 'good writing' to be the books, written or unwritten, which lead to Truth and Origin and are to be repeated and imitated: the Koran, pious tracts by theologians, oral traditions passed on by wise men, the Book of the Malay *Kerajaan* Order, the Book of Memory written in the soul of the wise. This has produced the frequent references in prologues of Malay works to previous authoritative books. To underline their moral authority they present themselves emphatically not as individual creation but as copy, imitation, borrowing. 'Bad writing' is unauthorized writing, the mere product of the uncontrolled fancies of an individual, a writing which forgets Origin and debases the Truth through the shadowplay of its mimic signs and inscriptions.

Within such a paradigm fiction can only be justified and be given an acknowledged status if it is seen to fulfill a subservient role as the handmaid of Truth. Fiction as a playful constructing of possible new worlds is allowed no place in it. This is the attitude towards fiction which we find in the Koran.

In opposing the Prophet and his message, his enemies frequently engaged the service of poets to attack the man and his message with the power of their words, a mighty weapon in then still largely illiterate tribal Arab society. Accordingly in Sura 26:221-6 the Koran delivers a harsh verdict on the poets:

> Shall I tell you on whom the Satans come down? They come down on every guilty impostor. They give ear, but most of them are liars. And the poets – the perverse follow them; hast thou not seen how they wander in every valley and how they say that which they do not? (Arberry 1983:381.)[17]

But this is not all the Koran has to say about poets. It also admits of the possibility that they may do some good, as appears from the way the same Sura (26:227) continues:

> Save those that believe, and do righteous deeds, and remember God oft, and help themselves after being wronged; and those who do wrong shall surely know by what overturning they will be overturned (Arberry 1983:381).

The Koran, then, admits the possibility that poets may produce good writing, if only they remember God during the act of writing and are thus properly inspired.

Proceeding from this positive view of fiction in the Koran the Sufis, who as mystics have an individualistic frame of mind and a penchant for

---

[17] For a discussion of the notion of poetry as lie in Arab poetics I refer to Bürgel (1974), Jacobi (1972) and Heinrichs (1969).

literature, have developed the doctrine of poetry as the 'bride of the Word'. According to this doctrine, poetry can be good writing if it allegorically adumbrates the Divine Word embodied in the Koran and lures the reader to it by its beauty, as the beauty of a woman attracts a man from behind her veil (Braginsky 1993:208-10).

A sterner attitude towards fiction, more in line with the negative view of the poets in the Koran, has been taken by the theologians. For them proper guidance (*dalil*, basically meaning 'a sign of something', 'a manifestation', 'proof' (see *Encyclopaedia of Islam* 1965:101-2), cannot be obtained from literature. It can only be derived from the Koran, the pious traditions and the writings of the theologians derived from their correct usage of terms (*istilah*). Witness for instance the following statement by Bukhari al-Jauhari as found in one version of his mirror for princes *Taj as-Salatin* (Crown of the Rulers) (1603):

> Maka hendaklah anak cucunya sekalian disuruhnya membaca kitab yang keluar daripada ceritera hadis Nabi salla 'llahu 'alaihi wa salam dan hadis segala nabi diceritera daripada pesuruh itu, dan ceritera daripada segala ulama yang muafakat dengan dalil Quran dan hadis segala nabi 'alaihi 's-salam itu juga sebenar-nya, dan membaca kitab ini, dan segala kitab yang dikarang segala ulama itu khabarnya daripada Quran dan Nabi itu, seperti Bustan as-Salatin dan Sifat as-Salatin dan Nasihat al-Muluk dan Sifat al-Muluk; dan lain daripada itu daripada segala kitab yang diperbuat ulama yang dikeluarkannya daripada istilah Quran dan hadis itu jua yang harus dibaca dan didengarkan segala ceriteranya dan diturut segala pengajarannya, maka beroleh pahala dan faedahlah adanya. (Mulyadi 1983:23.)

> (They should instruct their children and grandchildren to read books which derive from the stories of the Prophet, may God bless him and grant him peace, and from the traditions of the prophets which tell of the messengers [of God], and stories from the theologians which are consonant with the guidance given by the Quran and the true traditions of the prophets, upon them be peace. Let them read this book and books composed by the theologians, derived from the Quran and the Prophet, such as the *Bustan as-Salatin*, the *Sifat as-Salatin* [Characteristics of the Rulers], the *Nasihat al-Muluk* [Advice for Kings], the *Sifat al-Muluk* [Characteristics of the Kings]; and besides these books written by the theologians, derived from the correct usage of terms in the Quran and the traditions. It is those books they should recite and listen to and their teaching they should follow, obtaining merit and edification.)

This passage is preceded by a description of what is 'bad writing', that is, writing that does not edify and bring profit to man but leads him to harm by its lies:

> Sebermula barang siapa ada baginya beranak laki-laki atau perempuan, hendaknya anaknya itu jangan sekali diberinya bersahabat dengan orang yang jahil dan yang permainan berjudi atau penyabung dan yang perebana, dan jangan membaca hikayat yang tiada berfaedah adanya, karena dalam hikayat itu terbanyak juga dustanya kepada memberi mudarat dan tiada harus menyuratkan hikayat itu. Niscaya binasalah adanya dalam dunia dan akhirat, sebab nyata dustanya hikayat dengan (re)bana itu. Maka hikayat inilah dalam Tanah Melayu sangat masyhur kegemarannya perkataan dusta mengada-ada yang mengadakan dosyanya itu seperti

nyata yang tersurat itu pun tiada harus ditaruh dalam rumah hikayatnya. Lagi kafir barang siapa membaca dia atau menengar dia, seperti Hikayat Jawa Indraputra itu pun nyata dustanya, daripada dungu dan kurang budi juga segala yang membaca dia dan yang membenarkan dustanya itu. (Mulyadi 1983:23)

(If you have sons and daughters, do not allow them to befriend ignorant persons, gamblers, those who indulge in cock-fighting, and tambourine-players; do not let them read worthless *hikayat*, for the contents of these are for the most part lies which lead to harm and it is not proper to copy them. Those [who contravene this injunction] will be doomed both in this world and the next, for these *hikayat* recited to the accompaniment of the tambourine are obviously lies. As for these *hikayat*, the popularity of their lying stories that pretend to represent but really only represent sin is well-known. It is obvious that such writings should not be kept. Persons who listen to such stories as the Javanese Story of Indraputra are unbelievers. That these stories are lies is obvious; those who recite them and hold these lies to be true are stupid and lacking in character.)

Presumably, what Bukhari objected to in the *Hikayat Indraputra* was the Hindu-Javanese character of the world it held up to its readers. In his view, such writing was a lie. It only put people under a spell by its illusionary power; it was feigned representation (*mengada-ada*), not real representation (*mengadakan*). It was a lie because, for the theologian, it was a commemoration of a fallen, therefore non-existent order, a forgetting of God, a deviation from Origin. Typical of the scribal poetics of the Malay textual tradition, he exhorts his readers to counteract the influence of bad writing by not copying and keeping it.

A similar view concerning the *Hikayat Indraputra* was held by the theologian Nuruddin al-Raniri, as can be seen in his *Serat al-Mustakim* (Straight Bridge to Heaven) (completed 1644), a book on religious law (*fiqh*) and the observance of religious obligations (*ibadat*). In its 'Fasal pada menyatakan istinja' (Paragraph to discuss ritual cleansing) we find him condemning this *hikayat* and the *Hikayat Seri Rama* (Story about King Rama) as filth (*najis*), as a swerving away from origin, like the Torah and the Gospels:

Dan tiada harus bersuci dengan sesuatu benda yang dihormati pada syarak, seperti tulang dan kulit yang belum disamak atau barang sebagainya, tetapi harus istinja dengan Kitab Tauriat dan Injil yang sudah berubah daripada asalnya dan demikian lagi harus istinja dengan kitab yang tiada berguna pada syarak seperti Hikayat Seri Rama dan Indraputra dan barang sebagainya, jika tiada dalamnya nama Allah. (Mulyadi 1983:21.)

(And it is not proper to cleanse oneself with something which is respected according to the canon law, such as bones and untanned leather and other things; but it is proper to cleanse oneself with the Torah and the Gospels, which have deviated from their origin, and also it is proper to cleanse oneself with books which are useless according to the canon law, such as the *Hikayat Seri Rama* and *Indraputra* and the like, unless they contain the name of God.)[18]

---

[18] Another way in which Islam has dealt with romance has been to Islamize the genre in

Strict Muslims reject the performance of and attendance at *wayang* plays. Thus, in Kelantan, they consider the Wayang Siam sinful (Sweeney 1972:35-6). The reason will by now be clear: from the point of view of orthodox Islam to enjoy a shadow-play is to recite from the wrong book, namely the Book of the Devil (*mengaji dari kitab Syaitan*) (Siti Hawa Salleh 1970:86-110; esp. 90 line 19 and 20, 96 line 9)[19], a manifestly bad form of writing, motivated by the devious purposes of an evil author. To attend the *wayang* is to surrender oneself to a world of mere semblance and sinful seduction. It entails a turning to a pseudo-origin, a cosmic order toppled by the coming of Islam.

As I have already indicated, the *dalang* of the oral tradition, too, operates within a commemorative paradigm. Thus, for instance, in their ritual preparations for the enactment of their play, the *dalang* of the Wayang Siam invoke the help of the spirits in order to be able to perform it and they demonstrate their qualifications as *dalang* by becoming properly possessed by the spirits of their puppets in an act of trance (Sweeney 1972:273-9). And, typically, they consider the stories they tell to be the truth, not fiction. They denounce the invention of tales as *belawak*, a word meaning 'clowning', but in Kelantan Malay also 'lying' (Sweeney 1972:258, 268-9). To counter the accusations of the orthodox Muslims that they indulge in sinful fantasy, real *dalang* of the oral tradition have argued that the gods and genies of their stories do exist but are different manifestations of the *malaikat* (angels) created by God (Harun Mat Piah 1980:127-8; Sweeney 1972:277).

Even in the late 19th-century Malay world the writings of the paper-*dalang*, too, could still be taken as a form of commemoration and he, too, could refer to the pre-Islamic order and still find a measure of belief. This appears, for instance, from the occurrence of a warning in a manuscript of the *Hikayat Seri Rama* (1896) that Muslims are not to believe its story (Van Ronkel 1909:3-4).

A similar warning, and the advice only to laugh at the words of the

---

order to enlist its imaginative support for the propagation of the tenets of the Faith, in the same way that Spenser populated his Fairy Queen with ogres, dragons and knights-errant to lend attraction to his Protestant views (Frye 1976:29-30). This has given rise to an extensive body of Islamized romance. The *Syair Siti Zubaidah* discussed in this chapter is a fine sample of this genre. On Java – in the Malay world this did not happen – Islamized genres of *wayang* have been developed.

[19] Minangkabau oral literature, too, has incurred the censure of being *kapie* (*kafir*) and *jahie* (*jahil*). Performers of Sijobang, the poetic narrative about Anggun Nan Tungga – a popular entertainment in the area around Payakumbuh – may elicit an outburst of laughter when they start their performance with the following lines of verse:
Ampun dimintak ka nan banyak / ambo mangombang kitab setan / indak basyorak basumbillah / ontah badoso ontah tida / badan mbo sajo managguengkan. (I ask pardon of you all. / I am opening the Book of the Devil, / without religious law and without *bismillah*. / Perhaps it is sinful, perhaps not. / I alone bear the blame (Phillips 1981:35).)

dalang, is found in a *Hikayat Maharaja Boma* (Van Ronkel 1909:94). In his prologue its narrator, presumably to defend himself against possible criticism for telling a *jahil* story, mixes elements of the *dalang* with those of the *dagang*:

> Ini hikayat dikarang oleh fakir yang hina, maka dibaca oleh orang yang jauhari, maka dipatutkan oleh orang yang bijaksana, demikian mulanya. Ini hikayat Pandu [?] yang bernama Sang Sambah, anak Betara Kesna, yang terlalu indah-indah ceritanya dalang yang empunya cerita.
>
> (This story was written by a humble beggar, read out by a wise man and put into fitting words by a man of discretion, that is its origin. This is a story about Pandawa [?][20], who was called Sang Sambah, son of Betara Kesna, about whom the puppeteer, who owns the story, tells a tale that is of surpassing beauty.)

As the description of this act of writing as *mematutkan* indicates, the paper-*dalang* never quite relinquished the claim to commemorate. Yet as Islam came to dominate the centre of ideology, he had to yield his authority in this field more and more to the *dagang*. Commemoration and *mematutkan* were claimed as his prerogative by the *dagang*. Within the perspective of Islam the *dalang* was left only the spinning out of a tale (*memanjangkan*) and the providing of forgetfulness, the soothing of the emotions by its illusory power.

For Islam, however, the emotions, although these should be nurtured and vented occasionally, were to be kept under careful surveillance by the intellect (*akal*); emotions belonged to the carnal soul of man, the realm of lust, desire and illusion (*hawa nafsu*), they were part of his lower, animal nature (*haiwani*) (Siegel 1969:98-100). Islam could not recognize emotional catharsis as a path to salvation, as did the Old Javanese poetics with which the poetics of the *dalang* resound. In its eyes the *dalang* could only be a black magician, a mere purveyor of sinful pleasure, a figure at most tolerated in the margin (Braginsky 1986:197-8).

To deny all *memanjangkan* and to claim only to *mematutkan* is to deny the status of fiction to one's composition. It not only means to claim that one does not spin out fantasies, it also means to deny forgetting. It is to say that one's composition exactly matches the contents of the totality it claims to recall or copy, not only containing nothing more, but also nothing less.

It is this notion of *mematutkan* which resounds in the following passage, which I quote from the *Adat Raja-Raja Melayu* (Customs of the Malay Rulers). This work was written in 1791 at the command of Governor P.G. de Bruijn of Melaka by a Kapitan – probably the Kapitan Melayu of Melaka at

---

[20] If the fragment quoted in Van Ronkel is a correct rendering of the text of the manuscript, we may conclude that the author of the *Hikayat Maharaja Boma* has mistakenly identified Sang Samba, the hero of the *Bhomakavya*, as one of the Five Pandawa's. But perhaps the word Pandu is merely the product of a scribal error.

the time, Datuk Zainuddin Mahbub – at the request of the son of a Dutch notable who wished to be informed about Malay royal customs. The words in which the Governor imparts the instruction to the Kapitan to write a reliable account run (with some abbreviation):

> Semuanya itu hendaklah Kapitan ceritakan. [...[ceritakan semuanya [...] bagaimana adat semuanya tulis belaka [...]. Jangan kurang, tuliskan sekaliannya; jangan bertinggalan. (Panuti Sujiman 1982:55.)
>
> (You are to tell all, Captain, [...] tell all about it [...] write down everything that is considered custom [...]. Do not leave anything out, write down everything; do not omit anything.)

In his search for a proper source to repeat the Kapitan ran into difficulties, we are told: the oral experts in the matter of royal customs (*orang yang tahu adat benar-benar*) all proved to have died. At long last, when he had already begun to worry that he might have to admit to the Governor that no one could be found who knew the Malay customs properly, he found an expert, a mosque official (*lebai*) from Telangkira, one Abdulmuhit, who still knew everything by heart and gave him a reliable account, reciting as best he could from the Book of the Malay *Kerajaan* Order as inscribed by God in his memory:

> Maka dahulu Allah ba'dahu rasul-Nya, tuan itulah hikayatkan barang yang ingat ala kadarnya. Dan sebab tuan itu seorang lepaslah kemaluan segala orang Melaka. (Panuti Sujiman 1982:56.)
>
> (Then with the help of first God and then the Prophet, that gentleman set forth in narrative all he remembered to the best of his ability. And because of that gentleman the people of Melaka were saved from humiliation.)

In all Malay fiction there is a tension between the striving for the proper (*mematutkan*) and the desire to give in to the pleasures of amplification (*memanjangkan*), the urge towards wisdom, commemoration, mimesis and representation (*mengadakan*) and the seduction of giving in to desire and forgetfulness, to the creation of fantasies and illusions (*mengada-ada*), to impropriety.

Playful fiction – we would say literature – may seem a harmless playful supplement to serious texts. Yet because it tests values and rearranges them, tries out new modes of perception and indulges in flights of fantasy, it may lead to change and renewal in our constructions of reality as well. Where its language is separated from serious use, literature has something inherently parodic. Even where it strives to function in subordination to an ideological superstructure – where, in other words, it tries to be serious, good writing, grafted onto an authoritative Book – ultimately it is inherently subversive of such vehiculation and betrays its purpose by the disjunction between its serious intent and its pleasure in verbal invention. By the proliferation of signifiers such verbal invention leads to an unintentional polyinterpretability and a self-deconstructive slippage of meaning (Haidu 1977:885-6).

We have already seen that the paper-*dalang* often openly takes pride in his ability as a creator of fiction. The *dagang*, in contrast, takes no pleasure in his authorship. Characteristically he is wary of the threat posed to Origin and Truth by an uncontrolled play of the signifiers; therefore he exerts himself as best he can only to copy, repeat and represent and tries to avoid all spinning out of fantasies, all forgetfulness.

If a *dagang* indulges in playing the author he can only do so with a bad conscience. This appears, for instance, from the prologue and epilogue of a *Syair Burung* (Poem of the Birds) (Ms. Von de Wall 238, dated 1891; Van Ronkel 1909:360). With edifying intent this *syair* tells a story about birds discussing the tenets of Islam and the religious obligations to be performed. In the passages I quote, the narrator – behind whose mask we may surmise the presence of a copyist in the service of a Dutch patron – shows himself concerned lest the play of the signifiers of his fiction may subvert the serious signified he intends to convey. As his only excuse for committing the sin of indulging in creative authorship – an excuse he admits to be inadequate – he adduces that his writing is as much a consequence of God's will as was the appearance in writing of the Koran at the time of the Prophet:

> Bismillah itu permulaan kalam/ diturunkan Tuhan Khalik al-Alam / zamannya nabi alaihi-salam / diperjodohkan dakwat kertas dan kalam // sudahlah takdir Tuhannya nyata / jari membawa kalam melata / terhamburan kisah dengan cerita / ada yang sungguh ada yang dusta // setengah dusta lupakan diri / kalam dipegang dengan tiga jari / terkadang terhenti terkadang terlari / berhamburanlah kisah dengan peri // dengarkanlah tuan suatu madah / dikarangkan fakir didalam gundah / sungguhpun karangan tiada indah / di dalamnya banyak memberi faedah. (*Antologi* 1980:105.)
>
> Tamatlah syair sahaya surat / hati didalam sangat galurat / pekerjaannya banyak hendak surat / pekerjaan sedikit habis melarat // mencari hikayat tiadalah dapat/ menyuratlah sahaya mana yang sempat / perkataan yang satu menjadi empat / takutlah sahaya terkena upat // Allah dan rasul tiada suka / bohong pesona kepada siapa / tiadalah akhirat yang baka / dunia dan akhirat kena celaka. // janganlah tuan bersangka-sangka / hambalah tuan bekerjalah juga / tiada berbuat berjangka-jangka / seperti dihadapan tuan di Melaka. (*Antologi* 1980:110.)

(The invocation 'in the name of God' is the beginning of the Word / which has been sent down by our Lord, the Creator of the Universe. / In the times of the Prophet – on him be peace – / ink, paper and pen were joined together. // It is God's Will made manifest / that the fingers cause the pen to creep along. / Stories and tales pour forth, / some of them true and others lying. // Half lying and forgetting himself / your servant holds the pen between his three fingers, / and stories and tales pour forth, / as it now comes to a standstill, then hurries on again. // Good sirs, listen to these words, / written by a beggar who is sick at heart. / Although the work he composes is devoid of beauty, / he offers much in it that may edify.

Here ends the poem your servant has written, / his heart filled with deep sorrow.

III Dalang or dagang

/ As was his task he wanted to do much copying out / but after doing a bit of work he had already strayed off. // He looked for a *hikayat* to copy out but did not find one, / so he just wrote out whatever he was able to. / One story became four, / so that your servant now fears to be reviled. // God and the Prophet do not like it, / if one lies to anyone or puts him under a spell. / Then one will not enjoy the rewards of the everlasting World to Come, / and in this world and the next one will be accursed. // Do not mistrust your servant, o lord; / he assures you he will still do his work as he must. / He will not act as if he has all the time before him / in the presence of his lord at Melaka.)

PART 2

READINGS IN HEROIC EPIC, PANJI ROMANCE AND PARODIES

CHAPTER IV

The Kerajaan at war
The Syair Perang Mengkasar as heroic epic

1. Genre as a tool for interpretation

As any student of a culture foreign to him will know, in order to be able to satisfactorily produce and interpret utterances in the language of that culture, whether words, phrases or sentences, he must acquire a mastery of its linguistic system, a linguistic competence. In his writing and speaking he will, in order not to be misunderstood, take care to form his words, phrases and sentences according to the patterns codified in the linguistic system. And he will appeal to his familiarity with these same patterns in order to be able to perceive the utterances he hears or reads as coherent and meaningful.

For a time, perhaps, our student may think that, knowing the language-system, he can now adequately produce and interpret texts in that culture as well. What are texts after all, he may reason, but a series of words, phrases and sentences? Soon he will realize, however, that for the production and interpretation of texts as meaningful and coherent, in addition to linguistic competence he will also have to acquire a more general textual competence by immersing himself in the multitude of texts or encodations that are the shared property of that culture.

As Culler says: 'To naturalize a text is to bring it into relation with a type of discourse or model which is already in some sense natural and legible' (Culler 1975:138). This principle of writing and reading texts is called intertextuality. Julia Kristeva, who coined the term, has written: 'Every text takes shape as a mosaic of citations, every text is the absorption and transformation of other texts. The notion of intertextuality comes to take the place of intersubjectivity.' (Culler 1975:139.)

Culler has distinguished five ways in which a text may be brought into contact with and defined in relation to another text to make it intelligible, or, as he calls it, five levels of verisimilitude (I translate his term *vraisemblance*):

1. the socially given text, that which is taken as the 'real world';
2. a general cultural text, shared knowledge recognized by participants as part

of a culture, and hence subject to correction or modification, but none the less serving as a kind of 'nature';
3. the texts or conventions of a genre, a specifically literary and artistical verisimilarity;
4. the natural attitude to the artificial, where the text explicitly cites and exposes verisimilarity of the third kind (for example the foreword of an 18th-century novel in which the narrator explains how the manuscript of his true story came into his possession);
5. the verisimilarity of specific intertextualities, where one work takes another as its basis or point of departure and must be assimilated in relation to it (parody, irony) (Culler 1975:140-59).

In this chapter[1] I will concern myself with what Culler calls the level of literary and artificial verisimilarity, in other words with genre.

What is genre? It may perhaps be useful first to state what it is not. Genre, then, is not some static set of prescriptions or an unchanging canon of rules. Neither should it be seen as a historical entity, or be reified; a group of works itself is not a genre, but is informed by, based on a genre.

Rather, genre should be considered as a historically evolving regulative system of norms, conventions, expectations, that guide the construction and perception of literary works. The participants in a culture, whether subconsciously or consciously, are familiar with a number of genres: a system of genres that they derive from their intertextual knowledge of the literary tradition. In other words, they have, in varying degrees, mastered a certain literacy competence (Culler 1975:113-30). As the Russian Formalist Tynyanov has already indicated in his essay 'On Literary Evolution' (1927)[2], not only does genre regulate what specific functions may be assigned to what elements or devices of the literary work, but conversely it also regulates what elements may be assigned to what functions. Moreover, it regulates what artistic intentions or purposes may be pursued by the work (Striedter 1971:xxvii-xxviii, 1976:xxix, ixl, lxxvi, lxxxvii).

A writer who opts for one of the genres that the tradition offers him, rather than for another, makes this choice because its devices and intentionality – in whatever way he may choose to handle them himself – suit his own artistic purpose. Similarly, for the reader who identifies a work as based on one genre rather than another, a number of expectations will become operative concerning what devices he may expect with what function, and concerning what artistic intentions the work may possibly pursue.

As has been indicated by Tynyanov, who took the step of considering

---

[1] This chapter is a modified version of a paper which I wrote for the Fourth Indonesian-Dutch History Conference at Yogyakarta in 1983 (Koster 1986a). For a critical reaction I refer to Skinner (1985:308-12, 316-8) and Siti Hawa Salleh (1993a:54-5, 1993b:52-4).
[2] A full translation of Tynyanov's essay into German can be found in Striedter (1971:434-61).

both genre and its realization, the literary work, as a system, the notion of system implies not only an interrelatedness of the elements or devices, but a hierarchy between them as well, in which certain elements or devices are constitutive of the system. As he wrote: 'A system does not mean the coexistence of components on the basis of equality; it presupposes the pre-eminence of one group of elements and the resulting deformation of other elements' (Ehrlich 1980:199). As he has indicated, these dominant features, that he calls in Russian *dominanta*, not eternally given but subject to change, ensure the perceptibility of the literary work, not only as literature but as the realization of a certain genre: 'Nowadays we put a novel in correlation to the 'Novel' on account of the characteristics of its size and the way the plot is developed; once it was distinguished according to the presence of a love-intrigue' (Striedter 1971:451).

Tynyanov's concepts of system and *dominanta* are of great importance for the methodology of generic research. Traditionally scholars have been wont to try and define a genre by examining groups of works that were presumed to be realizations of it in order to isolate those features that all texts of the group had in common. As Hempfer has pointed out, this method results in the construction of mere taxonomies. The larger the number of features on which one bases one's taxonomy, the smaller will be the number of texts that will meet the requirements. On the other hand, the smaller the number of features one bases it on, the less the taxonomy will say about the specific constitution of the object classified. Thus, to give an extreme example, one may put into one class of red objects such diverse items as: the tiles of a roof, red cars, red flowers, red clothes, etc. (Hempfer 1973:136-7).

As Tynyanov's concepts of system and *dominanta* make clear, if we want to establish a genre, we are not simply to proceed in taxonomical fashion by abstracting smaller or larger numbers of features shared by works of a corpus. Rather we are to indicate that in the works compared shared elements occur that are similarly related in a hierarchy of dominant and dominated elements. To quote Stempel's definition of genre: 'The genre, in the final analysis, will be a system of compatibilities covered by a norm that is, so to say, the key to the genre' (Hempfer 1973:137-9). The main step in establishing a genre, thus, is to isolate its *dominanta*.

For our ability to interpret the texts of a tradition, familiarity with its genres is of utmost importance. About the genres that once regulated the production and reception of the texts of the Malay tradition, both those that one might consider as more serious and those that might be regarded as more playful, unfortunately we still know next to nothing. In this chapter I shall address myself to giving a characterization of the genre of the heroic epic.[3] This genre involves among other works many narrative poems in the verseform *syair* – notably those poems that have been classified by the Malayists as historical *syair* on war – but is also found in prose narrative.

Confronted with the large number of poems in the *syair*-form, Malayists have developed convenient taxonomies in which they distinguish the following types of *syair*:
1. *syair* which derive their theme from the Panji-tales;
2. romantic *syair*;
3. didactic or allusive *syair* having fruits, animals or flowers as protagonists;
4. historical *syair*;
5. *syair* which are adaptations of Javanese stories from *wayang*;
6. religious *syair* (Liaw Yock Fang 1975:293-317).

Within the class of historical *syair* they have discerned:
1. *syair* concerned with court events and the person of the ruler, describing the death, marriage or voyage of a ruler or a member of his family;
2. *syair* about events in the lives of non-royal Malay, Chinese or European personalities in social or political life;
3. *syair* that give a journalistic account of some recent spectacular event in a community, such as a great fire;
4. *syair* that chronicle the events of a war (Hooykaas 1951:106-8).

These taxonomies, while no doubt useful and even necessary, should not be mistaken for characterizations of genres. They may perhaps be based on the scholar's intuitive sense that certain works somehow have something in common, but they are not based on an explicit comparative examination of these works.

The first scholar to have made an explicit comparison in some detail of two so-called historical *syair* on war was Woelders (1975), in his *Het Sultanaat Palembang 1811-1825*. He compared the *Syair Perang Menteng* (henceforth SPM, Syair on the war with Muntinghe) with the *Syair Perang Mengkasar* (henceforth SPMR, Syair on the Macassar War).

The SPM, one of the texts from Palembang which Woelders edited in his study, is a poem written shortly after the war fought in 1819 between a Dutch force sent to Palembang under the command of H.W. Muntinghe to restore Dutch authority there, and the troops of Palembang's Sultan Badaruddin, a war that ended in victory for the Sultan (Woelders 1975:57).

The SPMR, with which Woelders compared the SPM, is the oldest preserved historical *syair* on war. Skinner published an edition of the only complete and oldest extant manuscript of the SPMR, a copy written out by

---

[3] An interesting study of a heroic epic that is in many ways comparable with the *Syair Perang Mengkasar* is provided by Tol (1990). I would like to thank Dr Tol for his advice concerning the spelling of Buginese and Macassarese personal names and toponyms.

Cornelia Valentijn on Ambon ca. 1710 (Cod.Or. 1626; Juynboll 1899:12-3). The aim of the introduction and notes Skinner added to the edited poem is mainly to give insight into it as a source of history but also to pay attention to it as literature.[4] He has proposed that the SPMR was written by a Macassarese *peranakan* Malay, Enci' Amin, shortly after the events that inspired its composition had taken place: the war fought from 1666-1669 between the VOC and the Sultanate of Macassar. Enci' Amin was the personal secretary of the Sultan of Goa, Hasanuddin. The Sultan of Goa, as the 'older brother', together with his 'younger brother', the Sultan of Tallo', led the oligarchy by which Macassar was ruled at the time (Skinner 1963:18-22, 42-3).

Woelders noted the following five points of similarity between the *Syair Perang Menteng* and the SPMR:
1. a strikingly similar wording in a number of quatrains;
2. the occurrence in both texts of declarations of courage and fighting spirit, usually introduced by the words *bercakaplah* ('he declared');
3. the comparison in both poems of the protagonists with heroes and gods from the *wayang*-stories or at least with Hindu-Javanese epic literature;
4. the occurrence of similar short, expressive descriptions of appearance and dress of the individual participants in the battle and of their attitude and behaviour in concrete situations of the battle, with the mention of the names of the prominent members of the élite;
5. a strong religious committment in the war against the Dutch and their allies, a war that is seen as one against unbelievers as prescribed by Islam.

In view of these similarities, Woelders suggested that the author of the SPM may have known the SPMR and was consciously or unconsciously influenced by it (Woelders 1975:431-4).

Although I do not wish to exclude influence as a possibility – the striking verbal correspondences might be seen as an argument for it – I would like to stress that a Malay scribe may well have written a *syair* remarkably similar to the SPMR without ever having set eyes on that text, namely, by applying the same generic conventions that inform the SPMR, conventions with which he may have become familiar through works other than that *syair*. With the exception of the first point of similarity, all the others Woelders has indicated, can be pointed out in historical *syair* on war that have no demonstrable link whatsoever with the SPMR.

One such *syair* I refer to is the *Syair Sultan Maulana* (henceforth SSM, Poem of My Lord the Sultan) from Kedah, the other the *Syair Perang Siak*

---

[4] Skinner (1963:37-8) was the first scholar to plead for a comparative examination of *syair* as an escape from an otherwise necessarily intuitive and impressionistic approach to them as literature. He justified the comparison of *syair* that are far removed from each other in time with the argument that the evolution of the Malay literary tradition was a very slow one and that the tradition was very stable.

(henceforth SPS, Poem on the Siak War) from Siak. The SSM has as historical background the naval actions of a Kedah squadron sent to help the Siamese expel the Burmese from Ujung Salang (Junk Ceylon). It was written during the second decade of the 19th century by a Malay scribe from Kedah, a state that was then under the suzerainty of Siam (Skinner 1985:31-32).[5] The SPS (Goudie 1989) has as a historical background to its main narrative (v. 228-507) the war fought on the Siak River from April to June 1761 between the fleet of the East Sumatran Sultanate of Siak under Raja Ismail and a Dutch squadron allied with the exiled Raja Alam of Siak. This squadron had been sent from Malacca to punish Siak for the massacre of the VOC garrison at Pulau Guntung in 1759. The *syair* as it is found in Ms. Klinkert 154 was probably written between 1781 and 1791 by a member of the Royal House of Siak (see Chapter V).[6]

As we have seen, to establish a genre it is not enough to show that certain works share a number of features: these must also be shown to occur in a similar configuration of dominant and dominated elements. In this chapter I will limit myself to describing the *dominanta* of the genre that informs the *syairs* on war I have mentioned above, that of the heroic epic. I will do so while concentrating mainly on one *syair*, the SPMR. To indicate the genericity of the features discussed, I will, where necessary, refer to the use of the same devices in two other *syair* on war, the SPS and the SSM.

The historical background of the SPMR is the war fought from December 1666 and July 1669 between the VOC and Macassar. At the time the war broke out, the Macassarese had subjugated most of Sulawesi, including their toughest opponent, the kingdom of Boné. To the great annoyance of the VOC, Macassar played an independent and disturbing role in the spice trade, playing off one European company against another and selling spices to the VOC's rivals, thus thwarting its efforts to establish a monopoly. Conflict was bound to arise, and in 1666 the VOC sent a fleet and soldiers to Macassar to demand satisfaction for the plundering of a stranded Dutch ship.

The commander of the fleet was the ambitious Admiral Cornelis Speelman, who brought with him as allies a group of Buginese exiles, led by the

---

[5] In the SSM, for point 2 of Woelders, see v. 288, 864, 867, 869. For point 3, see v. 158. For point 4, see v. 158-181, 821-883. For point 5, see v. 591. All my references to the SSM are to the edition published by Skinner (1985).
[6] Where I refer to the SPS it is to the edition by Goudie (1989). In the SPS, for point 2 of Woelders, see v. 238-44, 269, 273, 292, 304, 368, 377-9, 538-47, 574-5. For point 3, see v. 264, 310b, 417. For point 4, see v. 248-80, 394-7. For point 5, see v. 132b, 154c, 272d, 282d, 308d, 452a, 453b, 498b. For the interested reader I also refer to the corresponding passages in a variant version of the *Syair Perang Siak*, the Ms. Von de Wall 237, titled *Syair Raja Siak* (henceforth SRS), kept at the Museum Nasional at Jakarta and published by Kosim (1978). In the SRS, for point 2 of Woelders, see v. 13.8-14;,15.1, 15.5, 16.17, 20.13-15. For point 3 see v. 14.14, 17.4, 22.15. For point 4, see v. 13.18-15.10, 21.11-21.14. For point 5, see v. 7.17d, 9.1c, 15.4d, 24.12a, 24.13b, 27.1a.

Boné prince Arung Palakka, who was bent upon revenge for the humiliation inflicted by Macassar on the Bugis and eager to restore their as well as his own sense of self-esteem and honour. After some negotiations with Macassar, Speelman decided to exceed his instructions and went for all-out war. When his arms proved victorious – not least because Arung Palakka attracted massive Bugis support – and the fighting closed in on Macassar, even Macassar's allies began to defect to the VOC.

During the night of 2-3 November 1667, two nobles, Karaéng Bangkala and Karaéng Layo', who held a key position in the defence-line of Macassar, defected to the VOC, enabling Speelman to turn the Macassar defence-line, so that Hasanuddin had no option but to sue for peace. After a brief interval of peace from November 1667 to April 1668, following the conclusion of the treaty of Bungaya – a treaty that led, among other matters, to the ceding of the fortifications at Ujung Pandang to the Dutch – hostilities were renewed, to end in July 1669, when the royal citadel, Sombaopu, fell to the Dutch after fierce Macassarese resistance (Andaya 1981:73-136; Skinner 1963:288-92).

Skinner's introduction to the SPMR was one of the first, still too rare, efforts in Malay studies to try and give a full-blown interpretation of a text of traditional Malay literature. His introduction has always enjoyed considerable authority among historians attempting to come to terms with the 'historical' *syair*. His introduction and the accompanying notes to his translation are a valuable contribution to the question of to what extent factual correspondences may be seen between the narrative of the SPMR and works of modern historiography, notably those of Stapel.[7] As an interpretation of the text, however, they remain unsatisfactory. The reason is that Skinner, it appears, did not sufficiently 'follow the story', that is, he did not fully grasp the theme of the SPMR. As W.B. Gallie (in Culler 1975:224) has stressed, to grasp the theme of a novel means to have followed the story, and this entails a sense of its rightness and acceptability, a sense of 'the main bond of logical continuity', which makes its elements intelligible.

Reading the *syair* as a narrative that is as impartial and accurate as the lights and customs of the times would permit its author to tell (Skinner 1963:7-18), Skinner identified as the theme of the SPMR 'what happened in the course of the war between Macassar and its enemies'. For this proposition he found support in two verse-lines in the epilogue of the *syair*, which he considered a sufficient description by the author himself of the theme he intended to treat: *Tamatlah karangan Mengkasar alah* (This is the end of my composition about the defeat of Macassar, SPMR 524b) and *Tamat*

---

[7] Skinner's conclusion is that 'such historical value as the *sja'ir* possesses, lies mainly in confirming, rather than in refuting the picture of events already established' (Skinner 1963:12, 18).

karangan perang Mengkasar (This is the end of my composition about the Macassar war, SPMR 526a) (Skinner 1963:45-6).

Accordingly his main intertexts in reading the *syair* were those historical sources and studies concerning the Macassar War that are considered as more realistic and reliable by modern historiographers, such as the reports of Speelman to the authorities in Batavia, entries in the *Dagh-Register* kept at the fort of Batavia and the narratives constructed by Stapel (1922, 1936), rather than texts of the Malay or Maccasarese tradition.

That the intertexts, to which he gave preference in his reading, were not very rewarding, is apparent from the many elements of the narrative that Skinner was not able to naturalize. Thus, as 'shortcomings' and 'weaknesses' of the *syair* as historical narrative he characterized features such as:
1. an almost complete neglect of the economic factors of the war;
2. an absence of an appreciation of the tactical and strategic features of the campaign;
3. interest only in how the Macassarese conducted themselves in the fighting;
4. an episodic manner of presentation with little attempt to see the war as a whole or in any perspective;
5. a personality-centred narrative;
6. a concentration on court cabals and military incidents (Skinner 1963:7-9, 31).

These same intertexts must be the reason why Skinner – although noticing the black vs white character of the narrative – did not realize the thematic importance of the pervasive oppositions of praise and blame in the *syair*. Thus he argues:
1. that the theme of the *syair* is 'not so much concerned with the exploits of any hero, neither Speelman, because he is frequently reviled, nor Hasanuddin, since the poet would have had to praise his patron as a matter of course' (Skinner 1963:45);
2. that the eulogies for the Sultans of Goa and Tallo', and the 'citing' of the names of and the 'credit-giving' to the Macassarese nobles and prominent Malays were probably 'seen with unseeing eyes', the poet trying to keep such interruptions of the narrative to a minimum (Skinner 1963:28-30);
3. that the frequent contemptuous references to and abuse of the VOC and its allies are 'conventional', and therefore should not be taken too seriously (Skinner 1963:9-11, 16);
4. that the Macassarese are depicted as fighting with great courage was merely true, witness the Dutch sources (Skinner 1963:16).

As we see from these examples, praise and blame, although not unnoticed, are not seen in relation to each other. Either they are declared meaningless flourishes the poet is obliged to make in a situation of patronage, or they are read referentially as 'merely true'.

In the readers' activity of synthesizing the elements of a narrative into a theme, antithesis is a powerful operant. If a text presents two items – characters, situations, objects, actions – in a way which suggests an opposition, then, as Barthes (in Culler 1975:225) has said, 'a whole space of substitution and variation is opened to the reader'. As Lotman (1976:33-4) has pointed out, any regular pattern of similarities and differences, constructed on the basis of the contrastive comparison of specific elements, will result in signification: 'The principle of the contrastive comparison of elements is a universal structure-forming principle in poetry and verbal art in general'.

In a literary text, Lotman (1977:66-8, 249) says, a plurality of meaning and several overall systems of coherence can be constructed. In order to create these systems of coherence, these meanings, the reader has to decompose the work of art on the principle of similarity and opposition into a semantic field, a series of contrastive concepts that ultimately cohere in a final unifying antithesis. Lotman (1977:146, 171-2) calls this antithesis the 'archiseme'.

To identify the theme not only means to analyse the similarities and oppositions in the text, but also to construct a hierarchy in the systems of coherence and meaning that result, and to determine which of these systems is to be considered as the most powerful one. As Barthes (in Culler 1975:227) has said, meaning 'is a force which tries to subjugate the other forces, other meanings, other languages. The force of meaning depends on its degree of systematization. The most powerful meaning is that whose system takes in the greatest number of elements, to the point where it seems to encompass everything notable in the semantic universe.'

The theme Skinner proposed, as we have seen, gave him only limited possibilities to synthesize the elements of the narrative of the SPMR into a coherent system of meaning. Therefore, even though it may be read into the *syair*, it does not qualify as its 'most powerful meaning'.[8]

2. *The SPMR as a heroic epic*

In a reconsideration of his earlier conclusions, Skinner has come to recognize that the SPMR may perhaps be concerned with a hero after all, namely Sultan Hasanuddin of Goa. This because the society of the time, Skinner argues, would have regarded any narrative of events, whether in *syair* or *hikayat*-form, as inextricably linked with the person of the ruler, irrespective

---

[8] For a rejoinder to my criticism and a critical reaction to the argument subsequently developed in this chapter, I refer to Appendix F 'The *syair* as a historical source' and its notes in Skinner (1985:308-11, 316-8).

of the direct part played by him in the events narrated. With their belief in the Royal Power (*daulat*) of the ruler, Skinner says, the author and his contemporaries would probably not have made a distinction between his direct role, for instance as commander of an army in the field, and his indirect role, that is, as a source of moral authority and inspiration to his people (Skinner 1982:2-3).[9]

While one may wonder whether in reality no such distinction was made, the thematic relevance of the Royal Power of the ruler for the SPMR can indeed be confirmed by several passages in the poem. Thus Enci' Amin dedicates the SPMR to Hasanuddin with the words:

> Patik persembahkan suatu nazam / ke bawah duli makota alam / menceriterakan daulat syahi alam / mengeraskan syariat siang dan malam. (SPMR 13.)[10]
>
> (Your subject lays a poem / at the feet of Your Royal Highness. / It tells of the Royal Power of Your Majesty / who enforces sacred law by day and by night.)

And in the course of the narrative not only the courage and royal conduct of the ruler but also the willingness of his vassals to pledge to do battle for him, their fighting spirit in battle, as well as all sorts of favourable turns of events, are attributed to the inspiring influence of the ruler:

> Berkat daulat yang dipertuan / sekalian bercakap hendak melawan (SPMR 65c-d).
>
> (By the grace of His Majesty's Royal Power / all pledged their willingness to do battle.)
>
> Dengan berkat duli yang dipertuan / Bangkal dan Layo' patik melawan. (SPMR 451c-d.)
>
> (Thanks to Your Royal Highness / I will do battle with Bangkala' and Layo'.)
>
> Berkat keramat baginda duli / melawan musuh kuat sekali (SPMR 187c-d).
>
> (Thanks to Your Highness's miracle-working power / the enemy has been struck a hard blow.)
>
> Berkat keramat baginda duli / sungguh berperang patik sekalian (SPMR 478c-d).
>
> (Thanks to Your Highness's miracle-working power / your servants fight with dedication.)
>
> Jikalau ada daulat raja yang besar / selamat juga negeri Mengkasar (SPMR 129a-b).
>
> (As long as the Royal Power of our great ruler is there / no harm will come to Macassar.)
>
> Berkat daulat raja yang ghana / kepada rumah buruk disanalah kena (SPMR 261c-d).

---

[9] That the Malays also attributed supernatural power to kingship is shown by Milner (1983:23-49).
[10] I have made use of Skinner's translations, but have revised them where this seemed necessary.

(Thanks to the Royal Power of our victorious ruler / the only thing hit was a ramshackle house.)

This is even in one passage extended to Admiral Speelman:

> Berkat tuan kapitan amiral / Sanderabone bolehkan bekal (SPMR 445c-d).
>
> (Thanks to my Lord Capitan Admiral / Sanraboné will get its due.)

All favourable events thus are presented as reflecting favourably on the ruler, so that the narrator – appearing in the role of the Godseeking stranger to suggest his desire to produce a properly authorized account (see Chapter III) – in the prologue can indeed say that the *syair* relates the attributes or virtues (Arab: *asma*) of the ruler:

> Mohonkan ampun gharib yang fakir / menyatakan asma di dalam syair / maka patik pun berbuat sindir / kepada negeri asing supaya lahir // tuanku ampun fakir yang hina / sindirnya tidak betapa bena / menyatakan asma raja yang ghana // supaya tentu pada segala yang bijaksana. (SPMR 26-7.)
>
> (This destitute foreigner begs forgiveness / as he relates your fame in the form of a *syair*. / The reason I composed these allusive verses / was so that other countries might hear of the story. // This miserable, unworthy mendicant asks your forgiveness. / His verses are of little account. / They tell of the fame of our most lavish prince / so that all men of understanding may know of them.)

The SPMR shows a symbiosis of Royal Power and vassalage.[11] Above we have already seen that the *daulat* of the ruler motivates his vassals to go into battle and fight for him. Conversely, we may note that for Royal Power to shine forth, the possession of loyal vassals is an essential requirement, as is expressed in the lines:

> Daulatnya bukan barang-barang / seperti manikam sudah dikarang / jikalau dihadap segala hulubalang / cahaya durjanya gilang-gemilang. (SPMR 18.)
>
> (His Royal Power is of no mean order. / It is like a jewel fixed in its setting. / When waited upon by his officers / radiant indeed in his countenance.)

The finest expression of the importance of the vassals for royal power, can be found in the SSM, where the narrator in the epilogue says:

> Sebab diperbuat sair ikatan / supaya kerja nyata kelihatan / tetapi cara padang dan hutan / tiada manis sajak sebutan // sekadar maklum duli makota / perintah hamba sahaya semata / masing kerja baik dan leta / barang perintah di sinilah nyata // sebab pun kisah dinyatakan ini / supaya suka yang berani / barang yang culas kerja di sini / kemudian kalau takutnya fani // jika dibaca di tengah mualak / segala pahlawan bertambahlah galak / segala yang takut mau ditolak / kemudian lagi berani pulak // segala cetera perkataan beta / tiada sekali berbuat dusta / daripada baik atawa leta / seperti mana penglihatan mata // didengar dilihat

---

[11] As Milner (1982:105) points out, 'a subject improves his *nama* by working for his Raja, and a Raja improves his *nama* by having many loyal subjects'.

kelakuan pun serta / barang yang ada dilihat nyata / semuanya dengan sebenar dikata / Siam Melayu disebut semata. (SSM 1078-83.)

(I made this *syair* and poem in order that / it can clearly be seen how the ruler is served. / But its style is uncouth and rustic / and its verse is not sweet to the tongue. // So that His Majesty may know as well as possible / the disposition of his servants and slaves, / of each his service, whether good or bad, / and of each his dispositions is here made known. // The reason I make this story known / is in order that the courageous will rejoice. / All who are depicted here as remiss in their service / may perhaps find more courage on a future occasion. // When it is read out in public, loud and clear, / the heroes will even fiercer be. / They who were afraid will be inspired / and thereupon will take courage again. // In all the stories that I tell / not even once do I tell a lie. / Whether I speak of good or bad, / I have seen it all with my own eyes. // I heard it and saw it, took part in the actions. / All who were there I clearly saw. / About all I tell as well as I can; / Siamese, Malays, I mention them all.)

Pointers concerning the nature of the narrative in the SSM this passage provides – clues that are in fact relevant for our understanding of works like the SPMR, the SPM and the SPS as well – are:

1. that the narrative is concerned with the disposition (*perintah*) of the vassals of the ruler and with the way they serve him (*kerja*)[12];

2. that these are related in the *syair* to let the ruler know how his men serve him;

3. that the narrative either praises or blames: *baik* vs *leta*[13];

4. that the narrative has an exemplary function for both the brave and the fearful, a function mentioned in SPMR 533a with the words: *Tamatlah sudah kias ibarat* (This is the end of the parables and examples)[14];

5. that the poem, as a truthful account, is to make as complete a mention (*sebut*) as possible of the persons involved in the events of the war. This ties in with the feature of 'citing' or 'credit-giving' Skinner had already noticed in the SPMR.[15]

Now the contours emerge of a different form of narrative from those presupposed as feasible intertexts by Skinner in his reading of the SPMR: that of the genre of the heroic epic.[16]

The generic theme of works informed by the genre of the heroic epic may

---

[12] For the use of the word (*perintah*) in the sense of 'disposition', see the title of the text edited in Skinner (1982). The word is used in a similar meaning in the SPS (18a-b).
[13] Compare with SPS 272a-b for the element of praise and 372 for the element of blame; see in the SRS (15.10a-b).
[14] For *ibarat*, see SPS 4.
[15] Probably SPMR 206 may be interpreted in a similar vein.
[16] See Muhammad Yusoff Hasyim (1980:183-8) about the *Syair Sultan Maulana* as a '*syair sejarah yang bermotif heroisme*'. Following Frye (1973:248) I use the term heroic epic for a narrative about the great deeds done by heroes in the past, which is delivered by, or presents itself as delivered by, oral address. Like Frye I keep the term epic for its customary use as a term for the great literary epics, such as the *Aeneid* or *Paradise Lost*.

be briefly characterized as that of the *kerajaan* at war. The genre is mainly concerned with the praise of how the true *daulat* of the ruler and the true vassalage of his vassals manifest themselves in their heroic words, attitudes and deeds in council and in field. The negative pendant of this is the blaming of disloyal or unworthy vassals and – as a matter of course – of the enemy. Archisemic oppositions connected with this theme, that can be traced throughout the *syair*, are: true *daulat* vs false *daulat* and true vassalage vs false vassalage.

This theme is worked out in a narrative constructed with the help of the devices of formulaicness, that is, with the use of formulas, formulaic expressions and type-scenes. As type-scenes that are much in evidence in the heroic epic the reader will come to recognize: the council-of-war, the preparation of the army, the march-out to the battle, the flight, the report to the ruler, etc. In the following pages, in which I will discuss the SPMR as a sample of the heroic epic, the characteristic keywords of the type-scenes will be marked by an asterisk.

As the 'covering norm' of the genre of the heroic epic, that is, as its *dominanta*, I propose two features that are mutually related and determine each other. These two features, which I consider the characteristic expression of the generic theme of the heroic epic, are: the praising presentation – often, but not always, in the type-scene of the council-of-war – of the vassals uttering reassuring pledges and boasts (*cakap*) to the ruler, followed at more or less close range by the type-scene of the battle, in which the vassals are praiseworthily shown to redeem their pledges and boasts by matching their words with deeds. It is the combination of these two mutually related characteristics by which the reader may at a glance recognize a poem such as the SPMR as a heroic epic.[17] An example in a nutshell of this pledge-battle collocation[18] is:

---

[17] For the co-occurrence of these two features in the SPS see: the councils with pledges 237a-245a and 229a-305a in relation to the battle-scene in 393a-446a, that is resumed from 450c-459d. For a pledge outside a council-scene, see 273c-d. In the SRS, see 13.7a-13.14d and 16.12a-16.18a in relation to 18.19c-19.17a and 20.9c-21.1a in relation to 24.10c-24.19d. For a pledge outside a council-scene, see 15.5c-d. In Chambert-Loir (1982:61) attention is drawn to the occurrence of pledges to the ruler in the *Syair Kerajaan Bima* (v. 382-98). These are closely similar in structure to those in SPMR 46-64.

[18] In *syair* on war such as the SPMR, SPM and SSM the pledge-battle collocation, the characteristic feature of the genre of the heroic epic, is the dominant structuring principle. This does not, however, mean that the genre is only invoked in *syair* on war. The collocation can also be found in works where it is not the dominant structuring principle, as can be seen from the following example, which I quote from an Islamized work of romance, the *Hikayat Dewa Mandu*:

Maka sorak orangpun gemuruhlah bunyinya dan segala raja-raja itupun bercakaplah di hadapan raja Balia Dewaitu maka sembahnya:
'Daulat tuanku ya syah alam, dengan berkat duli yang maha mulia, patiklah melawan segala raja-raja yang di bawahnya Dewa Raksa Malik itu !' Setelah didengar oleh raja

Cili' Kalimata terlalu elok / menjadi ipar kepada raja di Telo' / barang di mana ketumbukan si Tunderu' / biarlah aku ke sana masuk // selang pun tidak berapa hari / Cili' Kalimata yang mengeluari* / berperang* tidak setengah hari / si Tunderu' melihat adalah ngeri. (SPMR 319-20.)

(Kaicili' Kalimata was a fine sight. / He was the brother-in-law of the King of Tallo'. / 'Wherever you see Palakka and his brigade / let me be the first to attack them'. // A few days later / Kaicili' Kalimata led an assault. / The fighting did not last beyond midday / and Arung Palakka, looking on, felt frightened.)

The SPMR may in fact be considered an amplification, in a number of moves, of this fundamental generic matrix.

A common variant of this matrix is one in which the narrator puts the line of action of the opposing parties into motion by a set of two councils-of-war with pledges and boasts, subsequently tracing both forces step by step in

---

Balia Dewa akan cakap segala raja-raja itu maka terlalu sukacita hati baginda serta memberi anugerah akan segala raja-raja itu dan menteri hulubalang serta rakyat sekalian itu masing-masing pada kadarnya.

Setelah keesokan harinya maka raja Balia Dewapun keluarlah dengan segala raja-raja dan menteri hulubalang dan segala balatentaranya berjalan berpasuk-pasukan beriring-iring baik pula rupanya seperti dalam tulisan, masing-masing dengan lakunya serta dengan tempik soraknya terlalu gegap gempita bunyinya. Setelah sampai keluar kota maka kelihatanlah lawannya sudah hadir menanti di tengah medan bersaf-saf, maka segala tunggul panji-panji segala raja-raja itupun seperti mega beratur rupanya [...].

Setelah bertemulah antara kedua pihak tentara itu lalu berperang terlalu ramai, yang indera samanya indera, yang cendera samanya cendera [...]. (Chambert-Loir 1980:74-5.)

(Thereupon the cheers of people rang out with a rumbling sound, and the kings swore solemn pledges in the presence of King Balia Dewa, saying: 'May your royal power flourish, O ruler of the world; by the grace of Your Royal Highness, your servants will oppose all the kings who are under the command of Dewa Raksa Malik!' After King Balia Dewa had heard the pledges of all those kings, he rejoiced greatly and distributed gifts to all the kings, ministers and military officers as well as to the commoners, rewarding each as befitted his rank.

Next day King Balia Raja came out with all the kings, the ministers and military officers, and all troops set off in squadrons accompanying him, looking as handsome as figures in a painting, bearing themselves proudly and cheering loudly with a rumbling sound. When they had arrived outside the town they could see the enemy, awaiting them in readiness in the middle of the plain, row upon row, with the pennants of all the kings looking like an ordered procession of clouds [...].

When contact had been made between the two combatant parties, a fierce battle ensued, spirits from heaven fighting with spirits from heaven, spirits from the region of the moon fighting with spirits from the region of the moon, [...].)

For some other instances of the pledge-battle collocation in the Hikayat Dewa Mandu, see Chambert-Loir (1980:92-3, 131-40, 141-54, 183-90). An example in a Panji story is found in the *Hikayat Misa Taman Jayeng Kusuma* edited by Abdul Rahman Kaeh (1976:292, 362). Not surprisingly, in the so-called epic *wayang* stories this pattern is also very much in evidence. For examples I refer to the *Hikayat Pandawa Lima* edited by Khalid Hussain (1964:122-3, 147-9). It can be traced back to Old Javanese *kakawin* such as, for example, *Bharatayuddha* by Empu Sedah (Zoetmulder 1974:256-63). If this is correct, it puts into question the theory of the Persian origin of the *hikayat*-style proposed by Brakel (1979b:8-33) mainly on the basis of a comparison of battle-scenes in Malay *hikayat* with such scenes in Persian literature. A problem of his theory remains the question what elements of the *hikayat* come from oral genres of Malay narrative.

IV The Kerajaan at war

a continually alternating reportage towards the culminating confrontation in battle. This variant of the matrix may be observed both at the beginning of the *syair* (SPMR 29-131) as well as where the poet tells of the resumption of the war after the end of the brief interlude of the peace of Bungaya (SPMR 442c-462).

The opposition true *daulat* vs false *daulat* and true vassalage vs false vassalage can be observed right from the start of the story of the war. As an example I shall compare the Dutch council-of-war, with which the actual story of the *syair* begins, with the Macassarese counter-council that follows it. This is how the *syair* presents the Dutch council-of-war:

> Berkampunglah* Welanda sekalian jenis / berkatalah jenderal kapitan yang bengis / jikalau alah Mengkasar nin habis / Tunderu' kelak raja di Bugis // setelah didengar oleh si Tunderu' / kata jenderal Welanda yang mabuk / berbangkitlah ia daripadu duduk / betalah kelak di medan mengamuk // akan cakap* Bugis yang dusta / sehari kubedil rubuhlah kota / habis kau ambil segala harta / perempuan yang baik bahagian beta // jika sudah kita alahkan / segala hasil beta persembahkan / perintah negeri kita serahkan / kerajaan di Bone Tunderu' pohonkan // setelah didengar oleh jenderal / cakap Tunderu' orang yang bebal / disuruhnya* berlengkap* segala kapal / seorang kapitan dijadikan amiral // putuslah sudah segala musyawarat* / [...]. (SPMR 31-36a.)

> (The Dutch and their allies were gathered together. / Said their savage commander-in-chief: / 'If we can defeat these Macassarese, / you, Arung Palakka, shall be king of the Bugis'. // When Arung Palakka heard / the words of the drunken Dutch general, he rose from his seat, saying: / 'I shall drive all before me on the battle-field'. // The accursed Bugis went on to say: / 'A day's bombardment will see the town in ruins; / you can have everything of value / and I'll have the pick of the women'. // 'After we've defeated them, / everything we take shall be offered to you. / Macassar shall be subject to you, / I ask for the throne of Boné'. // When the general heard / the words of the dunderheaded Arung Palakka, / he gave orders for all his ships to be fitted out / and appointed one of his officers as commander of the fleet. // When plans had been agreed upon, / [...])

The VOC fleet then sails to South Celebes and anchors at Barombong near Macassar, where it is sighted by the Macassarese. Then the *syair* launches into a lengthy laudatory presentation of the Macassarese counter-council, significantly introducing this passage with the exclamation of the narrator '*Pada sangkanya Bugis dan Welanda / dikatanya takut gerangan baginda*' (The imagination of the Bugis and the Dutch / saying that the king would be frightened) (SPMR 40a-b). Quoted with some abbreviations this passage is as follows:

> Berkampunglah* segala kaum Islam / menantikan titah syahi alam // akan titah baginda sultan / siapatah baik kita titahkan / tanyakan kehendak Welanda syaitan / hendak berkelahi kita lawan // menyahut baginda Keraeng Ketapang / Keraeng we jangan hatimu bimbang / jikalau Welanda hendak berperang / kita kampungkan* sekalian orang // [...] // bercakaplah* baginda Keraeng Popo' / mencabut sunderik yang amat elok / barang di mana ketumbukan si Tunderu' /

biarlah aku ke sana masuk // mengaru pula Keraeng Lengkes / mencabut sunderik serta memekis / jikalau sekadar Welanda dan Bugis / daripada tertawan remaklah habis // [...] // Keraeng Bonto Majanang saudara sultan / sikapnya seperti harimau jantan / barang ke mana patik dititahkan / Welanda dan Bugis saja kulawan // bercakap* pula Keraeng Jaranika / merah padam warnanya muka / Welanda Bugis anjing celaka / haramlah aku memalingkan muka // [...] // Keraeng Mamu berani sungguh / bercakap* dengan kata yang teguh / jikalau patik bertemu musuh / pada barang tempat hamba bertutuh // [...] // akan cakap* anak raja yang muda-muda / hendak berperang dengan Welanda / rupa sikapnya seperti garuda / sekaliannya anak saudara baginda // [...] / berkat daulat yang dipertuan / sekalian bercakap* hendak melawan // setelah habis sekalian bercakap* / semuanya beratur duduk mengadap / kecil dan besar hatinya tetap / karena anak raja-raja sekalian bercakap* // setelah sudah putus* musyawarat* / Enci' Amin dipanggil membuat surat* / [...]. (SPMR 42c-67b.)

(They gathered together – all good Muslims – / awaiting the Sultan's commands. // Asked the Sultan: / 'Whom had we best send as an envoy / to ask the devilish Hollanders what they want? / If they are bent on war, we shall fight them'. // Karaéng Katapang broke in: / 'Set your mind at rest, Karaéng; / if the Dutch mean to fight, / we shall assemble all our forces'. // [...] // Declared the noble Karaéng Popo' / as he drew his fine knife from its sheath: / 'Wherever Arung Palakka's column fights / just let me get in there'. // Karaeng Léngkésé broke in, / drawing his knife in a gesture of defiance: / 'If it is no more than Dutch and Bugis, / destruction is better than capture'. // [...] // Karaéng Bonto Majannang, the Sultan's [half-]brother, / tigerlike in his bearing, said: / 'Wherever I am ordered to go, / my only thought shall be to fight the Dutch and the Bugis'. Then came Karaéng Jarannika's turn. / His face a fiery red, he said: / 'Dutch and Bugis – those foul dogs! / May I be damned if ever I am disloyal to you!' // [...] // Karaéng Mamu was there, of unquestioned courage. / He pledged in words that could be depended upon: / 'If I should encounter the enemy, / wherever it may be, I'll smash him to pieces'. // [...] // The young members of the entourage declared / that their one wish was to fight the Dutch. Fierce as Garudas they looked, / all of them related to the Sultan. // There were hundreds of the bravest warriors, / in the service of our noble ruler. / 'With your Highness' blessing', they said, / 'we swear to resist the enemy'. // [...] // After all those present had given assurances, / they resumed their normal place in the audience-hall. / High and low, all were determined, / encouraged by the declarations made by the noblemen. // When the council was at an end, / Enci' Amin was summoned to draw up a letter.)

Between both councils a number of formal similarities may be observed. Both type-scenes are constructed upon the same frame of keywords: *berkampung* (to gather together), *bercakap* (to pledge) and *musyawarat* (to take council together). Both are opened by the words of the ruler and these elicit the pledges and boasts of the vassals. But then some differences may be noted. The first council is kept brief: only Speelman and Arung Palakka appear in it. The second one is a very lengthy affair: no less than 18 Macassarese noblemen and prominent Malays appear in it, mentioned by name (*sebut*), and presented one by one.

The first council, in which an epic preview of the outcome of the war is given to heighten the involvement of the public, will perhaps still make some sense to the modern reader – at least some sort of business is, it seems, transacted in it. But the second council is bound to puzzle him: no exchange of opinions, no debate, no plan that is discussed, and the one real issue that could have been debated – whom to send as envoy to the Dutch - is lost sight of as quickly as it is introduced. What can be the point of such a meeting? As the reader gradually comes to realize, instead of being concerned with plans or discussion, the council is taken up with a demonstration of courage and loyalty. The ruler initiates it by expressing his courageous determination to resist the Dutch, and it is these words which elicit the pledges of loyalty and boasts of courage of his vassals, introduced by the assurance to the ruler not to be worried. In presenting the pledges of the vassals the *syair* highlights the passion and sincerity of their words, the beauty and awe-inspiringness of their appearance, the fierceness of their gestures and movements, in short, their heroic stance or posture (*sikap*), comparing them to the male tiger or the bird of destruction (*garuda*), as opposed to the Dutch who are contemptuously referred to as damned curs. Heroic stance is presented in this meeting, and that is what the meeting is about: on the one hand it is a manifestation of the force of true *daulat* of the ruler, on the other hand a demonstration of the disposition (*perintah*) of true vassalage of the vassal, a confirmation of his reputation for loyalty and courage, a reputation ultimately to be backed up by deeds.

If we read the second council as a manifestation of true *daulat* and true vassalage, what about the first one? Now some significant differences may be noted. Speelman is presented as the drunken (*mabuk*) Dutch general. Of course one may wish to argue that this should be read referentially as a realistic portrait of a 17th-century Company servant – after all, the Dutch were notorious for their bibulousness. However, I prefer to argue that *mabuk* together with *bengis* (violent) should be read as opposites to those aspects of stance (*sikap*) that mark the ruler who possesses true *daulat*: mildness and gentleness (*lemah lembut*), grace (*manis*) and similar qualities necessary in a ruler who is to be able to exert a careful stewardship over the honour (*nama*) of his vassals.[19] Caught in the same framework as the Malay rulers, and therefore potentially a bearer of *daulat*, Speelman is thus from the beginning marked out as a ruler with false *daulat*.

Arung Palakka's vassalage, as well, stands in negative opposition to that of the Macassarese nobles and prominent Malays. Thus the *syair* not only pointedly omits details of *sikap* in its presentation of Arung Palakka, but also, in contrast to the Macassarese, whose words can be depended on,

---

[19] See Milner (1982:41-5, 98) for such qualities of behaviour as marks of veritable rulerliness. Speelman's overbearing behaviour, on the contrary, is considered *sombong*, see Milner (1982:43, 106).

presents Arung Palakka as a braggart (*dusta*), who makes a boast he manifestly could not (as the public well knew) back up with deeds – that is, by bombarding the town into ruins in just one day – and who thus shows himself merely puffed up with self-aggrandizement (*sombong, membesarkan diri*). Like master, like servant: Speelman's false *daulat* is matched by Arung Palakka's false vassalage. In the two councils true *daulat* and vassalage are thus opposed to false *daulat* and vassalage, an opposition that finds its formal correlative in the difference in diction in both type-scenes: the Dutch council practically non-formulaic, the Macassarese one couched in dignified traditional phrases.

The Western mediaevalist who looks at these council-scenes will have an experience of déja-vu. He may for instance call to mind the council-of-war with which Jordan of Fantosme (12th century) begins his *Chronicle*. In it King Louis of France broaches the subject of war with England to his nobles. King Louis, so the *Chronicle* tells us,

> Held a great council of all his good friends.
> Of the old king of England he was so thoughtful that the gentle King Louis was near to going out of his mind.

'Gentle King Louis' was first comforted by the Count of Flanders in fairly moderate language, but the Count of Blois was a stranger to moderation:

> Gentle King of St. Denis, rage possesses me in my body,
> I am your liege-man through faith and through homage,
> Ready am I to go fighting and find a host,
> Forty days will I serve you in the first rank,
> And I will do to King Henry, I believe, such damage
> That he will not indeed be restored to his complete possessions.[20]

Or he may call to mind the council-scene in that magnificent heroic epic, *The Song of Roland*, in which Turoldus presents the Saracen knights making their pledges and boasts to King Marsile at Saragossa to do battle with Roland and the Frankish army at Roncevaux, and of which I quote the following boast:

> There is an amurafle there from Balaguer,
> He has a well-proportioned body and his face is fierce and open.
> When he is mounted on his horse,
> He bears his arms very fiercely.
> He is reknowned for his bravery.
> If he were a Christian he would be a very worthy knight.
> He cried out in front of Marsile:
> 'I'll go risk my life at Roncevaux;
> If I find Roland, he shall be put to death

---

[20] Jordan, *Chronique* II, 46-59; RS 82:3, 206-8. The translation is quoted from Brandt (1973:122).

With Oliver and every last one of the Twelve Peers.
The French shall suffer an agonizing and shameful death.
Charlemagne is old and decrepit,
He will forsake the war he is waging.
He will abandon Spain to us and leave us in peace.'
King Marsile thanked him very much.[21]

Behind these texts may be perceived a feudal ideology not dissimilar to the aristocratic ideology which pervades Malay heroic epic. A similar concern with honour and reputation can be seen to motivate their protagonists, and a similar importance is attributed in them to heroic stance.[22]

As an example of how the story of a war-campaign may be worked out by the poet on the basis of the pledge-battle matrix, with the help of certain type-scenes, and with pervasive oppositions of praise and blame, I offer the story of the military expedition of the Sultan of Tallo' to Boné to suppress a Bugis uprising there. As Skinner indicates, this uprising must have taken place in February 1667, prematurely, because it erupted before Speelman had returned from the east, so that the Macassarese could easily suppress it (Skinner 1963:256).

When news (*khabar*) of the uprising reaches the Sultan of Goa, he calls his 'younger brother', the Sultan of Tallo', for a council-of-war. This council proceeds along similar lines to those described above in the council of the Macassarese and focuses on the pledge of the Sultan of Tallo':

> Serta datang baginda duduk / berdatang sembah seraya duduk / tuanku jangan berhati sibuk / biarlah patik ke Bone masuk // berbunyilah nobat genderang pekanjar / sultan di Telo' melompat berkanjar / bercakap* di hadapan sultan yang besar / Bone itu patik melanggar // segala hulubalang baginda sultan / sikapnya seperti harimau jantan / bercakap* di hadapan baginda sultan / Bone itu sungguh aku lawan // sultan di Telo' raja yang majelis / baginda bercakap* melanggar Bugis / segala yang mendengar habis menangis / seraya menyumpah Bugis iblis // mendengar sembah paduka adinda / sukacita hati kakanda baginda / menghimpunkan* hulubalang / yang muda-muda / akan mengiringkan* sultan yang muda // dengan sesaat putus musyawarat* / bagindapun kembali beristirahat / setelah berkampung* sekalian rakyat / menantikan titah maka berangkat*. (SPMR 153-8.)

> (The king of Tallo' entered the audience-hall and sat down, / doing homage as he did so. / 'Your Highness need not be worried. / Let your servant invade Boné.' // The royal drum and the war-drums were sounded. / The king of Tallo' made some defiant passes. / To his brother, the Sultan, he declared: / 'Your servant will attack

---

[21] The council-scene occurs in Laisse lxxii of the *Song of Roland*. The translation is quoted from Brault (1978, II:57-9). My thanks are due to A. Hagen of Utrecht University for pointing out the resemblances of the councils in the SPMR with those of the *Song of Roland*. Both he and Professor W.P. Gerritsen have kindly advised me about relevant literature.
[22] About the feudal ideology underlying the *Song of Roland*, see Jones (1963:49, 96-9, 105). For the earlier period, see Green (1965). For Malay aristocratic ideology on this point, see the concepts *malu* (Milner 1982:27, 72-93, 106-7, 131), *aib* (Milner 1982:74, 106) and *nama* (Milner 1982:46, 52, 63, 72-93, 94-111, 155).

Boné'. // All the warriors of His Majesty the Sultan / were fierce in bearing like male tigers. / In the presence of His Majesty they swore an oath: / 'We shall fight Boné in deadly earnest'. // The Sultan of Tallo', the handsome ruler, / swore that he would attack the Bugis. / All who heard him were moved to tears / and cursed the devilish Bugis. // Hearing his younger brother's declaration, / the Sultan was extremely pleased; / he ordered the young warriors to assemble, / to accompany the young King on his campaign. // In less than no time the council-of-war was over / and the King of Tallo' went back to his palace to rest. / When the troops had assembled / they awaited the royal command to set out.)

Now that the unanimity of the *kerajaan* has been expressed and confirmed the military campaign can begin. When the auspicious time comes the Sultan of Tallo' and his army are presented to us marching out (*berangkat/berjalan*) in a blaze of majesty. As the occurrence of the key-word *mengiringkan* (to accompany) shows, this march-out is of the variant royal march-out[23], which means that conventionally the scene is to be amplified with details such as the multitude of the followers who accompany the ruler, the pomp and circumstance of the occasion, all so many manifestations of the presence of true royal power (*daulat*):

> Antara selang beberapa hari / sultan berangkat* ketika seri / daulat baginda sangat berdiri / berarak dengan serunai nafiri // dipalunya genderang ditiupnya serunai / pahlawan berjalan* terlalu ramai / hulubalang mengiringkan* seperti sakai / baginda berarak seperti mempelai. (SPMR 159-60.)

> (A few days later / the King set out at an auspicious moment. / His Royal Power stood firm; / he was borne in procession to the sound of the fife and the trumpet. // The drums were beaten and the fifes shrilled. / The captains marched off, a great host of them. / The bodyguard followed behind, waiting on the King, / who was borne along like a bridegroom.)

Comparable royal march-outs worked out in similar detail can be indicated elsewhere in the SPMR:

> Sultan berangkat* ke Ujung Pandang / beraraklah dengan / serunai genderang / diiringkan* menteri serta hulubalang / senjata dan rakyat tiada terbilang // [...] // sultan berangkat* segera kembali / dengan segala rakyat serta menteri / ketika itu setengah hari / rakyat mengiringkan* berlari-lari. (SPMR 225-7.)

> (The Sultan went out to Ujung Pandang / in procession with the drums and fifes playing. / He was accompanied by his ministers and officers / and the long procession was bristling with weapons // [...] //. It was not long before the Sultan set off back, / followed by his retinue and his ministers. / It was then midday / and his men accompanied him, running along.)

All these royal march-outs, although built on the same frame-work of key-words, and executed with similar traditional details, can be seen to be adapted by the poet to the individual needs of the moment at which he employs the type-scene in his narrative.

---

[23] About *berjalan* type-scenes, see also Chapter II.

IV The Kerajaan at war   117

What the reader – or, at least, the modern reader – will often miss in Malay historical narrative are details that localize the scenes that are presented in time and place. This 'lack' of temporal and local specification is also characteristic of the way the poet tells us of the voyage the Sultan of Tallo' makes by ship to the scene of the battle: an adulatory amplification on the beautiful sight presented by the ships of the Sultan and his men 'takes the place' of a 'concrete' description of the voyage, as the modern reader would expect it:

> Kenaikan* sultan di Telo' / awan berarak tunjung berkeluk / kepada bunga setangkai baginda duduk / di hadapan menteri yang pitah mabuk // kenaikan* itu bernama pelang / ukirnya terus berkerawang / dicapnya dengan perada terbang / berkilat cahayanya amat cemerlang // indahnya tidak lagi bertara / selaku turun dari udara / jikalau ditentang di tengah segara / rupanya seperti setua anggara // dua ratus enam puluh orang berkayuh / dicapnya perada atas pengayuh / berkilat-kilat seperti suluh / tempik soraknya amat gemuruh // segala raja-raja dengan kenaikannya* / mustaid pula dengan senjatanya / masing-masing dengan gembiranya / terlalu ramai bunyi soraknya. (SPMR 161-5.)

> (The ship the King of Tallo' was to sail in / was carved with a pattern of clouds and curving lotus leaves. / The King had his quarters in the Flowery Column, / waited upon by his ministers, men of intoxicating eloquence. // The ship was of the type called *pelang*, / carved with fretted lines, / gilded with sparkling gold leaf, / so that it glittered and shone in dazzling fashion. // Its beauty was indescribable. / It looked as if it had come down from heaven. / Encountering it at sea / one would think it to be some monstrous animal. // It took two hundred and sixty oarsmen to row the ship / and the oars were gold-mounted. / They shone like so many torches. / The cheering and shouting was deafening. // Each lord had his own vessel / which was well armed. / They were all of them overjoyed / and their shouts rent the air.)

Just once, in the ensuing resumption of the march-out, are we given a geographical detail: the Macassarese disembark at Maros. Whereas in the first march-out the pomp and circumstance of *daulat* was central, in this march-out, kept brief in comparison to the preceding, the focus is on the eagerness of the Macassarese heroes, as true vassals, to offer battle to the enemy, as they promised in council to the ruler:

> Dari Maros baginda berjalan* / terlalu ramai dahulu-dahuluan / karena hendak bertemu lawan / barang yang berani di sanalah melawan // di jalan* tidak berapa lama [...]. (SPMR 166-7a.)

> (The expedition disembarked at Maros and marched off, / each man striving to be first, / for their desire was to meet the foe; / that would be the place for the brave man to fight. // They were not long on the march [...].)

Only at the moment when the battle has come, does the poet deign to pay attention to the enemy, the Bugis. Significantly their line of action is not presented as beginning with a council-of-war, that moment at which *daulat* and vassalage may be given their first and characteristic expression. Neither is any space given to their preparations for battle or to their march-out. The battle-scene in which they enter the narrative is given all the appearances of a 'Blitzkrieg' which overwhelms them, an effect to which the long description of the advance of the Macassarese preceding it can also be seen to contribute:

> [...[di Mampu perang* mula pertama / segala Bugis laknat yang ternama / dengan raja Mampu bersama-sama // perang* pun tidak berapa bentar [...]. (SPMR 167b-168a.)
>
> ([...] before they encountered the enemy at Mampu. / The Bugis, infamous for treachery, / together with the Raja of Mampu. // The battle did not take long; [...].)

All that the Bugis are introduced for here is to flee (*lari*), and the poet devotes considerable space to a damning presentation of their shameful flight, in which the crying, the fear and the unworthy conduct of the Bugis can be seen to contrast sharply with the joy, courage and heroic stance of the Macassarese eagerly rushing forward on their way to the battle:

> [...] larilah* Bugis dihambat Mengkasar / anak bininya terkisar-kisar / oleh raja Mampu yang cuak besar // larilah* Bugis keatas bukit / sekalian menjunjung bekal dan sumpit / setengah menangis setengah menjerit / setengah gementar habis memekik // tidaklah lagi akan kadarnya / tua muda lari* ke gua / beroleh aib lagi kecewa / sebab itulah orang tertawa-tawa. (SPMR 168b-170.)
>
> ([...] the Bugis fled, with the Macasserese after them. / Women and children were sent flying / in the flight of that arch-coward, the Raja of Mampu. // The Bugis fled up the hill, / clutching to their head their rations and blowpipes. / Some were in tears, some were crying out, / while others were shrieking in terror trembling in every limb. // Not one of them could hold his own, / young and old alike fled to the caves. / Shame and ignominy was their lot, / causing people to laugh derisively.]

Here again some geographical details are introduced: hills and caves. As Skinner points out, caves are indeed a characteristic of the landscape of the scene of battle. But a detail such as this is not, in my view, the point of the narrative and may well have been introduced by the poet to obtain what Barthes has called a 'reality effect'. As Barthes has argued, such items, which do not have a function in the plot, form a descriptive residue whose apparent role in the text is that of denoting concrete reality, of confirming the mimetic contract between writer and reader that the text is concerned with the real world as both know it (Barthes 1982:16).

If the mention of hills and caves is not the point of the story, what *is* meaningful is the choice of the Raja of Mampu as the opponent of the Sultan of Tallo'. In the Macassarese Court Diary it is recorded under the date equivalent to our 30 May 1667: 'Tuwammenang-ri-Lampanna (that is, the sultan of Tallo') and Karaéng Léngkésé' go to Boné to attack Matinrowe-ri-Bukaka (that is, the King of Boné, La-Ma'daremmeng)' (Skinner 1963:256, note 159b). But instead of the King of Boné, the Sultan of Tallo' is given

IV The Kerajaan at war

(and for that matter may really among others have had) the Raja of Mampu as his opponent. The same Raja of Mampu, who, as Bugis sources tell us, had already taken part earlier in a rising against the overlordship of the Macassarese (Skinner 1963:258, note 167d). Could it be that the poet chose the Raja of Mampu because this gave him the opportunity to confront the vassal fulfilling his pledges to the ruler, that is, the Sultan of Tallo', with a false vassal who had twice broken his oath of loyalty, the cowardly Raja of Mampu? The following scene, in which the captured Raja of Mampu is ridiculed and humiliated, hinges, it seems, on this confrontation:

> Sultan di Telo' terlalu murka / disuruhnya bunuh si Bugis tua / karena ia sangat durhaka / ke bawah duli memalingkan muka // raja Mampu datang menyembah / minta ampun barang yang salah / sudahlah dengan kehendak Allah / menjunjung Kuran seraya bersumpah // bertanya pula sahbandar yang pitah / berapa kali engkau sudah bersumpah / raja Mampu seraya menyembah / dua kali katanya tuanku sudah // segala yang mengadap suka tertawa / mendengar katanya si Bugis tua / kalau makan seperti sawa / ubi direbus dengan lemang jawa. (SPMR 171-4.)

> (The King of Tallo' was exceedingly angry / and ordered the old Bugis leader to be executed, / for he had been guilty of flagrant treachery / in rebelling against the Sultan. // Making obeisance the Raja of Mampu approached, / asking forgiveness for the wrong he had done. / 'What has happened in the past has been Allah's will', he said, / placing the Koran on his head and swearing loyalty. // The witty Syahbandar asked: / 'That makes how many times you've taken the oath of loyalty?' / Making obeisance, the Raja of Mampu said: / 'Twice, so far, Your Highness'. // The King's entourage roared with laughter / at the words of the old Bugis. / His capacity for eating his words was only equalled by a python / swallowing down boiled tubers and rice cooked in Javanese fashion.)

And with this scene of taunting and humiliation, the first move, namely the story of the war at Mampu, is rounded off, and a second move, in which the story of the war at Pattiro is told, begins, which is again opened with a brief march-out that suggests the rapid advance of the Macassarese army:

> Setelah sudah senda bergurau / baginda berangkat* ke negeri Patiro / hujan pun lebat menderau-derau / sekalian bertudung cilo-cilo. (SPMR 175.)

> (When they had finished joking / the King moved on to Pattiro. / The rain came beating down / and to shelter from it they wore their *cilo-cilo*.)

The ensuing fight (*perang*) and flight (*lari*) are told in two sequences that are given their overall unity by the imposition of a catalogue of the names of the Macassarese vassals who took part in the battle, the feature of *sebut* (mentioning by name) we have already discussed earlier. This catalogue is structured in the order of a battle-array. Rather than on what we would call the actual fighting, the focus of the poet is on the stance (*sikap*) of the Macassarese vassals as people of truly noble birth and on the corresponding lack of stance on the side of the enemy. Oppositions that can be seen are: the Macassarese heroes mentioned by name vs their nameless opponents; fight vs flight; *sikap* vs non-*sikap*; bears vs pigs, etc. The first sequence of fight and flight is kept short. First comes a brief fight that gives a praising presentation of the Macassarese:

> Keraeng Bonto Maranu kepala perang* / baginda itu raja yang terbilang / sadu perdana sikapnya terbang / putera marhum bangsanya sedang // Keraeng Lengkes raja yang garang / serta bertemu lalu berperang* [...]. (SPMR 176-7b.)
>
> (Karaéng Bonto Marannu was in the van, / a noted leader / and an outstanding warrior, ever alert, / a son of the late prince, of right noble descent. // Karaéng Léngkésé' was a fierce fighter. / No sooner did he encounter the enemy than he set to.)

This is immediately followed by a brief *lari* of the Buginese, that suggests their utter inability to resist the Macassarese onslaught:

> [...] Bugis pun lari* lalu ke seberang / seperti babi takut beruang (SPMR 177c-d).
>
> ([...] The Bugis fled across the river, / like so many pigs frightened of a bear.)

The second fight and flight sequence is amplified. First a long fight-scene is presented, again focussed on the heroic stance of the Macassarese:

> Daeng Mangepe' sayap yang kanan / kepada berperang* sangatlah perkenan / seperti beruang melihat makanan / terlalu banyak beroleh tawanan // Daeng Marupa sayap yang kiri / baginda pun anak raja jauhari / mustahillah kepadanya yang bernama lari* / kepada tunggulnya juga berdiri // baginda sultan menjadi tubuh / seperti umpama kota yang teguh / dengan tempik soraknya amat gemuruh / memberi dahsyat pada hati musuh // Keraeng Tompong menjadi ekur / bagindapun raja yang termasyhur / kepada berperang* tidaklah undur / Cili' Kalimata di sana bercampur // baginda itu raja yang terbilang / terlalu tahu akan kerja berperang* / tunggulnya merah berbelang-belang / kena asap setinggar turang-berturang. (SPMR 178-82.)
>
> (Daéng Manggapa commanded the right flank. / He liked nothing so much as fighting. / He regarded the enemy as a bear regards its victims / and took a great many prisoners. // Daéng Maruppa commanded the left flank. / The son of an illustrious prince, / he didn't know the word 'retreat', / and he took up his position by his standard. // The King himself commanded the main body of the army, / like unto a strong citadel. / Yelling and shouting at the top of his voice, / he struck terror into the heart of the foe. // Karaéng Tomponga led the rear-guard, / a most renowned prince, / who would never shrink from the fray. / Kaicili' Kalimata, too, was with him. // This latter was a well-known prince, / expert in the art of war. / His standard was a red, striped one, / begrimed with the smoke of the muskets.)

Searching for reference, Skinner on the line *terlalu tahu akan kerja berperang* comments: 'As well he [that is, Kaicili' Kalimata] might. He had been fighting for his brother Mandar Sjah and the VOC for close on twenty years', information for which he refers to *Corpus Diplomaticum Neerlando-Indicum* (Skinner 1963:259, note 182b). Would it not be better, one wonders, to see the line as a case of 'variation within identity', that pervasive artistic principle of the *syair* and the *hikayat* in general? (See Chapter II). Then the

IV The Kerajaan at war 121

line can be seen as a variation on similar lines in the same passage, whose function is to heighten the evocation of the heroic *perintah* (disposition) of the warriors: *kepada berperang sangatlah perkenan* (SPMR 178b) (he liked nothing so much as fighting) and *Kepada berperang tidaklah undur* (SPMR 181b) (he would never shrink from the fray).

A similar conclusion seems justified concerning the mention of Kaicili' Kalimata's banner in the *syair*, to which Skinner, with a reference to a passage in Stapel (1922) wishes, it seems, to attribute referential importance (Skinner 1963:259, note 182c). In the same passage (SPMR 179d) Daéng Maruppa is similarly provided by the poet with a banner, and, as passages elsewhere in the SPMR and in other heroic epics show, these banners simply belong to the landscape of scenes such as battles.

After this extended battle-scene the ensuing flight (*lari*) of the Bugis is also somewhat more extended than the previous one. This scene closes the second move of the narrative of the punitive expedition against the rebellious Bugis, the story of the battle at Pattiro:

> Larilah* Bugis berkawan-kawan / lintang pukang tidak keruan / hambanya tidak mengenal tuan / banyaklah pula yang tertawan (SPMR 183).
>
> (The Bugis fled in droves, / head over heels, without any semblance of order. / Servants no longer recognized their masters / and many were taken prisoner.)

Shame is piled on shame: there is no difference in stance any more between vassal and servant. Instead of preferring to die on the battle-field as a true vassal should, rather than to surrender (*daripada tertawan remaklah habis*, SPMR 47d), many Bugis choose ignobly to live and let themselves be taken captive by the enemy.

The journey of the Sultan of Tallo' back to Macassar is as glorious as his march-out, and includes, among other scenes, a hunting party. The narrative of the campaign is closed off with the scene of the just rewards being given by the Sultan of Goa to his 'younger brother', who has served him so well, and to the other vassals who took part in the campaign: ceremonial robes are distributed. This description of the ruler rewarding his loyal vassals may be contrasted to that of the shame and ignominy that was the lot of the disloyal Raja of Mampu and his treacherous Bugis:

> Paduka adinda dikarunia* / kain yang indah dari atas angin / kilau-kilauan seperti cermin / dipandang elok seperti pengantin // setelah sudah baginda bersalin / mengarunia* pula raja yang lain / pertama destar kedua kain / keris dan sunderik ditambahi cincin // segala raja yang mengadap / dikarunia* pula sekalian lengkap / [...]. (SPMR 200-202b.)
>
> (The young king was presented with a gift of raiment, / the choicest cloths from the regions to the West, / glittering as though they were made of glass. / He looked as handsome as a bridegroom. // When the king had donned his new robes / it was the turn of the other princes to receive their gifts: / first a head-cloth, then a *kain*, / a

kris and a cutlass, together with a ring. // All the nobles who waited upon the sultan / were given a complete set of gifts.)

3. *The heroic epic and modern historiography*

I began this chapter by introducing the principle of intertextuality that regulates the reading and writing of all texts: texts are always read and written in terms of other texts. When I say *all* texts, I mean to say that this principle is no less valid in the historian's criticism of his sources and in his writing of his own historical narrative. As Collingwood has argued in his book *The Idea of History* (first published 1946), in these activities the historian is guided by his 'historical imagination' or 'idea of history', that is, by a sense of what does and what does not constitute historical evidence and history. Collingwood considered this sense of history a universal and apriori faculty of mankind. In my view the 'historical imagination' is generic and culture-bound.[24] Collingwood's observations on how the historian criticizes his sources and constructs his narrative, as well as on the knowledge the historian is equipped with to be able to practise his profession, can be viewed without exception as confirmations of the operation of intertextuality in historiography.[25]

As the concept of intertextuality emphasizes, texts consist of, are made of other texts; they are irrevocably influenced by, permeated by, other texts; and their meaning only arises from their similarities to and differences from those other texts. Thus any text, no matter how much it may be intended to capture reality, or, to borrow 18th-century terminology, to 'imitate nature', is at the same time already pre-structured, stained and coloured by an already accepted description of reality, a culturally sanctioned vision which is codified in language, text and genre. This seems to be no less true in historiography, and this is what may be called its aspect of 'mythography'.

A work of theory that has gone into the 'mythographical' and literary aspects of historiography is White (1978). Historiographical narrative, White argues, is essentially the product of a fiction-making operation: using the same methods of emplotment employed by the literary artist, the historian

---

[24] For a plea to explode our apriori concept of history and develop an anthropology of history, see Sahlins (1983). My position here is in line with that of modern textualism, in which, crudely formulated, literature is given central importance and in which science and philosophy are treated as at best literary genres. For an exposition on textualism I refer to Rorty (1982:139-59). 'Philosophy', Rorty (1982:92) remarks, 'is best seen as a kind of writing. It is delimited, as is any genre, not by form or matter, but by tradition – a family romance involving e.g. Father Parmenides, honest old Uncle Kant, and bad brother Derrida.'

[25] See Collingwood (1978:244-5) about what I call intertextuality in the criticism of sources. For intertextuality in the construction of the historian's narrative, see Collingwood (1978:240-1). See Collingwood (1978:248) about the broad intertextual knowledge the historian has to acquire in order to be able to interpret his evidence.

encodes his facts by selection, suppression, highlighting, characterization and other such literary devices, into a coherent and meaningful whole. In constructing his narrative, White says, the historian, in response to imperatives that are generally extra-historical, ideological, aesthetic, or mythical, avails himself of specific kinds of plot-structures, certain culturally sanctioned types of configurations of events, accepted pre-conceptions of how events may be emplotted to become meaningful in a certain way.

Among others according to the adoption of different plot-structures, White has discerned a number of different modes in 19th-century historiography. In effect he points out a number of patterns of plot that historians at the time could and did appeal to intertextually in order to endow the events they narrated with a particular kind of meaning.[26] Elaborating Collingwood's idea that the historian fleshes out his factual framework – a framework for which he already selects his facts with a view to the sort of story he wants to tell – by deducing facts that 'must have occurred', by means of his constructive imagination, White has stressed that the historian augments what he has found in the historical record by projecting onto it those notions of possible structures of human existence and comportment that were present in his consciousness even before the investigation began (White 1978:59-60).

In this chapter I, too, have been concerned with something like a genre of historiography, namely with the heroic epic as it occurs in a poem in the *syair*-form. As I have tried to show, a work informed by this genre is based on conventions that are vastly different from those we are familiar with in modern historiography, but not dissimilar to those that were once in force in mediaeval Europe in genres such as the heroic epic and the aristocratic rhyme-chronicle. Not the least important difference with what we consider proper historiography now, and a difference so well known that it seems to need no special discussion, is the absence of the convention of having to give footnotes and references to documents preserved somewhere in existing archives. For the Malay, who was accustomed to a world of predominantly oral communication, not to give and not to expect such references was neither careless omission nor simple naiveté: the use of doing so just was not felt; reference tended to coincide with relevance.

Resuming my findings, we can say that the conventional theme of the genre of the heroic epic is that of the *kerajaan* at war. This theme is expounded in an exemplary story built on and pervaded by praising and

---

[26] For a brief exposition of all this the reader may turn to the essay 'The historical text as a literary artifact' in White (1978:81-100). Here he bases himself on Frye's theory of plot as proposed in his study *An anatomy of criticism* (first published 1957). I apply Frye's theory of plot in Chapters III.2 and III.3 in order to further define the genre of the heroic epic and characterize the genre of the Panji romance.

blaming antithesis. On the one hand, the ruler and his loyal vassals are extolled as presenting and manifesting true *daulat* and true vassalage in their heroic words, stance and deeds in council and in field. On the other hand, blame is contrastingly heaped on the disloyal or unworthy vassals and on the enemy, both the enemy ruler as well as his paladins. Thus, two fundamental archisemic oppositions dominate in the narrative: true *daulat* vs false – that is, an in some way flawed – *daulat*, and true vassalage vs false vassalage. These oppositions are worked out in an intricate network of other, related oppositions, as the narrative unfolds to the listener or reader. The *dominanta* or key-norm of the genre by which heroic narrative can be readily distinguished from other genres is that the plot is developed on the basis of a pledge-battle matrix. This matrix is worked out with the help of certain traditional type-scenes, such as: *berkampung* (to gather together), *musyawarat* (to take counsel together), *bercakap* (to pledge an oath), *menantikan ketika seri* (to await an auspicious time), *berjalan* (to set off), *berperang* (to do battle), *lari* (to flee), *khabar* (to report to the ruler), etc. These type-scenes may be fleshed out with certain details, comparisons, dialogues, etc., the variations in amplification resulting in shifts in emphasis, meaning and effect, as artistic purpose requires.

Goethe once remarked: 'But surely, Nature as it lies before us cannot be imitated: it contains so much that is trivial, unworthy: a selection is therefore inevitable' (*Dichtung und Wahrheit*, II.7). These words also apply to a work of historiography such as the SPMR.

By the constraints of the genre of the heroic epic, by its conventions, only certain matters are worthy of attention: the selection of events, their augmentation and construction into a narrative, all these acts are guided by the generic scheme of the heroic epic, for which the author has opted. In this scheme all is oriented towards an emphasis on the protagonists, on their public posture and stance of heroism and loyalty on council and in field. These are the kind of 'data' that are worthy of this genre of historiography. As in other genres of Malay historiography, there is no 'evocation of the past for its own sake' in Rankian fashion, no reconstruction of 'wie es gewesen ist'. Concomitantly, details that must serve to localize the events in time and place, a feature which Collingwood has considered an absolute must for narrative if it is to be considered historical (by the modern historian, that is), are relatively scarce, and, if provided at all, are not the point of the narrative. With its emphasis fully on the protagonists, the heroic epic scarcely tends to present events as the product of anonymous factors or underlying processes, nor can it conceive of history as something as abstract as the development through time of a nation, an institution or an idea. It will be clear that it is this 'alterity' (Jauss 1977) of Malay historiography which is the reason why its texts have only a limited appeal as a source for the modern historian. This is especially the case where Western sources – telling readily usable narratives that have all the appeal of apparent factuality on their side – are available in sufficient quantity.

May we now sit back comfortably and rest assured that the heroic epic is just fiction and that modern historiography – say, of the genre written by a Stapel or an Andaya – is the sole purveyor of unalloyed historical fact? May we limit ourselves to conceding that works informed by the genre of the heroic epic or one or more of the other genres operative in Malay historiography provide an interesting cultural perspective on what motivates Malay political action, while maintaining that the locus of the real facts, of the true events that actually happened, is to be found in the Western sources, only drawing on the Malay perspective to explain some facts for which the Western sources do not seem to provide an explanation? It may well be the only option the modern historian has, but I hope to have made clear that it cannot be chosen by him with an unhesitating and confident appeal to the fictionality or literariness of the one source vs the factuality or referentiality of the other.

As even the example of a Milner (1982:x, 72, 112-3) seems to suggest, the possibilities for giving credence to Malay works and for incorporating Malay historical narratives into our own modern genres of historical narrative are rather limited: for *facts* we prefer Western sources and historical works. This is generally accounted for by the argument that Western sources and historical works are intrinsically more factual, an argument that may well be thought to have something to it in the case of modern works, undeniably based on historical research as they are, where Malay works clearly are not.

Yet I wonder whether this is the real reason for our lack of belief. Commenting on the question why it took so long before Mendel's insights were accepted by botanists and biologists, Foucault (1976:224) remarked that it is not enough to speak the truth, but that one must be 'within the truth' (*dans le vrai*). It would seem that it may well be the commensurability or incompatibility of the Malay historical texts with the intertexts of the real, the cultural and the generic, rather than any intrinsic difference in factuality, that ultimately determines if and to what extent they may find credence with the judging historian.[27]

---

[27] It will be clear that I cannot agree with the summary of my argument recently given by Schulte Nordholt (1992:31). According to him I oppose Skinner's opinion that the SPMR contains reliable historical information and argue that the poem is basically concerned with representing moral issues in a quasi-historical setting in a narrative constructed with the help of specific literary conventions. In my view I have not argued for the quasi-historicity of the SPMR but for its alterity, which is altogether a different point.

CHAPTER V

Lest we become indifferent
Commemoration in the Syair Perang Siak

1. Narrativity, legality and the SPS

Storytelling is closely bound up with our need to moralize. If a narrative is to inculcate a moral, some concept of retributive justice must be assumed. Its agents must appear as the architects of their own fate: those who abide by the law are to be rewarded and those who trespass against it are punished. All narrative, from the folktale to the novel, from annalistic to fully developed historiography, is therefore in one way or another concerned with the topics of law, legality, legitimacy, or more generally authority. Narrativity, whether of the fictional or of the factual sort, presupposes the existence of a legal system against which, or on behalf of which, the agents struggle. In historical narrative there is always a conflict between desire and the law, the discourse of the real and the discourse of desire (White 1980:14-8).

In this chapter[1] I shall trace the conflict between the law and desire in the *Syair Perang Siak* (Poem of the Siak War, henceforth SPS), a history of the royal dynasty of Siak in the first half of the 18th century. In the course of my reading I hope to show how the SPS in a dialectics of remembrance and forgetfulness of the law tries to create an edifying, dignified, reconciliatory and consolatory vision of the past. As we shall see, the poem tries to provide the past with a proper moral by tracing the workings of just law and the shape of a meaningful order in the events of which it tells, yet, at the same time leaves considerable scope for all-too-human questions and doubts.

I will base my reading of the SPS on the edition published by Goudie (1989) of the oldest manuscript in which the poem has been preserved, namely Klinkert 154 which is kept in the Leiden University Library (Van Ronkel 1921:85).[2] This manuscript is a copy written out between November

---
[1] For a translation into Indonesian of this chapter by Drs. Al Azhar, Director of the Pusat Pengajian Melayu of the Universitas Islam Riau in Pekan Baru, I refer to Koster (1994a).
[2] Besides Klinkert 154 there are two other manuscripts containing the SPS, which have both been copied from it (Goudie 1989:17, 20). One is Von de Wall 273 which is kept at the Museum Nasional in Jakarta and is listed in Van Ronkel (1909:349) under the title *Syair Raja*

1849 and November 1850 at Senapalan (Pekan Baru) in the hinterland of Siak by a Siak man called Encik Mustafa. In a letter from Klinkert to the Executive Committee of the Nederlandsch Bijbelgenootschap dated Riau September 1864[3], I found that the manuscript was a gift from J.E. van Angelbeek, a member of the residency court of Riau (*Almanak* 1863:140) to Klinkert. Van Angelbeek told Klinkert that it had belonged to the Yamtuan Muda (viceroy) of Siak. That viceroy must have been Tengku Putra. He was a scion of the Arab dynasty that came to power in Siak in 1791 and ruled it in the nineteenth century. Tengku Putra was Yamtuan Muda of Siak until 1862, when he was exiled to Riau by the Dutch (Schadee 1918, I:78).

The SPS combines two literary genres. The second half of the poem, after which it has been named, is a heroic epic that deals with the war in 1761 between Siak and the Dutch, in which an important ally of the Dutch is the Siak prince, Raja Alam, who lays claim to the throne of Siak (SPS 228-508). The heroic epic is introduced by means of a genealogical chronicle (SPS 1-227). The narrative of the *syair* may be summarized as follows:

> The inhabitants of Bengkalis, a harbour town falsely claimed to be his dependency by the Buginese ruler of Johor, invite a ruler from the Minangkabau, Raja Kecik, to become their *raja*. He accepts their invitation and is duly installed amidst great rejoicings. Carrying out a surprise attack on Johor Raja Kecik inflicts a humiliating defeat on it. Subsequently he moves his capital from Bengkalis to Buantan, which becomes a bustling prosperous kingdom, attracting many foreign merchants and receiving emissaries from the Kompeni. (SPS 1-69.)
>
> Raja Kecik has two sons of equal status, Alam and Muhammad.[4] To his great sadness an armed struggle for power breaks out between the two brothers, which divides Siak into two camps and causes great misery. To put an end to the fighting, Raja Kecik decides that one of the two must leave Siak. After consultations with his men, Alam decides to leave, because he is unable to bear the humiliation of having to content himself the position of Yamtuan Muda. (SPS 70-109.)
>
> When Alam has left after having taken a tearful farewell of his relatives and the population, Muhammad remains behind a sad and listless man. He succeeds his father and has the regalia, part of which have been taken away by Alam, restored.

Siak. A transcription of this *Syair Raja Siak* has been published by Kosim (1978). The other manuscript is Klinkert 153, which is kept in the Leiden University Library (Van Ronkel 1921:85). According to its colophon its copying was completed on Riau on the 13th day of Jamadi 'l-awwal, AH 1281, which equals 15 September 1864. It should be noted that I limit my reading to the poem contained in quatrains 1-528, which is indeed centrally concerned with the Siak War and forms a coherent and finished work. In quatrain 529 it is obvious a new poem begins, as appears from the fact that it opens with the conventional formulaic exordium *Bismillah itu permulaan kalam / dengan nama Allah Khalikulalam* ('In the name of God' is the beginning of the words / in the name of God, the Creator of the Universe). This new, unfinished poem is not concerned with the Siak War.

[3] My translation of Klinkert's letter was published in Goudie (1989:249).
[4] Tenas Effendy, who is an expert in the genealogy of the sultans of Siak, kindly pointed out that the name of the second son of Raja Kecik was not Mahmud, as Goudie (1989) refers to him, but Muhammad.

He moves his capital from Buantan to Siak Sri Indrapura and carries out a successful raid on a Dutch factory. (SPS 109-31.)

Before Muhammad can realize his ambition to wage a Holy War against the infidel Dutch at Malacca, he falls ill and, after unsuccessful efforts to cure him, dies, a loss deeply mourned by his subjects. He is succeeded by his son Ismail. Because of Ismail's youth his uncle, Tengku Busu, and his cousin, Alam's son Muhammad Ali, act as regents. (SPS 132-227.)

Soon after Ismail has become sultan, news arrives from Malacca that a Dutch fleet will launch a punitive attack on Siak. Alam, who wishes to take revenge for the humiliation he has suffered, has joined the Dutch as their ally. After taking council with his men, Ismail orders the defences to be prepared and the fleet to be put in readiness. (SPS 228-92.)

A number of naval battles – almost always initiated by a scene in which Ismail takes council with his men – are fought. In these battles the Siak men, under the command of Muhammad Ali, offer fierce resistance. Among others tactics by putting a floating gun battery (*kota berjalan*) into action, they try to stop the relentless advance of the Dutch on the Siak River. However, all is to no avail and the invaders succeed in reaching Sungai Pinang, only a short distance from Siak's capital. There the retreating fleet of Siak entrenches itself behind a boom in a last-ditch effort to stop the enemy. An effort to destroy the Dutch fleet by sending downstream a flotilla of burning fire-ships fails. (SPS 293-480.)

When the Dutch, fearing the Siak men, show themselves reluctant to attack, Alam takes the initiative and persuades them to join him in an all-out attack. In the ensuing mêlée, in which Siak men fight side by side with the Dutch, the defenders are unable to discriminate friend from foe so that they are cast into uncertainty, and to their unutterable grief the inconceivable happens: the invaders succeed in capturing Siak Sri Indrapura. (SPS 481-508.)

After having taking a tearful farewell from his relatives and the population, Ismail goes into exile (SPS 509-20).

The SPS does not give the date of its composition, nor does it mention the names of its author and the person who commissioned its writing. Nevertheless, we can form for ourselves some impression of when and how the *syair* came into being, by searching its many passages of narratorial comment, spoken by a storyteller in the role of the truth-seeking *dagang*, for elements that may be read referentially and then combining these into a coherent picture.

From the internal evidence of the SPS we may conclude that the poem was written long after the Siak War by someone who had not been an eyewitness to its events and that the anonymous author made use of stories still current for the writing of his own narrative.[5] We also learn that the

---

[5] That the SPS was written long after the Siak War on the basis of stories still circulating is indicated by the narrator at the very beginning of the SPS when he states: *Tidak dipandanglah dengan mata / sekadar fakir mendengar cerita* (SPS 4c-d) (This beggar did not witness the events with his own eyes / but only heard the stories that were told). In the course of the poem he repeatedly draws attention to the fact that he bases himself on hearsay and stories by lines such as *itulah konon khabar berita* (SPS 25d) (that is the story as it is told), *demikianlah konon khabarnya gerang* (SPS 81a) (thus runs the story as it is told), and *puji dikenang sudahlah timpas* (SPS 131a) (According to the story of praise that is still

writing of the SPS was commissioned by a sultan or his viceroy. This high personage was a relative of the author and was his senior by two generations.⁶ The author, to whom the task of composing the *syair* was entrusted, was someone with the high court rank of *wazir* (Chief Minister).⁷ If my reading of the SPS is correct, the author calls himself a great-grandson of Raja Kecik.⁸

According to Goudie, the SPS was written in 1764 at Tambelan in the Tujuh Pulau Islands, on the orders of Ismail's uncle, Tengku Busu, who had followed him into exile. It was written to state Ismail's right to succeed Alam as Sultan of Siak and to keep the exiled family members together by

---

remembered the tide was low). The fact that he knew not ony the older history of Siak but also the history of the war and Ismail's exile, too, only from stories is confirmed by other statements. Thus, when he is about to tell the story of the final attack on Siak, the narrator announces that *cerita zaman baharu dibuka* (SPS 481a) (a story from the days of yore is only now revealed), and he opens his story of Ismail's exile with the line *perkataan banyak bukan suatu* (SPS 509a) (Many are the stories told about him, not just one).

⁶ The writing of the SPS was commissioned by someone, whom the narrator variously calls *(da)tuk* (grandfather) and *duli mahkota* (His Majesty). In the prologue the narrator states: *Dengan berkat duli mahkota / ibarat dahulu sudah nyata* (SPS 4a-b) (With the blessings of His Majesty / this exemplary tale of the days of yore is here made public). And in the course of a long passage of sad musings concerning the untimely death of Sultan Muhammad he remarks: *Tambahan fakir yang menyurat / malam dan siang di dalam gelorat / daripada tuk sampai dengan isyarat / perkerjaan ringan menjadi berat* (SPS 223) (Moreover the beggar who wrote this story / was deep sunk in sadness from morn to eve. / Because his grandfather came and gave him a sign / his duties once light became onerous). Later, apologizing for possible authorial shortcomings, the narrator says: *Fakir menyurat belum biasa / tambahan badan tidak kuasa / sebab dititahkan mahkota desa / jangan menjadi putus rasa* (SPS 280). (This beggar is not accustomed to writing, / moreover, the flesh is weak and frail. / He wrote his story because His Majesty commanded him / not to become indifferent). It seems likely that this grandfather/ruler is the same person as the ruler referred to as patron at the beginning of the SPS.

It seems hard to accept Goudie's reading of *tuk* in SPS 223c as *teruk*, a word meaning 'suffering' or 'to suffer'. A reading as *tuk*, short for *datuk* seems to me to be the more likely one. An argument in favour of this is found in verse line SPS 251a, where t-q obviously must be transcribed in this way: *dengan Tuk Salik jadi berempat*. Also, manuscript Klinkert 153 here has *datuk* (Goudie 1976:191). In theory another possible reading would be *tak*, but that also does not seem to make sense.

⁷ That the author was someone with the rank of *wazir* appears at the close of the SPS, when the narrator, pondering Ismail's sad fate, remarks: *Perang Siak tamatlah sudah / hati didalam sangatlah gundah / hari asar matahari rendah / duduklah wazir tunduk tengadah* (SPS 521) (The story of the Siak War is finished here. / The heart of the narrator is filled with grief. / It is late afternoon and the sun is low, / as the vizier sits deep sunk in thought).

⁸ This appears from lines SPS 278a-b, where the narrator closes off a lengthy account of how Ismail and his men prepared themselves to resist the Dutch attack with the words: *Terhentilah kisah cinda yang dikarang / akan puji-pujian sekalian orang* (SPS 278a-b) (Here ends the story of a great-grandson, which he wrote / in praise of all the men who took part). The Jawi text in line 278a here has c-y-n-d-(a)-y-q. Unless the word is a corruption the most likely reading is *cinda*. If this is indeed the correct reading, *cinda* should probably be interpreted as meaning 'great-grandson of Raja Kecik'.

giving them a sense of their history and destiny. In Goudie's opinion it later served as an instrument to state the right to rule Siak of Raja Akil, Sultan of Sukadana (1827-1849), who was one of the many members of the royal house of Siak in the line of Muhammad who fled into exile in 1791. In that year Said Ali, a member of the rival line of descent of Alam, grasped power in Siak and founded the Arab dynasty that ruled it in the 19th century. Said Ali was the son of Said Osman, an Arab who had served with Alam in the Siak War and had later married Alam's daughter (Goudie 1989:36, 39-43, 47-63).

Whereas it cannot be ruled out that an earlier version of the SPS was written at the time and place and with the purport surmised by Goudie, his theory is not borne out by the poem as we have it. In my view – an opinion I hope to substantiate in the course of my reading – the SPS as we have it must have been written during the reign of Ismail's son and successor, Sultan Yahya (1781-1791), on the orders of his Yamtuan Muda, the then already aged Muhammad Ali. I like to think that its author may well have been Tengku Muhammad, a son of Ismail's younger brother, Tengku Abdullah (Goudie 1989:36). Tengku Muhammad belongs to the generation of Raja Kecik's greatgrand-children and is known to have acted as *dalang* at his own marriage (Goudie 1989:36, 44, 68), something which requires considerable literary skill.

Let us now leave further considerations of the referential background of the SPS and its presumable aims and purports to a more suitable moment and turn to a rhetorical reading of the poem.

2. Comedies of memory

The heroic epic of the Siak War, the second half of the SPS, is opened by a scene in which Sultan Ismail takes council with his men. Tengku Busu and Muhammad Ali have not long been acting as regents over Siak, we are told, when news arrives from across the Straits that the Dutch plan to attack, in alliance with Alam who wishes to take revenge for the disgrace of exile he has suffered. The proceedings of the council are then described as follows:

> Demi baginda mendengar warta / tersenyum manis bertitah serta / khabar Melaka sudahlah nyata / sekarang apa bicara kita // berdatang sembah ayahanda dan kakanda / serta pegawai anum berida / barang yang mana kehendak Wilanda / patik sekalian sedialah ada // [...] // apatah guna patik ditimbang / menjunjung karunia kasih dan sayang / kepada niat malam dan siang / badan rebah jiwa melayang. (SPS 237-41.)

> (When His Majesty heard the news / he said with a gentle smile: / 'The report from Malacca is clear. / Now what is our opinion?' // His uncle and cousin approached respectfully, / as did his officials, young and old: / 'Whatever the Dutch may have in mind, / we, your servants, will be there to oppose them'. // 'What good would it

be to spare your servant, / who receives your bounty, kindness and love? / Day and night he has but one aspiration: / to fall in battle and give up his life.']

As is the case in the SPMR, the narrative of the heroic epic of the SPS is worked out in a series of moves. These are usually initiated by a council scene, in which pledges of loyalty to the ruler are uttered, and they tend to culminate in a battle-scene in which the heroes are shown to redeem their pledges by loyal service and the performance of deeds of courage.

In the scene quoted above, two wills are opposed: the lawful will of the Siak men to defend Siak, if need be at the cost of their lives, and the usurpatory desire of the Dutch to conquer it. The *kerajaan* order is obviously at stake, and the legitimacy of Ismail's rule, his *daulat*.

If a narrative is to maintain law and order, the simplest and most obvious way to emplot it is as a comedy of the moralistic variant: a story of how the good party wins and the wicked are punished. Such a story hinges on the opposition between just law and usurpation (Frye 1973:163-7). It is precisely this opposition that motivates the epic initiated by the above council scene, so that we may indeed say that it strives to emplot the events of which it tells as comedy.

Another way in which we may formulate the conflict motivating the plot of comedy in the heroic epic is to describe it as a struggle to prevent just law from being forgotten. The weapon deployed against forgetfulness in such a case is remembrance. The plot of comedy then not only opposes the law to illegitimate desire and propriety to impropriety, but also remembrance to forgetfulness.

In the story of the Siak War the protagonists are indeed shown as being involved in efforts to commemorate origins. They not only try to recall and thus confirm worldly law, as codified in the Book of the Malay *Kerajaan* Order. Besides this they invoke religious law, God's Writing as the manifestation of His Divine Will. The heroic epic strives to tell a double comedy of memory: a story of feudal order and God's Will successfully remembered and triumphantly confirmed.

In order to understand that we are to read the heroic epic as an invocation of feudal origin, it is helpful to picture it as a discursive arena. In this space by their fine pledges and boasts, by their great deeds and splendid stance, the heroes vie in trying to recall the example of (*ingat*), and thus to represent (*mengadakan*), the behaviour of the great heroes of the days of yore as codified in the Book of the Malay *Kerajaan* Order.

A confirmation that we must take the protagonists as involved in a commemoration of ancient origins, is the following description of Ismail's two younger brothers joining the fray in which they are represented as replicating, and therefore successfully representing, the behaviour of the heroes of the *wayang* stories and Hindu-Javanese epics[9]:

> Dipandang laku adinda kedua / laksana Ranjuna dengan Pandawa / akan perang wayang Korawa / selaku tidak sadarkan jiwa (SPS 417).

> (The way both brothers bore themselves / resembled that of Arjuna and the Pandawas, / about to offer battle to the Korawas of the *wayang* / as if they gave not a thought for their lives.)

The idea that we are also to see the protagonists as trying to commemorate religious origin, the law of God's Writing, appears from the fact that the war with the Dutch is presented as a struggle between believers, that is, protagonists of divine law, and unbelievers who try to obstruct God's Will. This theme can for instance be observed in the following passage in a battle-scene:

> Bunyi meriam bagaikan belah / tidak berhenti sebelah-menyebelah / ganggu tawakal kepada Allah / memakai jimat tegah Allah. (SPS 429.)

> (The guns boomed making a din as if they would burst. / The firing did not let up on either side. Those obstructors of God's Will / used charms forbidden by God.)

And, significantly, when setting off to confront the Dutch invaders, Sultan Ismail is depicted as the Vicegerent of God, that is, as a repetition of the great caliphs of Islam who led the Muslim community in the Holy War against the infidels:

> Lalu dipalu gong semboyan / dibongkarlah sauh penjajap sekalian / Khalifatullah di dalam kemulian / [...]. (SPS 314a-c.)

> [Then the signal gong was struck, / and the anchors were weighed aboard all the ships. / The Vicegerent of God set off in all his glory / [...].)

In the genealogical chronicle of the SPS, too, a comedy of memory may be indicated, notably in its opening story of the rise of Raja Kecik to greatness. The narrative sets in with an initial situation that evidently calls for the appearance of a Founding Father, a culture hero who will bring order to chaos:

> Tersebutlah kisah suatu peri / madah dahulu orang bahari / Buantan belum menjadi negeri / kayunya banyak akar dan duri (SPS 5)

> (Here the story is told, / a tale of our forefathers in bygone days, / of the time when Buantan had not yet become a *negeri* / but its dense forest was a tangle of creepers and thorns).

---

[9] The status of the *wayang* epics as ancient history has led to the incorporation of some of their prominent figures into the *silsilah* (genealogy) of rulers and to their playing a role in traditional histories. An example is the presence of Lord Bima, the second of the five Pandawa brothers, in the genealogy of the rulers of the Eastern Indonesian island of Bima and the prominent role he and his brothers play in the *Hikayat Sang Bima* written there (Chambert-Loir 1985:141-2, 159).

As is the case in the heroic epic, in the genealogical chronicle, too, the plot of comedy is worked out in a series of moves. The first move tells how a ruler from the Minangkabau, after having sought consensus among his men (*mencari mufakat*), decides to accept an invitation from the inhabitants of Bengkalis to become its ruler and how he successfully establishes himself there, thus setting to nought the false claim of Buginese-ruled Johor to the town as its dependancy (SPS 5-20).

The second one (SPS 21-46), which tells of a surprise attack in which the ruler conquers Johor and thus punishes it for its attempt to usurp his *daulat* (royal power), again is characteristically motivated by the will of the ruler, who acts in consonance with his people:

> Mufakat dicari dalam dan tohor / baginda hendak melanggar Johor (SPS 22a-b)
>
> (Through thick and thin they sought to reach agreement / for His Majesty wished to attack Johor).

And it ends in a resounding victory that fully proves the falseness of Johor's claim to greatness.

The third move begins in a similar manner:

> Baginda hendak membuat negeri / mencari bicara sehari-hari / mufakat dengan wazir menteri (SPS 47b-d)
>
> (His Majesty wished to build himself a negeri. / He consulted their opinions day by day / to establish consensus with his vizier and ministers).

Its culmination is a festive description of the bustle (*keramaian*) of the new capital, Buantan. As a sign of his true *daulat*, the ruler is pictured as being joyfully served by his numerous subjects and loyal ministers and receiving foreign merchants from far and near, as well as emissaries sent by the VOC.

Like the heroes in the epic, Raja Kecik, too, is to be understood as involved in a double effort to commemorate; in his words and deeds on the one hand he tries to invoke and imitate ancient wordly order and, on the other hand, tries to recall the Will of God. This can for instance be concluded from a scene which takes place on the eve of his attack on Johor, in which Raja Kecik is shown to invoke worldly and religious origins:

> Ke Tanah Merah sampai serta / kepada Allah doa dipinta / berkat Muhammad penghulu kita / jangan memberi nama yang leta // matahari masuk berayun petang / doa dipinta tangan tertelentang / berkat Datuk di Bukit Siguntang / janganlah apa aral melintang. (SPS 34-35.)
>
> (As he arrived at Tanah Merah / he uttered a prayer, beseeching God: / 'By the blessing of Muhammad, our leader, / may He not allow his servant's name to be dishonoured'. // The sun sank to hang above the horizon in the evening. / He beseeched God, praying with upturned hands: / 'By the blessing of the ancestors of Bukit Siguntang, / may no misfortune obstruct my path.').

The 'ancestors of Bukit Siguntang' is a reference to the story told in the *Sejarah Melayu* (see Shellabear 1982:16-21) that three princes, descendants of Iskandar Zulkarnain, miraculously appear at Bukit Siguntang (near present day Palembang). The youngest of the three, Nila Utama, as Seri Tri Buana, becomes the founder of the Malacca-Johor line of kings. The eldest, Nila Pahlawan, with the title Sang Sapurba founds the line of kings of Pagarruyung. In the SPS Raja Kecik's orgin is consistently associated with Pagarruyung.[10]

Significantly the narrator summarizes the story of Raja Kecik's rise to greatness with the words *itulah kisah usul mengindra* (SPS 70a). This line could variously be translated as 'That was the story of His Majesty's origins' or as 'That was the story of how His Majesty bore himself'. This suggests that we are indeed to view the deeds performed by Raja Kecik as invocations of origin, in other words, as acts of commemoration and mimesis, and are to read the story of his rise to glory as a comedy of memory. The feasibility of such a reading is confirmed by the existence of a Malay proverb, which says: *usul menunjukkan asal* (a man's behaviour shows his origin) (Wilkinson 1943, I:48; II:640).

Typically the heroic epic strives to be a literary expression of propriety. In this genre attention for the assumed fixed, proper relation between the stockphrases and what they refer to is given priority over the production of meaning through the contextually defined play of self-signifying terms. Putting it in Malay words: in the heroic epic *mematutkan* is to prevail over *memanjangkan*; consequently, true heroes must be shown to be really true heroes, successfully repeating the examples of their ancient predecessors and fighting the infidels, mindful of God's Will.

Proceeding from a belief in the pervading presence of an essentially uncontested linguistic field and a great communality of experience and social interest, the heroic epic is typically the theatre of unreflective action. Meaning is not something that need be discovered, but rather is something the heroes assume as their own, something they perform, something they declare formulaically, something they exude. The finer their words and gestures, the more violent and bloody their deeds, the more memorable the heroes are. And the better are their chances that they may inspire songs of praise and thus be remembered by later generations (Vance 1979:392-3).

---

[10] The opposition Minangkabau vs Bugis in the story of the rise of Raja Kecik finds an interesting parallel in the genealogical chronicle, *Tuhfat al-Nafis* (Dedication to the Splendid Endeavour, see Johns 1992:319-23). In the history of the Malay world in the first half of the 18th century, as it is told in the first half of that work, an important role is given to this opposition. This is symbolically indicated by the story of the cockfight in Cambodia between the cocks of the Buginese Opu, Daeng Rilaga, and the Minangkabau prince, Raja Culan, in which the Buginese cock wins because of the potency of the metal of its spurs (Raja Ali Haji ibn Ahmad 1982:45-6, fol. 49 II-50 I; Matheson Hooker 1991:181-3, fol. 49 II-50 I).

Although propriety dominates in the heroic epic, this does not mean that improper detachments of words from meaning are not a familiar phenomenon in it. We need only think of such examples as unkept promises, treason or cowardice, to see that such improprieties are a frequent phenomenon. As Bloch points out the inherent contradiction of representing linguistic transgression is never explored. The implicit discursive mode of the heroic epic is one of linguistic integrity. Where that fails the dominant strategy is recuperative: to attempt to translate improper words into proper deeds, thus restoring their propriety (Bloch 1983:100-3). Here we meet the principle of poetic justice: the narrative punishment of traitors, cowards and, of course, of the enemy.

An example of poetic justice in the SPS is, for instance, the story of how a Siak warrior, Encik Mangid, ignominiously fails to live up to his boastful words, when he is attacked by the Dutch. The narrator characteristically closes off this story with the comment: *Itulah orang sangat sombongnya / membuat berani seorang dirinya* (SPS 372a-b) (That was a man so puffed up with arrogance / he pretended to be brave all on his own).

What Encik Mangid is criticized for is his failure to represent, his inability to match sign with meaning. As I have shown in Chapter III, according to Malay poetics the possession of wisdom is the prerequisite for the capability to remember. Encik Mangid's behaviour is therefore a break in representation caused by a forgetting of self, by a lapse of memory which may befall those who lack wisdom and sense. Instead of *mengadakan* (representation) it proves to be merely *mengada-ada* (pretention).

What has been said here of the genre of the heroic epic is also very much true for the genre of the genealogical chronicle. There is, however, one difference between them: the scope they leave for improprieties. In the genealogical chronicle this scope is wider than in the epic, because the genre is of a more narrativizing character.[11]

Above we have already seen exemplified that the device of poetic justice is also used in the genealogical chronicle, namely, in the narrative punishment of the Buginese ruler of Johor. The fact that his failure, like that of Encik Mangid, is one of memory and representation is underlined by the story that he is so engrossed in his game of chess (*leka bercatur*), that is, is sunk into a state of such utter forgetfulness, that he does not notice the din of the attack, ignores all alarms and fails to act like a veritable ruler should do (SPS 41-4). Here, too, seeming *mengadakan* is shown to be really *mengada-ada*.

In a comedy of memory the prevalence of certainty of meaning – of *men-*

---

[11] For a discussion of a recent novel by Arena Wati in which, among others, the genres of the epic and the genealogical chronicle play an important part, I refer to Koster (1994b).

gadakan – is of paramount importance. Both in the heroic epic and in the genealogical chronicle, the importance of the certainty of meaning and the undesirability of opacities requiring interpretation is expressed by their association respectively with joy and sadness. Another opposition that may be aligned with that of certainty vs doubt and joy vs sadness is that of unanimity vs discord. In the epic the link of joy with certain meaning, for instance, finds expression in the description of the joyful eagerness with which real heroes unanimously set off for battle:

> Hilir berdayung berdahulu-huluan / umpama singa mencari lawan / bahananya sorak melangsi awan / galiblah hulubalang yang pahlawan (SPS 322).
>
> (They rowed downstream vying who would be first, / like lions in search of their foe. / The din of their cheers rent the clouds; / the heroic warriors were off in quest of victory.)

In the story of the rise of Raja Kecik, too, certainty of meaning is linked with joy and unanimity. This is concisely expressed in the three verse lines with which the story of the coming of the founder of the dynasty to Bengkalis is closed off and the story of the attack on Johor is initiated:

> Kerajaan baginda sudahlah tentu / tidaklah lagi berhati mutu / laksana emas sudah semutu / mencari mufakat pula suatu (SPS 21)
>
> (Now that the rule of His Majesty had securely been established / his spirits were no longer troubled. / Like gold that has been fully refined / he sought to establish consensus).

In the third move this association of joy with the absence of doubt and with the certainty of meaning is expressed in lines such as *tidak menaruh was dan sangka* (SPS 55d) (they did not foster any suspicions or doubts), *tidaklah lagi huru-hara* (SPS 62c) (there was no longer any confusion), and *tidak menaruh gundah gulana* (SPS 68d) (they did not foster any feelings of sadness). And the Johorese, for whom meaning has become unsettled because of their defeat, are accordingly depicted as being prey to the sorrows of uncertainty:

> Mana yang tinggal tidak bertentu / bercerai dengan anak menantu / remuk redam hatinya mutu / laksana kaca jatuh ke batu (SPS 46).
>
> (Those who did not flee felt completely unsettled, / parted as they were from their children and affines. / Overcome by sadness they were utterly shattered, / like glass that has fallen to pieces on stone.)

3. Dramas of forgetfulness

Although the genealogical chronicle and the heroic epic of the SPS should both maintain the plot of comedy, neither of them succeeds in doing so: both narratives have to admit extremely painful improprieties. In the heroic epic the main problem is Sultan Ismail's defeat, whereas in the chronicle it is the family-feud that almost brought the kingdom to the brink of destruction by civil war. In both, sign and meaning are ultimately seen not to match, and both thus turn from comedies of memory into dramas of forgetfulness.

We have already seen that the certainty of meaning is associated with joy. As the end of the heroic epic draws nigh and defeat becomes inevitable, from one full of joy the mood of Siak's warriors gradually and then increasingly turns into one of sadness, an indication that something incomprehensible is about to take place, that a shift is taking place from clarity to opacity, from propriety and remembrance to impropriety and forgetfulness:

> Orang Siak adalah duka / melihat kelakuan kafir celaka / didalam tembak bagai dijangka / berhanyut mudik juga belaka // [...] // Meriam Wilanda berbunyi selalu / pelurunya datang bertalu-talu / kapalnya sebagai berhanyut ke hulu / orang Siak adalah silu. (SPS 453, 456.)

> (The Siak men felt sad / when they saw the behaviour of the accursed infidels. / Under cover of carefully calculated gunfire / they kept drifting upstream with the tide. // [...] // The Dutch cannon boomed incessantly. / There was a constant hail of cannon-balls. / As their ships came drifting upstream / the men of Siak felt intimidated.)

And when the enemy fleet succeeds in reaching Siak's last line of defence, the boom across the river near its capital, the Siak men are completely flabbergasted:

> Tidak diangka sampai ke batangan / orang Siak bercengangan / tidak disangka diangan-angan / dia akan sampai ke batangan (SPS 496).

> (They had never expected the Dutch would reach the boom. / The Siak men were agape with astonishment. / Not even in their wildest fancies had they expected / that they would reach the boom.)

The sadness of opacity also dominates in the narrative of Ismail's exile. Significantly, his mood after his defeat is described in exactly the same terms as are the feelings of the Johorese after they have been robbed of the joy of certainty by the defeat Raja Kecik inflicted on them:

> Perkataan banyak bukan suatu / gundahnya hati tidak bertentu / remuk redam hati pun mutu / laksana kaca jatuh ke batu. (SPS 509.)

> (Many are the stories told about him, not just one. / His heart full of sorrow he felt completely unsettled. / Overcome by sadness he felt utterly shattered / like glass that has fallen to pieces on stone.)

In the genealogical chronicle we can trace the same movement from certainty to doubt, from joy to gloom and misgiving. This movement coincides with a movement from concord (*mufakat*) to discord (*tidak mufakat*):

> Tidak berapa lama antara / tiadalah mufakatnya dengan saudara / hampirlah negeri huru-hara / hendak menanggung duka sengsara // [...] // yang empat suku tidak bersatu / baginda melihat berhati mutu / remuk redam tidak bertentu / laksana kaca jatuh ke batu. (SPS 74, 80.)
>
> (It was not long before it happened / that discord arose between the brothers. / The kingdom was on the brink of chaos, / about to suffer great misery. // [...] // The Four Suku were no longer united; / noticing it His Majesty was overwhelmed by gloom; / he felt utterly shattered, was completely unsettled, / like glass that has fallen to pieces on stone.)

There need be no doubt that the heroic epic reflects well on Ismail as ruler and functions to praise the way in which he stood up to his task as the legitimate sultan of Siak in a time of crisis. Yet the awkward question remains, why, by what law, by what system of retributive justice, did Ismail have to suffer the humiliation of being defeated, dethroned and exiled? Surely, his conduct did nothing to justify this dramatic turn of events. Or were all the heroic gestures and words of the sultan and his men only so many empty promises, mere pretension? Were they after all just *mengada-ada* instead of *mengadakan*?

Similar problems are posed by the dramatic turn of events in the genealogical chronicle. Why was the promise of a narrative of one ruler succeeding another in an atmosphere of harmony and consensus not fulfilled? Why, by what law, by what system of retributive justice, did the royal house have to be torn apart by discord. Why did Alam have to suffer the disgrace of exile? And why did Muhammad have to fail to fully restore the dynasty's damaged *daulat* and turn the chronicle into a comedy again? Ever so many questions, ever so many nagging uncertainties, that do indeed fully justify the gloom of the protagonists.

The idea that the problems causing the dramatic turn of events – the breakdown of proper representation – after the reign of Raja Kecik may indeed be connected with a failure to commemorate, is confirmed by the way in which Muhammad tries to remedy this, in the hope that he may counteract the decline of the dynasty. The narrative of his efforts to do so significantly shows up a close parallel with that of Raja Kecik's rise to greatness.

Muhammad begins by re-establishing the consensus in the *kerajaan* and has the regalia, part of which has been taken away with him by Alam, restored again. The next step towards repairing royal power in Siak, Muhammad's removal of the capital to Siak Sri Indrapura, is motivated by his will, that acts in consensus with his people. The third step, his successful destruction of the Dutch garrison at Pulau Guntung, too, is motivated in a similar way (SPS 112-27). What Muhammad is doing is to try and represent royal power once more by acts of commemoration. As Raja Kecik, mindful of his glorious ancestors, once established his *daulat*, thus Muhammad, remembering and imitating his father's deeds, now tries to restore his own again.

Another commemorative weapon he employs shortly before his death, in a final effort to stem forgetfulness of the *kerajaan* order, is formed by his dying injunctions to his sons and grandsons:

> Baginda bertitah kepada putera / bawa baik budi bicara / hendaklah mufakat bersaudara / lebih kurang jangan berkira // sudahlah kepada aku seorang / dengan saudara jadi berperang / kepada kamu sahaja aku larang / jangan menaruh lara wirang. (SPS 156-7.)
>
> (The sultan spoke to his sons: / 'Behave well and exercise wisdom and discretion. / Maintain consensus with your brothers / and do not count your losses or gains. / Let it only be me, who fought a war against his brother; / I expressly forbid you / to foster the pain of disgrace.')

In his dying injunctions Muhammad refers to his conflict with Alam. This conflict unquestioningly forms a serious impropriety: a family-feud pitting brother against brother. It is a transgression of a law in the Book of the Malay *Kerajaan* Order which dictates that consensus and solidarity among relatives are of paramount importance. The failure to exercise wisdom and discretion breeds discord and disaster; that is the moral that Muhammad draws from what has happened – a lesson he enjoins his descendants to heed.

This retrospective reading by Muhammad of his struggle for power with Alam as having been caused by failures to commemorate finds confirmation in the narrative the SPS tells of how the conflict with his brother arose. Albeit discreetly and in a manner that preserves decorum as best it can, the SPS indicates two such failures, two acts of forgetfulness.

The first act of forgetfulness, that sets into motion the forces of disintegration, is committed by Alam: *Sudah berdaulat paduka anakanda / menaruh cemburu sama muda* (SPS 71) (When his son had already been invested with *daulat* / he began to feel jealous of his younger brother). Jealousy is a form of *hawa nafsu*, the indulgence of one's desires or lusts, forgetting one's rationality or higher self (*akal*). The most destructive forms this forgetfulness may take are the desire to aggrandize oneself and the giving in to contentiousness (Andaya Watson and Matheson 1979:118-9).[12]

---

[12] As is rightly pointed out in Andaya Watson and Matheson (1979:119-20), the *Tuhfat-al-Nafis* treats the history of Siak in the first half of the 18th century as an example of the destructive force of *hawa nafsu*, and thus makes its rulers themselves responsible for the decline of Siak's power. It should be noted that according to the *Tuhfat* the forces destroying Siak were unleashed by Raja Kecik, who broke his oath uttered in the mosque of Riau. The import of this oath was that if he intended any further harm or quarrelled with Sultan Sulaiman and the Buginese Yang Dipertuan Muda, he would never again be secure as long as he lived, and this would apply to his descendants, and to the sovereign power of his realm, which would be completely destroyed like a smashed *nipah* fruit and he would be smitten by the *besi kawi* (Raja Ali Haji ibn Ahmad 1982:69, fol.86 II-87 I; Matheson Hooker 1991:225-6, fol.86 II-87 I).

The second act of forgetfulness is committed by Raja Kecik. If he had heeded his duty as head of the family, he should have accepted responsibility and should have tried to solve the problem by reconciling his sons. In the SPS, however, he is shown to lay the burden on their shoulders.[13] And instead of reconciling them, he allows their animosity to continue, nay, even reinforces it:

> Lalu bertitah paduka baginda / apa diperkelahikan dengan saudara muda // di dalam negeri jangan berperang / engkau tidak dapat dilarang / jangan menjangka[14] lara wirang / pergilah engkau salah seorang. (SPS 84c-85.)
>
> (Then His Majesty the Sultan spoke: / 'What are you quarrelling about with your younger brother. / You should not fight within the confines of the realm. / I cannot forbid you to measure the pain of disgrace. / One of you two must leave.')

4. A revenge tragedy

As we have already seen, the end of the story of the Siak War in defeat forms a major breach of epic decorum. Obviously, one way in which the SPS attempts to solve the problem posed by this end – the problem that sign and meaning do not seem to coincide – is by suggesting that Ismail was bound to be defeated because he was attacked by an alliance of two powerful enemies, the Dutch and Alam. Another way in which the poem tries to restore

---

[13] There is another account of this episode, in which Raja Kecik is also seen to fail to take responsibility but is narratively exonerated by being shown to be mad. It is found in a genealogical chronicle, the *Sejarah Melayu* of the Royal House of Siak (Cod. Or. 7304, henceforth SMS, see Roolvink 1967:309), which, among others, consistently argues the claim of Raja Akil to be a descendant in the ancient line of Malay rulers who trace their origin back to Iskandar Zulkarnain and consistently denigrates Alam and his descendants. Raja Akil was a member of the royal house in the line of descent of Muhammad. He had fled into exile in 1791, when Said Ali, a descendant of Alam, had grasped power in Siak and established its Arab dynasty. In 1827 the Dutch rewarded him for his loyal services to them by making him Sultan of Sukadana (Goudie 1989:41). Muhammad Yusoff Hashim has published an edition of the SMS, renaming it *Hikayat Siak* and has assumed that it must have been written in 1855 by Tengku Said (Muhammad Yusoff Hashim 1992: 10, 28). Tengku Said – as was the possible author of the SPS, Tengku Muhammad – was a son of Ismail's brother Tengku Abdullah (Goudie 1976:388-9). Because Tengku Said refers to the text as a *Sejarah Melayu* (Muhammad Yusoff Hashim 1992:647) and in view of the fact that it sets out as a version of the *Sejarah Melayu*) it seems best to stay as closely as possible to that title. In the SMS we are told that Raja Kecik went mad for grief (*tiada tentu lagi gila*) after the death of his dearly beloved wife. When his grandees reported that his sons were fighting he replied: *Barangsiapa yang hidup, itulah anak kita* (Whoever survives, he is my son). Hearing the rumble of cannon he asked them what caused it, whereupon they replied: *Bedil anakda melawan orang Riau* (that is the sound of your sons offering battle to the men from Riau). And His Majesty was pleased (SMS in Muhammad Yusoff Hashim 1992:139-40, fol.450-1). This account agrees with that of the SPS in treating Kecik's behaviour as a failure of memory.

[14] Teeuw (1992:131) has proposed transcribing *panjangkan* instead of *menjangka*. It is unclear whether this is borne out by the manuscript. Here the word *menjangka* is taken to have a meaning similar to the word *berkira* used in Mahmud's dying injunctions (SPS 156d).

propriety is to argue that although Ismail showed himself a worthy ruler, because of his youth he could ultimately not be expected to be a match for his experienced uncle, a man who was quite as worthy to be sultan of Siak.

The SPS softens the shock of defeat further by having Alam inaugurate the final attack on Siak Sri Indrapura. Thus Ismail's *daulat* is ultimately seen not to have been disproved by the lying Dutch infidels (*kafir yang dusta*), but to have been eclipsed by the greater *daulat* of his senior relative. In this manner the *syair* ennobles the ignoble; it shows that power in Siak was not usurped by outsiders, but was instead assumed by someone with a legitimate claim, and that Ismail's defeat was a defeat with dignity.

There need be no doubt that the picture painted of Ismail's defeat as having been primarily brought about by a family-feud, rather than by the Dutch military intervention, does much to restore propriety. But this still leaves a number of equally distressing improprieties unsolved. One of these is that, if a family-feud caused the decline of Siak, the blame for it all would fall on Alam. As we have seen, it is he who unleashes the powers of destruction; and he does so out of jealousy, a form of forgetfulness.

Alam's mistake is that he fails to remember the law of consensus, codified in the Book of the Malay *Kerajaan* Order. According to this law consensus must be maintained among relatives. It demands that dynastic interests must overrule private considerations. How does the SPS cope with this impropriety? How does it exonerate Alam from causing the two intended comedies of memory – the story of Siak's rise and the epic of the Siak War – to turn into dramas of forgetfulness?

The answer is that the SPS restores propriety by emplotting the history of Siak's dramatic decline as a revenge tragedy. Within this scheme, the comedy of its glorious founding leads the dynasty to a sufficiently great height that its fall through the catastrophe of Ismail's defeat may indeed be properly abysmal. By turning Alam into an avenger, who is assisted in his revenge by the Dutch, the poem balances his improper act of forgetfulness with a proper act of remembrance. It presents Alam as remembering another law in the Book of the Malay *Kerajaan* Order, one that conflicts with the imperative of maintaining consensus in the family, namely, the grim law of *talio*. Throughout Alam's conflicts, first with Muhammad and then with Ismail, the poem portrays him as a man obeying this higher law and motivated by an honourable desire to *membalas lara wirang* (to avenge himself for the pain of disgrace) (SPS 234d, 239d).

With the words *lara wirang* (SPS 85c, 157d), the SPS refers to the humiliation that is inflicted on Alam by his having to yield supreme power in Siak to his younger brother. It is this humiliation that causes him to decide to leave Siak and go into exile, saying: *Biarlah mati aib ni jangan* (It is better to die than to endure this shame) (SPS 94d). The word *lara wirang*, repeated in a refrain-like manner in the course of the narrative of the SPS, cannot have failed to have a familiar ring to the audiences of the SPS. It must have reminded them of Panji tales, in which Raden Inu, the embodiment of noble manly virtues, is frequently depicted as roaming the world in exile, bent on regaining his honour, status and identity (Wilkinson 1943, II:650) (see also Chapter VI).

The idea that we are invited to see Alam's exile as a commemoration of Raden Inu's roaming is confirmed by Muhammad's reading of events, after Alam has gone into exile:

> Di dalam hati gundah gulana / dicari mufakat yang sempurna / saudara pun sudah pergi mengelana / sesal pun tidak lagi berguna (SPS 112).
>
> (His heart was filled with grief / as he tried to establish perfect consensus, / but now that his brother had already left to roam as a knight-errant / it was too late for remorse.)

The picture the SPS gives of Alam in exile is therefore an extremely dignified one: he is not ignominiously chased out of Siak, but leaves the *negeri* of his own free will and goes into exile as a *kelana* to regain his status and honour by his prowess in war. And Ismail does not fail as ruler but is the hapless scapegoat in a revenge tragedy, the catastrophe of which is the lost Siak War.

Tragedy tells a story of a fall from prosperity to wretchedness caused by an unexpected turn of the wheel of fortune. Just as comedy sets up an arbitrary law and then organizes the action to break it, so tragedy presents the reverse theme, that of the narrowing of a comparatively free life into a process of causation. In all tragedy some semblance of free will contends with a greater necessity – a higher law – and is defeated. Thus all tragedy leads up to an epiphany of law, of that which is and must be (Frye 1973:212).

Typically the tragic hero is someone on top of the wheel of fortune, who, as the highest point in the human landscape, seems to be the inevitable conductor of the powers about him. Too much happiness or too great success calls forth a response from them to reduce him to the sense of his human lot (Frye 1973:207).

The tragic hero is a scapegoat, who is both innocent and guilty. He is innocent in the sense that what happens to him is far greater than anything he has done should provoke, like the mountaineer whose shout brings down an avalanche. Simultaneously, he is guilty in the sense that he is a member of a guilty society, or lives in a world where injustices are an inescapable part of existence. These two facts do not come together but, ironically, remain apart (Frye 1973:42-3).

In a revenge tragedy the vision of the law appears in its most elementary form, namely, as the law of revenge; the hero provokes enmity or inherits a situation of enmity, and the return of the avenger constitutes the catastrophe. The plot of the revenge tragedy is a binary one: the original act provoking the revenge sets up an antithetical or counterbalancing movement, and the completion of the movement resolves the tragedy (Frye 1973:208-9).

Unlike the comedy of the melodramatic type, prescribed in the heroic epic, tragedy knows no villain and admits neither hissing nor applause. Although it may function as a cautionary tale, it ultimately seems to elude the antithesis of moral responsibility and arbitrary fate, just as it eludes the antithesis of good and evil.

By emplotting Ismail's defeat in the Siak War as the catastrophe in a revenge tragedy, the SPS therefore gives its narrative a disinterested, reconciliatory quality. Seen in this perspective ultimately neither Alam nor Ismail, nor indeed Muhammad, can be blamed for their deeds. They are shown to be merely the instruments of a power that eludes them, that of the law of revenge – a thoroughly reconciliatory vision, indeed.

The fact that the SPS strives to offer a reconciliatory vision is also perceptible in the many scenes that conjure up an image of the heroes as members of a family tragically divided who, nevertheless, still continue to feel much love and respect for each other. A fine sample of such a scene is the description of how a member of the family, Tengku Said, crosses the lines and visits Ismail, presumably in order to carry out negotiations with him:

> Tengku Said turun di kapal Wilanda / datang menghadap duli sri pada / berpeluk bercium adinda dan kakanda / jamjam durja luruh ke dada // seperti seorang syair merawan / kakanda bermohon adinda tawan / berdayunglah kelengkapan berkawan / khabarnya konon kepada lawan. (SPS 332-3.)

> (Tengku Said went aboard a Dutch ship / and presented himself before His Majesty. / The younger relative and the older embraced and kissed each other, / their tears streaming down onto their breasts. // Like a figure in a romance in verse[15], / when the older relative asked leave to depart, the younger tried to detain him, // and his ship accompanied that of the other, / so the story tells, on its way back to the enemy.)

Like a figure from romance – that is, indeed, the manner in which not only Ismail, but Alam, too, takes his leave from his relatives, when he goes into exile:

> Disapanya dengan manis muka / tinggallah kamu segala mereka / tinggallah sekalian adik dan kaka / tinggallah dengan sendi lega // tinggallah anak tinggallah

---

[15] The translation given of this line is not unproblematic. For one thing the text has *seorang* instead of *seseorang*. An alternative translation could therefore be 'Like a poet stirred by emotion', as Teeuw has proposed, but, as he has pointed out, in that case there is the problem that the manuscript does not spell the word *sya'ir* with a long *a*, as it should do if the word is to mean 'poet', but writes it with a long *i* and a short *a* (Teeuw 1992:133). In view of the context the translation offered here seems preferable.

> nyawa / tinggallah tidak lagi terbawa / baik baik encik saudara / mudah-mudahan bertemu jua. (SPS 103-4.)
>
> (He addressed them with a gentle face: / 'Farewell you all, my dearly beloved, / farewell my younger and older relatives. / Stay behind unencumbered with your sinews at rest. // Farewell, my son, farewell my life, / stay behind, since I cannot take you along with me. / Be on good terms with your relatives. / Who knows, we may yet meet again.')[16]

Significantly a closely similar tearful scene of parting, echoing that of Alam, takes place when Ismail, shattered by the blow of defeat, goes into exile, a heart-broken man:

> Tinggallah adik tinggallah kaka / tinggallah dengan sendi lega / kita ni jangan dikenang juga / jikalau untung bertemu juga // tinggallah kakak adik saudara / tinggal tidak lagi terbawa / jikalau ada hayat dan jiwa / mudah-mudahan bertemu jua. (SPS 510-1.)
>
> (Farewell my younger and older relatives, / stay behind unencumbered with your sinews at rest. / No longer think of me. / If fate so wills, we shall meet again. // Farewell my younger and older brothers, / stay behind, since I cannot take you along with me. / If I stay alive to see the day, / who knows, we may yet meet again.')

Both Alam and Ismail are thus shown to have suffered the pain of disgrace. Both are shown to be the victims of a quarrel that tragically turned friend (*kawan*) into foe (*lawan*).

In the story of Ismail's final defeat, too, this tragic motif of the *kawan* turned *lawan* emerges. When Alam launches the attack that will lead to the fall of the capital, we are told about the defenders: *Tidak tentu kawan dan lawan / seperti orang kemalu-maluan* (Unsure whom to treat as friend, whom as foe / they were at a loss what to do.) (SPS 504d). In other words, they are shown to be so embarrassed by the uncertainty whether they are confronting friend or foe – an uncertainty of meaning disruptive of representation and consequently of action – that they are thrown into a state of forgetfulness and fail to fight with their usual determination.

---

[16] Scenes of parting are an important component in the apparatus of type-scenes authors of romance use to construct their narrative. A good example of the type-scene of parting, taken from the *Syair Ken Tambuhan*, is the following passage in which Raden Inu takes leave of his love to go hunting for deer in the forest: *Raden berkata dengan cumbuan / emas merah ratna tempawan / kakanda bermohon kepada tuan / pergi mengaring perburuan // aria ningsun cahaya mahkota / tinggallah tuan jangan bercinta / Ken Tambuhan tunduk tiada berkata / seperti disahuti dengan air mata.* (Teeuw 1966:91-2.) (The prince said coaxing her with endearments: / 'My red gold, my precious one, / your older brother asks your leave to depart / to go ensnare game in the forest'. // 'My little sister, lustre of my crown, please stay here and do not be sad.' / Lady-in-Waiting Tambuhan looked downcast and remained silent; / it was as if she answered with her tears).

5. A tragedy of divine nemesis

Thus far we have seen that the revenge tragedy is put into motion by the jealousy of Alam. And we have seen that the SPS partly solves this impropriety by balancing his forgetting the law of consensus by his remembering the law of *talio*. I say partly, because Alam's jealousy is not really explained away by this.

According to Raja Kecik's reading of the event, Alam's becoming jealous is the consequence of a curse, that has unexpectedly struck the royal house. This appears from his reaction to the news that his sons are fighting each other:

> Baginda pun tahu lalu murka / merah padam warna muka. / Haram sekali tidak kusangka / akan menjadi mala pestaka. (SPS 82.)
>
> (When His Majesty learned what had happened he was furious. / The colour of his face turned a fiery red: / 'Never had I in the least expected / that a curse would befall us'.)

That Siak's *daulat* was undermined by a curse is indeed a major theme of the SPS. It is mainly in order to bring home this point that the SPS dwells extensively on the ill-starred reign of Muhammad and his untimely death.

In an effort to stop the working of the curse Raja Kecik decides to have either of his two sons leave into exile. When he has taken his decision he hopes that he has effectively counteracted it: 'By the miracle-working power of the saints, / may there not be the least shred of jealousy' *(Berkat keramat segala wali / janganlah apa mengali-ngali)*[17] (SPS 87c-d). But it is a fatal decision, because for the one source of trouble, the discord of the brothers, it only substitutes another, equally destructive one, the rancour and thirst for revenge of the exiled Alam.

The curse continues its destructive work unabated under the hapless, unaware Muhammad. When his brother has left to roam the Straits as a knight-errant he loses all zest for life:

> Tidaklah dapat baginda berpikir / akal hayatnya sudahlah mungkir / umpama perada yang sudah bakir / tiada berguna tulis dan ukir // [...] // telah selesai daripada itu / hilanglah akal menjadi mutu / (...) // dari itu datang berbeda / menanggung masygul di dalam dada. (SPS 114-117b.)
>
> (His Majesty had lost the ability to think; / his wits and energy had deserted him. / He was like gold foil that has been spoiled / and has become useless for inscribing and engraving // [...] / When that work had been completed / he lost his wits and was overcome by melancholy // From then on he was a changed man, / his heart filled with sadness.)

---

[17] Tenas Effendy (in Goudie 1989:89) translates this word as *mengira-ngira* or *berhitung-hitung*, meaning 'to calculate', apparently in the sense of 'making jealous comparisons' (see also SPS 156d).

By robbing Muhammad of his *akal*, that is, of his commemorative faculty, the curse saps his representational powers. As spoiled gold foil is useless for inscribing and engraving, so Muhammad, divested of his representational powers, is unable to be the author of his own fate and write the story of his own reign as a comedy, however much he tries.

That he is the under the sway of a higher power is also underlined in the description of the ailing monarch during his illness:

> Selama baginda mengidap rayu / lemah lunglai mendayu-dayu / laksana dendang di pucuk kayu / bagai dondangan[18] Indera Bayu (SPS 134).
>
> (While the sultan nursed his grief / he swayed languidly to and fro mumbling to himself. / He was like a crow sitting in the top of a tree, / as if rocked by the Lord of the Winds.)
>
> Isi istana sangat gelorat / melihat duli bertambah berat / laksana jung yang amat sarat / takut dipukul ribut barat (SPS 143).
>
> (All the palace folk were filled with great sadness / when they saw that His Majesty's condition worsened steadily. / He was like a junk that has been too heavily loaded / and fears the impact of the westerly squalls.)

That events may take an unlucky turn is subtly suggested right from the start of the *syair*. Amidst affirmations of Raja Kecik's ability to realize his own ambitions (*kehendak*) and be the successful author of the comedy of his rise to greatness, notes of uncertainty are intermittently struck. This is often done by having the protagonists say prayers to God before they engage in an important action: another act of commemoration. Thus, as we have seen above, on the eve of his attack on Johor Raja Kecik beseeches God that by the intercession of Muhammad and the ancestors at Bukit Siguntang He will not allow his servant's name to be dishonoured or any misfortune (*aral*) to cross his path.

An aim of saying such prayers may be to try and ensure that one's own ambitions (*kehendak, niat*) are authorized by supernatural authority. Besides prayer, another commemorative means used by the protagonists of the SPS to try and ensure themselves of supernatural backing for their actions is to establish the propitious moment for action by divination. Properly speaking, divination is an effort to enforce one's luck. We see Raja Kecik use this method as well when he plans his attack on Johor:

> Sudah mustaid sekaliannya / menantikan waktu dengan ketikanya / mencari langkah dengan saatnya / suatu pun jangan ada bahayanya (SPS 26).
>
> (When everything had been brought in readiness / they awaited the propitious hour and moment. / By divination they tried to establish the right moment for action, / so that nothing would be placed in jeopardy.)

---

[18] It seems best to follow the reading proposed by Teeuw (1992:131).

Whereas Raja Kecik is successful in forcing his luck, Raja Muhammad fails to obtain supernatural support for his kingship, as the narrator explains to us in the following passage:

> Niat duli khalifatullah / mengerjakan perang sabilillah / bilangan umat nabi Allah / lebih kurang tidaklah salah // dengan takdir Tuhan yang Esa / kodrat iradat amat kuasa / tidaklah sampai bagai dipaksa / kerajaan[19] duli mahkota desa. (SPS 132-3.)

> (It was the aspiration of His Majesty, the Vicegerent of God, / to serve God by fighting a Holy War. / But as for the allotted lifespan of the people of God's Prophet / whether it is extended or curtailed may not be gainsaid. // By the Will of the One God / Whose Might and Will are omnipotent, / the kingship of His Majesty / did not come about as divined.)

The mysterious power behind the curse, it now appears, is the Will of God. And the decline of the dynasty sets in, not only because of jealousy and dissent, but also, on a deeper level of understanding, because God has withdrawn His love from Siak:

> Tiada berapa lama antara / tiadalah mufakatnya dengan saudara / hampirlah negeri huru-hara / hendak menanggung duka sengsara // [...] // sudahlah takdir Khalikulbahri / alamat susah isi negeri / segala hulubalang dengan menteri / gundahnya tidak lagi terperi. (SPS 75-6.)

> (It was not long before / dissension arose between the two brothers. / It brought the kingdom to the verge of turmoil, / an omen that it would suffer great misery. // [...] // It was the Will of the Creator of the Oceans, / an omen that the entire kingdom would suffer. / The captains and ministers / were sad beyond description.)

It is also God's curse that makes Muhammad attract the enmity of the Dutch. This exonerates him from any possible criticism that he unwisely picked a quarrel with them and put the heavy load of a double enmity on the shoulders of his young son and successor:

> Kerajaan baginda di Inderapura / jayeng seteru tidak bertara / wartanya masyhur tidak terkira / Melaka hendak dikira-kira // sudahlah takdir Tuhan Ilahi / tidaklah dapat kita salahi / hilanglah asyik dengan birahi / hendak menjadi bantah kelahi // jikalau dikenang- kenang belaka / memberi pilu hati yang duka / wallah tidak diangka-angka / hendak menjadi mala pestaka. (SPS 127-9.)

> (The kingdom of His Majesty at Inderapura / was of unequaled prowess in war. / Its fame had spread beyond the boundaries of belief. / He now wished to make plans against Melaka. // It was the Will of God, our Lord; / we may not gainsay it. / All love and tenderness had now disappeared, / and were about to turn into strife and dispute. // The mere memory of it all / fills my heart with sadness. / By God, never would I have thought, even in my wildest fancies, / that a curse would befall us.)

---

[19] The reading *kerjaan*, chosen by Goudie (1989:112) does not seem to make sense.

Not only Muhammad and Ismail, but Alam and Kecik as well, – in short, all the members of the royal family – can now be seen to be the unaware victims of God, who has retracted his support from Siak. Thus the history of the dynasty in the first half of the 18th century – seemingly a shocking drama of forgetfulness – is emplotted as in reality not only a revenge tragedy, but, on a deeper level, a tragedy of divine nemesis: an epiphany of God's law that willed Siak's destruction. The SPS thus tells two tragedies, a revenge tragedy and a story of divine nemesis. In the first tragedy Ismail is the victim, in the second the dynasty as a whole.

As I already pointed out, in order to be able to moralize, we need some concept of retributive justice, some comprehensible moral mechanism, a legal order, in which human beings are given a degree of free choice: those who act in accordance with the law are rewarded, those who transgress it are punished. This mechanism is also essential to tragedy, where it may be seen to play two seemingly incommensurate roles.

To the extent that tragedy allows for a moral retributive justice, it may be used to domesticate incomprehensible necessity into moral necessity: the protagonists are then shown to have committed some transgression. On a more basic level, however, it serves to reveal the impotence of retributive justice in its inability to deflect the unintelligible, even amoral, forces of necessity: the protagonist does 'the right thing' but is destroyed (Owen 1986: 54-5).

The story of the conflict of Alam, first with Muhammad and then with Ismail, that is, the revenge tragedy told by the SPS, is a tragedy because it hinges on the conflict between two laws in the human order of things: the law of solidarity between relatives and the law of *talio*. Its central concern is with the paralysis of retributive justice, that arises from the conflict of these two laws.

In the second tragedy the SPS tells, that of the decline of the Royal House of Siak by divine nemesis, the human moral order is set in doomed conflict with an incomprehensible divine justice, that transcends the ambitions and aims of the human protagonists. This Will determines what must be according to its Own rules. Thus He proves to be the true Author of the plot of Siak's history, Who sets to naught all efforts by the protagonist, the Royal House of Siak, to be the author of its own fate.

6. *A Divina Commedia*

A simple drama of retribution, a story of crime and punishment, is not tragedy. In true tragedy all pretext of transgression is overwhelmed by the magnitude and mystery of a blind necessity. Although the central concern of tragedy is with the failure of the moral order, that does not preclude the possibility that to a certain extent it may also preach a moral. Thus, as we have seen, the revenge tragedy inculcates the lesson that kingdoms are built upon the prevalence of consensus and that jealousy is their undoing.

From the point of view of Islam, the story of divine nemesis should be predominantly read moralistically, that is, as a Divine Comedy of the successful working of God's Will. According to such a reading, the outbreak of the struggle for power between the two brothers, that led to Siak's demise as a major power in the Straits, may be understood as a just righting of the balance provoked by the excessive prosperity enjoyed by the kingdom.

For the pious, prosperity is a mixed blessing. It may lull man into forgetfulness of God and make him indulge in pride in his own power and achievements. Sweet though its taste may be, it may really be a ruse *(makr)* of God, Who uses this situation in which man is off guard as a snare to capture him and tempt him to worldly thought (Schimmel 1975:128, 160, 194, 198, 253). The extensive description of the beauty and prosperity of Buantan may well also have been intended to suggest the emergence of such a dangerous situation, in which Iblis may come to tempt man.

The blows God deals to Siak serve to humble its rulers and thus to reduce them to a sense of their human lot to live in this world as weak and frail exiles. Their fall from prosperity into wretchedness teaches Siak's princes the lesson of the instability and impermanence of all earthly glory. In the genealogical chronicle, *Tuhfat al-Nafis*, the mutability of man's fate is compared to the turning of a wheel: *Nyatalah manusia ini seperti keadaan lereng ma'alum adanya. Adapun kebesaran itu siapa-siapa yang dikehendaki Allah jua adanya.* (Clearly, the fate of human beings like us is like the turning of a chariot wheel. Authority will go to whomsoever Allah wishes.) (Raja Ali Haji ibn Ahmad 1982:407, note fol. 437; Matheson Hooker 1991:630, fol. 437.1). As the pious are aware, only God, Who is eternal, can be depended on. Thus Syaikh Ibrahim ibn Adham abandons all worldly power and possessions to which he is entitled as sultan of Irak *karena kerajaan dan kebesaran dan kemuliaan dunia lagi akan fana adanya, tiada akan kekal* (the government and greatness and honours of this world will come to an end, they will not be permanent) (Jones 1985:94-5).

As prosperity may bring misfortune by making man forget God, so adversity may be a blessing in disguise, because it makes man remember his Lord again and reminds him of his state as exile in this world. In the SPS overtones of the theme of man as exile, familiar from countless prologues by narrators of the *dagang*-type (see Chapter III, part 3), may indeed be heard. Thus the poem describes Ismail's exile after his defeat as follows:

> Selama duduk di tanah seberang / sakitnya bukan sebarang-barang / laksana perahu di atas karang / kawan yang rapat menjadi jarang (SPS 519).

(As long as he dwelt in foreign parts / the sorrows he suffered were indescribable. / He was like a proa that has stranded on the reefs. / Close companions had become scarce.)

This description has a close parallel in that given of the sadness of Alam's exile:

> Terkenangkan untung bukan suatu / anak miskin lagi piatu / remuk redam hati pun mutu / laksana kaca jatuh ke batu // terkenangkan badan duduk seorang / sakitnya bukan sebarang-barang / sampailah sudah ke negeri orang / sedikit yang ada banyak yang kurang. (SPS 107-8.)

> (I remember that many misfortunes befell him, / as he dwelt in poverty without kith or kin. / Overwhelmed by sorrow he felt utterly shattered, / like glass that has fallen to pieces on stone. // I remember he lived all alone, / and that the sorrows he suffered were indescribable. / Thereupon he arrived in a foreign land, / where he had little to subsist on and lacked very much.)

Read as a story with a moral the SPS admonishes us to follow the example of Ayub (Job), the archetype of all afflicted *dagang*, and bear the blows of fate with patience. As the Lord once took away all possessions from the innocent righteous Job and allowed Iblis to tempt him, to see if he would curse his Lord or remain steadfast in his submission to God's Will, thus he puts the faith of the princes of Siak to the test. In the SPS they are shown to heed Job's example, bearing the afflictions of exile with a steadfast heart, in the firm belief that God knows best.

'Say: O God, Master of the Kingdom, Thou givest the Kingdom to whom Thou wilt, and seizest the Kingdom from whom Thou wilt, Thou exaltest whom Thou wilt, and Thou abasest whom Thou wilt; in Thy hand is the good; Thou art powerful over everything.' With these words from the Koran (Sura 3.25; Arberry 1983:48) could one subsume the lesson taught by the exile of Alam and Ismail, whose fate recalls the sufferings which Ayub once had to bear. And that is the attitude the narrator enjoins us to take, when we ponder the fatal loss Siak suffered by the untimely death of Sultan Mahmud:

> Tidaklah boleh fakir katakan / kehendak Allah hendaklah sukurkan / baik dan jahat kita pikirkan / takdir Allah kita relakan (SPS 220).

> (This beggar may not gainsay it. / We must be grateful to God for what He has decreed. / While pondering whether it was good or bad, / we must consent to His Will.)

There is a strong tendency in Islamic reading and writing towards working with a dual interpretation of persons, objects and events, as both manifest and covert, literal and figurative. Consequently everything in the universe tends to be looked upon as endowed with a divine duplicity, functioning both as surface and as symbol. The SPS, too, seems to invite such a dual reading of the signifiers. Within such a mode of reading the history of Siak in the first half of the 18th century is only one of suffering if it is seen within a worldly perspective. This mode of reading may be exemplified by the words in which the Prophet exhorts his daughter Fatima to remain patient even in her extreme poverty, as we find them in a 17th-century Mirror of Kings, the *Taj us-Salatin* (Crown of the Rulers):

> Aku pinta kepada Tuhan [...] supaya dianugerahi-Nya kiranya sabar akan kami dengan kesukaran dunia ini yang ada pohon kebesaran akhirat juga; karena ganti satu duka yang ada di sini seribu suka jadi di sana, dan segala duka yang ada umpamanya dua tiga hari di sini itu lekas lenyap semuhanya, dan segala suka yang ada di sana itu kekal juga, dan tiada berkesudahan adanya. Maka hendaklah engkau sabar dan syukur dan rela akan kada-Nya itu, seperti befirman Ia dalam Kuran: XXX Qala Allahu ta'ala: Inna 'llaha ma'a 'l-sabirin. Ertinya: Bahwasanya Hak subhanahu wa-taala juga ada serta segala orang yang sabar. (Jones 1985:263.)

> (I beseech the Lord [...] that it may please Him to vouchsafe us patience with the difficulties of this world which are the means of greatness in the hereafter; for one sorrow occurring here is replaced by a thousand joys there, and the sorrows which last as it were only two or three days, all quickly pass away here – while the joys there are everlasting, they never come to an end. So you be patient, and be thankful, and be entirely satisfied with His ordinances; in accordance with His words in the Kuran: God the Exalted said: God is with the patient. Meaning: The Almighty and Exalted is with those who are patient.) (Jones 1985:264.)

If we limit ourselves to reading the SPS as a narrative that suggests that the suffering by the righteous in this world will ultimately be rewarded in the Hereafter, the poem's plot is only seemingly a tragedy, and in reality is a comedy. And if the SPS gives to its narrative of Siak's history, as a comedy of God's Ordinances, the implicit moral that God is with the patient and will ultimately reward them – and I think it does – the vision of the past it offers is a truly consolatory one.

7. Mediation and tragedy

To treat the SPS as a Divina Commedia means to stop at reading its narrative as a cautionary tale, that reminds inherently sinful, weak and impotent man of the Only Real Power. In such a reading the plot of the SPS is simply the triumph of God's just law. It is a mode of interpretation thoroughly sanctioned by Malay commemorative culture, with its strong emphasis on the necessity for those who seek true knowledge to turn away from the illusions of this world by recalling the Only Reality and Origin, God.

There need be no doubt that an important aim of the SPS is to trace the working of God's law in the history of Siak's decline. In order to prepare himself for his task of telling this story properly, in his prologue the narrator performs a commemorative act of self-erasure and submission to God's Will:

> Bismillah itu suatu asma / suatu disebut mula pertama / zat dan sifat keduanya sama / perhimpunan wujud sekalian nama // alhamdulillah puji yang sedia / bagi Allah Tuhan yang mulia / berkat Muhammad Sayid al-Anbia / jangan bernama yang sia-sia // astaghfirullah hambamu tobat / minta ampuni janganlah lambat / dipohonkan kepada Nabi dan Sahabat / pekerjaan maksiat jangan terjabat. (SPS 1-3.)

> ('In the name of God' is one of the attributes / that is invoked at the very beginning. / His Divine Essence and Attributes are one and the same. / All His names are the assembly of His Being. // 'Praise be to God' has of old been the praise / to God, our exalted Lord. / May by the grace of Muhammad, Lord of the Prophets / we not have a futile name. // 'May God forgive me', so Your repentant servant prays. / He begs Your forgiveness, pray be not slow to grant it, O Lord. / He beseeches the Prophet and his Companions / that he may not embark on a work of iniquity.)

As we have already seen, besides the religious order, the SPS also tries to uphold the *kerajaan* order by producing as dignified as possible an account of the painful power struggles among the members of the royal family, that minimizes or eliminates improprieties and preaches the moral that consensus forms the basis of dynastic greatness and prosperity, whereas disunity leads to disaster. In the prologue of the SPS the narrator indicates that he will give a proper account of events in which the *kerajaan* order is also confirmed. He does so by commemorating worldly authority, both that of the ruler and that of the sources on which he based himself, the stories that still circulated:

> Dengan berkat duli mahkota / ibarat dahulu sudahlah nyata / tidak dipandanglah dengan mata / sekadar fakir mendengar cerita (SPS 4).

> (By the grace of His Royal Majesty / the examples of the past are here made known. / This beggar did not witness the events of which he tells with his own eyes, / but merely heard the stories.)

Both commemorative acts we have seen the narrator perform above in Malay are called *mengingat*, a word which means so much as to heed the law or to recall that which is and must be (Wilkinson 1943, I:425). As we have already seen, this exemplary form of remembrance, this heedfulness of the law, is doubled on the level of the story by the protagonists of the SPS, who are shown to be engaged in efforts to heed religious and worldly law and abide by it in their actions.

In the SPS besides *mengingat* the narrator also performs another kind of commemorative act, which he calls *mengenangkan*, a term meaning to ponder over something with loving thoughts or vain regrets (Wilkinson 1943, I:555). This form of remembrance is therefore connected with the nostalgic and elegiac aspect of memory. This elegiac form of remembrance, too, is doubled on the level of the story. An example are the dirges (*ratap*) uttered by the subjects of Sultan Muhammad , in which they lament the great loss caused by the death of their beloved ruler and, amidst the traces left behind by his absence, undertake a vain effort to call him into their presence again:

> Bertagarlah ratap isi negeri / tuanku dimanalah patik cari // wahai junjungan mahkota lara / tinggallah negeri Inderapura / dengan hulubalang menteri wazira / dengan rakyat bala tentara // ayuhai junjungan mahkota patik / tuanku kemala tengah diratik / parasnya laksana kuntum dipetik / sejuknya seperti embun yang titik // tuanku raja yang bersilah-silah / turun temurun khalifatullah / sahid dermawan arif billah / junjungan sayidi dipelihara Allah // [...] // [...] // alamat duli ghaib dijulang / suramlah cahaya syamsu gemilang / sekalian jamjam mawar di balang / sungguhpun ada baunya hilang // [...] // sedang kuntum mengurai layu / kumbang melangsi mendayu-dayu / padam kemala desa Melayu / hilang disambar Garuda Bayu. (SPS 177-83.)

> (The laments of the entire population rang out: 'Master, where may your servants seek for you? / O sovereign, O hapless king, you have left behind the realm of Inderapura, with its military officers, ministers and vizier, / and the rank and file of the army. // O sovereign, king of your servants, / precious master, we are chanting litanies for you / who look as beautiful as a newly picked bud / and as fresh as dripping dew. // You, O master, are a king in a long line of princes, / who have been Vicegerents of God in unbroken succession. / Martyr to the Faith, bounteous, and wise in God's ways, / our sovereign, descendant of the Prophet, / God himself has you in his keeping. '// [...] // [...] // As an omen of the mysterious disappearance of Your Majesty while he was carried aloft, / the radiant light of the sun was dimmed. / Although the rosewater is all still there in the vial / its fragrance has vanished. // While the unfurled flower withers, / the bees buzz around it with a murmuring sound. / The lustre of the gem of the Malay lands has been extinguished, / as it was abducted by the winged steed of the Lord of the Winds.')

A remarkable characteristic of the narrator of the SPS is his oscillation all through the poem between these two types of remembrance, *mengingat* and *mengenangkan*. As an example I quote with some abbreviation the words with which he closes off his account of the death and burial of Muhammad:

> Tamatlah kisah marhum mangkat / di Inderapura bandarnya berkat / akal pendapat sudah singkat / laksana ikan di dalam pukat // tidaklah boleh fakir katakan / kehendak Allah hendaklah sukurkan / baik dan jahat kita pikirkan / takdir Allah kita relakan // daripada badan tidak beruntung / Allah dan Rasul tempat bergantung / duduk laksana seperti patung / mulut pun berat bagai disentung // habislah hari berganti bulan / duduk di dalam kesugulan / pikiran pun tidak berbetulan / umpama dimabuk pinang yang malan // [...] // tambahan fakir yang menyurat / malam dan siang di dalam gelorat / daripada tuk sampai dengan isyarat / perkerjaan ringan menjadi berat // dari pada badan[20] tidak bertuah / umpama

---

[20] Teeuw (1992:132) points out that manuscript Klinkert 153 here has a *lectio facilior* as *badan*. That, and the wording of verse line 523, indicate that this transcription is to be preferred to the problematic one as *padanan*, which Goudie proposes.

jintun tidak berbuah / terkenangkan marhum hilanglah arwah / sungguhpun miskin biasanya mewah. (SPS 219-24.)

(Here ends the story of His Highness / Who Passed Away at Inderapura, that blessed town. / My wits have failed me, / and I feel like a fish caught in a net. // This beggar may not gainsay it. / We must be grateful to God for what He has decreed. / While pondering whether it was good or bad, / we must consent to His Will. // Because our earthly body brings us no luck / we should rely upon God and the Prophet. / Here I sit helpless like a puppet, / the mouth of which can barely move, as if it has been fastened by a peg. // Days pass and turn into months / as I sit here in the midst of sorrow. / I am unable to order my thoughts, / as if befuddled by stupefying betel. // [...] // Moreover the beggar who writes this story / is deep sunk in sadness from morn to even. / Because his grandfather came and gave him a sign, / his duties, once light, have became onerous. // Because our earthly body does not bring good fortune, / it is like an olive tree that bears no fruit. / Remembering the late sultan I almost faint. / Though now so poor we used to be prosperous.)

Previously I have called the SPS a double tragedy. As the above fragment of narratorial comment confirms, we must indeed not stop at reading the SPS as a cautionary tale reminding us of the religious or the feudal order but must treat it as a tragedy.

The tragic experience is perhaps best subsumed in the words of Beethoven; above the opening bars of the last movement of his last string quartet, a movement which he entitled 'der schwer gefasste Entschluss' (the difficult resolution) the composer scribbled the words 'Muss es sein? Es muss sein' (Must it be? It must be) (Gardner 1971:34). To read a work as tragedy means to allow oneself to be torn between two conflicting attitudes: to confirm the law and to give in to desire, to resign and to protest. In the above fragment we see the attitude of the narrator oscillate between these two poles: between his duty and his desires, between the necessity to recall and confirm God's law that decreed the early death of Muhammad and the decline of Siak's power and prosperity, and his all-too-human longing to indulge in nostalgic dreams of its former glory.

The power of the SPS as narrative, we may now conclude, rests in its dual character: as a work of mediation that ultimately tries to confirm what is and must be; and as a tragedy that keeps asking the question whether things must really be as they are. The poem is a work of mediation to the extent that, in order to return to clarity of meaning, it not only solves improprieties but also removes contradictions by playing out cultural orders and patterns of plot against each other. It is a tragedy to the extent that it dwells on doubts, questions and feelings of bewilderment.

As we have seen, within one and the same narrative God's law which caused Siak's present poverty is confirmed, yet the human law which entitled it to a better fate is not relinquished. And within one and the same narrative both the law of consensus among relatives and the law of *talio* are allowed full scope and are confirmed. Thus man's need to believe in the existence of a moral order of things and his desire to see the Books of Religion and the *Kerajaan* Order confirmed, are satisfied in spite of contradictions.

It is the task of theology and ideology to find a solution for all contradictions and harmonize them into a coherence. In tragedy there is always a sense of some far-reaching mystery, of which the morally intelligible process of events is only a part. What ultimately remains in the SPS is the beauty and power with which the dilemma of conflicting orders is stated. Relatives should live in harmony, yet slighted honour may pit brother against brother. God is righteous but His ways are not ours. We cannot confine the Infinite nor bind Him to His own Prescript. But we must maintain our ways before Him. In the above fragment the narrator, faced with the impossible task of comprehending the incomprehensible and setting it forth in a manner that shows the working of a moral order, indeed repeatedly gives expression to tragic feelings of doubt, perplexity and paralysis.

As tragedy the SPS makes us ultimately suspend our moral judgement in favour of a sense of admiration for the human greatness of its heroes who grappled with fate. Thus, although affirming the instability of all earthly glory, the SPS, paradoxically affirms that very glory and greatness. And the poem invites us to sympathize passionately with the joys and sorrows of its protagonists as we give in to the poignant elegiac feeling of loss instilled by memories of what has been destroyed.

Within the perspective of Islam, and indeed also of that of the Malay *kerajaan* order, tragedy poses the problem that it leads to the forgetfulness of uncertain interpretation and thus endangers representation (*mengadakan*). It threatens to leave man gaping in a world of traces, which he must try to decipher, lost in exile among the opaque signifiers, unable to regress beyond their inertness. From the dayworld of the joyful certainty of meaning it threatens to abduct him into an uncanny nightworld of shadowy meanings, vague suspicions and doubts, in which things are not what they seem to be (*mengada-ada*). From a monologic discourse that speaks with the uncontradicted authoritative voice of the Truth, it risks leading us to a dialogic language, in which truth is at best equivocal and relative (Vance 1979:394-5).[21]

---

[21] That tragedy nevertheless may be conceived of within an Islamic context is also shown by Schimmel. As she points out, the first theological discussions in Islam were concerned with predestination and free will. Questions that arose were: If there is no agent but God, what is then the role of man? To what extent can his deeds and actions be attributed to him? What is the derivation of evil? And to what extent is man, like Iblis when he fell, caught between Divine Will and Divine Order? For many Sufi poets the predicament of Satan, caught

Characteristically, at the close of the SPS the narrator makes an emphatic effort to escape from this sad wasteland of uncertain interpretation and forgetfulness and tries to return to recall and the joy of certain meaning. Sitting down in meditation he tries to assuage his psyche, still confused by the incomprehensible mystery that caused the loss of Siak's greatness, and says a prayer:

> Allah Allah Malikulrahman[22] / karuniai[23] apa hambamu iman / dunia ini sudah meninggalkan[24] zaman / banyaklah makhluk tidak siuman (SPS 528).
>
> (My God, my God, King of Mercy, / pray grant your servant the strength of faith. / For the end of Time is at hand for the world, / yet many are the creatures who have not come to their senses.)

To pray can be a way to make the human will conform with God's Will. By his prayer at the last moment the narrator once again signals his wish to abandon all questions and doubts to return to obedience to the law, yet at the same time betrays his inability to do without them, because he is only human.

As we have seen, the SPS holds up a reconciliatory vision of the Siak War by emplotting it as tragedy. No one was to blame, it says; all the protagonists were merely the instruments of powers beyond their control. At the same time the poem inculcates the moral that consensus is the basis of greatness and that discord leads to disaster and the destruction of power. And that leads us back to the question when, by whom, and for whom the SPS as we have it was written. I have already indicated that in my opinion the work was written by Tengku Muhammad, a son of Ismail's younger brother, Tengku Abdullah. And I have said that in my view the poem was written during the reign of Ismail's son Yahya (1781-1791), on the orders of his Yamtuan Muda, the then already aged Tengku Muhammad Ali.

After the Siak War Ismail fled to Pelalawan in the hinterland of Siak, from where he was ousted with the help of Muhammad Ali. In 1765 Muhammad Ali succeeded Alam as sultan of Siak. In 1779, after the death of Alam, Ismail attacked Siak, reconquered the *negeri* and made himself sultan again. Muhammad Ali fled to the hinterland but surrendered to Ismail

---

between God's Will that no one should be worshipped except Himself, and God's order to prostrate himself before Adam, foreshadowed the difficulties man would have to undergo in this world. To be sure, Satan had read that one creature would be cursed by God, but, infinitely obedient as he was, how could he expect that it would be he himself? (Schimmel 1975:193-6).

[22] The manuscript here seems to have *Allah Allah malikulrahman*, rather than *Allah almalikulrahman*, which is the reading Goudie proposes.

[23] The manuscript seems to have *karunia nin*.

[24] Here the *lectio facilior*, given in manuscript Klinkert 153 as *meninggalkan* (Teeuw 1992:134), is followed.

when he was offered not just a pardon but even the function of Yamtuan Muda.

On his death in 1781, Ismail was succeeded by his son Yahya. During Yahya's reign the rival line of descent from Alam grew ever more powerful because of the machinations of the aggressive Said Ali. Said Ali was the son of Said Usman, the Arab ally of Alam in the Siak War who had married the latter's daughter. In his function of Yamtuan Muda of Siak, Muhammad Ali exerted himself to keep the rival factions in check and tried to curb Said Ali's ambitions. All was to no avail, however; in 1791, the year Muhammad Ali died, Said Ali seized power, and made himself sultan of Siak. Most of the descendants of Ismail fled from Siak into exile (Goudie 1989:37-45). Thus Said Ali founded the Arab dynasty of Siak that would rule over the kingdom until the Indonesian Revolution of 1945.

The purport of the poem argues in favour of the hypothesis that it was written for Muhammad Ali in the reign of Sultan Yahya. At that time there was a need for reconciliation. And at that time the importance of maintaining consensus within the royal family was a particularly relevant point to make. The SPS was not only written to edify its listeners by reasserting that unity leads to greatness, but was also intended as a means to rally the otherwise divided royal family in pity and admiration around a vision of the past that was dignified, consolatory and reconciliatory.

If the SPS failed to bring about peace between the family members, because it did not stop Said Ali from grasping power and inflicting the misery of exile on his relatives, the power of its consolatory and reconciliatory vision was nevertheless so great that it could be adopted as a *pusaka* by the descendants of Alam, in spite of their enduring feelings of enmity for the descendants of Muhammad, who figure so prominently in the poem.

This appears not only from the history of manuscript Klinkert 154, which shows that the SPS was once owned by a scion of the Arab dynasty, the Yamtuan Muda of Siak, Tengku Putra. It is also confirmed by the testimony of former officials who served in the palace of Pelalawan, a sultanate ruled by a brother of Said Ali and his descendants. Oral tradition has it that in an earlier version the SPS reached Siak in the reign of Muhammad Ali as Yamtuan Muda. Before the poem was read at his palace at Kampung Bukit Senapalan (present day Pekan Baru), on his orders it was first adapted to give a favourable portrayal of Alam, who was then still depicted as an enemy of Siak and friend of the Dutch (Tenas Effendy 1989:262).[25] After Said

---

[25] If the tradition of the reworking of the SPS at the command of Muhammad Ali is true, he may well also have ordered his own role in the Siak War to be shown in a more favourable light. In the account of the Siak War, as told in the SMS (Muhammad Yusoff Hashim 1992:153-5, fol.471-5), Muhammad Ali plays the role of a perjurer and traitor. When the Dutch threaten his father, Alam, with exile to Ceylon if Siak does not surrender to them, his

Ali had seized power, he and his brothers each had a copy of this new version made. Each year this SPS was solemnly performed in public both at the palaces of Siak and Pelalawan, a practice which was continued until as late as 1930 in Pelalawan (Tenas Effendy 1989:257-68).

Let us close this chapter with a look at the finest testimony of the fact that the Arab rulers of Siak and Pelalawan continued to use the SPS as an instrument of commemoration that left no one indifferent. We find it in the following description of the way in which the poem used to be publicly performed and of the emotions it would once set free in its audience, as it has been given by Tenas Effendy, an expert in the oral traditions of the Riau area:

> Pada masa dahulu, apabila Syair Perang Siak akan dibaca, maka diadakan semacam upacara khidmat di istana (baik istana Siak maupun di istana Pelalawan) untuk mengingat para pahlawan yang telah gugur dalam pertempuran-pertempuran itu. Dan waktu itu dipanggillah ke istana beberapa biduan yang elok dan merdu suaranya, untuk membacakan Syair Perang Siak. Suasana yang khidmat diresapi dengan irama syair yang berbagai jenis lagunya menimbulkan aneka perasaan bagi yang men – dengarnya. Pada saat sedih air mata akan berjatuhan dan isak sedu memenuhi ruangan. Tetapi bila syair sampai pada saat pertempuran, iramanya yang tegas menimbulkan semangat juang yang tak mau diam. (Tenas Effendy in Djaafar et al 1973:6.)

> (In former days, when the *Syair Perang Siak* was to be performed, a kind of solemn ceremony was organized in the palace (that of Siak as well as that of Pelalawan) in order to commemorate the heroes who had fallen in those battles. For the occasion several singers with a pleasing and tuneful voice were summoned to the palace to perform the . The solemn atmosphere was permeated with the rhythms of the *syair* of which the great variety of tunes to which it was sung aroused all sorts of feelings in those who listened. At moments of sadness tears would flow freely and sad sobs would fill the hall. But when the *syair* reached the moment of battle, its staunch rhythm would arouse a fighting spirit that would not be stilled.)

---

father begs him to help him. Breaking his oath of loyalty to Ismail, Muhammad Ali thereupon sinks his own battleship and has his wife wet all the gunpowder.

CHAPTER VI

A signifier-errant in exile
The Syair Ken Tambuhan as a Panji romance

1. The Syair Ken Tambuhan and the study of the Panji romance

In the previous chapter we have seen that the *Syair Perang Siak* (Poem of the Siak War) is a work mediating between contradictory norms. In the genre of the heroic epic and the genealogical chronicle, both predominantly oriented towards the direct confirmation of a particular order, such mediation is a highly unusual phenomenon. The fact that the author of the SPS availed himself of mediation bespeaks the problematical and controversial nature of the subject he had to deal with. In this chapter I will be concerned with a genre of which mediation is the essence and defining principle, the genre usually called the Panji story but more precisely characterized as the Panji romance.

In the Malay world the Panji romance has always enjoyed great popularity. One indication of this popularity is the proportionally large amount of manuscripts preserved which contain versions of it, either in prose or in verse form. As I shall argue the mediatory character of the genre must have been an important reason for its popularity. As an example of the genre I will read the *Syair Ken Tambuhan* (Poem of Lady-in-Waiting Tambuhan, henceforth SKT). An edition of this *syair*, telling the story of the love of prince Inu Kertapati of Kuripan for the Lady-in-Waiting Tambuhan, has been published by Teeuw (1966). For my reading I will base myself on this edition. From the evidence of the colophons of the many manuscripts in which this story has come down to us (Teeuw 1966:229-40), we may conclude that the oldest known manuscript containing it, ms. SOAS 12914, one of the seven manuscripts Teeuw has used for his edition, is a copy, written out at Bangkahulu, South Sumatra, in 1791. The story, as told in the edition by Teeuw, may be summarized as follows:

> Among the many princesses given in tribute and serving at the court of the kingdom of Kuripan is the 14-year-old princess of Tanjungpuri. Her original name is Puspakencana, but the king has called her Ken Tambuhan. The king has an only son called Raden Inu Kertapati or Raden Menteri. Because he has reached the age of 17, and is therefore nubile, his parents want him to wed. As his bride they choose the princess

of Banjarkulon, who is said to be a fitting match for him: an envoy will be sent there to ask for her hand.

But before this plan can be carried out, Inu Kertapati, on a hunt in the pleasure gardens, pursuing a parakeet he has shot down, strays into the forbidden compound. There he sees Ken Tambuhan, who is sitting there weaving a cloth, and he immediately falls in love with her. When she tells him the cloth is to be given as a betrothal gift to the princess of Banjarkulon, the prince declares that, now that he has met her, he will no longer go to Banjarkulon. Although Ken Tambuhan is afraid of the wrath of the king and queen, she succumbs to his entreaties and endearments and they spend several days together, making love as man and wife.

When the queen hears of this she is very angry that her son has demeaned himself by taking Ken Tambuhan as his wife and that the intended royal marriage may well not be realized. The king is of the opinion that his son has chosen well; after all Ken Tambuhan is of noble birth. The queen, however, will not allow herself to be persuaded by him to accept Ken Tambuhan. She requests her son to go hunting deer for her, pretending she craves their meat to eat. After he has left, she orders the executioner to take Ken Tambuhan to the forest and kill her. The executioner carries out the order. He grants Ken Tambuhan her last request which is to have her body placed on a raft covered with flowers, which is then set afloat on the river.

During the hunt Raden Menteri finds the raft and the body of his beloved. In desperation he follows her into the realm of death. When the king hears of his death and finds out that his son has committed suicide because the queen has had Ken Tambuhan killed by the executioner, he is furious. On his orders the executioner and his family are killed and the queen is removed from the palace and given the humiliating task of looking after the hunting dogs.

When the king, heartbroken over the loss of his son, has practised austerities for 40 days, the gods intervene; Batara Kala is ordered to go to Kuripan. Before going there he roams the pleasure gardens of the heavens in search of the flower, Gandapurawangi or Wijayamala. He obtains it from the heavenly nymph, Sugarba. The two lovers are brought back to life by the flower, and their marriage is celebrated with much ceremony and amidst great rejoicings.

News of the wedding reaches the king at Tanjungpuri – which, so the narrator reveals here, is identical with Banjarkulon, the capital of the kingdom of Daha – where the king and queen are mourning the loss of their daughter, who has mysteriously disappeared 13 years ago. The king of Banjarkulon/Daha visits his elder brother, the king of Kuripan, and Ken Tambuhan is reunited with her parents. The two kings decide to abdicate and Raden Menteri and Ken Tambuhan become king and queen of both Kuripan and Daha. After a tearful farewell Ken Tambuhan's parents return to Daha. Peace and mutual trust prevails between the two kingdoms, to the prosperity of both.

The efforts to define, amidst the seemingly amorphous mass of variants, what constitutes the Panji story have always been preceded by choosing the particular variant, which was considered the most complete and therefore closer to a presumed prototype, as a model. Thus, as the starting point for his comparison of nine Panji stories, both Javanese and Malay, Poerbatjaraka chose the lengthy Malay *Hikayat Panji Kuda Semirang*, because, in his view, this story 'contains elements, which *mutatis mutandis* are found both in the Javanese and in the non-Javanese Panji stories' (Poerbatjaraka 1940:vii). On the basis of the Panji stories which Poerbatjaraka compared,

Robson, in his 1969 edition of the *Hikayat Andaken Penurat*, proposed the following plot as typical of the Panji story:

> There were once in Java four kings who were brothers (sometimes these four have an elder sister, a nun; sometimes there are three brothers and a sister etc.). The eldest son was the king of Kuripan [Keling or Jenggala], followed by the kings of Daha [Mamenang or Kediri], Gagelang and Singasari. The king of Kuripan had firstly a son by a wife of low rank, then a son by the queen [Inu, the hero] and so on. The king of Daha's first child was a beautiful daughter [Galuh Tjandera Kirana], and so on. Inu and Tjandera Kirana were betrothed by their parents in infancy. One day Inu, who was fond of hunting, went on a trip with his friends into the forest, became separated from them in the chase, and happened to meet a beautiful girl, with whom he fell in love. This girl was of a lower rank than himself [the daughter of a *patinggi*, a *demung* or a *patih*]; but he took her as his mistress, thus incurring his mother's wrath. The mother had Inu's loved one killed, and in deep despair he left the palace to wander the countryside as a *kelana*, conquering many kingdoms. Meanwhile Tjandera Kirana also disappeared from the palace [of Daha] through the agency of the gods, and her brother the Crown Prince left home to seek her. After many adventures and after adopting many disguises, the princes and princesses were reunited, and Inu was married to Tjandera Kirana, who turned out to be another manifestation of his first love; they returned home and Inu became king in his father's place. (Robson 1969:10.)

If we compare the SKT with the above plot, we will note that its story seems to coincide with that of Raden Inu's first love for a girl of lower status; in the SKT he falls in love with a captive princess who serves at the court of Kuripan, a girl whose impaired status makes her an unsuitable marriage partner for him. Dubbing it the 'Angreni-motif', Poerbatjaraka has traced this tale of Raden Inu's first love, who has to die to make way for his destined mate, the princess of Daha, through the Panji stories he has compared (Poerbatjaraka 1940:156, 383). On the basis of his comparison of the main points of the contents of the Panji stories he examined, he considered it an integral part of its original plot (Poerbatjaraka 1940:341-2).

In spite of this partial coincidence, however, many elements defined as essential to the plot of the Panji story seem to be absent from the poem. Its narrative does not begin with the story of the four kingdoms of Java, but immediately plunges into the meeting of Raden Inu with his first love, at the location where, with the exception of some episodes at Daha, all the action will take place. Nor does it tell another story, which, according to the above schema, should precede the story of Inu's meeting with his first love, the story of the birth of the main protagonists, Raden Inu, Candra Kirana and their brothers and sisters. In most Panji stories their birth is brought about by the vows made by their parents to the gods in order to be blessed with children, and the main protagonists are born because gods are incarnated on earth as Raden Inu, Candra Kirana and their brothers and sisters. These stories of the vows and the subsequent incarnation, too, seem absent.[1]

In the SKT, Raden Inu has not been betrothed to the princess of Daha from infancy. After the death of his first love, Ken Tambuhan, he does not wander all over the countryside of Java as a knight-errant, performing great deeds of prowess in his disguise as a *kelana* and conquering many kingdoms and princesses, as he searches for the princess of Daha, who has been abducted from there. Instead he kills himself. In fact, in the SKT, apart from hunting, Raden Inu's only activity seems to be to woo and conquer his first love. Unless one takes the identity and name of Raden Inu's first love as a form of disguise, the element of disguise hardly seems to play a role in the SKT, whereas in what are accepted as full-blown Panji tales the narrative is brimming with scenes of physical disguise and often confusingly frequent

---

[1] Useful comprehensive studies of the Panji story have been contributed by Abdul Rahman Kaeh (1974, 1983) and Harun Mat Piah (1980). In the tradition of Poerbatjaraka these studies have among other features, made an effort to establish the sequence of episodes (*babak*) that constitutes a typical Panji story (Abdul Rahman Kaeh 1974:116-67, 1983:118-205; Harun Mat Piah 1980:58-68).
Thus Harun Mat Piah, taking as his point of departure the *Hikayat Dewa Asmara Jaya* has proposed the following outline: 1. the origin of the Javanese kings; 2. the kings of Kuripan and Daha make vows, desirous of having children; 3. the incarnation of gods and the birth of the main characters; 4. the events which precipitate Panji's roaming of the countryside; 5. the killing of Panji's love; 6. the hunt and the tournament (*sayembara*); 7. battles; 8. the illness of Panji or the princess of Daha; 9. the princess of Daha and Panji disguise themselves as man/woman; 10. the performance of *wayang*; 11. the final reunion and the marriage of the main protagonists.
The weakness of the studies of Poerbatjaraka and his followers is that they have failed to systematically develop a method for the comparison of stories. An insight which is lacking in all such traditional studies of the Panji story, which proceed by establishing a 'lowest common denominator of the Panji theme' (Robson 1971:13), but which has become common property in narratology since the publication in 1958 of the English translation of Vladimir Propp's *Morphology of the Folktale* (first published in Russian in 1927), is that, if we wish to compare the plots of narratives, we must identify function and context – that is, relations between elements rather than elements themselves – as the basic units of narration. To give a linguistic analogy, it is only within a specific context that we can determine the meaning and function of the word 'bit' (Dog bit man. Actor got bit part.).
An example from Propp: 'If, in one instance, a hero receives money from his father [...] and subsequently buys a wise cat with this money, whereas in a second case, the hero receives a sum of money for an accomplished act of bravery [at which point the tale ends], we have before us two morphologically different elements – in spite of the identical action [the transference of money] in both cases.' (Propp 1968:21).
In Panji studies, the first to be aware of the necessity for methodological reflection was Ras, who with great insight commented on the approach of Poerbatjaraka 'This comparative treatment [...] is a testimony to the utter ineffectualness of any effort to dig into the unwieldy mass of epic motifs provided by the often quite prolix Panji stories, unless one views these within the framework of the general structure of the plots of the stories concerned and is guided by a clear-cut theoretical starting-point' (Ras 1992:106).

changes of name and identity.² In view of such differences one may well see reasons to doubt that the SKT is a Panji story.

Therefore Teeuw has conjectured that the 'Angreni-motif' originated as an independent story about the tragic love between a prince and a common girl. This story then became part of the Panji story. Subsequently, after having been adapted to the characteristic features of the Panji story, it was again severed from it and used as main theme in several versions, found in works such as the SKT or the *Hikayat Andaken Penurat* (Teeuw 1966:xiv-xxxiv).

Robson, calling the 'Angreni-motif' a 'prelude', has suggested that it does not form part of the central elements of the Panji story, because the Middle

---

2   As a Panji story the SKT is obviously a very brief and simple work. Especially in Malay literature, Panji stories tend to be rather long and elaborate works, which take the form of a vast tapestry of narrative in which a profusion of lines of action is interlaced in a complex pattern. Many secondary characters share the stage with the principal protagonists and action may range freely over vast geographic distances. In the course of the narrative all the characters, even the servants, may have their names changed many times.
Techniques of narrative such as these were characteristic phenomena in Western late-mediaeval epic and romance, too. Since the second half of the 16th century Western critics, with an appeal to Aristotle's poetics, have come to reject these techniques. Thus Tasso criticized Ariosto's *Orlando Furioso*, a work still very much in the style of late-mediaeval romance, because in his view this work only aimed at offering variety of incident but did not trouble about producing a coherent story in which the various threads, in a converging pattern, move insistently towards a major knot. Tasso also rejected the poem as unacceptable because he found the length and profusion of characters too taxing for the reader's memory (Ryding 1971:9-17).
When Winstedt, discussing such sprawling Malay Panji stories as the *Hikayat Cekel Waneng Pati*, complained that 'the germ of nearly every Malay romance is a folktale or cluster of folktales, nearly always Indian and manipulated by men wildly ignorant of the unities of place and time' and that the reader becomes dizzy trying to recall the identity of the characters appearing in it, he was obviously speaking from this critical tradition (Winstedt 1977:58, 70).
This same critical tradition must have contributed towards the preference and positive appreciation Western scholarship has had for the shortest version of the story of Ken Tambuhan. This version, of which the manuscript is now lost, was the first Panji story to be published in a Dutch translation. It typically ends as a drama, with the death of Raden Inu and Ken Tambuhan (Roorda van Eysinga 1838).
De Hollander (1856:1), commenting on what is probably the same version, of which he published a transcription with notes, judged: 'Among the well-known Malay *syair* the *Ken Tambuhan*, although one of the least lengthy ones, occupies a significant place on account of the relative importance of its contents, for, with the exception of *Bidasari* and *Abdul Muluk*, the last-mentioned of which is known to be a very recent work, among the numerous poetic outpourings of the Malays one will hardly find any in which so much essential poetry is found and so little triviality; in which the leading characters have been so correctly depicted and sustained; in a word, in which a not unimportant subject is treated so well and gradually.'
That the same critical tradition is also present in the evaluation of Teeuw of the longer version of the story of Ken Tambuhan, which he edited, the SKT, can be seen from his comment concerning its plot that *sayanglah (dari segi mata kita) syair ini tidak berakhir dengan bab VIII, yaitu kematian dua kekasih dan pembuangan permaisuri yang ganas* (Teeuw 1966:xxxvi-xxxvii) (Unfortunately – from our points of view – this *syair* does not end with Chapter VIII, that is, with the death of the two lovers and the expulsion of the cruel queen).

Javanese Panji stories, the oldest texts of the genre preserved, do not contain the Angreni-motif (Robson 1969:11-2). In the introduction to his edition of the Middle Javanese Panji story *Wangbang Wideya*, he has accordingly omitted it from the plot he has proposed as reflecting the Panji theme's central elements:

> In Java, where the story is set, there are two kingdoms, Kuripan and Daha [various alternative names also occur], of which the former is the senior. The prince of Kuripan is betrothed to the princess of Daha but, before they can marry a complicating factor [or combination of factors] intervenes. [For example, the princess may be lost, or carried off, and have to be found, or a foreign king may attack and have to be defeated.] When the problems have been solved by the prince, in disguise and using an alias, then he can finally reveal himself and claim the princess. With their marriage the world returns to its former settled state. (Robson 1971:12.)

Obviously, this revised plot of the Panji story still does not really fit the SKT; the prince does not leave Kuripan in search of the vanished princess of Daha, nor does he disguise himself or assume an alias.

In this chapter I hope to show that, contrary to the opinions of Teeuw and Robson, the so-called 'Angreni-motif', as we find it for instance in a story such as the SKT, is a surface manifestation of the very structural core of the Panji story, so that the SKT is to all practical purposes a full-fledged sample of this genre. In order to be able to present my arguments for this view, I shall first perform my reading of the SKT.

2. *The SKT as a marriage story*

It is not difficult to see that a line of reading in the SKT is formed by the theme of marriage. In a traditional society such as the Malay, marriage – and especially a royal marriage – was a matter of pivotal social and economic importance. One did not conclude a marriage alliance primarily for reasons of individual love. Rather, marriage was an instrument to bolster or improve the family's social status and a means to keep together or increase the family holdings. And its aim was to produce an heir and thus to provide proper genealogical continuity.

One way in which one can read the SKT is as the archetypal drama of the son who, against the wish of his parents, insists on following his personal feelings and marrying a girl whose status is too low. By following his own desires rather than bowing to social obligation and marrying the princess his parents, concerned with the proper continuation of the genealogical line of descent, have chosen as a worthy mate for him, he endangers his unsullied lineage and transgresses against feudal social and economic order and propriety.

If we view the SKT in this manner, we will see that the queen stands on the side of the principle of the arranged marriage, and ruthlessly defends aristocratic lineage, status and real property. The opposite position is taken by the prince. In his view his individual feelings of love and desire override all other considerations. The king, although assuming the aristocratic view of marriage unquestioningly, is, nevertheless, not blind to the importance of individual love. Ken Tambuhan, on the other hand, yields to the dictates of her heart and gives in to her love for Raden Inu, yet never forgets her place and upholds the aristocratic view of marriage.

The aristocratic view of marriage is first stated by the king when he decides to ask for the hand of the princess of Banjarkulon; the wife to be sought must be suitable (*patut*, SKT II, 8d) and of equal status (*sebanding*, SKT II, 12d). What convinces the king that the princess of Banjarkulon is fit to be his son's wife is that, according to the prime minister, her appearance is like that of a heavenly nymph and that she is said to be of an indescribable beauty (*parasnya seperti bidadari / khabarnya elok tiada terperi*, SKT II, 14b-c). Beauty is a sign of royalty. At the root of his decision to seek a wife for his son lies genealogical anxiety; as the narrator points out, the prince had no brothers and sisters (*raden tu tidak bersaudara*, SKT II, 2d). Raden Inu's marriage is of crucial importance for the continuation of the royal line and the survival of the dynasty, and therefore not a matter to be trifled with.

Although the prince is unsure whether he really wishes to marry, as a dutiful son he decides to obey the wishes of his parents. However, no sooner has the decision to arrange his marriage been taken than a countermovement sets in, in which individual desire opposes the law of social obligation and filial duty. Significantly this desire is set in operation at night and is initiated by a dream.

That very night, when the prince has returned to his own palace and lies down on his couch, he is overcome by an intense desire for a wife (*hasratnya ingin hendak beristeri*, SKT II, 21d). He dreams that the moon falls down into his lap, but is snatched away by a giant with a loud voice, booming like the rumble of cannonfire (SKT II, 23-4). Whereas Raden Inu himself is unable to make out what his dream means, for the Malay audiences of the SKT its meaning will at once have been clear: he will obtain the beautiful wife he longs for so much, but she will be taken from him by force.

Before Raden Inu, Ken Tambuhan has a similar dream; she dreams that the moon falls down into her lap and that a huge snake (*naga*) coils itself around her waist (SKT I, 21). Like Raden Inu she is unable to make sense of the dream. The audiences of the SKT will have understood her dream as a portent that she will obtain a handsome husband but will be swallowed up by death, the *naga* being associated with the underworld and, presumably therefore also with death (Ras 1992:134; Zoetmulder 1982, I:1167).

In conjunction, these two dreams presage the coming meeting between the prince and Ken Tambuhan. This meeting takes place in what is the very locus of desire in Malay romantic literature, the pleasure grounds of the palace, where the prince has repaired with his companions to soothe his feelings of lovelorn longing by plucking flowers and shooting birds with his blowpipe.

Significantly the bird he shoots down is a love-bird (*serindit*, SKT III, 4, a sort of parakeet; Wilkinson 1943, II:453). In pursuit of the bird – clearly a symbol of the female pursued by male sexual desire, which is itself symbolized by the shooting of birds (see Frye 1976:104) – he looks into the forbidden compound where the princesses, given in tribute to his father, sit weaving cloth on the orders of the queen. The moment he sets eyes on (*terpandang*) Ken Tambuhan whose very demeanour is like that of the daughter of a king (*lakunya seperti anak para ratu*, SKT III, 12d), he is overwhelmed by desire (*birahi*) as if by an incurable malady (SKT III, 13).

The prince's attendant, Wiradandani, reminds his master of the law; he advises him not to enter the compound but to leave and forget about the girl. He points out that she is a captive princess (*puteri tawanan*) and is under the supervision of the queen, but that his parents will have no objection to his making her his concubine once he has married the princess of Banjarkulon (SKT III, 18-9). But now that the flames of desire have been ignited nothing can stop the prince. Ignoring the entreaties of his attendant he has the gate of the forbidden compound opened and enters, an act which marks a grave dislocation of paternal property and aristocratic propriety.

When they see him come in, all the other princesses flee. Only Ken Tambuhan stays behind. Approaching her unnoticed, the prince grasps her hand and addresses her with sweet and coaxing words. When he asks her from what kingdom she hails, how she has come to be in Kuripan, what is her name and what is the cloth she is weaving, she answers that she is called Lady-in-Waiting Tambuhan and that she is weaving the cloth on the orders of the queen as a betrothal gift to be presented when the hand of the princess of Banjarkulon is asked for the prince (SKT III, 32-5).

Overcome with desire the prince declares he will not go to Banjarkulon anymore (SKT III, 37b). In a vain effort to resist his advances Ken Tambuhan deliberately drops her spool and tries to escape while he searches for it. But the prince overtakes her and with soft endearing words succeeds in conquering her resistance and carries her into the bedchamber.

In his desire to possess Ken Tambuhan the prince not only infringes paternal property and aristocratic propriety but actually abjures paternal authority and inverts accepted social hierarchy as codified in the Book of the Malay *Kerajaan* Order. When Ken Tambuhan points out that she is only a slave in the possession of the king and expresses fear of the anger of the queen if she gives in to him, the prince swears that he will protect her from their anger and that henceforth his beloved will be his only sovereign (*yayi sahaja beta nin julang*) (SKT III, 51d).

Indeed, in his protestations of love the prince declares himself the slave of his beloved (*bukankah kakang hamba sungguh*, SKT III, 91a) (Am I not truly your slave?). He underlines his submission (*memperhambakan diri*) in several ways. One is that he addresses her as 'my divine queen' (*dewa susunan*, SKT III, 79a, 98c). Another is by making a gesture of homage: he places her hand on his head (*Diambil tangan lalu dijunjung*, SKT III, 105a).

The prince also utters a pledge which would normally only be made by a vassal to his overlord or by a royal consort to her husband: 'I will follow you, my lady, / even into the fangs of a snake' (*meski ke dalam mulut naga / tuan adinda kuikut juga*, SKT III, 58b-c). This pledge refers back to Ken Tambuhan's first dream – the dream about the snake – and it will be redeemed by the prince by his suicide on finding Ken Tambuhan's corpse in the forest.

Ultimately the desire of the prince finds its fulfilment when he makes love with Ken Tambuhan. Henceforth they are man and wife, as is expressed by the refrainlike repetition of the formula *laki isteri* in lines such as *beradulah raden laki isteri* (SKT III, 114a) (The prince slept with her as a man with his wife) or *santaplah ia dua laki isteri* (SKT III, 122d) (They took their repast as man and wife). Their union, then, is a form of marriage, namely a marriage based on mutual desire and love, or in other words a marriage of consensus.

In Indonesian cultures weaving is typically the task of nubile young women. To sit weaving a cloth – as Ken Tambuhan is depicted as doing at the start of the *syair* – is therefore in itself already a sign of her marriageability. Prior to their sexual union, the marriage of Raden Inu and Ken Tambuhan is already concluded when the prince picks up the spool Ken Tambuhan has dropped with the intention of escaping his advances. In myths found in Java, Bali, Lombok and Sulawesi there is a recurrent motif of a girl who promises to marry anyone who picks up her spool (Seltmann 1987:169-258, 262-3). As Derks (1985:43-8) points out the spool stands for the female sexual organ. By picking up Ken Tambuhan's spool, Raden Inu has therefore already in fact taken possession of her sexuality.

We have already seen that if Raden Inu is the reckless protagonist of desire and marriage by consensus, the queen is the equally unheeding champion of the law and all it implies: the purity of aristocratic lineage; the integrity of property and propriety; and the arranged marriage as the means of ensuring these. Her fury with the lovers knows no bounds when she hears that the prince has made Ken Tambuhan his wife – in her eyes merely a captive girl (*anak jarahan*, SKT IV, 12d), who therefore is without property and whose status is impaired so that her son's marriage to her will only bring the dynasty into disrepute (*nama yang keji*, SKT IV, 23b). Realizing that her plan for arranging the advantageous marriage with the princess of Banjarkulon has been thwarted, she swears she will punish Ken Tambuhan, *si cabul hendak mencapai bulan* (SKT IV, 11d) (that dwarf who wishes to lay hands on the moon) and reduce her to dust and ashes.

She directs her fury not only towards Ken Tambuhan, that slut who has turned her son's head, but even against her own flesh and blood: *Anak celaka yang bunuhan, mengambil bini anak jarahan* (SKT IV, 12c) (That wretched son of mine who deserves to be killed, of all people had to take a captive girl for wife). Ominous words that predict the fatal consequence of her blind fury: the suicide of the prince. Her countermove against desire in the name of the law is again announced by a dream; the prince dreams that a tiger – obviously a metaphor for the furious queen bent on death and destruction – seizes Ken Tambuhan and drags her off deep into the forest.

When the queen has verified that the prince has indeed gone hunting, she hurries to the pleasure garden where Ken Tambuhan is lodged. As she walks on cursing Ken Tambuhan she is again is compared to a tiger: *Bunyi kakinya berdegam-degam / seperti harimau akan menerkam* (SKT IV, 7a-b) (Her feet as she walked thudded along / like those of a tiger about to spring on its prey). And she is depicted as behaving in a fashion most undignified for a person of her rank and station:

> Tidaklah baginda mau melungguh / datangnya itu terlalu gopoh / berpancaran peluh daripada tubuh / lakunya seperti dihambat musuh (SKT VI, 9).
>
> (She refused to sit at ease, / arriving in a great hurry. / She was bathed in perspiration all over her body, / and behaved as if she was being pursued by an enemy.)

Her behaviour contrasts starkly with that of Ken Tambuhan, who, even when she makes her way to confront the angry queen retains her self-possession and dignity:

> Lalu ia turun berjalan / diiringkan Ken Penglipur Ken Tadahan / lemah lembut barang kelakuan / segala yang memandang belas dan kasihan (SKT VI, 19).
>
> (Thereupon she descended and set off, / accompanied by Lady-in-Waiting Ken Penglipur and Lady-in-Waiting Tadahan. / Gentleness and refinement permeated her demeanour; / all who beheld her felt affection and love.]

That the queen is indeed blinded by her fury becomes clear from the fact that her violent opposition in the name of proper genealogical continuity to the marriage of consensus of the prince effects the opposite of what it was to bring about. It is because she has had Ken Tambuhan secretly killed by the executioner – the king knows nothing about it – that the prince commits his desperate act of suicide. The prince was the only son of the king, only begotten by him after he had prayed long and hard and had made many vows to the gods. The criticism of her among the *rakyat* after Inu's suicide is well-deserved: *Marahnya tidak dengan akal / tidak dipikirkan puteranya tunggal* (SKT VII, 94b-c) (In her anger she failed to use her head. / She did not consider the fact that the prince was the only son of the king).

As we have already seen, the king agrees with the queen on the paramount importance of the aristocratic principle of the arranged marriage, yet he is a reasonable man, who considers matters carefully and is not a blind partisan of this as the only option. When he hears that Raden Inu has taken Ken Tambuhan for his wife, he is willing to assume that the prince is capable of choosing himself a wife and to agree with this choice (*pandainya anakku memilih isteri / semuanya hendak ia kuberi*, SKT IV, 8c-d). Against the anger of the queen, he even defends the suitability of Ken Tambuhan as wife for his son by pointing out that, even if she is a captive, she is not a slave but the daughter of a king, beautiful, kind and well-spoken.

Moreover, he has enough foresight to be aware that it may be unwise to forbid the prince to have the girl he has set his heart on as wife: *Kalau ia pergi barang kemana / sesal kita pun tidak berguna* (SKT IV, 16b-c) (He may well leave for who knows where, / and then all our regrets would be in vain). Losing his only son would endanger the continuity of his lineage. When his son suddenly announces his intention of going hunting in the forest, he is really worried that his son may be angry and therefore leave the kingdom. The queen's ladies-in-waiting are also aware of this risk. When they witness how the queen in her blind fury sends Ken Tambuhan to the forest with the executioner to have her killed there, they fear that when the prince finds out what has happened he will be enraged with the queen and that he may well leave and exile/kill himself (*entahkan pergi membuang diri*) (SKT VI, 52d). This fear becomes a reality when the prince commits suicide.

Impressed by their mutual love and unshakeable loyalty even unto death, the king commands that their bodies must be treated with equal respect *(keduanya itu disuruh samakan / karena ia sangat berkasih-kasihan / setianya teguh sangat setiawan*, SKT VIII, 28b-d). In his eyes Ken Tambuhan has fully proved her worth to be the wife of the prince. Here again his reasonableness contrasts with the obstinacy of the queen, who, even now still unrepentant of having had the girl killed, insists that her 'carcass' (*bangkai*, SKT VIII, 29b) should be left to rot in the forest. This is fresh evidence of her lack of self-control, of her inability to apply the law with discretion; a serious failing indeed for a person of her station. The angry reply of the king is fully deserved: *Janganlah engkau mencium surga* (SKT VIII, 31d) (Don't you try to kiss the heavens). The queen, who has accused Ken Tambuhan of presumptuous behaviour, has demeaned herself by her unqueenly behaviour. And now, having thus lost her right to be recognized as queen, she herself stands accused of presumption.

Whereas the queen demeans herself by her unrestrained behaviour, Ken Tambuhan shows her queenly qualities at every turn in the narrative, proving that it was no exaggeration when at the beginning of the story she was described in the following manner: *Lakunya arif bijaksana / akal bicaranya sangatlah sempurna* (SKT I, 14c) (Her behaviour was wise and discreet. / She had intelligence and common sense in plenty).

There need be no doubt that she loves Raden Inu as much as he loves her. When Raden Inu tells her that he will leave for the forest to go hunting for his mother, she has a premonition that she may perhaps soon die, so that she may never be able to fulfill her wish to requite his love (*matilah gerangan sekali nin aku / tiadalah sampai bagai niatku / membalas kasih kakang Inu*, SKT V, 65b-d). In her love she always puts his interest first, above her own, and her death is proof of her love for him, a demonstration of loyalty to the bitter end.

Although she gives in to desire and requites Inu's love, she never forgets the law, not even after she and Inu have been brought back to life again when the king, convinced that she has proved herself a worthy consort, has decided to let his son marry her and has proposed that Inu and his wife become king and queen of Kuripan. Even then, she retains her modesty as she humbly declines being worthy to become queen of Kuripan, saying to the prince:

> Menjunjung rahim patik sekarang / karena patik sudah terbuang / tuanku jangan berhati walang / patik tak patut disembah orang // patik nin sedia orang tawanan / asal dan bangsa tiada berketahuan / tiada suka orang sekalian. (SKT IX, 139a-140c.)
>
> ('Your servant is now entirely at your mercy / because she is a foundling without kith or kin. / Please, do not worry about her, my lord. / It would be unfitting for your servant to receive the homage of others. / She has always been a captive / whose origin and descent are unknown. / People do not like such a person.')

Upon the entreaties of the king to fulfill his wishes and become Inu's consort, she humbly replies that if he commands her she will not resist, but she still insists that she is unworthy of such high station:

> Patik tawanan yang hina leta / orang jarahan semata-mata // hinalah kelak seri pangeran / mengambil patik orang jarahan / bunda tuanku tiada berkenan / karena patik orang tawanan // raden tu sahaja salah pemandangan / patik dengar sudah bertunangan / di Banjarkulon puteri bilangan / kepada bangsa tidak berkurangan (SKT IX, 151c-153d.)
>
> ('Your humble servant is a mere captive of no consequence / just a prisoner taken in war and nothing more. // The prince only risks demeaning himself, / if he marries your servant, a mere prisoner-of-war. / His mother does not approve the marriage,

/ because your servant is a mere captive. // The prince has simply made a mistake. / I hear he is already engaged to be married / to a princess of consequence / of unblemished lineage.')

Precisely at this moment the narrative takes a crucial turn: the narrator reveals to us that Tanjungpuri is another name for Banjarkulon, the capital of the kingdom of Daha. When the king of Daha hears that his long lost daughter is in Kuripan and has become the wife of its prince, he decides to visit her there. Thus she now proves to be the very princess whom Raden Inu's parents have selected as a worthy wife for him. Desire and the law, marriage for love and marriage for power, are reconciled. Or one may also say, desire is converted into the law and order is restored. Ken Tambuhan proves to be doubly worthy to be Raden Inu's royal consort: both by the courage and devotion unto death with which she has loved her beloved and by her impeccable lineage and royal status. Retrospectively we will now see that the scene of the first meeting between the prince and Ken Tambuhan is fraught with dramatic irony (Green 1980:250-86): whereas the prince, when he picks up Ken Tambuhan's spool, unwittingly marries the very woman he has just declared he refuses to marry, Ken Tambuhan is unwittingly weaving her own betrothal gift.

3. Exile and return, signification and interpretation: the SKT as a romance

Until she is recognized as the princess of Banjarkulon/Daha, when her parents visit her in Kuripan, Ken Tambuhan only knows she is the princess of Tanjungpuri. She is apparently unaware that Tanjungpuri and Banjarkulon are identical. Why this is so becomes clearer when the narrator, besides revealing her true identity to us, also discloses how she has lost it: thirteen years ago, that is, when she was still only one year old, she had mysteriously disappeared from Banjarkulon, because she had been abducted and taken to the forest of Kuripan by the god Kesna. There she had been found by the king of Kuripan, who brought her to his palace.

As we have already seen at the beginning of the SKT, the king has provided the girl with a new name. By doing so, he has provided her with a new temporary identity, by an act which comes close to adoption. Even if the derivation is etymologically uncertain, it is interesting to consider the possibility that Ken Tambuhan's name may be explained with reference to the modern Javanese word *tambuh*, 'not to know, not to recognize' (Pigeaud 1938:550) as meaning 'Lady-in-Waiting Unknown' (see Teeuw 1966:xxxii).

Obviously, as well as being a love-story ending in marriage, the SKT may also be seen as a story about identity lost and regained. And, as will now also have become clear, the real hero who connects these strands of narrative is not, as I suggested at first, the prince, but Ken Tambuhan. It is she who proves her worth by her loyal love. Moreover the SKT is called Poem of Lady-in-Waiting Tambuhan. In his prologue the narrator also underlines that she is the heroine of the poem: *Inilah ceritera Ken Tambuhan, puteranya ratu jadi tawanan* (SKT I, 2a-b) (This is the story of Ken Tambuhan, the daughter of a king who became a captive). The contours that are now emerging are typically those of the plot of romance as it has been characterized by Frye (1976) for European literature.

According to Frye, the plot of romance consists of a circular movement from identity through alienation back to identity again. As Frye has pointed out identity equals being at home in an idyllic day-world, associated with happiness, security, peace, freedom, reality and the rule of just law. Alienation means to be outside, in a demonic night-world of exciting adventures which, however, involves separation, loneliness, humiliation, pain and other ills. This outside world is associated with illusion and anxiety or apprehension, absence of identity and tyranny.

Identity, thus Frye has explained, is a state of existence in which there is nothing to tell. It is existence before 'once upon a time' and subsequent to 'and they lived happily ever after'. What happens in between are adventures or collisions with external circumstances. The return to identity is a release from the tyranny of circumstances. The descent into alienation in the night-world begins with a break in consciousness which often involves forgetting one's previous state, the motif of amnesia. This amnesia is internalized as a break in memory and externalized as a change in fortunes, a reduction in social status. The plot of romance may then be described as a return movement back to identity, tracing a closed circle or a spiral, where the end is the beginning, transformed by and renewed by the quest (Frye 1976:53-4, 102-4, 173).

At the beginning of the SKT, we find Ken Tambuhan already in the phase of alienation, in which she has all but lost her memory of her previous identity and has received a new name. Her reduction in social status is indeed considerable; from the position of daughter of the king of Daha, who only recognizes the king of Kuripan as his older brother and superior among the kings of Java, she has sunk to that of daughter of an obscure king of Tanjungpuri. From being a free person who can go anywhere and do whatever she pleases, she has become a captive who has to work as a lady-in-waiting in the company of other captive princesses and has to obey the orders of the queen. From being an attractive marriage partner because of her high rank and wealth she has become a mere servant without any means of her own, dependent on the bounty of the king and queen, marriage with whom would only damage the reputation of a noble lineage like that of the prince of Kuripan.

The circumstances under which she has to live may indeed be described as tyranny. Instead of being treated as a nobly born lady, as she would be entitled to if her true identity were known, she is forced to put up with the humiliations to which the queen subjects her, for instance when she is given a public dressing down by the queen for having stayed with the prince:

> Inilah pekerjaan orang yang bidaah / sedap berkurung didalam rumah // tujuh hari sudah tiada bekerja / harapmu hendak menjadi raja (SKT VI, 26c-27b).
>
> (These are the actions of a liar, / to confine oneself cosily to one's room. // For seven days you have not worked. / You hope to become a personage of royal rank).

And it is she, not the prince, who is punished for their love, by the severest punishment possible, that of death.

On hearing her sentence of death Ken Tambuhan quite rightly laments to the executioner: *Jikalau ada ayah dan bunda / masakan demikian lakunya ada* (SKT VI, 88c-d) (How could they do this to me / if my father and mother were there). Having forfeited the bounty of the king and queen and forced to live in Kuripan without kith or kin Ken Tambuhan has no one to protect her. And as she is keenly aware, in Kuripan she is a person who can claim no rights nor hope for protection because her status is only that of an insignificant exile and an alien:

> Aku nin piatu di negeri orang / ada laksana seekor bilalang / permaisuri terlalu garang / barang lakunya siapa melarang (SKT VI, 131).
>
> ('Living in a foreign land without kith or kin / I am as powerless as an insignificant grasshopper. / The queen is a very fierce person. / Who can stop her from doing whatever she likes.')

But the tyranny of the queen is not the ultimate reason Ken Tambuhan has to suffer. There is another law, another power which ultimately decides everything, which everything must obey, namely the will of the gods who apportion fate. As we have seen, it is the god Kesna who has reduced her to her present condition of exile and loss of identity. Why has he done this? We are not told, but from a reading of other Panji stories we may infer that he did so to punish the king of Daha for not fulfilling the vow he had made when he prayed to the gods to grant him a child. Thus, in the *Hikayat Cekel Wanengpati* (Story of Valiant Knight Bachelor) the god Kala, angered because in his joy about the birth of his son the king of Kuripan has forgotten to fulfil his vow, decides to stage a *lakon* (shadow-play) about the prince of Kuripan and the king of Soca Windu and begins its action by having Raden Inu kidnapped by that king (Rassers 1922:32).

Aware that her fate ultimately lies in the hands of the gods, Ken Tambuhan places herself in their hands when the moment of her death has come: *Beta nin dagang tiada berguna / kalau ada kasihan Batara Kesna* (SKT VI, 94c-d) (I am an exile who is of no use, / but perhaps the god Kesna will take pity on me). Her prayer is indeed heard by the gods. Looking down from the heavens on the corpse of the princess, who even in death is as beautiful as a heavenly nymph, they take pity on her and say laughingly: *Hendak pun kita hidupkan pulang / kalaukan panjang perkataan dalang* (SKT VI, 151c-d) (Let us bring her back to life again, / so that the puppeteer may spin out his story). In order that thereafter the shadow-play may be spun out (*supaya panjang lelakon kemudian,* SKT IX, 3d), they order the god Kala to go to Kuripan with the heavenly flower, Wijayamala, and revive the lovers. Hidden behind the mask of the gods it is not difficult to discern the laughing storyteller who holds the fate of his heroes in his hands and enjoys the pleasure of drawing out his tale.

The shadow-play, which the gods set in motion by placing Ken Tambuhan in a world of alienation, is fraught with illusion and deceptive appearances. In the world at home, the day-world of identity, things are what they seem to be: the princess of Daha is the princess of Daha and therefore the destined mate of the prince of Kuripan. Not so in the night-world of alienation – an uncanny world of uncertain interpretation, the narrative of which is typically motivated by a misunderstanding; the daughter of the king of Banjarkulon/Daha – a ruler who is next in rank only to the king of Kuripan – and therefore the very princess who by birth and lineage is the most suitable mate for the prince of Kuripan, is taken for the mere captive princess from the obscure kingdom of Tanjungpuri she seems to be.

In different ways all the protagonists are in the grip of illusion. Ken Tambuhan is quite unaware of her true identity, understandably so, because she was separated from her parents when she was only a one-year-old baby. The king, who found her in the forest, the queen and Raden Inu, too, seem not to know that she is in reality the princess of Banjarkulon/Daha. The only two protagonists who could know are her two nurses, Ken Penglipur and Ken Tadahan, who must be considerably older than she. But, even when Ken Tambuhan is about to be killed by the executioner and when they may well have saved her life by telling who she really is, they still maintain that she is the princess of Tanjungpuri: *Dari kecil patik pelihara / tatkala didalam negeri Tanjungpura* (SKT VI, 132a-b) (Ever since you were a small child we have looked after you, since the time we lived in the Kingdom of Tanjungpura). This is indeed a striking case of amnesia. The most plausible reason for this lapse of memory seems to be narrative necessity: if they were to divulge the truth at this point, they would deprive the narrator of the chance to keep up the suspense and spin out his story.

Although the hold of illusion and deceptive appearance over the protagonists is strong, it is not total; whether consciously or unconsciously, they perceive signs that Ken Tambuhan may be of more consequence than her ostensible identity suggests. When the narrator first describes her he enumerates many of these signs:

> Parasnya seperti bidadari / sukar didapat mahal dicari // [...] / lakunya arif bijaksana / akal bicaranya sangatlah sempurna / sifatnya lengkap tujuh laksana // zaman itu sukar dicari / manisnya seperti Mandudari / [...] / cantik manis barang kelakuan / memberi hati bimbang dan rawan // sekaliannya heran memandang parasnya / kasih dan sayang rasa citanya / baik sekali budi bahasanya / patutlah dengan tegur sapanya. (SKT I, 13c-17.)

> (She looked like a nymph descended from heaven, / but rarely met and seldom found. // [...] / Her demeanour was wise and sensible. / Cleverness and wit she had in abundance. / Her appearance encompassed all the feminine charms. // At that time anyone who was her equal would have been hard to find. / Her beauty was like that of Mandudari. / [...] / Lovely and sweet was her every action, / filling one's heart with desire and tenderness. // All who beheld her appearance were amazed; / affection and love were felt by all. / Excellent were her breeding and her manners, / befitting her courteous speech.)

These signs that betray that she is really someone special are not lost on the king and queen of Kuripan, who love the foundling girl and favour her above the other princesses. These same signs are the real reason why the prince can fall in love with her. When the prince looks inside the compound and sees Ken Tambuhan, he asks his attendant, Wiradandani: [...] *Kakanda siapakah itu / lakunya seperti anak para ratu* (SKT III, 12c-d) (Elder brother, who may she be, / that girl whose bearing is like that of the daughter of a king). And, impressed by her royal demeanour, he humbles himself before Ken Tambuhan as he tries to win her heart, declaring himself her slave and vassal.

These very signs convince the king of Kuripan that his son has done well in choosing Ken Tambuhan as his wife:

> Ken Tambuhan itu pun anak raja / parasnya elok gemilang durja / sedap manis laku bersahaja / bagai dibuat dia sengaja // pada mata tiadalah jemu / segala yang memandang heran termangu / manis seperti laut madu / patutlah dengan anak Inu. (SKT IV, 18-9.)

> ('Even so, that Lady-in-Waiting Tambuhan is the daughter of a king. / Her appearance is beautiful and her countenance is radiant. / Pleasant and sweet is her modest demeanour, / as if she cultivates such a behaviour. // The eye never tires of gazing at her. / All who behold her gape with astonishment. / She is sweet like a sea of honey; / indeed a proper wife for my royal son.')

Yet, the power of illusion is so strong that, even if they notice the signs of Ken Tambuhan's real identity, neither the king nor his son perceive that Ken Tambuhan is the very girl whose hand will be sought for the prince.

Only the queen, in her overhasty desire to safeguard the interests of the dynasty, turns a blind eye to these signs. She insists that a captive is a captive and that Ken Tambuhan is indeed what she seems to be. As far as the queen is concerned, if the girl claims to have the right to be treated as a lady of the noblest lineage and not to have to work, she is only pretending to be what she is not (*bidaah*).

Illusion is only lifted when Ken Tambuhan regains her identity; until this happens, the other protagonists, with the exception of the queen, only vaguely or unconsciously sense her high birth and station, which shines through the semblance of outward appearances as a jewel shimmers through a veil of dust. Indeed, in the phase of illusion most of the protagonists, finding themselves in a situation of half-knowledge and vague inklings, have to cope with the difficulty of interpreting, of deciphering the signs which surround them.

Thus, both Ken Tambuhan and the prince have difficulty in making out what is predicted by the many dreams by which they are visited and by the portents they observe. Each time, this uncertainty about meaning is described as a very disturbing experience. This is how the narrator describes Ken Tambuhan's reaction to her first dream at the beginning of the SKT:

> Terkejutlah ia lalu jaga / heran berpikir seketika / dalam hatinya adalah duka / mimpi nin apa artinya juga (SKT I, 22).

> (She was startled from sleep and then was wide awake. / Astonished she was lost in thought a while. / Her heart was filled with sadness; what could be the meaning of her dream?)

The prince, too, is completely unsettled by his first dream, which fills him with a dejection, from which he can only find relief by his excursion to the pleasure gardens:

> Raden terkejut arwah melayang // pikirlah ia seorang dirinya / menaruh gundah dalam hatinya / betapakah gerangan takbir mimpinya / bertambah heran akan dirinya. (SKT II, 24d-25.)

> (He was lost in his own thoughts. / His heart was filled with misgivings; / how should his dream be interpreted? / He felt more and more amazed.)

Uncertainty and foreboding also characterize Ken Tambuhan's reaction on hearing about Raden Inu's dream in which a tiger drags her off into the forest:

> Menangislah ia dengan perlahan / seperti diberitahu akan kematian / hilanglah arwah didalam badan / terkenangkan nasib peruntungan // betapa gerangan celaka badanku / datanglah gerangan perceraianku / tidaklah lama rupanya aku / bersama-sama dengan kakangku. (SKT IV, 39-40.)

> (She began to weep softly, / as if she had received news of someone's death. / She almost swooned, / as she pondered her sad fate and fortune. // 'How then shall misfortune strike me? Perchance our separation is now at hand. / Apparently not long will I / remain in the company of my love.')

This sadness about the uncertainty of meaning also overwhelms Ken Tambuhan when at night, unable to sleep, she ponders the news that Raden Inu will leave to go hunting in the forest on his mother's orders:

> Terasalah hati Ken Tambuhan / seperti diberitahu akan kematian / hilanglah arwah tiada berketahuan / lalu menangis perlahan-lahan // ia berpikir dalam beradu / matilah gerangan sekali nin aku / tiadalah sampai bagai niatku / membalas kasih kakang Inu // dimana diketahui bicaranya orang / masakan tampak ditengah terang / puteranya orang masakan hilang / aku juga merasai seorang. (SKT V, 64-6.)

> (Ken Tambuhan felt / as if she had received news of a death. / She almost fainted and felt confused / and thereupon began to weep softly. // As she lay on her couch she thought to herself: / 'Perchance this means I will now die, / and will not be able to fulfill my deepest desire, / to requite the love of the prince. // How can I know what people are talking about? / How can it ever be revealed? // Why should someone else's child have to die? / I will be the one to suffer the consequences.')

As we see in these passages, the uncertainty of meaning is among other means expressed by the words *gerangan* (perchance, maybe) and *rupanya* (apparently); the protagonists are assailed by a distressing suspicion that they are perhaps being deceived by illusory appearances. One of the vehicles for expressing this distress is the word *heran* (astonished, struck with wonder, bewildered, confounded). This word refers to a state of mental tension or perplexity, inducing a loss of consciousness, a state of forgetfulness (*lupa*), in which the rational self-control (*akal*) of the interpreter, in other words his senses, are completely disintegrated by the overwhelming experience of his inability to grasp the meaning of the sign to be interpreted and by the concomitant rise of a desire (*birahi*) or longing (*rindu*) to appropriate it (see Braginsky 1979:7-8; Siegel 1979:251-9).

Obviously, then, the narrative of the SKT, and, more specifically, the story of Ken Tambuhan's love for Raden Inu, is very much concerned with interpretation. The central object of interpretation is Ken Tambuhan herself, who – to coin a new term – could be described as a 'signifier-errant', the meaning of whom is to be deciphered by the other protagonists. One of the many ways in which her status of a sign requiring interpretation is underlined is indeed by the many descriptions of the feelings of astonishment provoked in the beholder by her beauty, such as for example: *Sekaliannya heran memandang parasnya* (SKT I, 17a).

In this search for interpretation the queen – an unbending and ruthless advocate of the view that things are what they seem to be and the heedless champion of representation and propriety – plays the part of a misreader. For her, in spite of all indications to the contrary, Ken Tambuhan remains a mere captive, unworthy to be the wife of her nobly born son, a reading which is finally refuted when Ken Tambuhan really proves to be the princess of Banjarkulon/Daha.

The king and the prince admit the possibility that things may not be what they seem. They leave scope for interpretation, for the possibility that the seemingly improper may prove to be proper after all and thus allow for the possibility of a break with representation. Although they remain in the grip of illusion for a long time, they intuitively produce a correct reading.

Before the correctness of this reading has been finally proved by the recognition of Ken Tambuhan's identity, they find themselves continually groping for meaning while yet shrouded in opacity; time and again they have to find their way guided – or led astray – by a knowledge that is only partial, by vague suspicions and uncertain and hesitant recognitions.

Another source of anxiety, of uncertain interpretation – both for the prince and for Ken Tambuhan – is the fate that the gods – and behind them the narrator – hold in store for them, as we can see from the reflexive, pensive way (*terkenangkan nasib peruntungan*) in which they react to the dreams and portents that predict crucial turns in the narrative, witness the passages I quoted above.

The SKT, then, is not only a marriage story, the heroine of which is Ken Tambuhan – if we read it on a more abstract level, it is also a drama of interpretation, in which she enacts the role of the pivotal signifier to be interpreted. To turn her into a 'signifier-errant' the narrator – hidden behind the mask of the god Kesna – abducts her from Daha. He exiles her from the clarity and openness of the day-world of identity, a world in which her meaning is fixed (*tentu*) and is a matter of commemoration by formulaic repetition, and parachutes her into the opacity of a night-world of alienation and forgetfulness, where her meaning is open to interpretation (*gerangan*) and is to be laboriously deciphered. In the SKT the first symbol of this opacity we meet is the dense and impenetrable forest of Kuripan, where the king finds Ken Tambuhan.

The reason Ken Tambuhan provokes problems of interpretation is that she is a signifier allowing for conflicting interpretations, an unsettling experience indeed. On the one hand apparently she may be read as a mere captive princess of no consequence, on the other hand by her behaviour she continually gives those who behold her the impression that there is more behind this sign than meets the eye. From behind the screen of what she seems to be, the shimmering of another identity can be perceived, that of a great lady of the noblest birth.

Ultimately all misunderstandings and misinterpretations are swept aside, as is the rule in the Panji story. But, before they are cleared away, the narrator of the SKT exerts himself as best he can to keep his protagonists – and with them also his audience or readers – in suspense, even to mislead them so that he may spin out his story (*memanjangkan*) at great length, before Ken Tambuhan's identity and with it propriety (*patut*) is finally restored, so that nothing much else remains to be told. Being quite familiar with Panji stories in which the prince of Kuripan always marries the princess of Daha, the public will have already suspected that Ken Tambuhan is not some mere obscure captive princess but the princess of Daha, his destined bride, hidden in disguise by the art of the narrator.

As I have previously pointed out, Ken Tambuhan's loss of identity is figured as a fall into a state of exile (*dibuang, dagang, piatu*). Concomitantly her regaining of her identity is figured as a movement of return (*pulang*). The culmination of this movement of return is the reunion of Ken Tambuhan with her parents and the subsequent marriage of the girl, now acknowledged as the princess of Daha, to Raden Inu. Her exile is also figured as a lapse into forgetfulness, into a state of amnesia. Accordingly her return is effected through a restoration of memory. In other words, in the course of the plot Ken Tambuhan from being a signifier-errant, open to conflicting interpretations, therefore uncontrolled and exceeding the limits of the Book of the Malay *Kerajaan* Order, is transformed back into what she was at the start: a signifier bound to a signified which supervises it and thus again operating within the constraints of the Book. Sign and meaning coincide again.

We have already seen that the queen accuses Ken Tambuhan of lying (*bidaah*) in order to play the great lady. What she stands accused of, then, is pretension. In a way the accusation is right, but the only pretension she is unwittingly guilty of is to be a captive princess of dubious status. She does not pretend to be a noble lady; on the contrary, she proves by her appearance, her behaviour and her deeds that in reality she is just that. And for this she is duly rewarded, by receiving the exalted position of consort of Raden Inu and Queen of Kuripan.

By contrast the queen, who to all appearances should indeed be just what she seems to be – queen of the highest ranking kingdom of Java and a worthy consort for its king – proves to be only pretending and undeserving of this high estimation. That her claims to high status are only pretensions appears from her rash behaviour, manifesting a lack of self-control; from her failure to do justice; and from her deeds of wilful deception. She is punished accordingly by being stripped of all her dignity. She is publicly humiliated by being thrown out of the palace and being ordered to look after the hunting dogs. Poetic justice takes its course.

Ken Tambuhan, we may say, moves from a state of disjunction between sign and meaning to one of conjunction between both. From having involuntarily held out an illusion, she moves to representing reality. From unwitting pretension (*mengada-ada*) she moves to mimesis (*mengadakan*) (about these terms, see Chapter III, part 5). In spite of some outward indications to the contrary, her deeds and words prove to be grounded repetitions of the behaviour of a person of truly noble origin, as this is codified in the Book of the Malay *Kerajaan* Order. The sway of representation is restored.

Omina – signs in the Book of the Universe – signal the correctness of this reading. On Ken Tambuhan's death the sky becomes gloomy and overcast, the sun goes into hiding as if in mourning, birds call as if they want to spread the news that something calamitous has happened. Far away the rumbling of thunder may be heard, while a gentle breeze begins to blow, making a soft sound like a barely audible dirge. Warm rain drizzles down and a rainbow appears (SKT VII, 1-4). Observing these omina but unable to grasp their meaning, the king of Kuripan and the population are amazed (*heran*, SKT VII, 4c). Other omina confirming her truly royal status are observable when Ken Tambuhan's corpse is found in the forest by the prince; it gives off a sweet odour like that of spikenard (*baunya seperti narawastu*, SKT VII, 33a).

As I have indicated in Chapter III, parts 3, 4 and 5, according to Malay poetics, the act of mimesis – grounded repetition – involves a gesture of return to Origin. The hiatus between the empirical presence of the signifiers and an immanent or transcendent signified at the origin of all is bridged by an act of unforgetting what is written in the soul in the Book of Memory. This act of unforgetting requires wisdom. It is therefore significant that Ken Tambuhan is described as a wise and discerning person (*lakunya arif bijaksana / akal bicaranya sangat sempurna*, SKT I, 14b-c). It is through her wisdom that she is capable of mimesis, of recall. It causes her intuitively to remember and imitate the behaviour befitting the sort of person she really is, a truly noble lady.

For a model of this behaviour the narrator refers to the *Hikayat Seri Rama*, when he eulogizingly compares Ken Tambuhan's royal demeanour with that of Queen Mandudari. Mandudari is the beautiful and loyal wife of King Dasarata. When Rawana demands she be given to him as wife, she takes him in by a ruse; from the excretions from her skin (*daki*) she fashions a copy of herself, Mandudaki, which her husband, who knows nothing about what she has done, gives to Rawana (Achadiati Ikram 1980:155-8). By acts of commemoration of queenly behaviour, by acts of unforgetting which break the spell of illusion as exemplified for instance in the figure of Mandudari, Ken Tambuhan is thus able to regain her temporarily obscured identity. This process of unforgetting is figured in the plot as a movement of return.

The trajectory of the queen leads in the opposite direction, because she is blinded by fury. In this state she loses her power of discrimination (*akal*) and is unable to remember how a proper queen should behave and imitate that behaviour. As people criticize her, blaming her for the death of the lovers: *Apatah gunanya orang yang bebal / marahnya tidak dengan akal* (SKT VII,

94a-b) (What use is such a stupid person? / In her anger she failed to use her head). And she herself concedes ruefully, as she laments over the corpse of her son: *Bundamu tuan akalnya buta* (SKT VII, 121c) (Your mother, oh my son, / was blinded by her fury and lost her head). Instead of being a self-possessed queen she proves to be a shrew who allows herself to be ruled by her fierce passions, which the narrator expresses by comparing her to a tiger or a devil. Her behaviour, instead of *mengadakan* (to represent) is really *mengada-ada* (to feign, to pretend); instead of a grounded repetition of origin, it is an empty repetition, a swerve away from origin, which belies her claim to royal status.

4. Divine couples: another plot of exile and return?

Throughout the SKT yet another origin is invoked: divine origin. Both the prince and Ken Tambuhan, as children of kings of Java, are of divine origin. Introducing the prince, the narrator directly states his divine origin as an explanation of his strikingly handsome appearance: *Parasnya tidak lagi bertara / asalnya turun dari udara* (SKT II, 2a-b) (He was of peerless beauty; / his lineage had descended from heaven). Throughout the poem Ken Tambuhan's divine origin is also suggested. Thus we are told time and again that she looked like a heavenly nymph (*bidadari*).

More specific indications of their divine origin are given in comparisons referring to well-known figures in the Book of Hindu-Javanese Mythology. Thus Raden Inu, grieving at the side of his dead beloved, sighs:

> Aria ningsun Yangyang Kusuma / parasnya seperti Nila Utama / pertemuan kita dari selama / remaklah kakang mati bersama (SKT VII, 44).
>
> ('My little sister, Yangyang Kusuma, / whose beauty is like that of Nila Utama, / that we would meet was of old ordained by fate; / rather would I die together with you than to be separated from you again.')

These mythological allusions are a common phenomenon in Middle Javanese and modern Javanese as well as Malay Panji stories and will most probably have been derived from them rather than from the Old Javanese *kakawin*. Nevertheless, to understand their meaning it is helpful to take a look at the story with which they are concerned, as it is told in a *kakawin*, namely *Arjunawiwaha* (The Marriage of Arjuna) composed about AD 1030 by Mpu Kanwa. It is the work which, according to Zoetmulder, marks the beginning of East Javanese *kakawin* (heroic epic in an Indian metre) literature. In *Arjunawiwaha*, the nymph Nila Utama (Tilottama) figures together with another nymph, Suprabha. In the SKT the prince also compares Ken Tambuhan with this other nymph, whom he calls Dewi Sugarba, the Malay form of her name (SKT III, 99c).

Arjunawiwaha tells how Arjuna, one of the five Pandawa brothers, is rewarded for his epic exploits in defeating a demon king who has attacked Indra's heaven. As a reward Arjuna may stay in heaven for seven celestial days to enjoy the fruits of his valiant behaviour as king on Indra's throne. After he has been solemnly installed, his sevenfold marriage with seven celestial nymphs is celebrated. He consummates these marriages one by one. The first nymph to be led into the nuptial chamber is Suprabha, who has helped Arjuna by seducing the demon king into betraying the one spot where he is vulnerable. She is followed by Tilottama and the five other nymphs. When the seven months, equal to the seven celestial days, have expired Arjuna returns to earth (Zoetmulder 1974:234-7).

If Ken Tambuhan is compared to Arjuna's first two heavenly wives, then the prince is likened to Arjuna returned to earth. Thus, when he leaves Kuripan to go hunting in the forest, the ladies-in-waiting, amazed by his beauty, throng together and cannot refrain from addressing him:

> Aduh susunan seri pangeran // baik paras utama jiwa / patut diadap menteri punggawa / tidak berbanding di Tanah Jawa / entahkan penjelmaan segala dewa // sekianlah rupa Sang Ranjuna. (SKT V, 3d-5d.)

> ('Oh, lord and master, glorious prince, // so handsome to behold, my life-spirit ! / You are truly worthy to be served by ministers and military officers. / You are unrivalled in the Land of Java. // Who knows, you may be an incarnation of the gods. // That is the very appearance of Lord Arjuna.')

Interestingly, in the SKT the nymph Sugarba (Suprabha) – who here seems to be identified with the nymph Nila Utama (Tilottama) (SKT IX, 47-8) – also plays a role in the plot. She appears as the guardian of the revivifying flower, Wijayamala or Gandapurawangi, in search of which the god Kala roams the gardens of heaven (SKT IX, 6-71). The healing flower is a motif widespread in Javanese and Malay Panji stories. We also find the heavenly flower, Gandapurawangi, in the Malay Panji story *Hikayat Dewa Asmara Jaya*, where it is used to heal Panji who has been cursed by a god (Harun Mat Piah 1980:77).

The flower's other name, Wijayamala, already occurs in a *kakawin*, namely *Bhomakavya* (The poem about Lord Bhoma). There we are told that a flower of this name is in the possession of Bhoma, another name for the demon king, Naraka, who spreads death and destruction throughout the heavens. Bhoma has been given the flower by his mother, the Earth Goddess. It is taken from him by Krishna's (Wisnu's) *garuda* (winged mount) in a battle, in which Krishna's son, Samba, and his ally, Arjuna, are killed. After killing Bhoma, Wisnu uses it to revive them as well as some of his enemies, Bhoma excepted (Zoetmulder 1974:312-20). It is also found in the *Hikayat Sang Boma*.

Above we have already seen that the prince also likened his love to Yangyang Kusuma. Here again, although the comparison has probably been inspired by other Panji stories, a look at an Old Javanese *kakawin* is illuminating. The work in question is *Smaradahana* (The Burning of Kama) by Mpu Dharmaja. Again we are reminded of a divine couple: Yangyang Kusuma is another name for Ratih, the goddess of love and consort of the god of love, Kama (Klinkert 1947:1044).

To Ratih's immense sadness her husband has to leave her to carry out the order from Indra and the other gods to bring Siwa, who is doing severe penance on Mount Meru, out of his meditation and make him desire his spouse, Uma, who is still virgin. Kama's efforts to disturb Siwa by attacking him with his flower-weapons, succeed and in a dream Siwa sees Uma sitting on his lap. Awaking an instant later and noticing Kama's presence, he assumes his terrifying shape and scorches Kama to ashes with his fire.

Besought by Indra to revive Kama, Siwa consents to let him live again, but only in an immaterial form. When news of Kama's death reaches Ratih, she is overcome with grief. The sage, Wrhaspati, acquaints her with Siwa's decision that she and her husband shall both continue their existence in invisible form, she in women, he in men. When she expresses her profound repugnance for such a formless life, which can hardly be called a life at all, and pleads that they be granted a rebirth, the sage assures her that this will definitely happen in the future.

Ratih now accepts her fate and decides to follow her husband in death. She goes to the place where he was burnt and throws herself into the flames, which Siwa causes to flare up again. The couple meet, but, as they are bodiless, they cannot unite. Therefore Kama enters the heart of Siwa and Ratih that of Uma. From the moment Siwa is struck by Kama's arrow, the passion of love takes possession of his heart. Now he unites with Uma.

Later, on a pleasure trip, Uma sees the ashes of the god and goddess of love. Moved by compassion and gratitude she obtains from Siwa the promise that they shall be reborn. After several other rebirths Kama finally descends to earth as king of Java. Ratih is reborn in Janggala (Kahuripan), where she is known as Kiranaratu. Thus by grace of Siwa His Majesty Kameswara now reigns in Dahana (Daha), with Dewi Kirana as queen (Zoetmulder 1974:291-5).

That we may also consider the possibility that the SKT is alluding directly to *kakawin* literature could be concluded from the explicit mention of the title of a *kakawin*, *Kresnayana* (The story of Kresna) by Mpu Triguna. In a *memakai* (dressing) type-scene (about this type-scene, see also Chapter II) occurring just after Raden Inu's ominous dream in which a tiger seizes Ken Tambuhan, we are told that the prince *beranting-anting Kesnayana* (SKT IV, 52b) (He wore drop-earrings like in the Story of Kesna). But of course, here again, the author may simply have been inspired by another Panji story.

From a glance at Zoetmulder's dictionary of Old Javanese it appears that in Panji stories in the genre *kidung* (poems in Middle Javanese in a Javanese or some other Indonesian metre) the type-scene of the dressing of the hero or heroine (on which the *memakai* scenes in Malay literature are obviously modelled) was probably already a favourite occasion for the author to indulge in mythological allusion.

If we look under the lemma *gringsing* in Zoetmulder (1982, I:545-6) we will learn that, in the *Kidung Malat*, we may find lines such as *sabuk geringsing Smarantaka* (a sash on which was depicted the story of the Death of Smara); *asabuk geringsing Pandawajaya* (he wore a sash on which was depicted the story of the Victorious Pandawas); and *alancingan gringsing Ramayana*. And for instance in the *Kidung Wangbang Wideya* we can find *alancingan gringsing Suprabaduta* (he wore trousers depicting the story of Suprabha's espionage mission) (canto 3, 67b) (Robson 1971:187). In the *memakai* scene in the SKT in which *Kresnayana* is mentioned, the prince is indeed also depicted as wearing trousers of *gringsing* cloth (*berlancingan geringsing*).

That the reference to *Kresnayana*, if not inspired by another Malay Panji story, may have been prompted by a *kidung* rather than a *kakawin* will strike us as even more likely if we note that in *Wangbang Wideya* (canto 3, 26a) we find a dressing-scene, in which we are told that Panji *arja akeris atrap-trap Kresnayana anatar wilis* (Robson 1971:166-7) (He looked fine, wearing a kris inlaid with a scene from the *Kresnayana* on a green ground). In fact, to a large extent the SKT and this *kidung* share the same mythological allusions.

Yet another possible source of mythological allusion is indicated by the fact that in the dressing-scene in the SKT we are told that Raden Inu *berlancingan geringsing wayang* (SKT IV, 50a) (he wore trousers depicting a scene from the shadowplay). Here one could think of a *wayang purwa lakon* such as *Suprabaduta*, which, as we have seen, is also alluded to in *Wangbang Wideya* (Robson 1971:35).

Finally, it must be said that besides appearing as written *kidung*, composed for a literate audience, the Panji stories themselves also circulated in oral form, namely in the performances of the *wayang gedog* (Ras 1976:56). It is therefore also quite possible that the author borrowed his mythology from there.

However, let us now return to *Kresnayana* to try and grasp the meaning of the mention of its title in the SKT. This *kakawin* tells how king Kresna abducts princess Rukmini, daughter of the king of Kundina, on the eve of her marriage to the king of Cedi. He does so on the promptings of her mother who has always hoped to have him for a son-in-law.

Rukmini's mother informs Kresna of the impending marriage by sending a female attendant to him. The attendant makes him fall in love with a detailed description of Rukmini's charms and tells him that he is the only man Rukmini desires for a husband. She also tells him that it is the ardent desire of Rukmini's mother that he carry her off before it is too late. He need not wait for an auspicious day; a *gandharwa* marriage (a marriage by sexual consummation with mutual consent) will suffice. When the couple has eloped, the army of the king of Cedi pursues Kresna but is defeated. Rukmini's brother, Rukma, who attacks Kresna in his hiding place, is also defeated by him, but Kresna spares his life. Ultimately Kresna triumphantly carries his bride to his kraton (Zoetmulder 1974:284-8).

The implication that Raden Inu may indeed be identified with Kresna is also underlined by the fact that, on his accession to the throne, he is given the title Batara Kesna (SKT XI, 48a) (King Kesna). His father, too, goes by the title of Batara Kesna (SKT X, 26b). In the SKT the god Kesna actually plays an important role in the plot. It is he who gets the *lakon* under way by abducting the princess of Daha and bringing her to Kuripan (SKT X, 2c). And it is he for whose pity Ken Tambuhan hopes when the moment of her death has come (SKT VI, 94d).

Curiously, Ken Tambuhan's prayer that she may be helped by Kesna leads not to his intervention but to that of the god Kala (SKT IX, 4a, b). In most Panji stories it is indeed Kala who acts the role of *deus ex machina*. Conceivably, the author of the SKT considered Kesna and Kala as identical figures, which seems to be indicated by the fact that the nymphs the god Kala meets on his tour of the heavenly gardens surmise that he must be the god Bisnu (Wisnu) (SKT IX, 8a, 19b). If that is so, we may conclude that, in the SKT, the god Kesna is not only instrumental in getting the *lakon* under way but also intervenes when matters threaten to get out of hand and end improperly with the undeserved death of the lovers.

What can the meaning of all these intertextual echoes be? What is the relationship between the myths to which they refer? And what is the connection between all these couples with whom the SKT allusively compares the prince and Ken Tambuhan: Ranjuna and Segarba/Nila Utama, Kama and Yangyang Kusuma, Kesna and Rukmini?

Obviously, all these mythological stories to which allusions are made to have in common that they are concerned with marriage. *Arjunawiwaha* and *Kresnayana* respectively deal with the winning of a bride by the performance of heroic deeds as a *ksatrya* (member of the warrior caste) and by abduction. One of them, *Smaradahana*, has as its main theme the consummation of marriage through the indispensable love induced by Kama and Ratih. By allusions to these myths the marriage of Raden Inu and Ken Tambuhan is represented as a repetition, a commemoration of these exemplary divine marriages of days of yore and the SKT is turned into an allegory of the power of the love between man and woman.

Ranjuna and the nymphs Segarba and Nila Utama, as well as Kama and Yangyang Kusuma, are clearly instances of couples who have been united in heaven. By the suggestion that Raden Inu and Ken Tambuhan may be incarnations of these heavenly couples, born on earth in different families, their marriage is figured perhaps not as a reunion of two lovers as man and wife but as a reunion of a husband and wife. This reunion takes place after a period of separation, in which they have been searching for each other, full of longing.

If Raden Inu and Ken Tambuhan are in fact incarnations of a heavenly husband and wife – Ranjuna and Segarba or Kama and Yangyang Kusuma, incarnated in the son of the king of Kuripan and the daughter of the king of Daha – then they are twin-souls (*jodoh*), tied by a cosmic law, namely that of karma (*untung*). And in that case it is their karma that they should meet in this world. This is the argument which Raden Inu uses to persuade the reluctant Ken Tambuhan to give in to his desires, saying:

> Sudahlah gerangan untungmu tuan / dengan kakanda pertemuan // dimanakan dapat tuan salahkan / kehendak dewata tuan ridhakan. (SKT III, 61c-62b.)
>
> ('Perchance it was your fate, my lady, / that you should meet me. // How can you gainsay what it decrees? / You had better resign yourself to the will of the gods.')

As Ratih follows Kama into death so as to be reunited with her husband, so Raden Inu commits suicide in order not to be separated from his long lost twin-soul. The prince promises to do so, saying:

> Tuanku seperti Yangyang Kesuma / parasnya seperti bulan purnama / kakanda mencari dari selama / akan bela mati bersama (SKT IV, 65).
>
> ('You, my lady, are like Yangyang Kusuma / whose beauty is like that of the full moon. / All my life have I searched for you, / in order to follow you in death and die together with you.')

He confirms this promise on finding her corpse in the forest:

> Aria ningsun Yangyang Kusuma / parasnya seperti Nila Utama / pertemuan kita dari selama / remaklah kakang mati bersama // janji nin tidak kakang ubahkan (SKT VIII, 44a-45a).
>
> ('My little sister, Yangyang Kusuma, / whose beauty is like that of Nila Utama, / that we would meet was of old ordained by fate; // rather would I die together with you than to be separated from you again.')

But what is the meaning of the comparison with the couple Kresna and Rukmini? In *Kresnayana* they are not represented as a heavenly couple. If we may assume that the author of the SKT really was familiar with that work – which cannot be stated with any certainty[3] – and meant them to

---

[3] That a direct relation between an Old Javanese *kakawin* and a Malay work may

figure as an example of a heavenly couple, separated by incarnation in different families on earth, perhaps he confused *Kresnayana* with another *kakawin*, *Hariwangsa* [Hari's Wisnu's Lineage] by Mpu Panuluh (Zoetmulder 1974:250-5).

This *kakawin* tells the same story of the abduction of Rukmini, but with significant differences. One of these is that in *Hariwangsa* Kresna and Rukmini are represented as incarnations of Wisnu and his consort, Sri, so that the time before their marriage is a time of separation and their marriage itself becomes a reunion. Both protagonists are conscious of their origin, which influences all their thoughts and feelings (Zoetmulder 1974:289).

Above I have described the characteristic plot of romance as a *nostos* (return), a circular movement from a happy state of identity and reality, through the anxieties of loss of identity, of alienation and illusion, back again to identity. I have also indicated that the fall into alienation is accompanied by a certain amnesia. We will now perceive that, in a sense, yet another return movement is suggested in the SKT by the allusions to the divine couples I traced above; we are invited to see the sexual union and marriage of Raden Inu and Ken Tambuhan as in reality the reunion, after a long separation, of a divine husband and wife.

For Raden Inu and Ken Tambuhan their identity as a divine couple – not, of course their divine origin as such – is only a vague intuition, a half-suspicion that they have met before somewhere in some other existence. Here we find another instance of the element of partial amnesia. There is return in the sense that a marriage is restored. But the return remains incomplete, because the couple does not return to heaven but remains imprisoned in the shadowplay of the great illusion of creation (*tinjomaya*, Ras 1982:25).

Whereas in the story of Ken Tambuhan's return to her original worldly identity as princess of Daha amnesia is fully removed by the process of unforgetting, it is not fully lifted in the suggested story of the return of a divine couple to their reunion in marriage; in the world – not, of course, in heaven – the identity of the lovers as a divine couple remains a matter of conjecture. A hint that the reunion is nevertheless accompanied by an increased awareness of their possible identity as a divine couple, seems to be implied by the change of name Raden Inu undergoes after his marriage,

---

sometimes be demonstrated may be seen from the comparison of the Malay *Hikayat Sang Boma* with the *kakawin Bhomakawya* by Teeuw (1946:21-38). As has been pointed out by Robson in a paper read in 1990, the opening of the Malay *Hikayat Pandawa Lima* is without a doubt a rendering of the Old Javanese *kakawin Bharatayuddha* (Robson 1992:36). In his paper Robson has argued that prestigious Javanese culture was thoroughly imbibed by Malays, who familiarized themselves with it in Java and propagated its values and norms in Malay literary works which were, however, also adapted to Malay tastes.

when he succeeds his father: he receives the title of king Kesna.

In the SKT, then, in a sense we have a story in which the heroine appears in a double disguise: she is not only the princess of Daha disguised as a mere captive princess from some obscure kingdom, there is also the suggestion that she is a goddess or nymph incarnated into the illusory shape of the princess of Daha. And, in his identity of her heavenly twin-soul, Raden Inu, too, may be said to be a figure in disguise.

5. Mediation as the function of the Panji romance

In a wide-ranging study of the Panji story, first published in 1973, which includes a comparison with the Ngaju Dayak creation myth, Ras has put forward the proposition that '[t]he story about the union of Raden Inu with Candra Kirana, interpreted as the union of Wisnu and Sri may [...] be defined as an ancient, pre-Hindu-Javanese, creation myth retold in quasi historical terms in the cultural setting of eleventh century Hinduized Java' (Ras 1992:151).

According to Ras (1992:134-5),

> '[b]y the identification of the prince of Koripan with Wisnu and that of the princess of Daha with Dewi Sri, the story gains an extra dimension, and becomes an allegorical representation of the union of the god Wisnu with the goddess Sri, repeated or re-enacted on earth in this royal marriage. [...]. It becomes the re-enactment of an oft-repeated cosmic drama in which the creator and lord of the Upperworld unites with the goddess representing the primeval waters and the Underworld, which is auspicious for the fertility of the earth and the good fortune of the human community.'

Interpreted in this way, Ras argues, 'the drama of Panji and Candra Kirana was an appropriate stage-play to be performed on the occasion of every pre-Islamic royal wedding in Indonesia'. According to him the stage performance of the Panji drama could in the end become 'a purely conventional procedure having little to do indeed with any mystical [Ras obviously means mythical here] preoccupation of the theme or its possible aspects of ancient tribal division, initiation ritual, the phases of the moon, etc'. In his opinion 'it is this social function of the Panji drama as the conventional stage-play for royal weddings in the twelfth-fourteenth centuries rather than its deeper religious meaning which explains the large number of existing Panji stories both in Java and outside'.

According to Ras (1992:151-2), his comparative study

> 'enables us to isolate a number of features and motifs from the seemingly unwieldy, "amorphous mass" of Panji stories which we can now recognize as being essential to the theme. It may thus eventually become possible, if not to find a prototype, then at least to classify the existing stories as more or less faithfully reflecting that prototype. [...] [T]his comparison brings us very near to Rassers, who regarded as the

most ancient core of the Panji story the myth relating to the coming into being of the Javanese world and the primeval marriage of the first human couple, who were the ancestors of the Javanese people and the founders of Javanese society.'

As we have seen above, in the mythological allusions in the SKT the god Wisnu (Kesna) does indeed assume a prominent place, which confirms the feasibility of reading the poem as an allegorical representation of the marriage of Raden Inu and the princess of Daha as that of Wisnu and Sri. But, as we also saw, the poem may also be read as an allegory of the power of love which reunites twin-souls, as it once reunited Kama and Ratih even through death.

My reading of the SKT also shows that for the interpretation of this poem the mythical dimension is indeed – as Ras concedes for the later Panji stories in general – of marginal importance; the most prominent theme of the poem as a work of the genre of the Panji story is that of the socio-economic and status problems involved in the choice of a marriage partner, and, on another level, its narrative may be read as a drama of signification and interpretation.

Both Rassers and Ras treat the Panji story as a distorted vestige of a vanished system. As the conclusion of his study of the Panji tale Rassers asserted that in Java 'a certain connubial arrangement obtained, which permitted certain marriages whilst prohibiting others' and that '[t]his would mean that the Panji myth is here putting us on the track of a primitive exogamous social organization' (Ras 1992:119).

For the Panji story in Bali Boon has argued that it may perhaps be better to see it as an active commentary on current social possibilities than as a distorted vestige. In his view there is

> 'no need to posit some sort of Ur-moiety or primordial dual organization to explain the myths. Rather, every pre-arranged marriage in fact establishes contradictions similar to those that motivate both the Panji tales and the South Asian epics. [...] In Bali the *Ur*, so to speak recurs. Thus protostructure bows to social action.' (Boon 1977:179.)

Above we have already seen what are the contradictions which attend the pre-arranged marriage of the prince of Kuripan and the princess of Daha in the SKT: the demands of individual happiness vs the laws of social hierarchy; sexual desire vs social obligation; love for love's sake vs love for the sake of the status, power and property.

The narrative of the SKT mediates these contradictory demands by giving full scope to the demands of desire, yet converting the individual choice of the lovers into something as preordained as if it were dictated by social law, namely by the rules of kinship. And it suggests that their love even conforms to yet another law, a cosmic law: their karma from a previous existence in which they were a divine married couple. Lovers, marriage partners of matching status and perhaps even twin-souls from another existence: what marriage could surpass in quality this thrice blessed and guaranteed union?

On the one hand, the SKT asserts the aristocratic model of marriage; it endorses the upper-class belief that worth and birth are synonymous, and that only aristocracy is fit to marry aristocracy. Yet, on the other, it also suggests that a marriage into the aristocracy is possible after all, whatever one's social or economic status, provided one can prove one's worth, as Ken Tambuhan does.

Meritorious as Ken Tambuhan has proved herself, she must ultimately also be found to be of proper status for Inu's marriage partner. By showing the elective affinity of the lovers to be in reality thoroughly in keeping with the biopolitics of the dynasty of Kuripan and Daha, the SKT posits the possibility of an accommodation of the desire to choose one's marriage partner individually to aristocratic family practice. Accommodating desire and the law of descent, contesting as well as affirming the principles of genealogy and noble property, the SKT is thus a work of a bivalent, dialogical and mediatory nature.

Presumably the tensions which motivate the SKT as a marriage story were not restricted to royal marriages, but also played a role in marriages between members of other classes of Malay society. This seems to be the reason why not only royal audiences but listeners from other social strata as well could apparently identify themselves emotionally with its heroine and hero. By allowing for individual exceptions in the rigid system of social hierarchy and privilege and thus opening up the possibility for their episodic relocation and cyclic relegitimation, the SKT by literary means helped to prevent Malay culture from becoming rigid and fossilized (Bloch 1983:159-97; Wittig 1978:182-9; Boon 1977:192-202).

As a drama of signification, too, the SKT is a work of mediation. As we have seen, Ken Tambuhan may be regarded as a signifier-errant who, in a circular movement of exile and return, connects two orders of signification. She is temporarily exiled from a state of transparent identity, in which her meaning is fixed and is a matter of commemoration by formulaic repetition, into a state of opacity, alienation and forgetfulness.

In her initial state of identity as the princess of Daha the heroine is a signifier bound to the signified of the Book of the Malay *Kerajaan* Order which supervises and fixes its meaning. The princess is a princess; the sign coincides with meaning. In this state of identity, propriety (*patut*) and representation reign. The meaning of the heroine is self-evident. She can be simply understood as an invocation, commemoration, representation of origin, as a grounded repetition (*mengadakan*).

By a change in fortune and a form of amnesia, she is made to fall out of this joyful world of clear meaning, to be temporarily turned into a signifier-errant whose meaning has been set adrift and is a matter for interpretation and conjecture. In this state there is an improper disjunction of sign and meaning; although apparently a mere lady-in-waiting and daughter of an obscure king of Tanjungpuri, Ken Tambuhan acts and looks like a princess of the highest birth. In this state of alienation and forgetfulness the invocation and commemoration of origin is problematized. Representation is temporarily disrupted by a proliferation of meaning (*memanjangkan*) in a play of semblance (*mengada-ada*) and reality (*mengadakan*).

The central interest of the Malays in the SKT must undoubtedly have lain in the story about Ken Tambuhan's exile and signifier-errantry, because it allows a temporary carnivalesque freedom from the compulsion of the serious monological Voice of communally accepted Truth by its playful disruption of communal repetition and its thematization of individual interpretation. Ultimately, however, the SKT restores identity and returns to the proper order prescribed by the Book of the Malay *Kerajaan* Order and to representation. Thus the SKT both confirms and denies the feasibility of invoking and commemorating origin and both confirms and denies the power of language to represent, another instance of the poem's mediatory dialogical nature.

It is important to note that, paralleling the oppositions between the production of meaning by communal recall and by individual interpretation, the SKT shows two contrapoised tendencies, one towards the heroic epic and one towards the lyric. The co-presence of these two literary types is also characteristic for romance in Western mediaeval literature (Bloch 1983:174-8).

The epic strain in the SKT manifests itself insofar as the poem is a narrative of action taking place in time and space, characterized by a diminished interiority of the subject, utterance – both that of the narrator and that of his protagonists – being oratorical and public in nature. In the heroic epic all that counts is the signified, the great deeds which are recounted.

The lyric strain shows insofar as the SKT has passages of contemplative stasis, transcending the boundaries of time and place and halting the flow of the narrative. In such passages we see a fetishistic amplification of words for their own sake, as the verbs and adverbs of a narrative of action give way to a markedly nominalizing language, leading attention away from the signified to revel in the proliferation of the signifiers. Whereas, in the epic, the narrator and his characters speak as the spokesmen of their society addressing it as their audience in public speech, in the lyric the speaker's voice is that of an individual, overheard by us while uttering his personal feelings and emotions.

When a Minangkabau Malay copyist, apparently discussing Panji stories in *syair* form or animal and flower *syair* parodying this genre (for these, see Chapters VII and VIII), once remarked to Overbeck that 'a *shaer* was read not so much for the story as for the delight one experiences from witty dialogue and in finding one's own feelings, passion or self-pity well expressed' (Overbeck 1934:111), he showed a keen awareness of the importance of the lyrical aspect in romance.

In the SKT the lyrical element is indeed strongly present. All through the poem we meet it in the numerous outpourings of feelings of love, passages in which the prince tries to comfort his beloved or entice her by sweet words of endearment (*membujuk, bercumbu*). Time and again such outpourings bring the narrative of the SKT to a standstill, almost to the point of eclipsing it, so that one is indeed made to feel that the emotions of the lovers are more important than the fate that befalls them in the narrative.

A particularly fine example is the following passage, in which we may not only note the device of an ever-varied naming, but may also discern forms of repetition and parallelism that seem to be characteristic for lyric song:

> Tidaklah kakang mau bercerai / dengan adinda emas urai / adalah kakanda laksana murai / barang kemana terbang berderai // jika tuan menjadi air / kakang menjadi ikan di pasir / kata nin tiada kakanda mungkir / kasih kaka batin dan zahir // jika tuan menjadi bulan / kaka menjadi pungguk merawan / aria ningsun emas tempawan / janganlah bercerai apalah tuan // tuan laksana bunga kembang / kakanda menjadi seekor kumbang / tuanlah memberi kakanda bimbang / tiadalah kasihan tuan akan abang // jika tuan menjadi kayu yang rampak / kakanda menjadi seekor merak / tiadalah mau kakanda berjarak / seketika pun tiada dapat bergerak // dewa susunan emas juita / tangkai hati cahaya mata / sayangnya terbuang air mata / harganya seimbang badan beta. (SKT III, 74-9.)

> ('I will not part from you ever again, / my little sister, my precious golddust. / I am like the fork-tailed robin, / that flies everywhere with a whirring sound. // If you, my lady, turn into the waters, / I will turn into the fish that rests on the sandy riverbed. / I swear I will never go back on these words / I love you with all my body and soul. // If you, my lady, turn into the moon, / I will turn into the moping owl. / My sweet little sister, my precious gold, / my lady, please, never part from me. // If you, my lady, are like the flower in bloom, I will turn into the bumble bee. / You, my lady, are the source of my anxiety. / Will you not take pity on me? // If you, my lady, turn into the shady tree, / I will turn into the strutting peacock. / I will not even take one step away from you. / Not for a moment can I stir from here. // My goddess and queen, my precious gold, / artery of my heart, light of my eyes, / what a pity you have wasted all those precious tears, / which I value as much as I would my own life.']

6. *The SKT and the generic plot of the Panji romance*

Now that I have discussed the characteristics of the SKT as a work of the genre of the Panji romance, the question remains whether these characteristics are indeed typical of this genre. If the Middle Javanese poem *Wang-*

bang Wideya, as the oldest Panji story we have, may be considered as a representative sample of the genre, as has been suggested by Robson, the answer must be affirmative. The story of this poem may be rendered as follows:

> The princess of Daha, whose beauty is like that of the heavenly nymph Suprabha, has been betrothed to the prince of Kuripan, Raden Makaradwaya, whose beauty is like that of Arjuna, but two months before their marriage is due to take place the princess disappears. She is found in the forest by the prince of Kembang Kuning, who takes her back to Daha. Because Raden Makaradwaya has meanwhile become infatuated with another princess, the king of Daha marries his daughter to the prince of Kembang Kuning, but she refuses to allow him to consummate their union. Hearing of the marriage, the prince of Kuripan is furious. He goes to Daha in disguise and, pretending to be a person of low status, born of the union between a man of the highest caste, the brahmanas, and a peasant woman of the *wesia* caste, he calls himself Wangbang Wideya and establishes himself at its court with the rank of *pangalasan*, a minor official. There the prince demonstrates his superiority in the arts (canto 1); defeats the king of Lasem who attacks Daha because he desires to possess the princess (canto 2); refuses the gift of women offered him by the king of Daha as a reward; shames the king of Daha and the prince of Kembang Kuning by his superior mastery of the arts, carries off the princess and unites with her in the bedroom. At last he reveals his identity, marries her, and finally all are reconciled.

Within the scope of this chapter I cannot present a detailed examination of the validity of my characterization of the Panji story for *Wangbang Wideya*. Leaving that to the diligence and ingenuity of the interested reader, I shall limit myself to discussing only one important shared feature, the most important one, because in my view it forms the structural core of the genre: that the hero of the Panji story is typically involved in a movement of return from exile and false identity, which is effected through acts of mimesis of kingly behaviour.

Whereas in the SKT the exile and loss of status of the protagonist is effected by an outside force, in *Wangbang Wideya* it is brought about by a wilful act of the protagonist himself. But whatever superficial differences there may be between the SKT and *Wangbang Wideya* in the way in which the narrator gets his story under way and works it out in detail, once we have grasped that the return from exile and false identity through acts commemorating kingly behaviour forms the structural core of the Panji story, it is not difficult to see that as actants Ken Tambuhan and Raden Makaradwaya structurally play the same role and go through the same plot.[4]

---

[4] In Propp's role-oriented analysis, each character is defined by a 'sphere of action'; according to him certain actions and only these are appropriate to a particular character. Reinterpreting Propp, the French structuralist Greimas (1966) has developed an actantial model, which defines 6 actantial roles in their mutual relation, that of *sujet*, *objet*, *destinateur*, *destinataire*, *adjuvant* and *opposant*. Dolezel, finding Greimas' system too limited, in 1972 proposed a more open system of characteraction configurations (Wittig 1978:200).

Robson has already suggested that the Panji stories are transformations of the same generic plot, when he pointed out that they do not form links in a chain making up a cycle, but that each one is a rounded story in itself. 'Each story', Robson says, 'appears to contain the same (or a very similar) *nucleus* of plot, embroidered with narrative detail in varying amounts and of varying content, thus giving rise to the different titles bestowed on the various works' (Robson 1969:11).

But what about the 'Angreni-motif', the episode of Panji's first love, who has to die to make way for his destined bride, Raden Galuh? Is that not a feature in which the SKT differs completely from *Wangbang Wideya*? My answer would be: no, it is not. Not if we realize that the 'Angreni-motif', too, is a particular surface manifestation of the deep-structural core of the Panji story: by showing unflinching courage even in the face of death, Ken Tambuhan effects yet another act of mimesis of royal behaviour, refuting her seemingly humble origin, and thus brings about her ultimate return to her true identity.

This is confirmed by a Balinese Panji story, the *Geguritan Pakang Raras*, a work showing surprising similarities with the SKT. In the *geguritan* first Raden Inu, and subsequently Galuh Candrakirana, can be seen to move through the same basic pattern of plot, which is worked out into different surface transformations. The first move is clearly a variant of the 'Angreni-motif', but with Raden Inu in the role of Angreni. Whereas in the first move Raden Inu is the main protagonist and signifier-errant to be interpreted, in the second one it is Raden Galuh who plays this role, as appears from the following summary:

> Raden Inu of Jenggala [Kuripan], handsome as the god of Love, dreams that the goddess Ratih has come. While hunting in the forest to assuage his desire, he is overtaken by a storm which carries him to the pleasure gardens of Daha. There he changes into the clothes of a commoner in order not to be recognized. When he meets Raden Galuh, whose beauty is like that of the nymph Suprabha, he pretends not to know whence he hails and tells her that he lost his way in the forest during a storm, while accompanying his mother, a humble peddlar of wares.
>
> Under the name of Pakang Raras, Inu is adopted as the brother of Raden Galuh and assigned quarters in the palace. He teaches Raden Galuh to play the gender, instructing her among other accomplishments to sing the episode from Arjunawiwaha about the espionage mission of Suprabha and Arjuna to defeat the demon king. This only makes them all the more enamoured of each other and finally, protesting his love and everlasting faithfulness, he unites with her in the bedroom.
>
> When the king hears of the illicit affair from a lady-in-waiting, he summons Pakang Raras to the palace and orders him to accompany the *patih* to the region of Pajarakan, ostensibly to restore order there, but in reality to be killed there by his companion. Aware that he is to be killed, Pakang Raras persuades the *patih* to kill and bury him in the graveyard of Daha. When the *patih* asks him about his real identity, he tells him that his blood will provide the answer; if it has a foul smell he is a mere commoner (*sudra*), but if it has a sweet odour he is a nobleman (*menak*).

When Pakang Raras is stabbed, his blood smells sweet, rain begins to drizzle, thunder rumbles, a rainbow appears and the earth trembles, a sign that a royal person has died. Guided by a voice from heaven Raden Menteri's servants find his corpse, and on the orders of Shiwa a white crow revives him.

From a farewell letter left by Pakang Raras, Raden Galuh learns that he is in reality Raden Inu. When she learns that her love for Pakang Raras has been betrayed to the king, she leaves Daha in anger to roam the forest of Jenggala. There she meets a man, De Bekung, and his wife, who are of lowly birth and poor, making a living by burning lime and peddling it. She tells the couple, who are struck by her great beauty, that she does not remember who her parents are and that she has lost her way in the forest.

They take the girl home to look after her. Meanwhile Raden Inu's return to Jenggala is celebrated with much rejoicing. To make amends to the gods for his not fulfilling his vows upon the birth of his son, the king has the appropriate ceremonies performed. On behalf of Raden Inu, the Arya Demang is sent to Daha to ask for the hand of Raden Galuh. There he hears that she has disappeared. When the king of Daha learns from one of Arya Demang's men that Raden Inu is the same person as the Pakang Raras he had killed he offers his apologies. Back in Jenggala, the Arya Demang reports the disappearance of Raden Galuh.

While hunting in the forest Raden Inu happens to come to the house of De Bekung. Meeting Raden Galuh and her servant outside, he immediately has the feeling that she must be his beloved. When he asks her who she is she does not answer. Her servant tells the disbelieving prince that she is a mere commoner and palace servant. When he has heard from De Bekung that she was found by him in the forest, he makes himself known to her as Raden Inu, and tells her how he was killed by the *patih* of Daha on her father's orders.

When the king of Jenggala hears that Raden Galuh has been found, he orders preparations to be made for the wedding. Hearing that his daughter has been found, the king of Daha is overjoyed. Accompanied by the queen, he travels thither to take part in the festivities, together with many other kings. After the wedding the rulers all return to their kingdoms.[5]

It would fall outside the aim and scope of my book to try and trace the manifold ways in which the basic plot of the Panji story and its actantial scheme could be concretely worked out; the treatment of such a subject – a very worthwhile line of inquiry – would require a separate monograph.[6] What is clear is that basically the author of a Panji story had two options to choose from: one was to emphasize its epic strain, the other to opt for its lyrical potential. The choice made decided the devices that were to be used.

If the author chose for the epic strain, as happened in Panji stories in prose such as the *Hikayat Cekel Wanengpati* (Rassers 1922) and the *Hikayat Misa Taman Jayeng Kusuma* (Abdul Rahman Kaeh 1976), and decided to produce a narrative packed with adventures and battles, it meant that he

---

[5] I made this summary of the *Geguritan Pakang Raras* on the basis of the summary published in Baroroh Baried et al (1987:92-105).
[6] A fine model for a monograph of this kind is provided by Wittig (1978), in the form of a detailed structuralist study of the genre of the Middle English Verse Romance on the basis of a large corpus.

would have to let his hero and heroine roam all over the Javanese world, as they both, simultaneously or one after another, went through the generic plot of imposed or self-imposed exile and loss of identity followed by a return through acts recalling their true status as persons of noble birth.

The authors of the SKT and the *Geguritan Pakang Raras* – to be sure, with different degrees of emphasis – chose to write a lyrical Panji story, which made it necessary to limit the geographical setting to the adjacent kingdoms of Kuripan (Jenggala) and Daha. And it seems likely that they chose to set it forth in verse which was sung rather than in prose, because this device seemed to suit this artistic aim better.

CHAPTER VII

A fishy story
Exercises in reading the Syair Ikan Terubuk

1. Scholarly lore about the SIT and intertextuality

In a first reading the Malay *Syair Ikan Terubuk* (henceforth SIT), or Poem of the Terubuk-fish, will hardly impress one as a text that deserves the attention of the literary connoisseur. Probably most Western readers would once again find their feelings on *syair* in general confirmed. As Blagden so bluntly expressed it: 'To the Western mind they (*syair*) are an intolerable bore' (Blagden 1913:101). And Winstedt's remark about short *syair* seems fully justifiable: 'Few of the short sha'ir have literary merit, being to European taste at any rate monotonous in theme and rhymes. The Sha'ir Ikan Terobok dan Puyu-Puyu, the verses on the Shad and the Climbing Perch, are among the cleverer and less trite.' (Winstedt 1977:193.)

In the nineteenth century *syair* were very popular among the Malays (Wilkinson 1913:87). The fact that the SIT must have been popular may be concluded from the great numbers of manuscripts and lithographs of it. These all hail from the Riau area and Singapore. Differences between the various texts are considerable, and upon closer examination they may lead to interesting differences in effects and, accordingly, in interpretations. The Malay scribal tradition of the nineteenth century had a great deal of flexibility and each copying is a moment that deserves attention in its own right. That is why in this chapter, in which I present a reading of the SIT,[1] I will restrict myself to an interpretation of only one manuscript, Von de Wall 242,[2] which is preserved in the manuscript collection of the Museum Pusat

---
[1] This chapter is a revised version of a paper I wrote jointly with H.M.J. Maier for the Fourth European Colloquium on Malay and Indonesian Studies at Leiden in 1983 (Maier and Koster 1986).
[2] From the findings of Meijer (1984:5-8) it appears that most of these manuscripts, the one I use included, date from the mid-19th century. Comparing ten variants of the SIT available in eight manuscripts and two lithographs, Meijer has discerned three versions, without, however, being able to indicate an original manuscript by means of the construction of a stemma. He did not publish the manuscript I use for my reading, manuscript Von de Wall 242 (Van Ronkel 1909:356) of which a transcription has been published in *Antologi* (1980:156-66). He decided not to do so because in his view this manuscript owing to its many textual differences was not representative for the variant of the SIT under which he classed it (Meijer 1984:15-6).

in Jakarta (*Antologi* 1980:156-66). To begin with, I offer a synopsis of this version.

> In the waters of the Straits of Malacca there lives a prince, the Terubuk-fish, passing his days in sad longing for a beautiful princess, the Puyu-puyu-fish, who dwells in a pool near Tanjung Padang. Eventually the prince can no longer bear his feelings of lovelorn longing and he summons his ministers for advice. He implores them to help him to take her by force – if they do not, he will go to Ceylon. Each of his fish-ministers, each even more formidable than the other, makes his pledge of willingness to give his life in fighting for his ruler. The council closes after some warnings that an attack on Tanjung Padang may fail.
>
> Meanwhile, Princess Puyu-puyu sits on her throne in the pool, full of fear about possible dangers, a fear which all too soon is vindicated: the eel, who has attended the council of Prince Terubuk, comes to warn her that an attack is impending. The princess summons her ladies-in-waiting for a council in which some of them pledge their willingness to give their lives in resisting the imminent attack, whereas others show rather less courage and fighting spirit. Princess Puyu-puyu confesses herself not to be unwilling to give in to Prince Terubuk, but it would be an impossible union, she remarks: his state lies in the sea and her own state on the land. As she sits down in despair and indecision, the council gradually gets out of control. Her insignia-bearers and their colleagues arrive at the council and start pledging their willingness to sacrifice their lives in battle for the princess, but then the Sebahan-fish, taking pity on the princess, tells her not to trust in these pledges of her friends and servants but to ask God for help instead.
>
> Following this advice, the princess starts to pray and soon her prayers are heard: in a rain-storm, amidst flashes of lightning, the ancestors descend from Heaven bringing a Pulai-tree from Tanjung Balai to the pool, and the princess jumps to safety in its top.
>
> Meanwhile Prince Terubuk, no longer able to suppress his longing, has collected his warriors, and has set out for the pool at Tanjung Padang at the rear of his armada. The Pari-fish, who has been sent ahead to reconnoitre, discovers that Princess Puyu-puyu is gone: he is told that she is in Heaven. On hearing this, Prince Terubuk returns in despair, and consoles himself with another fish, a whale.

Thus one could summarize the SIT. Western readers, like Klinkert, Wilkinson, Winstedt and Hooykaas, have never been able to make much sense of this *syair*. Even Overbeck, no doubt a most perceptive reader of Malay literature, did not know how to interpret it. He, too, had to confess that for him the story was 'curious and partly obscure' (Overbeck 1934:117). Is it just a silly, trivial story about two fish who could not get each other because they were not destined for each other? Is it nothing but another amusing story of boy-cannot-get-girl? Was this *syair* written only to soothe the lovelorn feelings of readers and listeners? Or was it to serve some more serious purpose?

In a desperate attempt to give the *syair* some coherent interpretation Klinkert proposed the following reading: 'The whole seems to be a skit on a marriage proposal by one of the rulers of Malacca that is mentioned in the *Sejarah Melayu*' (Klinkert 1868:370).

Both Winstedt (1977:193) and Hooykaas (1947:73-5) simply took over the interpretation Klinkert offered – as scholarship so often does –, and so did Liaw Yock Fang (Liaw 1975:302) and the *Antologi* (1980:10). The only commentator who did not just repeat this learned opinion was the amateur Overbeck: looking for the corresponding passage in the *Sejarah Melayu* texts available to him, he remarked that he could not find any such passage. Neither can I.

Klinkert's attempt at interpreting the SIT is a fine demonstration of intertextuality, the most vital principle of writing and reading alike – texts are always written and read in terms of texts with which both reader and writer are familiar, and they are made meaningful against the background of this familiarity.

Of course Klinkert was not the only Malayist who has – albeit implicitly – made use of intertextuality: any scholar had to relate the SIT to some other texts to make it meaningful; just like any reader, no matter which text he is reading, has to relate it to other texts to make sense of it. Overbeck, for instance, approached the SIT as an example of the group of Malay animal and flower *syair*; the *Antologi* classified it as an example of a symbolic *syair*; Winstedt labelled it an erotic and didactic *syair*, and Wilkinson (1913:87) saw in it a work that discussed Malay theology. These classifications are certainly not without their uses; the isolation of a corpus of Malay texts which share certain formal features was necessarily followed by a second step in which they were classified according to themes that could be imposed upon them. In each of these thematizations a certain feature was foregrounded – and thus a pervasive interpretation of the SIT seemed guaranteed.

The SIT does indeed deal with animals, as Overbeck claimed: it is a story full of fishes – shoals of them. Overbeck goes even further than this. 'The stories contained in the Malay animal and flower shairs are based on real incidents', he wrote (Overbeck 1934:108). This could have been a rewarding line for interpretation, but unfortunately nobody ever examined this more deeply. For some reason it was taken up again in the introduction of the *Antologi*. Here another quality of the SIT is foregrounded: its symbolic quality – the SIT should be read as an allusion (*sindiran*), and as such it is an example of the symbolic *syair* that were written in the form of symbols and metaphors (*perlambangan dan kiasan*) for some political, financial or romantic affair (*Antologi* 1980:7-8). The didactic qualities of the SIT could be foregrounded in an interpretation, as well, as Winstedt did. And even Wilkinson's suggestion that the SIT should be interpreted in religious terms – a remark which he seems to have made in a weak moment – could be worked out: only by prayers to Allah and the ancestors can we find our way out of our problems.

In the following I propose other reading possibilities. In an effort to break the transmission of learned lore about the SIT, I went to the text itself for a systematic reading in which I cast my net of intertextuality as far as I could: I used both Western texts and Malay ones – as other readers before me have also done.

Now, as Culler has pointed out (1981:100-18), intertextuality is a diffuse concept; in one way or another we have to order our familiarity with texts in order to make it operational. I propose to discriminate between generic intertextuality, in which a particular text is made meaningful on the basis of a set of norms thought to inform a group of texts, and specific intertextuality, in which reading and writing take one or more specific texts as a starting-point for the production of meaning. Both types of intertextuality occur in any literary system but it is obvious that generic intertextuality is dominant in a literary tradition like the Malay one in which variation on existing formulas, narrative patterns, and themes is stronger than the invention of new ones.

A reader who is a little more familiar with the *topoi* and devices of Malay literature will be struck by the amount of this variation as soon as he starts out to read the SIT more carefully.

2. Confirmations and frustrations: heroic epic or romance?

The first experience of *déjà-lu, déjà-vu* presents itself at the very beginning, in the initial situation of the lovelorn hero, pining away (*rindu*) after having set eyes on his beloved:

> Duduk merawan siang dan malam / terkenangkan puteri didalam kolam (SIT 2r1).
>
> (He sat down full of melancholy day and night, / his thoughts filled with the princess in her pool.)

This scene reminds us irresistibly of the beginning of *syair* such as the *Sair Buah-Buahan* (Poem of the Fruits), *Syair Bunga Air Mawar* (Poem of the Rose), *Syair Kumbang dan Melati* (Poem of the Beetle and the Jasmine Flower), *Syair Burung Pungguk* (Poem of the Moping Owl). These all start with a similar description of *rindu* (lovelorn longing). And the subsequent scene, in which Prince Terubuk requests his ministers to mediate (*tolong*), will bring to mind the *penolong* (helper, mediator) who also plays such an important role in these *syair*.

The reader will have another experience of *déjà-lu, déjà-vu* when he notices that the request for mediation is made in what he gradually realizes is a council of war: the vassals of the ruler pledge their willingness to give their lives for their ruler in battle, a scene that we have already come across many times in reading heroic epics such as the *Syair Perang Mengkasar* (Poem of the Macassar War), *Syair Perang Menteng* (Poem of the War with

Muntinghe), *Syair Sultan Maulana* (Poem of My Lord the Sultan), and *Syair Perang Siak* (Poem of the Siak War). In the course of this council we come across a reference to the unsuccessful attack of the swordfish on Singapura, a story with which we are familiar from other Malay historical texts, such as the *Sejarah Melayu*. Here the story is told to warn Prince Terubuk not to launch an attack on the Pool of Princess Puyu-puyu at Tanjung Padang.

The council of war of Prince Terubuk – a rather unusual one as it ends with these warnings – is duly followed by its counterpart: the council of war of Princess Puyu-puyu, which turns out to be even more unusual than that of Prince Terubuk. The royal servants certainly do not show a very warlike spirit; and, halfway through the council, the leech (*lintah*) disturbs the dignified atmosphere of the proceedings by starting to dance and to sing erotic *pantun*, which brings the reader back to the abovementioned texts on lovelorn animals and flowers, in which the exchange of *pantun* is an essential feature. The dignified atmosphere is restored when the insignia-bearers (*bintara*) enter the council and pledge their resolute willingness to fight – once again we are in a work like the *Syair Perang Mengkasar*. The encouraging effect of these pledges is, however, spoilt again all too soon, this time by the words of the Sebahan-fish:

> Sekaliannya cakap tidak berguna / tuanku juga akan terkena (SIT 9v 8)
>
> ('All these pledges are of no use;/ you, my lady, too, will get hurt.')

The princess is advised to pray instead of preparing for war so that Allah and the *sangyang dewata* (the gods) can help her. It is a strange prayer indeed: not only is Allah called upon, but so are the ancestors and the gods – an unusual combination. Ultimately it proves to be the ancestors who here, at this crucial moment, play the role of the *penolong*. They send down a tree, and thus help Princess Puyu-puyu to escape from both the *rindu* and the attack of Prince Terubuk.

The clash that the reader of epic has learned to expect does not materialize. The only thing that does take place as it should is the council of war – albeit a short one without pledges. Prince Terubuk decides not to wait any longer and to have his ships prepared, a scene which is duly followed by that of his army on its swim to battle. The outcome is a disappointment, not only for Prince Terubuk but also for the reader: the battle-scene does not materialize as expected, the vassals are not able to back up their pledges with deeds, and, moreover, the *rindu* of Prince Terubuk is not fulfilled either.

Towards the end of the SIT the reader is led back to the initial situation: again the prince sits down in lovelorn longing. A new move sets in: the prince sets his eye on the Gelasa-fish and, experienced as he is in the handling of love-potions, he manages to become friends with her – only to find that his heart cannot forget his beloved Princess Puyu-puyu. And for the third time the reader finds himself back at the initial situation: once more the prince sits down in sadness. This time he manages to console himself with, of all fishes, a whale – and they lived happily ever after (*leka bergaul bersuka ria*, SIT 11v 4d).

Above I have given a short description of the vicarious pleasures and displeasures, the confirmations and frustrations of his expectations that await the reader when he brings his more or less amorphous knowledge of Malay texts to bear on his reading of the SIT. Against the background of this diffuse intertextuality two groups of features seem to stand out: the one group centred on lovelorn longing, the other centred on loyalty to the ruler.

Accordingly, two themes may be perceived to be competing for domination in the narrative in that they both seem to offer a pervasive interpretation of the SIT. This discovery is not really surprising: within the Malay literary system there are a great number of *syair* that centre on the theme of lovelorn longing, and there are also a great number of texts that focus on the loyalty of the vassal towards his ruler. By discovering these two themes in the SIT, this *syair* can be related to two generic intertextualities, namely romance and heroic epic. In texts that are read in terms of the first genre, the theme of lovelorn longing is an all-pervasive one; in texts that are read in terms of the latter the theme of warlike heroism dominates. Connecting the SIT with these two generic intertexts offers interesting perspectives for reading.

First romance. One of its typical schemes of scenes is as follows: the hero sets eyes on a beautiful girl and sits down overwhelmed by longing until he can no longer bear it. He then calls in the help of a mediator (*penolong*) who either helps him as a *postillon d'amour* or teaches him some knowledge (*ilmu*) by which he can make the girl love-sick so that he may ultimately satisfy his longing.

This pattern is playfully parodied in animal and flower *syair*, as appears from the apt summaries of such *syair* given by the poet of the *Sair Buah-buahan* (Poem of the Fruits) in the catalogue of *syair* for rent at the end of this work. (About romance, and more specifically the Panji-story, see Chapter VI).[3]

> Pertama sair sang Capung / terbang di sawah di daun kangkung / menahan rindu tiada tertanggung / pada Balang ia minta tulung // [...] // keempat burung Bayan dan Nuri / menanggung rindu sehari-hari / Nuri meminang tiada diberi / yang menulung Tekukur jauhari. (*Antologi* 1980:86 vs. 63v 2, 63v 6.)

---

[3] For a fuller discussion of the animal and flower *syair*, and more specifically the *Sair Buah-Buahan* as parodied romance I refer to Chapter VIII, part 4. What is parodied in the SIT and the *Sair Buah-Buahan* is not the plot of romance, as it has been described in Chapter VI, but certain type-scenes and type-episodes and other characteristic motifs.

(First there is the poem of Mister Dragonfly. / He flew about in the ricefields and among the swamp spinach leaves. / He suffered unbearably from longing / and he asked the Grasshopper to mediate for him. // [...] // Fourth there is the poem of the Parakeet and the Parrot, who was torn by longing day after day. / The Parrot proposed but was turned down. / It was the Turtle-dove who mediated.)

As for the other generic intertext, the heroic epic, this genre has the following scheme of scenes: a dual set of councils of war with pledges of loyalty and willingness to go into battle by the vassals to their respective lords, and then a battle in which the vassals prove or disprove their loyalty. The courageous words of promise and boasts of the heroes are to be fulfilled in battle (about the heroic epic, see Chapter IV).

Now the SIT has some striking features of both these intertexts: the heroic epic and romance. We can read and interpret the text as a play upon both. Of course this double play develops simultaneously through the SIT, but for the sake of convenience I will describe it along separate tracks of reading. First I will show how the SIT can be read against the background of romance, then how it may be read against the background of the heroic epic.

As I already showed in my description of the sequential process of reading, the SIT starts out with an exposition of the situation of *rindu* (lovelorn longing): the prince sits down filled with longing for the girl he has seen, and then he twice calls in the help of *penolong* (helpers) (SIT 2r 7 and 2r 9). Thus the play upon the intertext of romance sets in. An inordinate amount of space is given to the description of the promises of the *penolong* – not one, not two, not three, but scores of them being described, and they turn out to be bizarre helpers at that. They are neither *postillons d'amour* who bring a message to the girl nor teachers of a special *ilmu* (magic) to win the girl's heart. Here they are presented as a bunch of swashbucklers, and the description of their boasts demands so much verbal acrobatics that the initially assumed intertext of romance almost disappears from sight: is this really romance, we start to wonder?

Only after the council of war of Prince Terubuk has ended and when the focus of the narrative has shifted to the other side, to Princess Puyu-puyu, is the attentive reader again reminded that the narrative is framed on the type-scene pattern of romance: she is described as sitting down filled with sadness, and the parallel of her situation with that of the lovelorn Prince Terubuk is formally confirmed in the verbal correspondences between the two passages:

Gundah gulana tidak ketahuan / lalulah pulang muda bangsawan / setelah sampai ke Tanjung Tuan / siang dan malam igau-igauan (SIT 1v 9) // [...] // duduk merawan siang dan malam / terkenangkan puteri di dalam kolam. (SIT 2r 1).

(He was utterly distraught with grief./ Thereupon he went back, that noble youth. / When he arrived at Tanjung Tuan / he raved day and night. // [...] // He sat down full of melancholy, / his thoughts filled with the Princess in her pool.)

> Adapun akan puteri bangsawan / sehari-hari duduk merawan / hatinya gundah tidak ketahuan / siang dan malam igau-igauan (SIT 5r 9) puteri semayam di atas tilam / terlalu gundah hati di dalam (SIT 5v 1).
>
> (As for the noble princess, / day after day she sat down sunk in melancholy. / Her heart was utterly distraught with grief. / She raved day and night. // [...] // The princess sat down on her mat. / Full of sadness was her heart. / She sat down plunged in misery day and night.)

And indeed, a *penolong* turns up, a messenger from the other side: the eel arrives to inform the princess that Prince Terubuk is coming to take her by force. But again: what a strange *penolong* this is! He is not a messenger from Prince Terubuk himself but a traitor, and he does not hold out prospects of sweet love and happiness but of calamities and battles.

The ensuing council of war at the court of Princess Puyu-puyu throws us into further confusion: the vassals who pledge their loyalty seem to be rather convincing *penolong* but then, surprisingly, they urge their Lady to succumb to the desire of Prince Terubuk, and the essence of *rindu* is effectively summarized by Princess Puyu-puyu herself:

> Puteri menyahut manis suara / sekaliannya itu benar saudara / daripada seorang baik berdua / tetapi akhirnya beta kecewa (SIT 7r 3).
>
> (The Princess answered in a sweet voice: / 'All that you say is right, my sister. / It is better to be two than to be alone, / but in the end I will be disappointed.')

The mention of *ilmu nisa* (the knowledge of the magic by which one can win a woman's love) by one of the vassals is another confirmation that we are after all reading a parody on romance, and this theme is elaborated upon by the clownish leech, who sings erotic *pantun*. Only after the leech has been literally knocked out, does the atmosphere become serious and heroic. The pledges of war become increasingly bellicose, but the debunking remarks of the Sebahan-fish – to offer battle would be useless – confuse us again. Eventually the real *penolong* appear – the ancestors – but it is not the initiator of events, Prince Terubuk, who is helped, but the object of his *rindu*, Princess Puyu-puyu – another frustration to our expectations.

The Prince's *rindu* remains unfulfilled because Princess Puyu-puyu escapes to Heaven and the ensuing attempt to free himself of his longing for her is unsuccessful. In four lines Prince Terubuk manages to accomplish what he was not able to do in scores of quatrains: by means of an effective love-potion he wins another girl, yet *rindu* persists. A third scene of longing is accordingly initiated, and this time sadness turns into happiness within two quatrains: he marries a whale and the marriage is a happy one.

Already at a very early moment in the SIT we are put on another track of reading. After the short exposition on the *rindu* and the sadness of Prince Terubuk we find a scene that reminds us of the epic – the ruler summons his ministers. The ministers come and pay homage to their lord, who smiles at seeing his *daulat* (royal power) confirmed. The scene continues as it should in an epic: the ruler asks his ministers for their opinion – *Sekarang apa bicara kita*, 'Now what is our opinion' – a key formula of the council-scene (see Skinner (1963:241b, 458d, 465b) and Goudie (1989:124c, 237d, 299d) – and poses the issue: he wants to gain the hand of the Princess Puyu-puyu. The ruler's honour is at stake and he appeals to his vassals' own sense of honour – *apalah nama tuan sekalian?*, 'What will be your reputation, gentlemen?' This emphasis on the fear of the ruler of losing his honour seems an unusual feature for a council of war: the ruler's honour should not be discussed and the loyalty of the ministers should not be questioned. And our uneasy feelings – that maybe this is not a heroic epic after all – are further confirmed by the words:

> Jika tidak adik ditolong / pergilah adik ke negeri Selong (SIT 2r 9).
>
> ('If you don't help me I will go to Ceylon.')

These are certainly not words that manifest the self-confidence of a ruler with *daulat*. At first the vassals exhaust themselves in pledges to their lord, thus trying to strengthen his confidence that he will manage to get the girl with their help, and they do this in a very orderly way: each pledge takes two quatrains of boasting. This formal regularity is broken by the words of the Siakap-fish: his words take nine quatrains and their contents correspond to this formal divergence – they do not contain a pledge of loyalty but a warning. Thus our expectations concerning how the council will proceed are confused: a vassal should not discourage his lord. The warning consists of another fishy story, namely that told in, among others, the *Sejarah Melayu* about the attack of the sword-fish on Singapore, which ended in their death, and of some wisecracking. It makes Prince Terubuk hesitant about the good outcome of his expedition, and, in spite of the exhortations of his vassals to leave right away, he prefers to postpone it: 'With this full moon I cannot go' (*purnama ini tiadalah sempat*, SIT 5r 7d). Thus the council ends in indecision, in spite of all boasts and pledges – not a very usual development in heroic epic.

Then the perspective is switched to the council of Princess Puyu-puyu. The link is made by the only fish that is able to mediate between land and sea, between fresh and salt water, that slimy creature the *belut* (the eel). When the warning of the *belut* is reported to her, the princess similarly summons her ladies to gather for a council; and it is significant for the difference in atmosphere that she calls them *kawan* (friends) and not *menteri* (ministers) or *hulubalang* (officers). The words in which the council is elaborated remind us not of the heroic epic but rather of works of romance, such as Panji stories (SIT 6r 2, 6r 3). When she asks her ladies for advice – *apalah bicara engkau belaka*, 'Now what is your opinion?' – the heroic epic resurfaces, only to disappear again in the council that follows because the princess does not show any kind of *daulat* or authority and her friends do not show much heroism either:

> Apakan daya kita nin perempuan / dimanakan kita boleh melawan (SIT 6r 9c-d).
>
> ('What can we women do about it? / How can we offer resistance?')

A picture of the council is created that is the complete opposite to the council of Prince Terubuk. Indeed it reads like an opposition between male and female: the pledges of the ladies are full of indecision and gradually turn into eroticism instead of heroism (SIT 6r 8c-d), and finally the girls even start to praise the prince as a desirable husband:

> Jikalau seperti Batara Muda / ibarat kata semuanya ada (SIT 7r 2c-d).
>
> ('A person like the young lord / has all it takes: parables and fine words.')

Is this really a heroic epic *syair*? And before the council can develop a serious mood, the leech disrupts whatever atmosphere of seriousness there is by her dancing and singing. *Pantun* and eroticism certainly do not form part of a heroic epic. With the arrival of the insignia-bearers (*bintara*) a more serious atmosphere develops: pledges of loyalty are made and the royal power of the princess is emphasized, but this demonstration of heroism is all too soon disrupted again – *sekaliannya cakap tiada berguna*, 'All their making of pledges is of no use' (SIT 9v 8c) – says the Sebahan-fish. And here our expectations that we may be reading a heroic epic collapse completely: we are not told of preparations for a battle but about prayers to the gods and Allah; we do not hear a heroic story of a bloody battle but a curious story about the climbing of a tree. On the side of Prince Terubuk appearances are kept up for a while longer. The army marches out, although not in the splendour and glory that might have been expected. Even worse than this is to follow: the heroes are unable to fulfil their pledges and boasts. The SIT cannot be read as a heroic epic after all, it is just a play on that genre.

3. Historiography and other intertexts of reality

There are a number of elements in the narrative that resist integration into the intertextualities that I have thus far used to establish order in the SIT, elements that are too precise to have narrative functionality, no matter whether we read the SIT as romance or as heroic epic. We experience these elements as stumbling-blocks. Most of them are place-names. Are they merely insignificant notations, used for constructive reasons only, to fill a rhyme or create a rhythm? Here they follow in the order of their occurrence.

VII A fishy story 209

Prince Terubuk lives in the sea of the Straits of Malacca (SIT 1v 2); Princess Puyu-puyu lives near Tanjung Padang (SIT 1v 7); the residence of Prince Terubuk is specifically located at Tanjung Tuan (SIT 1v 9); Prince Terubuk speaks about going to Ceylon (SIT 2r 9); in the pledges of loyalty to Prince Terubuk mention is made of Bukit Batu (SIT 4r 1), Bukit Pengarah (SIT 4r 3) and the sea of Mengkalis (SIT 4r 4), which are all to be attacked, and 'if our time has not yet come to die, we will only stop when we are in Siak' (*Jika belum ajalkan mati / ke tanah Siak tempat berhenti*, SIT 4r 5); Tanjung Tuan is mentioned again as a place of residence of Prince Terubuk (SIT 6r 6); Tanjung Balai is the place from where the tree that serves Princess Puyu-puyu as an escape route descends (SIT 10v 1); in the attack of the fleet of Prince Terubuk his people are said to have reached Teluk Pedada (SIT 10v 7); and finally Prince Terubuk reaches Tanjung Padang to find Princess Puyu-puyu gone (SIT 11r 1).

Apart from Ceylon, and apart from Malacca and Tanjung Tuan (both of which lie on the Peninsula), all these place-names can be located in the Siak area. Obviously Prince Terubuk is associated with the Peninsula and the Princess Puyu-puyu with Siak, and we could read the attack of the Prince as presented in the SIT as an opposition between the Peninsula and the East Coast of Sumatra, or more specifically as referring to an attack by someone who lived in Malacca or Selangor on someone living in Siak.

Now, is it possible to connect this fishy story of attack and war with the theme of lovelorn longing? And is it possible to specify this war? As is so often the case, the most stubborn stumblingblock offers a clue: the mention of Ceylon. At the start of his council Prince Terubuk says: 'If you do not help me, I will go to Ceylon', *Jika tidak adik ditolong / pergilah adik ke negeri Selong*, SIT 2r 9c-d), and this sentence can be connected with a passage in the *Sejarah Melayu* (Genealogy of the Malay Rulers) of the royal house of Siak, (Cod.Or. 7304, henceforth SMS). The SMS[4] is a genealogical chronicle starting as a version of the *Sejarah Melayu*, which subsequently turns into a history of the royal house of Siak to culminate in the reign of one of its exiled descendants, Raja Akil, as sultan of Sukadana (1827-1849) (Goudie 1989:36; Roolvink 1967:309).[5] Here we have a case of the specific intertextuality that we can use alongside generic intertextuality for the production of meaning:

> Dan kepada sehari-hari berperang juga sampai enam bulan, negeri Siak tiada juga alah. Dan dua kali mengambil serdadu ke Melaka. Dan kapitan kapal pun terlalu marah kepada Yamtuan Raja Alam: 'Dan Tuan Raja dibilang negeri Siak boleh diambil tiga jam kerana rajanya kanak-kanak kecil, akan sekarang kita lihat rupa perangnya seperti orang yang biasa lagi berani, dan jikalau tiada juga alah hari

---

[4] All quotations from the SMS are from the edition by Muhammad Yusoff Hashim (1992).
[5] For details about the SMS, see Chapter V, note 13.

esok, mesti Tuan Raja kita hantarkan ke Sailong'. Dan bagindapun tersenyum. Kata baginda: 'Jikalau kita hantarkan ke Sailong ini kapal tiada juga sampai di Sailong'. [...] Hatta baginda [Ismail] sampai di Pelalawan maka Yang Dipertuan minta perahu kepada Maharaja lalu baginda keluar ke Riau dan akan negeri Siak pun alah. [...] Dan Yamtuan Raja Alam pun masuk ke dalam kota. (SMS in Muhammad Yusoff Hashim 1992:154-5, fol. 473-5.)

(And every day they fought until six whole months had passed, but still Siak did not suffer defeat. And twice they went to bring soldiers from Malaka, and the captain of the ship was very angry with His Highness Raja Alam: 'And Your Highness said that Siak could be taken in three hours because its raja was only a small child! But now we see that the way they fight is like that of people who are battle-hardened and full of courage. And if they do not suffer defeat tomorrow, we will have to take Your Highness to Ceylon!' And His Majesty smiled, and said: 'If we are taken to Ceylon, this ship surely will not make it to Ceylon'. [...] Then His Majesty [Ismail] arrived at Pelalawan and His Highness requested a ship from the Maharaja and thereupon His Majesty set out and sailed to Riau and Siak surrendered. [...] And His Highness Raja Alam entered the capital.)

In short, Raja Alam is threatened by the Dutch with exile to Ceylon if he does not immediately see to it that Siak surrenders to them. Yet more information from the SMS is necessary to understand this passage. The Dutch in Malacca had sent an expedition to Siak to take revenge for the Pulau Guntung massacre in which a garrison of the VOC had been killed by Siak troops. From another specific intertext with which historians are more familiar, namely Netscher (1870), we know that this expedition took place in 1761.

During the preparation for this expedition the Dutch had contacted Raja Alam who was all too willing to help them: he saw a chance to regain the throne of Siak that he had lost to his stepbrother Muhammad who had subsequently forced him into exile. Alam married a sister of the famous Buginese Daeng Kamboja who resided in Selangor, and while he roamed the Straits of Malacca Sultan Muhammad of Siak died and was succeeded by his young and inexperienced son Ismail. Raja Alam allied himself with the Dutch in order to drive this Ismail out of Siak. Pressed by the Dutch threat of being banished to Ceylon if Siak did not surrender to them, he managed to bring about its capitulation, and Ismail had to flee into exile.

The most stubborn stumbling-block in the SIT – Prince Terubuk's reference to his having to go to Ceylon if his men do not help him to get Princess Puyu-puyu – puts us on the track of the SMS. And the relation with this specific intertext opens up the possibility of another interpretation of the SIT: Prince Terubuk could be identified with Raja Alam, Princess Puyu-puyu could be identified with Sultan Ismail – and the SIT would be concerned with the story of how Raja Alam attacked Siak and managed to drive Sultan Ismail out. The case for this interpretation of the SIT is further strengthened by a number of elements that can be made meaningful through the specific intertextual relations with the SMS as well as through other specific intertextual relations that corroborate this interpretation, namely with the *Syair Perang Siak* (Goudie 1989, henceforth SPS)6 in which the war in Siak between Raja Alam and Sultan Ismail is also extensively described.

In the SIT Princess Puyu-puyu is presented as an indecisive creature – and so is the Sultan Ismail of the SMS, who must be persuaded by a vassal to offer resistance and not to yield the throne of Siak to his uncle when he is attacked (SMS in Muhammad Yusoff Hashim 1992:153-4, fol. 475-6). The attack of Prince Terubuk is pictured as coming through the sea of Mengkalis, near Bukit Batu (SIT 4r 1, 4r 4) – as did the attack of the Dutch and Raja Alam in the SMS and the SPS. Princess Puyu-puyu escapes unharmed – just like Sultan Ismail in the SMS (Muhammad Yusoff Hashim 1992:155-6, fol. 475-6) and SPS (509-20).

In her despair Princess Puyu-puyu is presented as *duduk berpangku* (SIT 2r 6, 'sitting on the lap') and as *semayam dipangku* (SIT 8v 1, 'residing on the lap'), – which tallies with the description given in the SPS of the youthful Sultan Ismail:

> Tiang kerajaan duli tuanku / ayahanda dan kakanda kedua memangku (SPS 232c-d).
>
> (His Royal Majesty, pillar of the realm, / nursed on their laps by his uncle and cousin.)
>
> Tiada berapa kerajaan baginda / dipangku oleh ayahanda dan kakanda (SPS 233a-b).
>
> (The realm of His Majesty had not for long / been nursed on their laps by his uncle and cousin.)

Thus, there are indications enough for the SIT to be read as a narrative that alludes to the war fought between Alam and Ismail for the throne of Siak.

In this light, the SIT reads like a satire. What is remarkable in its presentation of the war is the even-handed way in which this satire is directed at both parties and this seems to tie in very well with the detached way in which this conflict is presented in a text like the SPS.

What both texts have in common is the marginal role that is attributed to the Dutch: the conflict is an internal one of the House of Siak. In the SPS the neutrality of perspective lends a tragic colour to the events described: the conflict has a certain inevitability, it is presented as a *mala petaka* (curse, SPS 82; 129; see Chapter V) brought down on the House of Siak by Allah's Will. In the parody of the Siak War in the SIT this neutrality of perspective is

---

6   The SMS also plays an important role in my reading of the *Syair Perang Siak* (Chapter V) because of its many intertextual relations with that text.

given expression in a tragicomedy: in the end no one comes out of it the better off and the councils and expedition are ridiculed.

The next thought that may occur to us is: if we may read the SIT as a satire on the war between Alam and Ismail, then why the play on schemes of action of romance? Here one may think of the fact that the Malays used the word *meminang* in a double way: it means to ask for the hand of a girl, but it also means to lay claim to an area, as appears from the SPS:

> Jikalau Wolanda datang meminang / di laut darah niat berenang (SPS 393).
>
> ('If the Dutch come and propose / we will certainly swim in a sea of blood.')

Prince Terubuk did both: he proposed a marriage to Princess Puyu-puyu, who is closely associated with land (SIT 7r 6): *Muda di laut beta di darat*, 'he is in the sea, I am on the land'. The theme of *rindu* is an ideal way of giving expression to claims of both love and land.

Yet the narratives of the SMS and the SPS do not cover completely that of the SIT, and comparison of the SIT with the narrative that Netscher has constructed of this war (Netscher 1870:111-27) leaves some of its elements unexplained: Prince Terubuk does not stay in Tanjung Padang as Raja Alam did in Siak; Princess Puyu-puyu escapes via Tanjung Balai north of Siak, whereas Sultan Ismail escaped via Pelalawan south of Siak. But, of course, such a covering is not necessary. And that the text offers us so much more, that it can lure us into so many sidetracks, is a fine proof of Malay literary genius: the SIT is a very dense texture indeed.

Even now our reading of the SIT is not yet finished. We could pose the question: why, of all animals is the *terubuk*-fish used as the hero? And again, the elements that do not exactly fit into the parodied schemes of romance or heroic epic offer us the key; the place-names give a strong hint that these warlike events can be connected with Siak. If we want to understand why this is so, another kind of specific intertexts – also intertexts of reality – may be brought into play: Western texts on the Siak area that deal with local lore and biological phenomena.

Nieuwenhuyzen (1858) tells us that *terubuk*-fishing is the most important means of livelihood in the Siak area. Gramberg (1877) speaks of organized fishing on a large scale. The key function which the *terubuk* plays in the life of the people of Siak explains why this animal was chosen to be the hero of the SIT: he is simply the most important animal, and the other fish, its congeners, are indeed its vassals. As Nieuwenhuyzen (1858:437) tells us:

> 'With the new and full moon large shoals of these [*terubuk*] fish visit the Brouwers Straits [Laut Mengkalis] and continue their trek until they reach the estuary of the Siak River, whence, after a period of three or four days, they return to the sea'.

And Gramberg (1877:304) tells us: 'Most probably they come from the northern entrance of the Straits of Malacca, whence they descend to the Brouwers Straits at regular times and in large shoals'.

The correspondences with the SIT are striking: the *terubuk*-fish is as restless as Prince Terubuk, and the Prince's attack on Siak begins through the Laut Mengkalis, just like the journey of the *terubuk*. Even the full moon mentioned by Nieuwenhuyzen tallies with the Prince's visits to the area: 'I was there at full moon', he tells his vassals in council (SIT 2r 6), and when the fleet of the Prince finally sets out, it is again full moon (SIT 10v 5).

Also, it is conceivable that the bewildering multitude of names of fish have been a little exercise in memory for the first readers and listeners of the SIT, who lived so close to the sea. And one wonders in how far the pledges of the fish and their behaviour in the SIT were in playful accordance with the associations that its one time Malay audiences had concerning the nature of these fish. The aggressive tone of the sharks (*ikan jerung, ikan yu*) has a familiar ring even for us, and for the eel (*ikan belut*), our own culture also provides a fitting ichthyological intertext: it is the ideal mediator between salt and fresh water, and it is a slimy creature, certainly not to be trusted. This fish was obviously also chosen because its name is a pun on the word *belot*, meaning to go over.[7]

Nor is it very surprising that the *puyu-puyu* fish was chosen to play the role of Princess of the fresh-water fish. It is at once a very common and a strange fish. It is able to leave the water, climbs trees in search of insects, and, just like the *terubuk*, it usually lives in shoals (Koningsberger 1915:398). Moreover, the narrative needed a fish that could escape, and this *puyu-puyu* fish was a very appropriate subject for this as well: it could climb its way out via a tree, symbol of land. Could this tree also be read as connected with the tree of life – the most radical way to stay alive that is in close contact with the immortal gods? And why was the *pulai*-tree *(Alstonia scholaris)* of all trees chosen? Skeat, basing himself on information from Siak, tells us that the *pulai*-tree is a very special tree, associated with bees – are they the insects a *puyu-puyu* is looking for? – and surrounded by magical practices. In the SIT this tree is imbued with magic, too: it is a gift from heaven that should not be chopped down (SIT 11r 8). The search for more specific intertexts on the *pulai*-tree and wax-collecting may result in more specific explanations (Skeat 1900:204-5).

The *Encyclopaedie van Nederlandsch-Indië* offers some more informa-

---

[7] In Maier and Koster (1986) it was suggested that for Malay readers of the SIT the eel must have been a disgusting animal because it was *haram* (forbidden by religion). It only rarely happens that an interpretation is disproved. Dr. Umar Junus of the University Malaya did just that in a very original and convincing manner; when I visited him in 1983 he took me to a Restoran Padang and ordered a dish of deep-fried *belut*. Does the eel stand for Alam's son Muhammad Ali or for his son-in-law Tengku Said? (See Chapter V.)

tion: the *pulai* grows in coastal areas – like Siak – and its light wood is used among other things to make floats for fishing-nets. Therefore it has a close connection with fish. Moreover it is a very high tree and, as such, a very suitable means for the *puyu-puyu* to come as close as possible to heaven (*Encyclopaedie* 1917, I:32).

In this connection the ceremonies of the *Jinjang Raja* as recorded by Gramberg are also worth noticing (Gramberg 1877:308-11). This is a woman who is called in to help when the *terubuk*-fish does not appear in the Laut Mengkalis at the appropriate time. She tries to lure them into the waters around Siak by performing rituals, first near Bukit Batu, then on the island of Bengkalis, where the god of the Terubuk is believed to have his residence. During these exercises in magic, she is generally recognized as the 'raja of Siak', a role that she keeps until she has made the necessary contacts with the spirits and the *terubuk* finally appears in shoals in the estuary of the Siak River, near Tanjung Balai. Is Princess Puyu-puyu an echo of this *Jinjang Raja*? Are her prayers an echo of the coaxing prayers of the *Jinjang Raja*? And is the shady *pulai*-tree (*rindang dengan rampaknya*) an allusion to the spells that the *Jinjang Raja* spreads over the sea near Siak, so that Prince Terubuk's armada enters the Siak estuary? That this entry would not take place without problems had already been predicted to one of Prince Terubuk's vassals in a dream (SIT 4r 2-4) and it comes true:

> rakyat sampai ke Teluk Pedada / berjenis-jenis banyak perkara (SIT 10r 7),
>
> 'The soldiers reached Teluk Pedada / many were their kinds and many their problems'.

Nieuwenhuyzen (1858:437-8) offers us yet another intertext: he tells us that, according to the local population, some beautiful sharks live on the mainland of Sumatra and that the *terubuk* pays regular visits to Siak from the north because of a passionate desire to make love with them. On finding out that this is impossible they leave again – just like Prince Terubuk.

These are mere suggestions, possibilities – the reader may relate the SIT to these specific intertexts in order to extend its interpretations; the SIT may echo these intertexts in one way or another; and no doubt there are many more stories to which the SIT can be related if we wish to elaborate the interpretations I have suggested so far, and these may even lead to interpretations which I have not been able to conceive of. The SIT, it is clear, is embedded in an intricate network of intertextualities, some threads of which we may be able to trace or reconstruct – without ever accomplishing anything like completeness or exhaustiveness.

Reading is a fragmentary activity that depends on the knowledge that we ourselves are willing and able to bring to bear on it. Reading is a pleasure that is intrinsically incomplete and pleasures may be various. Of course we cannot pretend to be Malay readers, but maybe the people of nineteenth-century Siak, on hearing or reading this *syair*, smiled and laughed for the same reasons that modern readers now do.

I want to bring in one last intertext that may perhaps help us to another interpretation not only of the shoals of fish that crowded this fishy story, but also of the occurrence of the *pulai*-tree: the leader of the Dutch expedition to Siak of 1761 to which the SIT, as we have seen, alludes, was named Jan Janszoon Visboom,[8] that is, literally translated, 'fish-tree'.

---

[8] For yet another line of reading connected with the central theme of my book – one on which I only hit after the publication of this chapter – I refer to the Introduction. Another fascinating sample of a satirical animal-fable is the *Syair Raja Tedung dan Raja Katak* (Poem of the Cobra King and the Frog King; ms. Klinkert 161, see Van Ronkel 1921:89). This poem satirizes the accommodation of the Buginese princes into the political structure of the kingdom of Johor in the first half of the 18th century. A transcription with introduction has been published as an MA thesis (Massier 1988). I also refer the interested reader to my interpretation of the *Syair Nuri* by Sultan Badaruddin of Palembang (?) as a political allegory and a nostalgic letter from exile (Koster 1996).

CHAPTER VIII

The soothing works of the seducer and their dubious fruits
Interpreting the Sair Buah-Buahan

1. Muhammad Bakir and his Sair Buah-Buahan

To write about a work that even such a usually sympathetic reader of Malay traditional texts as Hans Overbeck (1934:138-45) has dismissed as the product 'of very inferior quality' by a 'real penny-a-liner who could dash off anything required for the market' and as a text 'lacking the refinement of thought and word found in the "real" Malay shaer' is an act that stands in need of some justification. In this chapter I hope to show that the work concerned, the *Sair Buah-Buahan* (henceforth SBB) or Poem of the Fruits is not only of interest from a scholarly point of view but is an artfully contrived work of literature that bespeaks familiarity with important works and genres of the tradition.[1]

The SBB, which was published in transcription in *Antologi* (1980:37-86), consists of a main story telling about the tribulations of some fruits in a garden who are in love, and two subsidiary stories, one about the love of a faithful Chinese for his wife, and the other about two bees who teach people how to make garlands of flowers inscribed with poems. The *syair*, that was completed on 22 November 1896 (1r 1, 62r 5-62v 2), was written by a certain Muhammad Bakir, more fully named Muhammad Bakir bin Syafyan bin Usman bin Fazi (Van Ronkel 1909:28; *Antologi* 1980:196, 81r 6b), who operated a lending library at Langgar Tinggi, Kampung Pecenongan in Batavia, and who is also known to have made a living as a teacher of Koran recitation to children (*tukang ajar anak mengaji*) (Van Ronkel 1909:28). The manuscript in which the SBB is contained – a *codex unicus* that now has the inventory number ML 254 – was acquired by the Bataviaasch Genootschap at

---

[1] This chapter was first published in 1986 (Koster 1986b). I hereby particularly wish to express my gratitude to Dr Hendrarto Poesposoetjipto and his wife, Dr Shanti Sastrosatomo, for generously allowing me to enjoy the hospitality of their house at Duren Tiga, Jakarta, where, in the inspiring surroundings of a garden full of *sawo* and *jambu* trees, I wrote the first version of this chapter.

the turn of the century together with a number of other manuscripts that are of similar provenance.

Whether spurred on by financial necessity and the demands of his readers – if we may believe his words in the epilogue of the SBB he was jobless at the time he finished the Poem (63r 4c-d) – by an artistic ambition or both, Muhammad Bakir proved himself a fertile author. Other works known to be from his pen are the short *Sair Sang Kupu-Kupu dengan Kembang dan Belalang* (Poem of the Butterfly, the Flowers and the Praying Mantis), which tells of a butterfly who wilfully robs many flowers of their honey until he meets his fate in the *femme fatale* Praying Mantis (Van Ronkel 1909:354; Overbeck 1934:135-7); the two *wayang*-stories *Wayang Arjuna* (the Play of Arjuna) (1897) (Van Ronkel 1909:28-9) and *Wayang Pandu* (the Play of Pandu) (Van Ronkel 1909:22-5); and the very bulky (1800 pp.) romance with an Islamic background, *Hikayat Sultan Taburat* (Story of Sultan Taburat), a tale brimming with quests, disguises, erotic conquests and battles (Van Ronkel 1909:194-203; Overbeck 1934:145-6).[2]

Manuscript lending libraries like that of Muhammad Bakir must have played an important role in the formation of an urban readership which could support the transformation of the Malay textual system between roughly 1870 and 1920 from a dominantly oral-aural one into a modern one in which writing, reading and print prevailed (Maier 1988:101-59). Batavia had many such libraries, all in those districts that were predominantly *peranakan*-Chinese or close by them (Salmon 1981:16).

In the SBB the *peranakan*-element is conspicuously present, both on the level of the story and on that of the narration. Following Rimmon-Kenan (1983:1-5, 86-98), by story I mean the narrated events and characters, and by narration I indicate the act or process of production of the story that is perceptible in the voice of a narrator. In the story of the SBB the Chinese

---

[2] Chambert-Loir by a careful examination *in situ* of the manuscripts in the Museum Nasional at Jakarta has unearthed the rare and precious find of a corpus of 25 texts written down by the hand of one person, Muhammad Bakir, of which a dozen are his original works. As he points out, this collection is of great importance for our knowledge of Malay literary life and may provide us with insights into the Malay literary system. On the basis of scraps of evidence derived from the texts Chambert-Loir manages to piece together a considerable amount of data concerning Muhammad Bakir's life. He points out that although his family-name Fadli (Fazi) sounds somewhat Arabic, it is not, in fact, an Arab family name. According to him Muhammad Bakir's origin remains obscure: he may have been a Malay, a Javanese or even a *peranakan*-Chinese. Chambert-Loir notices that in one manuscript he signed his name in Javanese *aksara* and in one manuscript even in Chinese characters, but explains this as probably the fancy of an educated man rather than as any evidence of his origin (Chambert-Loir 1984:49-50). Chambert-Loir has generously put his still unpublished provisional transcription of the SBB at my disposal. While referring to the edition of the SBB in *Antologi* 1980 for the convenience of those readers who do not have access to Chambert-Loir's transcription, I have in fact followed the latter's transcription, in order to retain the Betawi flavour of Muhammad Bakir's language.

element appears not only in details of geographical setting such as the Chinese graveyard at Sentiong, but even in the human characters of the faithful Chinese and his wife.

In the narration the Chinese element manifests itself in the fact that the – as we shall see very garrulous – fictional narrator (*fakir*, 'this beggar'; *hamba*, 'your servant'; *saya*, 'your slave'; *pengarang*, 'the writer'; *dalang*, 'your storyteller') at times adresses his counterpart, the fictional narratees (*pembaca*, 'the reader'; *tuan*, 'dear sirs'; *kau*, 'you'), as *baba dan nona* ('*peranakan*-Chinese gentlemen and ladies').[3] Whereas the real author, Muhammad Bakir, in view of his name was probably not a *peranakan*-Chinese, his real readers may well have been mainly Chinese. Let us begin interpreting the SBB by giving a summary of its story:

Part 1
1r 1-2v 6: In the Garden Sukasari (Flower-Pleasaunce), hanging over a pool, lives Princess Grape (*anggur*), whose beauty and gentle manners far surpass those of her companions Rambutan, Sugar Apple (*serikaya*), Duku and Rose Guava (*jambu air mawar*). Her maidservants are Langsat, Kokosan and Cempedak (a type of jackfruit), a pock-marked girl with such an insolent manner and of such easy virtue that only Jackfruit (*nangka*) in the forest would make a fitting husband for her (1r 1-2v 6).

2v 6-9r 4: One day the marriageable young ladies, who have all learned to read, in order to amuse themselves (*suka*, 2v 7a) take turns reading out to each other the *Hikayat Sultan Taburat* and other stories about people in love in the days of yore (2v 3c-2v 4b), but the stories only make them more sad (*duka*, 2v 6d) and troubled by longing. In this tense atmosphere the girls now start to quarrel (3r 7-7v r): when Cempedak suggests that Sugar Apple is absent because she is afraid of Grape, Rambutan, too shy to take a turn in the reading, takes this as an insinuation aimed at herself; when Kokosan is sent with Cempedak to fetch Sugar Apple and invite her to join in the reading of the *Hikayat Raja Pandawa* (Story of the King of the Pandawas), the *Hikayat Raja Bermadewa* (Story of King Bermadewa), the *Hikayat Raden Cekel* (Story of Prince Bachelor)[4] and the many other *hikayat*, 40 in all, that Anggur may rent (6v 5c-6v 7d), Kokosan blames the fact that she has to miss

---

[3] For *fakir* in the SBB, see 1r 1a, 13v 13b, 17v 8b, 62r 7a, 62v 1a, 64r 2d. For *hamba*, see 29r 5c, 43r 2a, 61v 7a, 63v 1b. For *saya*, see 9r 4b, 9r 4c, 27v 5b, 28v 6a, 36v 2d, 36v 3c, 45v 7a, 55v 8a, 62r 4a, 62v 5a, 62v 6a, 63r 2c, 63r 3a, 63r 3b, 63r 3c, 63r 4a, 63r 4b, 63r 5a, 63r 6a. For *pengarang*, see 1r 4a, 13v 13a, 24v 1d, 25r 5a, 28v 1d, 40r 7c, 43r 3d, 43v 1c, 43v 5d, 51v 8d, 54r 5d, 54r 7a, 57v 2d, 63r 4c For *dalang*, see 33v 2c. Of course, these references need not always be taken as fictional. Thus it is hard not to take the *saya* who speaks in the instructions to the borrowers at the end of the poem as referring to the real author.
[4] The *Hikayat Raden Cekel* is probably the *Hikayat Cekel Wanengpati* (Story of Valiant Knight Bachelor).

hearing the stories on Cempedak, and a verbal exchange in saucy Batavia Malay ensues. On their return with Sugar Apple, who has dodged gossipy Custard Apple (*buah nona*) to avoid being slandered for being out alone, Cempedak scares the girls out of their wits by imitating the voice of a man at the door and is roughly scolded by Duku. Thus the girls spend their days listening to the stories of princesses enamoured of fine princes, thus hoping to comfort themselves, but really only losing their grip on their own feelings more and more (*hatinya jua akan dilibur / padahal pikiran suda melantur*, 8v 1c-d), completely forgetting all else (*sampai tiada ingat kanan kiri*, 8v 4c) under the spell of the *hikayat* (*hikayat jadi penawar*, 8v 3a) and each longing for the prince of her own dreams to appear.

9r 4-11r 2: In the Garden Dukasari (Flower-Gloom), which only the sad visit, a place so beautiful that whoever enters it feels as if he is gripped by spirits and fairies (9v 3), lives Prince Pomegranate (*delima*), an accomplished young man with all the marks of good breeding, who, though loved by men and women alike, is still unmarried. His companions are the young men Jackfruit (*nangka*), Mangosteen (*manggis*) and Langsat.

11r 2-16r 8: One night prince Pomegranate has a dream in which he sees a light, which is as beautiful as a bird with resplendent feathers (*cahaya seperti burung rupanya / bersinar-sinar bulu sayapnya*, 11r 5a-b) and which he wants to possess. Waking up from his dream with a start (*bangun*[5] *dengan terkejut*, 11r 6a) he sadly wonders what the meaning of his dream can be (*apa gerangan arti mimpinya*, 11r 8c). To soothe his anxiety (*meliburkan diri*, 11v 2c) he decides to go and shoot birds with his blowpipe (*sumpitan*, 11v 4d) in the Garden Sukasari. He dresses (*bersikap**, 11v 5b), takes his repast (*santap**, 11v 5d-12r 2d), goes on his way accompanied by his many companions (11v 5d-12r 2d) to soothe his anxieties by the hunt (*hendak diliburin pikiran ingatan*, 11v 7c) and only when he has reached the door to the Garden does he feel restored to his senses again (*setelah sampai di pintu taman / hati Delima jadi senyuman*, 12r 5a-b), and from being sad (*duka*), he becomes glad (*suka*, 12r 6a-b) again. He shoots a parrot (*nuri*) and without giving the matter any further thought (*tiada dibicarakan dahulu perkara / dengan akal budi bicara*, 12r 3c-d), he enters the garden with his companions to pursue the bird. As they proceed through the garden its beauty overwhelms them and casts its spell on them more and more. Wanting to return they are somehow loath to do so (*mau pulang rasahnya oga*, 13r 10d) and they feel as if they have forgotten how to return (*rasahnya tiada ingatkan pulang*, 13r 11b). In their pursuit of the bird they reach the house of Grape, where the bird disappears. Now they hear the voices of the girls

---

[5] The occurrence of an asterisk behind a word indicates that the word in question is a keyword in a type-scene.

reading out aloud the *Hikayat Bidasari* (Story of Lady Bidasari), the *Sair Rinum Sari* (the Poem of Rinum Sari), the *Hikayat Sultan Taburat*, the *Sair Nasihat* (the Poem of Admonition), the *Sair Kembang Merabat* (the Poem about the Creeping Flowers) and the *Hikayat Merpati Emas* (the Story about the Golden Dove[6]) (13v 5a-13v 7a), a sound like the buzzing of bees sucking honey from the flowers (*kumbang menyeri*, 13v 3b). Spying through the fence Pomegranate sets eyes on (*terpandang*, 13v 11a) Grape, Mango (*mangga*) on Rambutan, Mangosteen on Duku (13v 10-14 v8) and they are driven mad by lovelorn longing:

> Akan terpandang pada Anggur rupawan / hati Delima menjadi rawan / datang rindu suda ketahuan / menarik napas kepilu-piluan (13v 11)
>
> (When his eyes fell on the beautiful Princess Grape / the heart of Prince Pomegranate was filled with tenderness. / He realized that he had been overwhelmed by lovelorn longing; / as he drew his breath he felt sad at heart)

Mango dares to address sweet words to Rambutan who has come to see who is there spying on them through the fence:

> Mari adinda mari gusti / kakanda hendak bertemu siti / jikalau ada keridhaan hati / kakanda minta rahim yang pasti (15v 5)
>
> (Come here, younger sister, come here, my Queen. / Your older brother wants to meet your ladyship. / If it may please you to consent, / your older brother begs to be assured of your mercy)

When she sees him and his comrades she flees to report she has seen three men and the reading of the stories is stopped.

16v 1-17 v7: Pomegranate decides to return to his palace. If they hang around Grape's palace like coolies, it may provoke calumny (*fitnah*), while for them, as people of high birth, it should not be difficult to win the hand of the girls later. They return all the more filled with longing and almost out of their wits (17v 6b-c).

17v 8-19r 2: At Sukasari the girls search the garden for intruders. When none are found they return home and are not allowed to go out any more by their parents who fear someone will eat of the fruits.

19r 3-29r 6: Several years later Pomegranate passes the now deserted house (*ruma*) of Anggur and his feelings of longing return in full force. He orders Soursop to fetch Banana and requests Banana's help (*tolong*) to ask

---

[6] The *Hikayat Merpati Emas* may well refer to the *Hikayat Merpati Emas dan Merpati Perak*, dated 19 September 1887, and described in Van Ronkel (1909:174-5). The *Hikayat Bidasari*, if it ever existed, must have been a prose version of the story of Bidasari several versions of which exist in *syair*-form (see Van Hoëvell (1843), Klinkert (1886) and Tuti Munawar (1978)). Overbeck (1934:144) has suggested that the *Sair Rinom Sari* mentioned in the SBB – the *Antologi* transcribes *ribut sari* (13v 5b) – may be based on an episode from Muhammad Bakir's *Hikayat Sultan Taburat*.

for the hand of Grape (*pinang*, 20v 1c-20v 5b). Banana wisely advises him to write a respectful letter to her parents stating his wish, and Soursop delivers it at the garden. Banana negotiates the bride-price for him. They are married (*nikah*, 23v 2) at Imam Date's (Tuan Imam Kurma) house, alms are distributed, prayers are said to ward off evil and a feast (*kondangan*, 23r 4-26r 8) is held where, amidst the din of a contest for the singing of religious chants to Chinese tunes (*mengadu dikir lagu cina*, 25r 5d) accompanied by the timbrel (*rebana*), the marriageable boys (*anak jejaka*) Sawo, Jackfruit and Mangosteen set eyes on (*terpandang*, 24r 6-25r 4) the confined girls (*anak larangan*) Sugar Apple, Cempedak and Duku. After the feast, when even Imam Date has gone home with his pockets full of alms, the enamoured fruits promise each other to be always faithful to each other (*berteguh-teguhan janji dengan setia*, 26v 7a) and, as a token of this, Mango gives Rambutan a bracelet, Sawo gives Sugar Apple a ring, Jackfruit gives Cempedak a costly hairpin to stick into her bun, and Mangosteen gives Duku a shoulder-cloth (26v 4-27v 4). Grape and Pomegranate are so happy with each other that they promise to be faithful to each other forever. They pray to Allah never to separate them until their hour of destiny (*janji*) has come, and to allow them to follow each other in death (*bela*), and their prayer is heard (*kabul*) by Him (27v 5-29r 5).

29r 6-33v 4: Now lovelorn Mango, succumbing to his desires, writes a letter full of *pantun* and sweet words to Rambutan who wisely does not answer it so as not to injure her reputation. At his wit's end he lets Cucumber bring him to Maize, a white-bearded ascetic who lives in the Chinese cemetery at Sentiong. Requested to help (*tolong*, 31v 1), Maize teaches him a powerful spell (*hikmat*) by which 'what is untrammeled is enthralled and what has been forgotten is remembered again' (*barang terlepas jadi terikat / barang yang lupa jadi teringat*, 30v 1). Driven mad with longing, Rambutan now agrees to marry him. They appear before witnesses at the house of the chief of the town district (*bek*), where a ceremonial meal is eaten and they marry (*nikah*) at Imam Date's house, with prayers said by the Bilal Yam.

33v 5-35v 6: Sawo, weak and grown thin with longing, is rejected by Sugar Apple because he is poor. Hearing from Mango how Maize has helped him, Sawo, too, goes to Maize and requests him to help (*tolong*, 34v 6). Using the secret knowledge (*ilmu*) he is taught, he makes Sugar Apple mad with longing, but when she wants to meet him he feigns coolness towards her. Sugar Apple now throws herself at him, making her mother so ashamed that she quickly arranges the marriage that is again performed by Imam Date.

36v 7-36r 4: Mangosteen, though poor, is accepted as son-in-law by Duku's family because he is not only handsome but also well-behaved.

36r 5-36v 1: Cempedak is missing for seven days and nights. Has she run away? Was she dragged off by spirits and fairies? Did she follow a man from

VIII The soothing works of the seducer and their dubious fruits 223

Kampung Bali? Or was she perhaps taken along by a ropemaker? Finally she is found at Jackfruit's house and her marriage, too, is concluded.

36v 2-37r 3: The fruits, now happily married, love each other very much, most of all Grape and Pomegranate, whose prayer to God was granted and who remained a faithful pair to the end as is exemplified in the following story.

Part 2
37r 4-45v 6: A faithful Chinese (*baba setiawan*) has a dearly beloved wife who is ill and to whom he has pledged loyalty until death do them part (*suda berjanji tempo dahulunya / berteguhan janji dengan cintanya*, 40v 8a, b). In spite of all the money he spends on doctors and medicines, her health does not improve.

One day she craves for Grape and Pomegranate, who are found at last and bought at a high price by her husband at the garden Sukasari. When she eats a part of both fruits she dies. To console himself, her bereaved husband has a fine grave built, surrounded by a fence (*diperbuat hek jadi penglibur*, 41r 4c) on which beautiful flowers grow which attract many insects and birds. He instructs his neighbours that when he dies he wants to be buried next to his wife. On his grave must be planted a Cempaka, on her grave a Melati. When he returns thirsty from the grave he eats the remaining bits of Grape and Pomegranate, immediately dies to his neighbours' great surprise and is buried next to his wife as he has requested.

Part 3
45v 7-61v 7: On the graves – no one knows from where they have come – appear two beautiful beetles. The male, called Green Beetle (*kumbang hijau*), sits on the Cempaka, the female, called Lustre of the Cempaka (*seri cempaka*), sits on the Melati. During the day they suck the honey from the flowers and at night, when the moon is clear, they exchange *pantun* (*jawab menjawab*), such as (he)

> baik tuan menyiram bunga / baik siram bunga Cempaka // tuan jangan hati setenga / di mana tempat dibela jugak
>
> (It is better to water the flowers, my lady, / it is better to water the Cempaka flowers. // Do not harbour doubts, my lady; wherever it may be, I will follow you in death)

and (she)

> buat apa siram Melati / jikalau bakal pohonnya mati // buat apa cinta di hati / jikalau tiada janji yang pasti
>
> (Why water the Melati / if the shrub is destined to wither anyway? // Why cherish love in one's heart / if there are no promises one can rely on?) (52r 4, 53r 7)

and dance wildly like *ronggeng* (dancing girls), only to return to their trees when the face of the moon turns pale like that of a newly-wed.

Now it so happens that the people of that time are still ignorant of how to make garlands of flowers with fine engravings (*bunga gubahan dengan ukiran*, 55r 6b) to give to a sweet girl. To distract themselves (*melibur diri dengan pikiran*, 55v 3b) with some fun and to teach humanity this useful art, the beetles fly to the *negeri* and drop a garland in front of a craftsman (*tukang pandai*, 56r 6c) who takes it home to copy it (*tiru*, 56v 1d). Then Green Beetle makes a garland of flowers on which *pantun* are engraved that make people forget everything (*lupa pikiran lupa ingatan / melihat kumbang punya buatan*, 57r 3c-d). They fly to the *negeri*, drop one bud on the head of the princess so that she may smell it and one bud on the *raja* for him to rejoice in. When the princess reads the poems written on her flower she realizes this must be the work of Green Beetle because his name is written on it. Mad with longing (*mabuk rindu*, 60r 5b) the *raja* and the princess instigate a search for him, hoping he may perhaps become the soother of their cares (*kalaukan kumbang jadi penglibur*, 60r 4a), but he is nowhere to be found. The craftsman is now ordered to make garlands of flowers with writing engraved on them, just like Green Beetle had made them. Nowadays they are still made and sold and, when there are newly-weds, people order them and it has been like that from the beginning until now.

2. A didactic fruit-fable

Any summary is already an interpretation, a biased report by someone whose view is necessarily limited by whatever reading experience he happens to have had. In it the reporter naturally tends to foreground those elements in the text that contribute to the construction of those lines of reading which he considers feasible in the light of certain intertexts. In all reading and writing the constitutive principle is intertextuality: in order to construct or perceive meaning in a text, one necessarily falls back on one's familiarity, both conscious and unconscious, with other texts, with other encodations, with already accepted signifying practices of a culture. Only against the foil of other texts – no matter whether they are taken up, prolonged, cited, transformed or refuted – does the text one writes or reads acquire its particular meaning and thrust (Culler 1981:100-18).

One way in which we may fruitfully read the main narrative of the *syair*, Part 1, is as a didactic text, notably as a fruit-fable. In his famous *Abhandlungen über die Fabel* or Tracts about the Fable, the 18th-century German critic Lessing (1955:16) has argued that *fabulae* and *exempla* are minimal forms of narrative that are derived from sayings, proverbs and maxims and he has shown how one may create a narrative from them:

> 'The weaker usually becomes the victim of the more powerful. That is a general statement, at which I think of a whole series of other things, one of which is always stronger than the other; [...]. Now my statement goes: the marten devours the woodgrouse; the fox the marten; the wolf the fox. Devours? Maybe, too, he does not devour. That certainly is not precise enough for me. I therefore say: he devoured. And lo and behold, my statement has turned into fable.'

In the case of the SBB it is the poem itself that provides suitable proverbial intertexts. By occasional *sententia*-like comments the narrator provides the reader with a clue for how he may begin to decipher the allegory of the narrative. Thus referring to the boy-fruits he remarks:

> Kalau kurang kuat akarnya / tentu rubu akan pohonnya / pohon rubu apa jadinya / tentu tiada dapat makan buanya (17v 3).
>
> (If its roots are not strong enough / the tree will certainly fall. / If the tree falls what will become of it? / Its fruits can then certainly not be eaten.)

And about the girl-fruits he comments:

> kalau suda bua dimakan kalong / seorang tiadalah bole tolong (18v 7).
>
> (Once the fruits have been nibbled at by the fruit-bats / there is no one who can do anything for them)

The fruits may then be seen to stand for the nubile boys and girls, who must preserve their moral integrity and chastity if they hope to be an attractive marriage partner. At first, when they give in to *hawa nafsu* (animal passion), this integrity and chastity are threatened. The use of their *akal* (reason) finally saves them and they are rewarded with married bliss. By listening to this tale about these all-too-human fruits, with whom they could easily identify themselves, the (young?) public could derive useful examples and moral guidance (*mengambil ibarat*) for similar situations in their own love-life. This is also confirmed by Overbeck's observation that the Malays often cherished animal and flower *syair* as an *ars amandi* (Overbeck 1934:111, 134), as a manual of courtship.

That this is a way in which the SBB's main narrative may be read is also underlined by the comment with which the narrator closes Part 1 of the poem:

> Demikian ibarat zaman sekarang / peliharakan diri jangan sembarang-barang / biar tau pantang dan larang / sebab zaman sekarang wang kurang (36v 3).
>
> (This is its lesson for these our times: / that one must not trifle with taking care of oneself. / It makes known what is not done and prohibited, / because nowadays money is hard to come by.)

Whereas a reading as didactic fable proves quite effective in Part 1, it does not yield interesting results in Parts 2 and 3. A hint that these do not primarily lend themselves to an interpretation as didactic narrative is given by the narrator at the beginning of Part 2 when he remarks – and his remark seems to concern the entire remainder of the *syair* – that the public *bole juga iseng-iseng dengarkannya* (37r 3a) (may as well listen to it to while away the time).

3. A referential reading

Overbeck, too, noticed the importance of proverbs and sayings for deciphering the allegorical riddles that animal and flower *syair* present to the reader. He acknowledged their didactic function but emphasized that they had a topical and satirical slant. In his view, with the exception of such poems as the *Syair Unggas* (Poem of the Birds) in which birds discuss the tenets of Islam and the *Syair Pelanduk Jenaka* (Poem of the Wily Mouse-deer), the animal and flower *syair* are poems based on real incidents in which the non-human names of the chief actors often are pairs familiar from Malay *pantun* and proverbs, such as *pungguk* (the moping owl) and *bulan* (the moon); *kumbang* (the beetle) and *kembang* (the flower); *pipit* (the sparrow) and *enggang* (the hornbill); or may have been chosen from the character attributed, sometimes locally, to some animal or flower (Overbeck 1934:108). According to him, the stories in the SBB probably treat local events that were well-known at the time the *syair* was written. It is not unlikely that some of the animal and flower *syair* may indeed be read as allusions to real events, as in the case of the *Syair Ikan Terubuk* (Syair of the Terubuk-Fish) (see Chapter VII). This line of reading cannot be substantiated for the SBB, because intertextual relations with biography or historiography cannot be indicated.

Overbeck's marked preoccupation with referential readings – in fact the ruling passion of all Malayists of his generation – also shows in his strong emphasis on the mimetic potential of the animal and flower *syair*. No matter whether they were based on real incidents or only on probable ones, here at last he found a group of works that allowed glimpses of the real life and feelings of the common Malay beyond the court chronicles, fairy-tales and conventional romantic stories of princes and princesses (Overbeck 1934: 109). As for the Malay *syair* from Java, a class into which he also put the SBB, they were 'little realistic stories' that were not without points of interest (Overbeck 1934:138).

Read mimetically, against intertexts of reality (Culler 1975:140-1) such as our geographical, social and cultural knowledge of Batavia at the time of its writing, the poem undeniably does make fascinating reading: the descriptions of the reading out of *hikayat* and *syair* that once really were hired out and some of which really were written by Muhammad Bakir and can still be inspected in the Musium Nasional in Jakarta; the instructions for borrowers at the end of the poem; the rhymed catalogue of *syair* for rent with which it closes, in which some works still extant are mentioned; the descriptions of the way in which boys and girls court each other; the descriptions of marriage ceremonies; the scenes of merrymaking at the *kondangan*; the many points of geography still familiar even now, such as Sentiong, Kampung Bali and so forth, that locate the story, down to such details of social organization and hierarchy, like the role of the local authorities at the level of the *bek* neighbourhood; from the Dutch word *wijk*), or where to look for a bad girl who has eloped – all these elements, when read referentially, cooperate to effect a lively and colourful vision of what non-European Betawi society may well have been like at the end of the nineteenth century.

Yet a general mimetic reading leaves far more elements unaccounted for than it explains. What are we to do with the prince and princess and what of their ladies-in-waiting, retainers, palaces and pleasure gardens? Are we to take all these elements as references to Betawi reality? And what are we to do with those quaint fruits and beetles as protagonists?

4. Parodied romance

An intertext against which to read the SBB, more fruitful than that of historical Betawi reality as we know it, is a generic one (Culler 1975:145-8), that of the genre of the Malay animal and flower *syair*. Anyone who has read, for instance, the *Syair Bunga Air Mawar* (Poem of the Rose), the *Syair Burung Pungguk* (Poem of the Moping Owl), the *Syair Ikan Terubuk* (Poem of the Terubuk Fish), the *Syair Kumbang dan Melati* (Poem of the Beetle and the Jasmin Flower), the *Sair Sang Kupu-Kupu dengan Kembang dan Belalang* (Poem of the Butterfly, the Flower and the Grasshopper), the *Syair Nyamuk dan Lalat* (Poem of the Mosquito and the Fly) and the *Syair Nuri* (Poem of the Parrot) (*Antologi* 1980), as he or she proceeds to read through Part 1, will have an increasing sensation of having seen this all before. It will gradually dawn on him or her that the pattern of the narrative of Part 1 closely follows similar patterns in these *syair*. An apt summary of it can be found in Muhammad Bakir's description of some animal and flower *syair* for rent in his library as based on an identical scheme of type-scene:

> Pertama sair sang capung / terbang di sawah di daun kangkung / menahan rindu tiada tertanggung / pada Balang ia mintak tulung (63v 2) // [....] // keempat burung Bayan dan Nuri / menanggung rindu sehari-hari / Nuri meminang tiada diberi / yang menolong Tekukur jauhari (63v 6).

> (First there is the poem of Mister Dragonfly. / He flew about in the ricefields and among the swamp spinach leaves. / He suffered from longing, unbearably / and he

asked the Grasshopper to mediate for him. // [...] // Fourth there is the poem of the Parakeet and the Parrot, / who was torn by longing day after day. / The Parrot proposed but was turned down. / It was the Turtledove who mediated.)

This pattern, with its keywords *rindu* (to long for) and *tolong* (to mediate), is triggered off each time by the keyword *terpandang* (to set eyes on), and is repeated several times in the main narrative of the SBB.

The generic theme of these animal and flower *syair* is the effort to soothe lovelorn longing. A fundamental opposition on the basis of which this theme is developed (Lotman 1977:146, 171-2) is that important Islamic antithesis of *akal* vs *hawa nafsu*. According to Malay Muslim thought *akal*, the faculty of reason implanted by Allah into all human beings to differentiate them from other creatures, is the fundamental requirement for good, orderly and happy society to prevail.

In the pre-Islamic age (*jahiliah*), before the Divine Revelation through Muhammad had taken place, *akal* lay inert and people acted irresponsibly, from base interest and animal passion (*hawa nafsu*). The Prophet activated the dormant *akal* of his followers, awoke them from their moral sleep and made them aware (*sedar*) of their higher common interests. As long as *akal* prevails over and controls *hawa nafsu*, good community and order are guaranteed. When *hawa nafsu* gets the upperhand, chaos and strife will reign and people will only act from selfish interest caring only for their own comfort like mere beasts (Kessler 1978:221).

The main story of the SBB may be described as an effort by its protagonists to soothe their particular form of *hawa nafsu*, their lovelorn longing (*rindu*), at first unsuccessfully by giving in to the dangers of seduction, but finally successfully by allowing themselves to be guided by their *akal*. The thematic importance of *rindu* is immediately stated in the prologue when the narrator tells us that he

> mengarang sair buah-buahan / dalam kebun berhati rawan / menanggung rindu tiada tertahan (1r 4b-d).
>
> (wrote a syair about some fruits, / who, feeling dejected in their garden, / were suffering the torment of an unbearable longing.)

The transition from *hawa nafsu* to *akal*, from the confusing sadness of *rindu* to the peaceful and quiet happiness of marital bliss, takes place in a series of moves which are repeated until all the fruits are safely wed. Oppositions related to the fundamental one of *hawa nafsu* vs *akal* are: *duka* (to be sad) vs *suka* (to be happy), emblematically expressed in the names of both gardens; *lupa* (to forget) vs *ingat* (to remember); *terikat* (to be under a spell) vs *tahu pantang dan larang* (to know what is not done and prohibited); using *hikmat* (magic) and writing secret loveletters vs *pinang* and *lamar* (formally to ask for the hand of a girl); behaving like *kuli* (coolies) vs acting like *orang berbangsa* (people of noble birth), and so forth.

Once *akal* (reason) has begun to assert itself, when the boys return home to try and gain the hand of the girls by socially acceptable means, it still suffers occasional setbacks before its final triumph: Mango writes a letter full of *pantun* and sweet words to Rambutan and his *hikmat* (magic) drives her mad with longing; by the use of *hikmat* Sawo causes Serikaya to throw herself at him. The *penolong* (mediator) may be either on the side of *hawa nafsu* (animal passion), like the ascetic Maize, or on that of *akal*, like Banana. Ultimately all the fruits enter the safety of *akal* (reason) through the joys of happy marriage. Even Cempedak, a fruit that is beyond the pale of civilization (*taman*, garden), is married. In keeping with her nature she elopes with the only fruit fit to be her husband, Jackfruit in the forest (*nangka di rimba*).

What all these animal and flower *syair* have in common is that they resound with echoes of romance. Once we have noticed this, we will realize that there is, after all, one line of reading in which the seemingly discrete elements of Betawi reality in the SBB can be related. To be able to perceive it we have to turn to those same conventional tales of princes and princesses beyond which Overbeck had hoped to be able to look by means of the animal and flower *syair*. In the SBB the traces of romance are perceptible from its very beginning (about romance, and more specifically about the Panji story, also see Chapter VI).

First there is the overall narrative scheme with which the main story of the SBB begins. This scheme, that can be found in many romances, shows a very close parallel to that of a Panji-story like the *Syair Ken Tambuhan* (Poem of Lady-in-Waiting Tambuhan) edited by Teeuw (1966):

1. Once upon a time in a certain kingdom there was a nubile princess, who was of such perfect beauty that she had no rival in all the land of Java and only a prince of the noblest birth would be worthy to become her husband. Her ladies-in-waiting were Ken Such and Ken So; now one day it happened that [...] (SKT I, 3-18);

2. At that time in another kingdom there was a young and handsome prince who had all the accomplishments that a young man should have but was not yet married. His retainers were so and so; now one day it happened that [...] (SKT II, 1-7).

Within this scheme a number of motifs familiar in romance are used. One which we notice is the reading out of texts to a gathering of listeners, and the description of the emotions of tender love and passionate longing aroused by the sweet voice of the performer. An example of this from the *Hikayat Misa Taman Jayeng Kusuma* (Story of Misa Taman Jayeng Kusuma) is:

> Maka Raden Putera Negara pun [...] membaca sastra kakawin itu. Terlalu manis suaranya seperti dapat diminumkan rasanya. Gemar segala yang mendengar dia. Mangkin jauh malam mangkin baik pula merawankan hati segala yang mendengar dia. (Abdul Rahman Kaeh 1976:33.)
>
> (Then Raden Putera Negara read out [...] the text of the poem. His voice sounded very sweet, as if it could be drunk [like a sorbet]. All who listened to him delighted. The more the night drew on, he stirred up tender feelings in the hearts of all who listened to him.)

Pomegranate's dream, his shooting of birds to soothe himself and his being guided to the woman of his dreams, Grape, by a bird are also motives very much at home in Panji-stories, notably in those that tell the story of how Raden Inu happens to meet his beloved to whom he is bound by karma. Again the *Syair Ken Tambuhan* edited by Teeuw (1966) may serve as a parallel. The SBB so closely imitates the style in which this well-known episode is told that it often verbally echoes that text. Some of these verbal echoes are brought about by the fact that the SBB avails itself of a sequence of type-scenes, each framed on their own characteristic keyword, a device, that is widely used in the telling of Panji-stories. In the synopsis of the SBB and in the following comparison these keywords have been marked with an asterisk.

In the *Syair Ken Tambuhan* Raden Inu dreams that the moon falls into his lap but is immediately snatched away by a giant. Frightened by the dream (*terkejut*, SKT II, 24d), he wakes up and sadly wonders (*pikir*, SKT II, 25a; *gundah* SKT II, 25b) how his dream may be interpreted (*betapakah gerangan takbir mimpinya*, SKT II, 25c). Awake early, he takes a bath (*mandi**, SKT II, 31a) dresses (*memakai**, SKT II, 31c), takes his repast (*santap**, SKT II, 33a), takes a betelquid (*sirih**, SKT II, 33d), and, because he does not feel well on account of the dream, he decides to go and comfort himself by enjoying himself in the garden (*bermain-main ke taman*, SKT II, 35b) plucking flowers (*mengambil bunga-bungaan*, SKT II, 35c) and shooting birds with his blowpipe (*menyumpit burung*, SKT II, 35d). He goes on his way with all his retainers (*lalu berjalan** / *diiringkan* oleh segala kedayan*, SKT II, 37a-b) and only when he sets eyes on the garden with *angsoka* trees does the prince feel happy again (*serta terpandang taman angsoka* / *baharulah hati baginda nin suka*, SKT II, 50c-d). In the garden he shoots a love-bird (*serindit*, SKT III, 4b), a small blue-crowned hanging parrot) that falls down into the dense *cempaka* trees inside the walled forbidden compound where Ken Tambuhan, on the orders of the Queen, is weaving a cloth as a gift for Raden Inu's marriage. It alights on the cloth, refusing to be caught by Ken Tambuhan, and Ken Tadahan tells her that it is a messenger of love (*burung nin memberi kasmaran*, SKT III, 7d). Ignoring his retainers' warnings Raden Inu has the door to the compound opened, and setting eyes on Ken Tambuhan he falls head over heels in love with her:

VIII The soothing works of the seducer and their dubious fruits 231

> Serta terpandang hatinya berdebar / lakunya tidak lagi tersabar / arwah melayang berahi terkibar / bagai penyakit tiada tertambar (SKT III, 13).
>
> (The moment he set eyes on her his heart began to throb in his breast, / and he behaved as if he could not control himself any longer. / He felt faint and desire stirred in him / like a malady that could not be cured.)

At first he seeks to soothe his passion by uttering sweet seductive words (*bujuk*) to his beloved:

> Aria ningsun warna gemilang / paras yang elok tiada kepalang / kepada tuan sudah terpandang / tidaklah dapat kakanda pulang (SKT III, 43).
>
> ('My darling, my resplendently fair / whose beauty is without equal / now that he has set eyes on you, my lady / your older brother cannot retrace his steps.')

He ultimately finds relief from his longing by sexual union in the bedroom with the object of his love:

> Ia pun lalai seketika / kain tersingkap pinggang terbuka / rupanya seperti taruk angsoka / Raden mencium melakukan suka (SKT III, 109).
>
> (For a while as if under a spell he was oblivious of everything: / her dress had been swept aside and her loins were uncovered, / looking tender like the supple shoot of the Angsoka tree. / The prince kissed her and had his way with her.)

In the SBB the imitation of this well-known episode omits the bedroom scene and ends with the sweet seductive words (*bujuk*) Mangga addresses to Rambutan.[7]

The appeal for help to a powerful ascetic to teach *ilmu* (esoteric knowledge) and *hikmat* (magic) in the SBB can be related to the motif of the appeal to a god, ascetic or fairy for help in gaining the love of a lady or for some other purpose. This motif is widespread in all sorts of romances and romantic episodes in *wayang*-stories. Thus in the *Hikayat Pandawa Lima* (Story of the Five Pandawas), in a dream Sang Bimanyu, who is in love with Siti Sundari, requests the help of the god Betara Marapati who gives him an object by means of which he can, unseen by others, enter his beloved's bedroom (Khalid Hussain 1964:32-3). In one version of the *Hikayat Cekel*

---

[7] The same motifs are treated in a very similar manner and with similar style and diction in the *Hikayat Andaken Penurat* (Story of Andaken Penurat) published by Robson (1969:20-2, 26-38). Another parallel is provided by the *Syair Bidasari*. In the versions that have been published, the dream motif, the motif of the hunt that leads to the meeting of the hero with the heroine with whom he immediately falls head over heels in love, as well as the subsequent *bujuk*-scenes, all occur and are presented in a similar style and diction (Van Hoëvell 1843:76-125, 58-69 (in jawi); Klinkert 1886:318-31; Tuti Munawar 1978:53.6-66.5). The motif of the hunt leading to the meeting of the hero and the heroine occurs in all sorts of Panji-tales, and can even be found in the oral tradition of the Wayang Siam, notably in the *ranting*-stories where it is adapted to suit the Rama-characters (Sweeney 1972:264-5). For a fuller discussion of the type-scenes and their sequence in the *Syair Ken Tambuhan* I refer to Chapter II. About type-scenes in heroic epic, see Chapter IV, part 2.

Wanengpati (Story of Valiant Knight Bachelor), Aria Wangsa (Raden Inu) goes to a graveyard and, by concentrating his thoughts, calls up Betara Shiwa whom he requests to find his son, Ki Desti Pengarang, for him (Winstedt 1977:241). In the *Hikayat Misa Taman Jayeng Kusuma* Raden Kembar Dahang of Temasik requests the help of Ajar Brahma Sakti to kill Dalang Sungging Anom, whom he has been unwise enough to hire in order to soften up the resistance of his wife, Raden Galuh, to his amorous advances by his sweet words (Abdul Rahman Kaeh 1976:175-6). And in the love-story with Muslim setting, *Hikayat Dewa Mengindra* (Story of Dewa Mengindra), Sutan Muda learns all sorts of magic tricks from the Fairy King, Kumala Sakti (Juynboll 1899:133).

The oath of the royal fruits to be forever faithful and their prayer to Allah that He may never separate them until their hour has come finds a close parallel in the *Syair Ken Tambuhan* edited by Teeuw (1966). Thus, when Raden Menteri has told Ken Tambuhan of his dream that foretells their separation, he enjoins her:

> Mohonkan tolong pada dewata / janganlah bercerai kedua kita / jikalau sesuatu hal emas juita / biarlah kakang mati serta (SKT IV, 44).
>
> ('Request the gods that by their intercession / the two of us may not be separated. / If something should befall you, my gold, my life, / then it is better that your older brother die together with you.')

He assures her of his everlasting loyalty saying that *kakanda mencari dari selama / akan bela mati bersama* (SKT IV, 65a-b) (All my life if have been searching for you / to follow you in death and die with you). And, on hearing of their deaths, Raden Menteri's father describes their love thus:

> Sudahlah untung dengan janjinya / jatuh kasih pada hatinya / daripada hidup sampai matinya / janganlah bercerai dengan isterinya (SKT VIII, 34).
>
> ('It must have been his fate and destiny / that he should fall in love with her. / It was his wish that neither in life nor in death / would he ever be separated from his wife.')

Other variants of the story of Ken Tambuhan, too, show similar parallels. The motif of following one's husband or lord in death is a widespread one, both in *wayang*-stories (Khalid Hussain 1964:78-80, 114, 116, 126-7, 155-6) and in Panji-stories (Abdul Rahman Kaeh 1976:133, 274, 374, 410).

But what about the longing of the sick wife of our faithful Chinese for Grape and Pomegranate in Part 2? It will now be clear that it leads not only to the coming of the fatal hour but also to the suicide (*bela*) of her truly loyal husband who, like his wife, dies by eating the fruits and thus joins her by his 'Liebestod' (suicide for the sake of love), so that the story is indeed an exemplary tale of conjugal love as the narrator claims. May her craving for the fruits perhaps be taken as a realistic element in the story, since it is true that people who are ill often do like to eat fresh fruit?

Possibly the narrative plays freely with two motifs of romance. One could be the sudden craving for a rare form of food (*mengidam*), a device that is often employed in romance to bring about the separation of the lovers and a new round of adventures. Thus in the Panji-story *Syair Ken Tambuhan* published by Klinkert (1886:105), as well as in a number of other variants of this story (Teeuw 1966:xxi), after having been reunited and become King and Queen of Kuripan, the hero and heroine are once more separated, because the pregnant heroine requests her husband to search for the fabled *buah pauh janggi* or double coconut (Cocos maldiva or Lodoicea seychellarum, see Wilkinson 1943, II:221). A variant of this motif occurs in the *Hikayat Kuda Semirang Sira Panji Pandai Rupa* (Story of Kuda Semirang Sira Panji the Clever and Handsome) where the angry Queen separates the lovers by sending Inu to hunt for a tigress, for the meat of which she pretends to have a craving, and, during his absence, has Ken Martalangu killed (Harun Mat Piah 1980:1968). According to Wilkinson (1943, I:417) this also occurs in Muslim romances such as the *Hikayat Indra Nata* (Story of Indra Nata), the *Hikayat Kuraisy* (Story of Kuraisy) and the *Syair Puteri Akal* (Poem of the Clever Princess).

The other motif that comes to mind is that of healing an illness by eating flowers. This motif is widespread in Panji-stories. In the *Hikayat Galuh Digantung* (Story of the Princess Who was Hung on a Tree) the illness of the princess is cured by the eating of the flower, Gandapuraloka, that Inu, after many tribulations, has finally managed to obtain in a garden in the abode of the gods (*kayangan*). In the *Hikayat Dewa Asmara Jaya* (Story of Dewa Asmara Jaya) it is Panji who, fallen ill because of the curse of a god, is healed with the flower, Gandapurawangi, that his son by Princess Candra Kirana, after many adventures, brings to him from the heaven of the gods (Harun Mat Piah 1980:76-8). But, if all these heroes and heroines of romance successfully recover by eating the flowers, why then, one may wonder, do our loyal Chinese and his wife die? A puzzling story indeed.

Part 3 also resounds pervasively with the echoes of romance. Here a prominent feature is the exchange of strings of *pantun*. In the *Hikayat Kuraisy* on the island in Lake Lela Ajaib, where Kuraisy finds Princess Hairani Asyikin, people amuse themselves by singing them (Van Ronkel 1909:142). Another feature is making garlands of flowers. In romance making garlands of flowers occurs as a distracting pastime to soothe one's troubled emotions. Thus in the *Hikayat Pandawa Lima* Siti Sundari, in love with Sang Bimanyu, goes with her maids to a garden where they make garlands of flowers to soothe themselves (Khalid Hussain 1964:28). And writing poems or letters on flowers, too, is a motif familiar in romance. In the *Hikayat Pandawa Lima* we are told of Sang Bimanyu, who is in love with Siti Sundari:

> Maka diambil bunga pandan disuratnya kekawin terlalu manis bunyinya, katanya tuanku nyawa, tiadalah kuasa lagi kakanda menahan rindu dendam. Jikalau tiada tuan kasihan beta baiklah mati daripada sengsara ini. (Khalid Hussain 1964:30.)

> (Then he took the flower of a pandanus and wrote a poem on it with very sweet-sounding words, saying: 'My dearly beloved, your older brother no longer has the strength to bear his feelings of yearning and desire. If you do not take pity on me, it is better that I die rather than to endure this suffering.')

And, in the *Hikayat Misa Taman Jayeng Kusuma*, Sira Panji's beloved, now in the guise of the nun, Lara Sari, writes a letter of farewell to him on a *bunga puding* (Abdul Rahman Kaeh 1976:215).

Even some of the protagonists of the SBB may have been borrowed from romance. Thus, in de *Hikayat Indraputra* (Story of Indraputra), on Indraputra's arrival at Lake Samundra that is wide as an ocean, where the sand is of gold, the pebbles are of diamonds, the gravel of pearls, the grass of saffron, the ground of musk and the river is of rosewater, we are told:

> Syahdan di tepi tasik itu beberapa pohon kurma dan pohon anggur dan delima. Maka Indraputra pun hairan melihat kekayaan Allah taala. Maka Indraputra pun makan buah-buahan. (Mulyadi 1983:66-7.)

> (Furthermore, on the shore of the lake there were several date-palms and plants of grape and pomegranate. And Indraputra was amazed when he saw the riches of Allah, may He be Exalted. Thereupon Indraputra ate the fruits.)

We find these fruits once more united in the *Syair Bidasari* edited by Van Hoëvell (1843:69, 48 (jawi)), in the garden where the merchant has hidden Bidasari to protect her from the envy of the queen, a garden, we are told, where *ditanamnya zabib anggur delima* (he planted raisins, grapes and pomegranates). In the version of the *Syair Ken Tambuhan* of De Hollander (1856), the parakeet that leads Andaken Penurat to the secluded garden where Ken Tambuhan is weaving *terbangnya hinggap di pohon delima* (came flying and perched on a pomegranate tree) (Version De Hollander in Robson 1969:Appendix I, 45b), and in the *Hikayat Andaken Penurat* (Story of Andaken Penurat), it also alights on a pomegranate tree (Robson 1969:36.6).

Whereas the Chinese and his wife obviously cannot have been borrowed from romance, the Cempaka and the Melati are ubiquitous in it. The protagonists of Part 3, the beetles, may also very well have flown in from the gardens of romance in which they invariably fly about as animal symbols of seduction. When the nun, Lara Sari (Raden Galuh), in the *Hikayat Misa Taman Jayeng Kusuma*, has left Sira Panji and hides in the forest under a *pohon beringin*, the flowers of which are in bloom, we are told:

VIII The soothing works of the seducer and their dubious fruits 235

Kumbang pun banyak menyeri bunga beringin itu, berdengung-dengung seperti suara laki-laki yang baik paras memujuk isterinya dalam peraduan, demikianlah (Abdul Rahman Kaeh 1976:216).

(Numerous beetles sucked the honey from the flowers of the banyan-tree, with a buzzing sound just like that of the voice of a handsome man who coaxes his wife in the bedchamber.)

In the *Syair Raja Mambang Jauhari* (Poem of Mambang Jauhari), Mambang Jauhari, on hearing of the great beauty of Princess Kusuma Indra who dwells in the Garden Asmara Brangta, changes himself into a beetle to abduct her (Juynboll 1899:20-1). And in the *Hikayat Berma Syahdan* (Story of Berma Syahdan) we even find a Green Beetle, into whose form Princess Nur al-'Ain has changed herself to lure Berma Syahdan to her (Juynboll 1899:163-4).

What is the effect of these echoes of romance? It seems the answer must be: parody. A work may be read as parody when it borrows formal-stylistic or contentual elements from another work or genre and handles these in an incongruous manner, with comical or satirical effect.[8] We do not have to look far to find out why romance is parodied: the parody supports the critical view apparently taken in the SBB of romance in the SBB as a source of *hawa nafsu*.

Now an opposition becomes visible between *nafsu*-dominated pre-Islamic *jahil* romance and *akal*-dominated Islamic Betawi reality. Pre-Islamic romance prevails until the zenith of *hawa nafsu* is reached in the *terpandang* scene. The SBB only just stops short of the bedroom-scene that would have followed in a Panji-tale. The rise of *akal* and reality sets in when the reading of the stories is stopped. The boys abandon the example of the desiring and conquering Panji-style hero and return to the world of rationality and the law: *pantang dan larang, pinang, lamar, nikah*. Parodical incongruity results from the conflict of both worlds and a complete inversion of all values is accomplished when the behaviour of the lover in the princely style of Panji as extolled in romance is condemned as the behaviour of mere coolies.

5. Reading from the Book of the Devil

But why does pandemonium break loose the moment the reading of the stories is started? What is the meaning of that curious episode in which quarrels break out among the girl-fruits? However much this episode gives us the feeling that we are looking directly at the real life of the common

---

[8] My definition is modelled on that of Rotermund, quoted in Karrer (1977:35). Karrer presents a useful overview and synthesis of the babel of theories of parody.

anak betawi (native Batavians), it still points not so much to reality as to other Malay works. For instance, to the story in the *Hikayat Merong Mahawangsa* (Story of King Merong Mahawangsa) that tells how Syaikh Abdullah accompanies Iblis (the Devil) on a tour of the world in order to come to know his works among mankind (Siti Hawa Salleh 1970:86-110), a trip that finally brings him to Kedah and leads to its conversion by him to Islam.

Wherever Iblis goes, the *hikayat* tells us, people start to quarrel and murder each other and commit all sorts of other sins at his instigation. The way in which he seduces them to evil action is sometimes described as causing them to *mengaji* – a word meaning 'to recite from the Holy Koran' – from the *kitab syaitan* (the Book of the Devil) (Siti Hawa Salleh 1970:90 line 19, 90 line 29, 100 line 6-10). Pandemonium breaks loose, it now appears, because the Devil has been conjured up by the reading of the stories. To read romance is to read from the Book of the Devil (see Chapter III, part 5).

The narrator of the SBB also indicates that the Devil is at work by his remark that they quarrelled *selaku dijura ole si penggoda* (as if troubled by the Seducer, 3v 4d). And this is not the only place where Iblis is at work: when Pomegranate hopes to soothe himself in the garden Sukasari he is said to *menurut nafsu setan* (follow his devilish desires, 11v 7d). With his companions he pursues the bird *laksana orang kena pencoba* (like someone who has been stricken by the Tempter, 13r 13b) and the deeper they penetrate the garden of Grape, the more they feel *serasa tergoda jin dan setan* (as if seduced by evil spirits and devils, 13v 2d). Then the boys and girls set eyes on each other at the *kondangan* because they *sampainya hati tergoda iblis* (had the heart to allow themselves be seduced by the Devil, 24r 4d). Mango writes his illicit loveletter to Rambutan *sebab tergoda nafsu iblis* (because he was urged on devilish desire, 29v 5a). His magic makes her mad with longing *seperti tergoda jin dan setan* (as if she had been temped by evil spirits and devils, 31v 8d). Even the beetles are said to behave *seperti anak setan* (like children of the Devil, 54r 4a) when they dance like *ronggeng* and exchange their strings of *pantun*.

The Malay public expected literary works to provide profitable examples and soothing pleasure in varying degrees of dominance (see Chapter I). In the SBB romance, being the work of the Devil, is not only ostensibly rejected as a source of profitable examples – but it is also denied the power to soothe. This power is often claimed in romance, for example, in a passage in the prologue of the *Hikayat Andaken Penurat*:

> Maka barangsiapa membaca dia atau menengarkan dia, jikalau orang itu ada menaruh percintaan sekalipun, maka hilanglah percintaannya sebab mendengar hikayat inilah yang meliputi dendam akan kekasihnya (Robson 1969:fol. 1).
>
> (Now no matter who reads this work or hears it being read, even if he should be

nursing a grief, then his grief will vanish because of hearing this story, which can soothe all feelings of yearning and desire, especially in those who may be longing for a loved one.)

In the SBB all protagonists, not only the boys and the girls, pursue the same aim: to soothe their lovelorn longing. The faithful Chinese tries to soothe his longing for his beloved by building her a fine grave and having himself buried next to her; the beetles soothe themselves by venting their feelings in strings of *pantun*; and the princess and the *raja* hope to cure the *dendam dan birahi* (yearning and desire) that Green Beetle's verses have awakened in them by hearing more amorous poems by him.

Superficially the SBB may seem a mere jumble of barely connected tales; seeing hardly any connection between Part 1 and Parts 2 and 3 Overbeck, in interpretative desperation, proposed that from Part 2 onwards the SBB formed a second *syair* based on a Chinese poem treating Chinese legendary material (Overbeck 1934:143).

The fact that the SBB does in fact possess a remarkable coherence, appears not only from the pervasiveness of the romantic theme of trying to soothe one's yearning, but also from the careful way in which the narratives are linked up by pairs of protagonists: Pomegranate and Grape, by being eaten by them, link up with the Chinese merchant and his wife; who link up, via the Cempaka and the Melati, with Green Bee and Lustre of the Cempaka who, by their gifts of garlands and poems link up with the *raja* and the princess. It is not difficult to see here a parody of the motif of the reincarnation of karma-bound twin-souls (*jodoh*), a feature of the Panji-story (see Chapter VI, part 4). The pervasive theme of soothing lovelorn longing is accompanied by an equally pervasive parody of romance that underlines the critical view of the power of romance as a *penawar* (antidote) to soothe feelings of yearning and desire (8v 3a) apparently offered by the SBB. It seems to be medicine but is really poison.[9]

Have we now savoured all the flavours that the fruits have to offer? It is clear that there is still more to taste when we realize that fruits are invari-

---

[9]   Chambert-Loir (1991:99) has cast doubt on the feasibility of my reading of the SBB as one text. As he points out, Muhammad Bakir has put his signature at the end of the first story (my part 1 of the text contained in ms ML 254). In his view this somewhat supports Overbeck's view that the second story of the SBB, treating of the love of a Chinese *peranakan* for his wife, is a separate poem, which possibly has its origin in some local Chinese legend. He suggests that, instead of a 'local Chinese legend' as Overbeck proposed, it may have been a *syair* by a *peranakan* Chinese which Muhammad Bakir copied.
However, as my reading of the poem shows, there is a remarkable coherence between the narratives of the text contained by ms ML 254 as a whole; in fact, the stories fit into each other like Chinese boxes, one tale receding into another. That the text of ML 254 is to be read as a whole, in spite of the signature, is also clear from the fact that the narrator explicitly invites the readers to read the second story as exemplification of an important point made by the first (*Antologi* 37r 1, 37r 12).

ably part of the romantic landscape and are there to be plucked by the heroes and heroines to soothe themselves. Fruitful intertexts from the *Hikayat Misa Taman Jayeng Kusuma* may be:

> Maka Raden Inupun berjalanlah pada segenap pohon bunga dan buah-buahan itu menghiburkan hatinya (Abdul Rahman Kaeh 1976:57).
>
> ('And Raden Inu went to all the trees with their flowers and fruits to soothe his feelings.')
>
> Maka sepanjang jalan itu pedati segala para puteri itu singgah mengambil bunga dan buah-buahan. Lipurlah sedikit hatinya segala para puteri dan para putera itu oleh bermain sepanjang hutan itu. (Abdul Rahman Kaeh 1976:123.)
>
> ('And everywhere along the road the princesses had their carts make stops to pluck flowers and fruits. The feelings of the princesses and princes were somewhat soothed because they disported themselves everywhere in that forest.')

The fruits can thus be regarded as symbols for the soothing power of romance and as standing for the dubious fruits that the reader will reap by reading these *penawar*.

Here a number of Islamic intertexts can provide useful pointers for interpretation. On the one hand that outlandish pair Pomegranate and Grape hold out promises of soothing, even heavenly bliss, as can be seen from the *Hikayat Iskandar Zulkarnain* (Story of Iskandar the Two-Horned). During his wanderings through the Land of Darkness Iskandar meets Asrafil who, at Allah's Command, gives him a bunch of grapes (*serantai zabib*), saying:

> Inilah karunia Allah taala akan dikau, maka makanlah olehmu akan dia selama hidupmu dan tiadalah merasai lapar dan dahaga lagi. [...] Barangsiapa makan dia tiadalah dirasainya penyakit selama hidupnya itu. (Van Leeuwen 1937:226.9-15.)
>
> ('This is a favour which Allah in His bounty has granted you. Eat it as long as you live and you will never feel hunger or thirst ever again. [...] Whosoever eats it will never feel sickness as long as he lives.')

Desiring to possess the grapes, the Devil, disguised as an old man, successfully tricks Iskandar into exchanging them for a seemingly attractive apple. When he has eaten it, however, the apple proves to expose him to hunger and thirst once again (Van Leeuwen 1937:226-7).

In the *Hikayat Muhammad Hanafiyyah* (Story of Muhammad Hanafiyyah), the Devil, this time disguised as a beggar, tries unsuccessfully to trick the Prophet into giving him a bunch of heavenly grapes that Gabriel had brought for the Prophet's grandchildren, Hasan and Husain (Brakel 1975: 118-9). The idea that deadly poison may lurk behind their attractive appearance appears from a passage in the *Hikayat Merong Mahawangsa* where a story is told that the Devil, on his tour with Syaikh Abdullah, approaches a man who has retired to the forest to acquire the magical power of a great hero and warrior by the un-Islamic, *jahil* and romantic means of *bertapa* (practising asceticism). The Devil promises to fulfil all his wishes if he will eat the *buah delima* he holds out to him. Seeing that the pomegranate glows with a bright lustre (*bercahaya-cahaya buah delima itu*), the ascetic, seduced by its beauty, eats the fruit and the consequences are fatal:

> Maka menjadi kelam matanya, tiadalah sedar akan dirinya, menjadi gilalah orang yang bertapa itu. Maka penghulu syaitan itupun ghaiblah di matanya dan buah delima yang di tangannya itu / pun hilanglah. Maka orang bertapa itu pun bertempik dan melompat berlari-lari kesana kemari di dalam hutan itu, jadi gila haru-biru. (Siti Hawa Salleh 1970:94 line 25-95 line 9.)

> (Then the ascetic's eyes grew dim, and he fell into a trance as he went mad. And the leader of the devils disappeared from his sight and the pomegranate which he held in his hand also vanished. Thereupon the ascetic burst out shouting, jumped up, ran about hither and thither in the forest and went completely crazy.)

The conclusion is clear: eating such dangerous fruits will make one a prey to the moral sleep (*tiadalah sedar*) and the chaos and madness (*hutan*, *gila*) of *hawa nafsu*. The reader of romance reaps dubious fruits indeed.

6. The seductive garden of literature

The gardens, too, have symbolical potential and may be regarded as standing for the literary work and its lurking dangers. This danger is subtly suggested in the description of the garden Dukasari:

> Siapa masuk dalam kebun itu / hatinya bimbang sudalah tentu / yang berhati masuk disitu / seperti terpegang jin dan hantu // siapa masuk di kebun jadi duka / teratur buah-buah tiap-tiap ketika / Durian Manggis ada juga / semuanya itu bua yang berharga // berhati duka berhati bimbang / karena banyak pohon bercabang / teratur dengan sepanjang-panjang / seperti perhiasan jin dan mambang // tiada lagi ingatkan pulang / banyak pohon tiada berselang / bagusnya bukan alang-kepalang / jasad serasa bagaikan hilang. (9v 3-6.)[10]

> (All those who enter that garden / will feel anxious, that is for sure. / Those who dare to enter it / will feel as if seized by evil spirits and ghosts. // All those who enter the garden will become sad. / Row upon row of fruits are there in every season, / durian and mangosteen, too, are there, / all of them fruits which are expensive. // They will feel anxious, they will feel sad, / because there are many trees full of branches, / ranged in endless rows / like ornamentations made by ghosts and spirits. // They will not remember to return. / Many are the trees standing there packed together without a break, / of such a beauty that it cannot be described, / so that they will feel they are going out of their mind.)

And as can be seen in the synopsis, the spell cast by the beauty of the garden

---

[10] The perspicacious remarks of Braginsky (1979:4-11) about beauty as the potentially dangerous characteristic of literature are particularly relevant for a proper understanding of this passage.

Sukasari on the boys who venture to enter it has an equally pernicious effect on them.

The idea that it is not unjustified to consider the gardens as symbols of the alluringly attractive, but potentially dangerous, literary work and to regard the fruits as the fruits of reading is corroborated by Abdullah ibn Abdulkadir al-Munsyi. In the foreword to his *Hikayat Panja Tanderan* (first published in 1835), a translation into Malay of a Tamil version of the collection of didactic animal fables *Pancatantra*, Abdullah says:

> Maka adalah diumpamakan fakir hikayat ini seperti suatu taman yang amat permai lagi dengan indah-indah perbuatannya. Maka adalah dalamnya itu beberapa pohon buah-buahan yang amat lazat citrarasanya dan beberapa bunga-bungaan, yang amat harum baunya (Abdullah 1919:5).

> (Now this beggar likens this *hikayat* to a garden which is exceedingly beautiful and has been laid out with great allure. In it there are several trees with fruits which are exceedingly delicious to the taste and several kinds of flowers, the scents of which are exceedingly fragrant.)

First, Abdullah tells us, a wise (*bijaksana*) man goes in and, on seeing the trees with their fine fruits and flowers, he craves for them and plucks the fruits. Full of joy he leaves the garden and, when asked by his friends how he has profited from (*faedah*) his visit, he answers:

> Hai, sahabatku, telah kulihat akan segala ajaib dan khasiat dalamnya, serta kumakan buah-buahan yang terlalu lazat rasanya dan kupersuntingkan bunga-bungaan yang terlalu harum baunya (Abdullah 1919:6).

> ('O, my friends, I have seen all the wonders and special properties of it, and I have eaten the fruits which are exceedingly delicious to the taste and I have stuck the flowers which are very fragrant into my hair.')

And his friends rejoice and also wish to enter the garden. But now a stupid (*bebal*) man enters the garden, and this is what happens:

> Apabila ia masuk ke dalam taman itu, serta ia melihat segala buah-buahan dan bunga-bungaan dalam taman itu, lalailah ia, serta dengan malasnya hendak tidur, serta heranlah ia akan dirinya, dengan tercengang-cenganglah ia kesana kemari; tiadalah ia teringat hendak mengambil buah-buahan dan bunga-bungaan itu (Abdullah 1919:6).

> (When he entered the garden and saw the fruits and flowers in it, he fell into a trance and became so sluggish that he felt like sleeping and surprised he went hither and thither, his mouth agape with wonder; and he did not remember that he wanted to pluck the fruits and the flowers.)

When the stupid man comes out of the garden empty-handed he is severely criticized by his friends.

Drawing as the moral of this fine parable of reading *bahwa orang yang berakal itu niscaya dikiaskannyalah segala cerita dan hikayat itu, maka diperolehnyalah faedahnya* (that intelligent people will surely derive instruction from the tales and stories and thus profit from them), Abdullah exhorts his readers, especially the young, not to read his *hikayat* just *sebab suka mendengar lagunya sahaja* (because they like to hear its melody) or *sebab hendak tertawa sahaja* (because they just want to have a laugh), but, following the example of the wise man, to read his work for the lessons it provides by the allusions to (*kias*) and examples for (*ibarat*) human behaviour which the animal heroes of its stories embody (Abdullah 1919:7). Abdullah's admonition may well be extended to the readers of the SBB as well: preserve your *akal* and do not let yourself be deceived by mere alluring literary beauty that does not serve some moral purpose as well. The riches of Allah's creation, the literary work included, require discriminating use.

7. Irony, writing, Origin and authority

If the SBB may be read as a didactic fable dressed in the garb of allegory, there are two forces that prevent it from remaining merely moralizing and allow the poem to transcend its exemplary function. One we have already met on the level of story, namely parody. Let us now turn to her twin sister on the level of narration, irony.

We have an ironical, or, what amounts to the same, an unreliable narrator, when we have good reasons to suspect that there must be a discrepancy between the views and values the narrator expresses and those we feel the 'implied author' – that personifying term for the total set of implicit choices and evaluations governing the work – to have (Rimmon-Kenan 1983:94, 100-3, 140).

In traditional oral and oral-aural textual systems, irony, unless it is pretty well labelled as such (the 'stable irony' of the 'reliably unreliable narrator'), is virtually inconceivable. Typically the public oral performer is speaking for everyone to everyone about what every adult already knows and asking no questions. In the insistently repetitious, imitative, participatory noetic economy of oral tradition, with its close identification of author, audience and materials, there is no place for the inquisitive, distancing and divisive mode of irony (Ong 1977:272-302). The pervasive presence in the SBB of the device of the unreliably ironical narrator is one of the features that mark this text out as a work of the period of transformation of the Malay textual system, in which writing, reading and ultimately print came to prevail over oral-aural modes and media of expression.

To those who may hear her voice, irony already announces her presence in the prologue of the SBB and sets the tone for what will be her dominant concern all through the poem: writing and its authority. In the prologue the fictional narrator addresses his narratees thus:

Dengarlah tuan karangan fakir / yang hina miskin alfakir hakir / yaitu disebut namanya Muhammad Bakir / di Kampung Pecenongan tempatnya hadir // kisah dikarang buah-buahan / dalam kebun berapa rupa warnahan / ajaib sekali Kuasa Tuhan / buah anggur menanggung kecintahan (1r 1-2).

(Listen, gentlefolk, to the writing of this beggar, / who is lowly and poor, a worthless mendicant, / namely he who is called Muhammad Bakir / and lives at Kampung Pecenongan. // He has written a story about fruits / in a garden of several forms and colours. / Truly marvelous is the Power of the Lord; / a grape felt the pangs of love.)

Significantly the narrator calls himself *fakir*. This term indicates a role in which, by convention, traditional Malay authors frequently cast the narrator (or speaker) of their texts. The narrator as *fakir* by convention is reliable. The term *fakir*, that has been derived from Sufi mysticism, means something like 'a spiritually poor mendicant who has completely abandoned himself (*tawakkul*) to Allah's Divine Will'. By using it, traditional Malay authors expressed their religious conviction that man does not owe his creative powers to himself but can only create by submitting himself completely to the One and Only Author (Braginsky 1979:1-4; Muhammad Naguib al-Attas 1970:100; see also Chapter III, part 3).

The ultimate dependence of all human endeavour, writing included, on the Divine Will has found manyfold expressions in Sufi literature. In a mystical poem, written in imitation of the poetry of the seventeenth-century Sumatran mystic Hamzah Fansuri, this belief is expressed by the fine simile of the puppets and their Puppeteer:

Ketahui olehmu hai anak dagang / dirimu itulah yang diumpamakan bayang / cahaya maasyuk gilang-gemilang / itulah wujud yang bernama dalang (Doorenbos 1933:82).

(Know ye, oh foreign trader / that it is your self which is likened to the shadows on the screen. / The light of the Beloved is radiant; / that is Allah's Being which is called the Puppeteer.)

In a chronicle about early nineteenth-century Bima, the *Syair Kerajaan Bima* (the Syair of the Kingdom of Bima), the same pious attitude is expressed:

Inilah kisah suatu syair / dikarang seorang khatib yang fakir / bukannya hamba berbuat sindir / nyatalah Allah yang empunya takdir (Chambert-Loir 1982:9).

(This is a story, a *syair* / which was written by a beggarly preacher. / It was not your servant who made the poem. / It was clearly Allah who willed it so.)

Quite in line with this pious attitude is the confirmation of Allah's omnipotent *Kuasa* (Power) for which nothing is impossible to create, however miraculous it may be.

We can imagine that, listening to the prologue of the SBB, the unwary listener may well have nodded assent at hearing Islamic views and attitudes properly expressed by the narrator. But perhaps he has listened more critically and then he may have had the uneasy feeling that something was wrong with these statements. If the Power of the Lord is sincerely praised, is it not somehow incongruous that It is praised for bringing about something as ridiculous as making a grape feel the pangs of love, an event that is strange indeed! And the word *ajaib* (marvelous) must have reminded him of the many passages in romance in which this word, functioning as a marker of the fabulous nature of the work, is used in ironical assertions by the narrator of the truth of his tale.

Such a passage of romance that asserts the truth of the wonders it tells about by reference to Allah's Omnipotence is the one in the *Hikayat Indera Bangsawan* (Story of Indera Bangsawan) in which a friendly giant (*raksasa*) gives the hero a demonstration of the magical powers of a *sarung kesaktian*:

> Hatta maka diambillah oleh raksasa akan sarung kesaktian itu dan dimasukkannya pada tubuhnya itu. Seketika maka ia pun menjadi kanak-kanak. Maka Indera Bangsawan pun heranlah melihat kebesaran Allah subhanu wa taala itu menjadikan atas hambanya serta mengucap syukur kepada Allah taala. (*Hikayat Indera Bangsawan* 1978:16.)

> (Thereupon the giant took the magical *sarung* and put it on. In the twinkling of an eye he turned into a small child. And Indera Bangsawan marvelled when he saw the wonders which the Greatness of Allah – praise be unto Him and may He be exalted – worked upon His servants and he gave thanks to Allah may He be exalted.)

However absurd it may seem to the modern reader, it is not entirely impossible that those among the listeners who were only accustomed to the world of oral tradition may have even accepted the assertion of truth of the narrator of the SBB in the manner of the narrator of romance as a seriously intended one. One witness to the possibility that the traditional Malay audience was much more inclined to accord belief to the tales it was told than we can now imagine is a Malay who, in the March 1934 issue of the journal for teachers *Majallah Guru*, stated:

> Dahulu daripada tiap-tiap cerita atau hikayat dewa mambang dan sebagainya disangkanya benar belaka. Katanya: sekalian itu betul telah berlaku pada zaman dahulu tetapi tiada mau lagi jadi pada zaman ini, karena perkara hairan-hairan seperti itu telah alah oleh mukjizat Nabi kita, dan kayangan pun telah runtuh apabila diperanakkan Nabi kita. (Penulis Lama 1964:62-3.)

> (In the past each tale or story of gods and spirits and suchlike beings was thought to be absolutely true. People said: all this is true and happened once in the past but it will not happen again in the present because strange things like these have been conquered by the power of our Prophet and the heaven of the gods was already toppled when our Prophet was born.)

And in 1906 Wilkinson wrote that the Malay peasant believed that in the not so distant past 'birds and animals could talk, heroes and princesses enacted in real life the wildest dreams of romance and mighty magicians [...] walked the earth, turning all that opposed them into stone, as indeed many a rock testifieth to this day [...]' (Wilkinson 1906:43-5).

Whether the listener really accepted the narrator's assertions at face value or not is of little importance here. What matters is that we now clearly see that he could choose between two levels of comprehension: the ostensible meaning held out to him by the voice of the narrator and the one really intended, unobtrusively spoken by the low voice of the 'implied author' for whoever has ears to hear.

Irony is divisive indeed. And its effect is to suggest: the wonderful world in this poem, like in romance, in reality is only a world in words, dear public, conjured up for your pleasure by the writing of an author and existing on his authority. This theme is underlined by the frequent references in the prologue to the activity of writing (*dikarang*, 'it was written'; *pengarang*, 'writer') and the explicit mention by name of the real author of the SBB, Muhammad Bakir, that seems not to be devoid of a certain authorial self-awareness and pride.

In the course of Part 1 irony regularly resurfaces and draws attention to the activity of the writer behind the narrator's back. When the narrator has told us that in the heat of the quarrel Cempedak has blurted out a secret affair of Kokosan's, he closes the episode with the tongue-in-cheek comment:

> Berkelahi mulut satu persatu / seorang tiada ada yang bantu / mujur tiada yang jalan disitu / jadi rahasialah masi utu (5v 8a-6r 1b).
>
> (They had a brawl, giving each other tit for tat / and there was nobody to do anything about it. / Luckily just then nobody passed by there; / that is why the secret is still intact.)

Telling about the *kondangan* (feast) and what happened there he remarks:

> Tua muda hina dan dina / pendekar alim dan bijaksana / semua datang kondangan disana / hanya tiada pengarang durjana (24v 1).
>
> (The old and the young, the lowly and the humble, / the rowdies, the scholars and the wise, / all came to attend the feast there; / only your ne'er-do-well writer was not there.)

In these passages the now strangely limited, and then again inexplicably unlimited, knowledge claimed by the narrator make us alert to the presence of irony and one effect is that the fictional convention of the omnipresent and omniscient narrator is foregrounded and exposed as just that.

For the Malay public passages such as these may also have resounded with the echo of assertions of truth customary in oral-aural traditional historiography of the type in which the authority of a text is strengthened by underlining that the narrator has been present at the scene he describes and has been an eyewitness to the events. A fine example could be the almost Herodotian way in which, in the epilogue of the *Syair Sultan Maulana* (Poem of My Lord the Sultan) that treats Kedah's role of ally of Siam in a war at sea against the Burmese at the end of the first decade of the nineteenth century, the author through his narrator stakes an emphatic claim to truth for his tale:

> Segala cetera perkataan beta / tiada sekali berbuat dusta / daripada baik atawa leta / seperti mana penglihatan mata // didengar dilihat kelakuan pun serta / barang yang ada dilihat nyata / semuanya dengan sebenar dikata / Siam Melayu disebut semata (Skinner 1985:1082-3).
>
> (In all the stories that I tell / not even once do I tell a lie. / Whether I speak of good or bad, / I have seen it all with my own eyes. // I heard it and saw it, took part in the actions. / All who were there I clearly saw. / About all I tell as best I can; / Siamese, Malays, I mention them all.)

The limited knowledge of the narrator, that important source of irony, also makes its appearance when the narrator, still describing the events at the *kondangan*, remarks:

> Ada yang tertawa ada yang masygul / ada anak perawan duduk berkumpul / ada yang tertawa mesem-mesem simpul / entalah justa entalah betul // [...] // demikian kata pengarang durjana [...] (25r 2a-25r 5a).
>
> (Some were laughing loudly, others were sad. / Some young girls were sitting together, / some of them smiled to hide their blushing. / I do not know whether it is a lie or the truth. // [...] // Thus says your no-good writer [...].)

In this passage, as well as in some of the examples quoted in the preceding paragraph, two elements appear that deserve to be noticed: the term *justa* (*dusta*), 'lying', as a way in which the narrative may be qualified, and the self-deprecatory manner in which the narrator indicates himself as *pengarang durjana*, 'your ne'er-do-well writer'. Terms such as these may well have reminded those among the public who were familiar enough with the Holy Koran of that Sura where the poets are roundly condemned as mere liars possessed by the Devil:

> Shall I tell you on whom the Satans come down? They come down on every guilty impostor. They give ear, but most of them are liars. And the poets – the perverse follow them; hast thou not seen how they wander in every valley and how they say that which they do not? (Sura 26 Al-Su'ara, vs. 221-6; Arberry 1983:381; see also Jacobi 1972.)[11]

The qualification of the narrator as *pengarang durjana* draws attention to the presence behind him of the 'implied author', who, at the expense of the

---

[11] This is not the only way in which the Prophet viewed the poets, as I point out in Part 5 of Chapter III.

narrator, shares with the more perceptive among the public the fun of exposing him jokingly as a mere liar.

The public will also have enjoyed the irony of the passage near the end of Part 1 where the previously so doubting narrator, having told how the enamoured fruits Sawo, Jackfruit and Mangosteen promised everlasting loyalty to their loves Sugar Apple, Cempedak and Duku, and as a token of this gave them gifts, such as a costly hairpin for her bun to Cempedak, and a shoulder-cloth to Duku, confidently asserts the truth of his tale in the following manner:

> Maka sebab itu awal mulanya / jadi Nangka Cempedak suka ditusuknya / ditusuk sama kayu di kepalanya / supaya jadi lekas matangnya (27r 4) [...] // sampai sekarang akan jadinya / beli duku selampai jadi bungkusannya. (27v 1a-b.)
>
> (Now that is how it has come about / that Cempedak likes to be pricked by Nangka, / and have a piece of wood stuck into her head / so that she may quickly ripen. // [...] // To this day it still will happen; / if you buy a duku fruit you will wrap it in your shoulder-cloth.)

Similar ironical passages close Part 2 and Part 3. The story of the faithful Chinese whose wife craved for Grape and Pomegranate is first asserted to be true:

> Sampai sekaranglah kesuda-sudahan / mana yang sakit mintak buah pilihan / sampai sekarang kalau orang sakit / mintak makan anggur delima sedikit (44r 6).
>
> (To this very day it has always been so / that whosoever falls ill asks for choice fruits. / To this day when someone falls ill / he will ask to be given some grapes and pomegranates to eat.)

But then the narrator adds: *Demikian awal mulanya / enta betul enta justaknya* (That is its origin and beginning / I do not know whether it is a lie or the truth). And that Green Beetle taught ignorant (*bodo* 54r 8c) – because still *jahil?* (unenlightened by the Divine revelation to Muhammad) – humanity the 'useful' (*berguna*, 54r 7d) art of making 'soothing' garlands of flowers with fine engravings on them is evidently true, the narrator assures us: *Tempo dahulu awal mulanya / sampai sekarang dikerjakannya* (It all began in the days long gone by, / and is still done to this day) (61v 6a-b).

In oral-aural traditions it is quite acceptable that a narrator tries to establish the truth and authority of his report of events that took place in the past by referring to the still visible traces caused by them as evidence that they really once happened. Thus the *dalang* of the Wayang Siam, usually loath to admit that they invent tales – which they denounce as *belawak* (clowning lying; fooling someone) – and firmly convinced that the events in their repertoire did occur locally, each can quote evidence substantiating the correctness of their belief in their historicity, e.g. that therefore seven palms are still to be seen in Singgora (Sweeney 1972:258, 268-9; Wilkinson 1943,

II:28). The *Sejarah Melayu* (Genealogy of the Malay Rulers), too, contains many fine passages of such etiological explanations. A good example is the Sixth Story in the version of Abdullah ibn Abdulkadir Munsyi published by Situmorang and Teeuw (1952:51-2) that tells of the exploits of the strongman Badang, the champion of the *Raja* of Singapura. According to this story Badang was so big that when he fell down from a tree his fall caused a rock to split, and this rock, Batu Belah (the Split Rock), may be seen to this day. He was also so strong, that, in a trial of strength against the champion of the *Raja* of Keling, he could hurl a rock to the far bank of Kuala Singapura, where it may be seen to this day on the extremity of Tanjung Singapura.[12] It seems likely that the echoes of oral-aural assertions of truth such as these must have contributed significantly to making the public of the SBB enjoy the fun and laugh.

We have already seen that on the recommendation of the narrator Parts 2 and 3 may best be read just for fun to while away the time, rather than for edification and good examples. That we may take his advice seriously appears when we read both parts not only for the story but also bathed in the light of ironical narration. In both parts of the SBB this ironical narration is as important as – if not more important than – the story. And in both it again predominantly thematized the *sebab* (cause), *awal* (origin) and *mula* (beginning) of the events narrated on the level of story.

To be able to join the Malay public in the fun it must have had here, we have to return once more to Islamic belief, notably to that in the Safely Preserved Tablet of Fate. According to this belief, that is based on passages in the Koran (Sura 85.22 and 97.1), Allah, the Prime Mover, with His Pen (*kalam*) has written the decisions of His Divine Will (*takdir, iradat*), the archetypes of all that is destined to be until the coming of the Day of Judgement, on the Safely Preserved Tablet of Fate (*al-lawh al-mahfuz*). One side of the Tablet is turned to Asrafil for his guidance but the other side none has seen save Allah alone (*Encyclopaedia of Islam* 1986, V:698; Wilkinson 1943, II: 66; see also Chapter III, part 5).

In the homiletic poem *Syair Dagang* (Poem of the Trader Far From Home), in which man is advised to welcome the hardships of spiritual poverty and to entrust himself entirely to God's Will, this belief is expressed thus:

---

[12] A related form of argument, but one that works a reverse manner, is the explanation that can now be heard on Karimun Besar for the presence of two large shallow depressions in the rock near Pasir Panjang. People tell that they were made by Badang, who stood there, spanning the sea between Karimun and Singapore with one foot on each island (Matheson 1985:6-7). Here the past, in the form of a story, credited as true because it occurs in the *Sejarah Melayu* is adduced as explanation for a phenomenon in the present.

> Itu pun kehendak Tuhan Ilahi / menurunkan untung kepada azali / kepadaku seorang serta terbahagi / dimana kan lagi disalahi (Doorenbos 1933:21); tiadala saya ada terkatakan / kehendak Allah gerangan tuan / sudah tersurat yang demikian / tiadalah lagi dapat disalahkan (Doorenbos 1933:28).
>
> (That is the Will of Our Lord Allah, / Who has ordained our fates from on high at the beginning of time. / When my lot has been apportioned to me, / how can I ever object to it? // [...] // I cannot gainsay it; / maybe Allah has willed it so. / When it is already written / one can no longer object to it anymore.)

One example which occurs in a work of historiography is the following passage quoted from the *Syair Perang Siak* (Poem of the Siak War), in which the narrator enjoins the audience to accept gratefully as Allah's Will that Siak suffered defeat at the hands of the Dutch and *Raja* Alam when it was attacked by them (according to modern historiography in 1761):

> Sudahlah dengan takdir Allah / tiadalah dapat lagi disalah / di luh mahfuz suratan terjumlah / barang yang datang disyukurkanlah (Goudie 1989:527).
>
> (It is the Will of Allah; / it cannot be gainsaid anymore. / It all stands written on the Well-Preserved Tablet; / whatever may come to pass, we must render thanks unto Him.)

The playful ironical references in the SBB to the Writing of Allah's Pen must not of course be taken to imply disrespect or unbelief, but are in the nature of a playful distancing of deeply-held Islamic convictions. Such a distancing is a familiar phenomenon in for instance Arab literature, where the poets playfully quote and ironize passages from the Koran and the *hadith* (traditions about the Prophet) in their verse. One effect such distancing has, seems to be to prevent these convictions from being trivialized and from becoming mere formulae, repeated automatically and without reflection.

The play of irony in Parts 2 and 3 is in fact started in Part 1, when the shared 'Liebestod' of Grape and Pomegranate is motivated. When the pair prays to Allah never to be separated, the narrator stresses that their prayer can only be fulfilled if Allah does indeed will it and exhorts the faithful to accept his decision:

> Suda takdir yang melakukan / tiada siapa dapat salahkan / barang janjinya ditakdirkan / Anggur Delima tiada dipisahkan (28v8 a-29r 1b).
>
> (Divine Providence determines the course of events. / No one can object to it. / Their destinies had been foreordained; / Grape and Pomegranate were not separated.)

Little inconsistencies and ambiguities indicate that irony is intended and these point to the presence of the joking 'implied author'. At first the inattentive among the public may have been tricked into hearing only laudable piety by the narrator's comment that *semuanya itu dengan takdir /*

mengharap Tuhan empunya nasir / jodo kuat tak bole mungkir (28v 1b) (all that depends on Allah's Decree. / One must have hope in the help of the Lord. / The strong bond between twin-souls cannot be disavowed), but if this was so, the next line will no doubt have startled them: *Di atas pengarang duduk berpikir* (to the writer falls the task of finding some way out) (28v 1).

The occurrence of such inconsistencies and the ambiguous reference to a *yang kuasa* (Powerful One) (36v 8a-b) from whom the couple hopes to obtain fulfilment of their prayer drew attention to another source of authority in whose power it is to decide the fate of the protagonists, the writer, who may indeed grant their wish that they *mati bersama-sama dalam ceritahan* (die together in the story) (29r 2d).

This play on the two writers is continued all through Parts 2 and 3. Now that we are alert to its presence, we realize that an explanation can finally be given for the mysterious sudden illness and death of the loyal Chinese and his wife on eating Grape and Pomegranate: *Dengan takdir orang yang mengarang / datang sakitnya jua sekarang* (By the decree of the writer / he immediately fell ill) (43v 3). And why does the writer want his poor protagonists to go through all this suffering and death? The jocular and surprising answer of the 'implied author' is: *Sebab pengarang mau panjangkan / di belakang kali mau disebutkan* (Because your writer wants to draw out the story / and wants to tell about them later) (43v 1c-d).

First the wife dies by the *takdir di dalam tulis* (decree of his writing) (43r 7c) that makes her eat the fruits with fatal consequences, and then it is the turn of her husband. But before carrying out his authorial will and making him die, the 'implied author' has previously made the narrator ask the fictional reader to tell whether the hour of death of her husband has come, because *kita tiada ketahui untung suda atau belum* (we do not know whether his time has already come or not) (42v 8d). The *tulisan yang kuasa* (the writing of the powerful one) (44r 2b) is also the real force behind the events and actions in Part 3.

All pretence is dropped and the 'implied author' steps into the full light, when the narrator, commenting on that miraculous event of beetles making garlands of flowers engraved with poems, is made to remark: *Ajaib sekali kodrat semesta / tiadalah kuasa Rabb ul-izzata / demikian saya katakan* (Truly marvelous is the Power over all. / The Lord of All Honour does not have this might: / it is I who say so) (55v 7a-c).

Now that we have seen how the activity of the writing author is continually being thematized by the ironical manner of narration, it becomes possible to discern one more level of allegory in the SBB, namely to read the Green Beetle as a symbol for the writing author. A pointer that we may indeed do so is, for instance, the fact that the narrator explains the singing and dancing of the beetles as events that happen *diatas kumbang empunya mau* (because the Beetle wanted it) (46r 3). Perhaps the strongest hint in this direction is that the princess, having read the poems Green Beetle wrote on the flower he dropped on her, concludes: *Kumbang Hijau ini pekerjaanya / karena dalam sair ada namanya* (This is the work of Green Beetle / because his name is in the *syair*) (60r 1a-b). Not only the writing author but also the signing author, who possesses the copyright of his text, is thus, it seems, introduced.

If the reading of Green Beetle as the writer is indeed justified we may discover a naughty thrill in the following passage that occurs in the episode where we are told how people wonder where the beetles have come from: *Pagi sore kumbang bertutur / ada yang berkata kumbang melantur* (46r 1c) (From morning to evening the beetles kept on chattering / some said the beetles had strayed (or: talked nonsense)).[13]

We have already seen that Green Beetle may be seen as an animal symbol of seduction. If that is so we may now conclude that the writer, too, is presented as a seducer and that we see him at work in the portrait of Green Beetle.[14] And indeed, behind the narrator, we may discern the 'implied author', who, after previously condemning romance as the Book of the Devil (see also Chapter III, part 5), now himself indulges in reading from precisely that Book, when he parodies familiar motifs from it and treats us to strings of erotic *pantun* that *memberi rusak hati jejaka perawan* (cause heartbreak to young men and girls) (51r 5d). Thus irony silently subverts the didactic moralizing in Part 1 about the devilish dangers that lurk behind the beauty and pleasure of literature.

The seemingly diabolical, but in fact fictional, nature of the works of the writer is ironically underlined when the narrator tells us:

> Lakunya kumbang selaku iblis / akan berpantun berbagai jenis / banyak pantunnya tiada ditulis / tinggal pengarang duduk menangis (54r 6).
>
> (The bees behaved like devils / and sang all sorts of *pantun*. / Many of these *pantun* were not written down, / which leaves only your writer who sits down in tears.)

Irony is complete when not only the soothing works of the seducer, but even the seducer himself, Green Beetle, are nowhere, we are told, to be found.

The SBB, we may conclude, does not deserve the harsh verdict that

---

[13] For the double meaning of the word *melantur*, see Abdul Chaer (1976:212).
[14] Interestingly, the *dalang* of the Wayang Siam, the performer of Mak Yong (Sweeney 1972:34-6) and the performer of Sijobang (Phillips 1981:16) are reputed to be able to attract women and to possess special powers to seduce them. The seductive *dalang* is of course also a regular feature of Panji romances.

Overbeck – perhaps also prompted by that dislike of Batavian Malay of his generation of scholars – has passed on it as a work of literature. Of course, a poem's literary excellence cannot be 'proved': at the end of the eighteenth century the more sensible literary scholars had already wisely abandoned efforts to do so as fruitless. What I hope I have been able to achieve is that the reader may have become willing to try and see the SBB with new eyes and, who knows, may perhaps even have been persuaded to see what I have seen in it.

From a purely scholarly point of view the SBB is, no doubt, a highly interesting text. Parody, irony of the unreliable narrator and playful foregrounding of fictionality, rare phenomena in the oral-aural Malay tradition, mark the poem as a work of deeply ingrained literacy. In it the literary work in the modern sense of a unique construction produced by a self-aware author, proud of his originality and creativity, makes its appearance.

And perhaps I may now add one more allegorical reading to the ones that have already been proposed. If we may say that the appearance of Green Beetle heralds the coming of the original literary writer, may we not recognize his faithful shadow, the slavish imitator, in the figure of the *tukang pandai* (craftsman)?

Bibliography

Abdul Chaer
1976   *Kamus dialek Melayu Jakarta-Bahasa Indonesia*. Ende: Nusa Indah.
Abdul Mutallib Abdul Ghani (ed.)
1983   *Syair Siti Zubaidah Perang Cina*. Kuala Lumpur: Dewan Bahasa dan Pustaka.
Abdul Rahman Kaeh
1974   Hikayat Misa Taman Jayeng Kusuma; Sebuah cerita Panji Melayu. [MA thesis University of Malaya.]
1976   (ed.) *Hikayat Misa Taman Jayeng Kusuma; Sebuah cerita Panji Melayu*. Kualu Lumpur: Dewan Bahasa dan Pustaka.
1983   *Panji Narawangsa; Analisa struktur dan fungsi dalam hubungannya dengan pendidikan*. [PhD thesis IKIP Malang.]
Abdullah al-Munshi
1919   *Hikajat Pandja Tanderan, jaïtoe jang dinamaï oleh orang Melajoe Hikajat Galilah dan Daminah*. Leiden: Trap. [First edition 1835.]
Achadiati Ikram (ed.)
1980   *Hikayat Sri Rama; Suntingan naskah disertai telaah amanat dan struktur*. Jakarta: Penerbit Universitas Indonesia.
Almanak
1863   *Almanak en naamregister van Nederlandsch-Indië voor 1864*. Batavia: Landsdrukkerij.
Andaya, L.
1981   *The heritage of Arung Palakka; A history of South Sulawesi (Celebes) in the seventeenth century*. 's-Gravenhage: Nijhoff. [KITLV, Verhandelingen 91.]
Andaya Watson, B. and V. Matheson
1979   'Islamic thought and Malay tradition; The writings of Raja Ali Haji of Riau (ca. 1809-ca. 1870)', in: A. Reid and D. Marr (eds), *Perceptions of the past in Southeast Asia*, pp. 108-28. Singapore: Heinemann.
Antologi
1980   *Antologi syair simbolik dalam sastra Indonesia lama*. Jakarta: Departemen Pendidikan dan Kebudayaan.
Arberry, A.J. (transl.)
1983   *The Koran interpreted*. Oxford: Oxford University Press. [Reprint.]
Bakhtiar, L.
1976   *Sufi; Expressions of the mystic quest*. New York: Avon.

Baroroh Baried et al.
1987　　　　　*Panji; Citra pahlawan Nusantara*. Jakarta: Departemen Pendidikan dan Kebudayaan.

Barthes, R.
1982　　　　　'The reality effect', in: Tz. Todorov (ed.), *French literary theory today; A reader*, pp. 11-7. Cambridge/Paris: Cambridge University Press.

Besserman, L.L.
1979　　　　　*The legend of Job in the middle ages*. Cambridge, Mass./London: Harvard University Press.

Blagden, O.
1913　　　　　'Criticism', in: *Noctes orientales; Being a selection of essays read before the Straits Philosophical Society between the years 1899 and 1910*, pp. 98-105. Singapore: Kelly and Walsh.

Bloch, R.H.
1983　　　　　*Etymologies and genealogies; A literary anthropology of the French middle ages*. Chicago/London: University of Chicago Press.

Boon, J.A.
1977　　　　　*The anthropological romance of Bali 1597-1972; Dynamic perspectives in marriage and caste, politics and religion*. Cambridge: Cambridge University Press.

Braginsky, V.I.
1975a　　　　*Evolyutsiya malayskogo klassicheskogo stikha*. Moskwa: Izdatel'stvo Nauka.
1975b　　　　'Some remarks on the structure of the Sya'ir Perahu', *Bijdragen tot de Taal-, Land- en Volkenkunde* 131:407-26.
1979　　　　　'The concept of the beautiful (indah) in Malay classical literature and its Muslim roots', Paper persidangan antarabangsa pengajian Melayu mengenai bahasa kesusastraan dan kebudayaan Melayu pada 8-10 HB Sept. 1979 sempena 25 tahun pengajian Melayu Jabatan Pengajian Melayu University Malaya, Kuala Lumpur.
1986　　　　　'Some traces of the theory of *rasa* in Malay classical literature; Remarks on the problem of Hindu-Moslem synthesis', in: W. Morgenroth (ed.), *Sanskrit and world culture*, pp. 191-7. Berlin: Akademie Verlag.
1988　　　　　'A preliminary reconstruction of the Rencong version of the "Poem of the Boat" ', *Bulletin de l'École Française d'Extrême-Orient* 77:263-301.
1990　　　　　'Hikayat Shah Mardan as a Sufi allegory', *Archipel* 40:107-35.
1991　　　　　'Evolution of the verse-structure of the Malay syair', *Archipel* 42:133-54.
1993　　　　　'Universe-man-text; The concept of literature in Malay-Indonesian Sufism', *Wostok* [forthcoming].

Brakel, L.F.
1975　　　　　*The Hikayat Muhammad Hanafiyyah; A medieval Muslim-Malay romance*. The Hague: Nijhoff. [KITLV, Bibliotheca Indonesica 12.]
1979a　　　　'Hamza Pansuri; Notes on: yoga practices, lahir dan zahir, the "taxallos", a difficult passage in the Kitāb al-Muntahī, Hamza's likely place of birth, and Hamza's imagery', *Journal of the Malaysian Branch of the Royal Asiatic Society* 52-1:73-98.

1979b	'On the origins of the Malay hikayat', *Review of Indonesian and Malaysian Affairs* 13-2:1-33.
Brandt, W.J.	
1973	*The shape of mediaeval history; Studies in modes of perception.* New York/London: Yale University Press.
Brault, G.J.	
1978	*The Song of Roland; An analytical edition; Vol. II, Oxford text and English translation.* University Park/London: Pennsylvania State University Press.
Bürgel, J.Ch.	
1974	' "Die beste Dichtung ist die lügenreichste"; Wesen und Bedeutung eines literarischen Streites des arabischen Mittelalters im Lichte komparatistischer Betrachtung', *Oriens* 23/24:7-102.
Chambert-Loir, H.	
1980	(ed.) *Hikayat Dewa Mandu; Épopée malaise.* Paris: École Française d'Extrême-Orient.
1982	(ed.) *Syair Kerajaan Bima.* Jakarta/Bandung: Lembaga Penelitian Perancis untuk Timur Jauh/École Française d'Extrême-Orient.
1984	'Muhammad Bakir; A Batavian scribe and author in the nineteenth century', *Review of Indonesian and Malaysian Affairs* 18:44-72.
1985	(ed.) *Ceritera asal bangsa jin dan segala dewa-dewa.* Bandung: Penerbit Angkasa dan École Française d'Extrême-Orient.
1991	'Malay literature in the 19th century; The Fadli connection', in: J.J. Ras and S.O. Robson (eds), *Variation, transformation and meaning; Studies on Indonesian literatures in honour of A. Teeuw*, pp. 87-114. Leiden: KITLV Press. [KITLV, Verhandelingen 144.]
Clara van Groenendael, V.M.	
1985	*The dalang behind the wayang; The role of the Surakarta and the Yogyakarta dalang in Indonesian-Javanese society.* Dordrecht/Cinnaminson: Foris. [KITLV, Verhandelingen 114.]
Collingwood, R.G.	
1978	*The idea of history.* Oxford: Oxford University Press. [First published 1946.]
Culler, J.	
1975	*Structuralist poetics; Structuralism, linguistics and the study of literature.* Ithaca: Cornell University Press, London: Routledge and Kegan Paul.
1981	*The pursuit of signs; Semiotics, literature, deconstruction.* Ithaca: Cornell University Press, London: Routledge and Kegan Paul.
Dakers, C.H.	
1939	'The Malay coins of Malacca', *Journal of the Malayan Branch of the Royal Asiatic Society* 17, I:1-12.
Derks, W.A.G.	
1985	*Sumbang; Incest in de Indonesische mythologie.* [MA thesis Katholieke Universiteit Nijmegen.]
Djaafar, T. et al. (comp.)	
1973	*Cerita-cerita rakyat di daerah Riau.* Pekanbaru: Badan Pembina Kesenian Daerah Propinsi Riau.

Doorenbos, J. (ed.)
1933   *De geschriften van Hamzah Pansoeri, uitgegeven en toegelicht.* Leiden: s.n. [PhD thesis Rijksuniversiteit Leiden.]

Drewes, G.W.J.
1977   *Directions for travellers on the mystic path; Zakariyyā' al-Anṣārī's Kitāb Fatḥ al-Raḥmān and its Indonesian adaptations.* The Hague: Nijhoff. [KITLV, Verhandelingen 81.]
1987   'Reality? Or delusion?', *Bijdragen tot de Taal-, Land- en Volkenkunde* 143: 363-8.

Drewes, G.W.J. and L.F. Brakel (eds)
1986   *The poems of Hamzah Fansuri.* Dordrecht/Cinnaminson: Foris. [KITLV, Bibliotheca Indonesica 26.]

Duggan, J.J.
1973   *The Song of Roland; Formulaic style and poetic craft.* Berkeley: University of California Press.

Ehrlich, V.
1980   *Russian formalism; History, doctrine.* Fourth, revised edition. The Hague: Mouton. [First published 1955.]

Encyclopaedia of Islam
1965   *The Encyclopaedia of Islam.* New Edition. Vol. 2, fascicules 38-40. Leiden: Brill.
1971   *The Encyclopaedia of Islam.* New Edition. Vol. 3, fascicules 59-60. Leiden: Brill.
1986   *The Encyclopaedia of Islam.* New Edition. Vol. 5, fascicules 89-90. Leiden: Brill.

Encyclopaedie
1917   *Encyclopaedie van Nederlandsch-Indië.* Vol. 1. 's-Gravenhage: Nijhoff, Leiden: Brill.

Foucault, M.
1976   *Archaeology of knowledge.* New York: Harper and Row.

Frye, N.
1973   *Anatomy of criticism; Four essays.* Third printing. Princeton, N.J.: Princeton University Press. [First published 1957.]
1976   *The secular scripture; A study of the structure of romance.* Cambridge, Mass./London: Harvard University Press.

Gardiner, F.C.
1971   *The pilgrimage of desire; A study of theme and genre in medieval literature.* Leiden: Brill.

Gardner, H.
1971   *Religion and literature.* Oxford/New York: Oxford University Press.

Gellrich, J.M.
1985   *The idea of the book in the middle ages; Language theory, mythology and fiction.* Ithaca/London: Cornell University Press.

Goudie, D.J. (ed.)
1976   A critical edition of the Syair Perang Siak with a consideration of its literary and historical significance. [MPhil thesis University of London.]

1989 *Syair Perang Siak; A court poem presenting the state policy of a Minangkabau Malay royal family in exile*. Kuala Lumpur: Malaysian Branch of the Royal Asiatic Society.

Gramberg, J.S.G.
1877 'De troeboekvisscherij', *Tijdschrift voor Indische Taal-, Land- en Volkenkunde (TBG)* 24:298-317.

Green, D.H.
1965 *The Carolingian lord; Semantic studies on four old High German words: balder, fro, thuhtin, herro*. Cambridge: Cambridge University Press.
1980 *Irony in the medieval romance*. Cambridge: Cambridge University Press.

Gullick, J.M.
1958 *Indigenous political systems of Western Malaya*. London: Athlone Press.
1982 'The condition of having a raja; A review of *Kerajaan*, by A.C. Milner', *Review of Indonesian and Malaysian Affairs* 16-2:109-29.

Haidu, P.
1977 'Repetition; Modern reflections on medieval aesthetics', *Modern Language Notes* 92:875-87.

Hanitsch, R.
1903 'On a collection of coins from Malacca', *Journal of the Straits Branch of the Royal Asiatic Society* 39:183-202.

Harun Mat Piah
1980 *Cerita-cerita panji Melayu*. Kuala Lumpur: Dewan Bahasa dan Pustaka.

Havelock, E.A.
1963 *Preface to Plato*. Cambridge, Mass.: Belknap Press of Harvard University Press.

Heinrichs, W.
1969 *Arabische Dichtung und griechische Poetik; Hazim al-Qartagannis Grundlegung der Poetik mit Hilfe aristotelischer Begriffe*. Beirut/Wiesbaden: Steiner.

Heins, E.
1982 'A note on the structure and function of melody in *syair*-performance', *Indonesia Circle* 29:15-7.

Hempfer, K.W.
1973 *Gattungstheorie; Information und Synthese*. München: Fink.

Hikayat Indera Bangsawan
1978 *Hikayat Indera Bangsawan*. Jakarta: Departemen Pendidikan dan Kebudayaan.

Hoëvell, W.R. van (ed.)
1843 *Sjaïr Bidasari; Een oorspronkelijk Maleisch gedicht*. Batavia: n.n. [Verhandelingen van het Bataviaasch Genootschap van Kunsten en Wetenschappen 19.]

Hollander, J.J. de
1856 *Sjaïr Kén Tamboehan; Een oorspronkelijk Maleisch gedicht met aantekeningen uitgegeven*. Leiden: Brill.

Hooykaas, C.
1947 *Over Maleise literatuur*. Leiden: Brill.

1951	*Perintis sastera.* Groningen/Djakarta: Wolters.
Ismail Hamid	
1983a	*Kesusastraan Melayu lama dari warisan peradaban Islam.* Petaling Jaya: Fajar Bakti.
1983b	*The Malay Islamic hikayat.* Bangi: Penerbit Universiti Kebangsaan Malaysia.
Jacobi, R.	
1972	'Dichtung und Lüge in der arabischen Literaturtheorie', *Der Islam* 49:85-99.
Jauss, H.R.	
1977	*Alterität und Modernität der mittelalterlichen Literatur; Gesammelte Aufsätze 1956-1976.* München: Fink.
1984	*Aesthetic experience and literary hermeneutics.* Translated by Michael Shaw. Introduction by Wlad Godzich. Minneapolis: University of Minnesota Press.
Johns, A.H.	
1992	'*Tuhfat al-Nafis*: not a precious gift?', *Bijdragen tot de Taal-, Land- en Volkenkunde* 148:319-23.
Jones, G.F.	
1963	*The ethos of the Song of Roland.* Baltimore: Johns Hopkins University Press.
Jones, R. (ed.)	
1985	*Hikayat Sultan Ibrahim Ibn Adham; An edition of an anonymous Malay text with translation and notes.* Lanham: University Press of America, Berkeley: Center for South and Southeast Asia Studies, University of California.
Juynboll, H.H.	
1899	*Catalogus van de Maleische en Sundaneesche handschriften der Leidsche Universiteits-Bibliotheek.* Leiden: Brill.
Karrer, W.	
1977	*Parodie, Travestie, Pastiche.* München: Fink.
Keeler, W.	
1987	*Javanese shadow plays, Javanese selves.* Princeton, N.J.: Princeton University Press.
Kern, R.A.	
1940	'De beteekenis van het woord dalang', *Bijdragen tot de Taal-, Land- en Volkenkunde* 99:123-4.
Kessler, C.S.	
1978	*Islam and politics in a Malay state, Kelantan 1838-1969.* Ithaca/London: Cornell University Press.
Khalid Hussain (ed.)	
1964	*Hikayat Pandawa Lima.* Kuala Lumpur: Dewan Bahasa dan Pustaka.
Klinkert, H.C.	
1886	*Drie Maleische gedichten of de Sjaïrs Ken Tamboehan, Jatim Noestapa en Bidasari.* Leiden: Brill.

1947   *Nieuw Maleisch-Nederlandsch woordenboek.* Leiden: Brill. [Reprint.]
Koningsberger, J.C.
1915   *Java, zoölogisch en biologisch.* Buitenzorg: n.n.
Kosim, H.R. (ed.)
1978   *Syair Raja Siak.* Jakarta: Departemen Pendidikan dan Kebudayaan.
Koster, G.L.
1986a   'The *kerajaan* at war; On the genre heroic-historical *syair*', in: Taufik Abdullah (ed.), *Papers of the Fourth Indonesian-Dutch History Conference, Yogyakarta 24-29 July 1983,* Vol. 2, pp. 29-72. Yogyakarta: Gadjah Mada University Press.
1986b   'The soothing works of the seducer and their dubious fruits; Interpreting the Syair Buah-Buahan' in: C.M.S. Hellwig and S.O. Robson (eds), *A man of Indonesian letters; Essays in honour of Professor A. Teeuw,* pp. 73-99. Dordrecht/Cinnaminson: Foris. [KITLV, Verhandelingen 121.]
1988   Review of P.L. Thomas, *Like tigers around a piece of meat; The Baba style of Dondang Sayang* (Singapore 1986), *Review of Indonesian and Malaysian Affairs* 22-2:204-10.
1990   'Auteurschap als noodzakelijk kwaad; De verteller als vreemdeling in het Maleise sjair-dicht' in: W.L. Idema et al, *Het beeld van de vreemdeling in westerse en niet-westerse literatuur,* pp. 202-21. Baarn: Ambo.
1992   'Reluctant authorship; On the role of the narrator as a trader far from home (*dagang*) in the Malay *syair*', *Newsletter of the Indonesian Studies Program* 2-3:16-21.
1994a   *Peringatan dalam Syair Perang Siak.* Translated by Al Azhar. Pekan Baru: Pusat Pengajian Melayu Universitas Islam Riau.
1994b   'Harga diri dan rasa kemelayuan; Beberapa catatan tentang Sudara', *Dewan Sastera* (oktober):54-65.
Koster, G.L. and H.M.J. Maier
1982   'Variation within identity in the Syair Ken Tambuhan examined with the help of a computer-made concordance', *Indonesia Circle* 29:3-14.
1985   'A medicine of sweetmeats; On the power of Malay narrative', *Bijdragen tot de Taal-, Land- en Volkenkunde* 141:441-61.
Kramers, J.H. (translator)
1985   *De Koran uit het Arabisch vertaald.* Amsterdam/Brussel: Elsevier. [Reprint.]
Leeuwen, P.J. van (ed.)
1937   *De Maleische Alexanderroman.* Meppel: Ten Brink. [PhD thesis Rijksuniversiteit Utrecht.]
Lessing, G.E.
1955   *Gesammelte Werke; Band IV.* Herausgegeben von P. Rilla. Berlin: Aufbau Verlag.
Liaw Yock Fang
1975   *Sejarah kesusastraan Melayu klassik.* Singapura: Pustaka Nasional.
Lord, A.B.
1960   *The singer of tales.* Cambridge, Mass.: Harvard University Press.
Lotman, Y.
1976   *Analysis of the poetic text.* Ann Arbor, Mich.: Ardis.

1977   *The structure of the artistic text.* Translated by Ronald Vroon and Gail Lenhoff. Ann Arbor: Department of Slavic Languages and Literature, University of Michigan.

Maier, H.M.J.
1988   *In the center of authority; The Malay Hikayat Merong Mahawangsa.* Ithaca, N.Y.: Cornell South East Asia Program.

Maier, H.M.J. and G.L. Koster
1986   'A fishy story; Exercises in reading the Syair Ikan Terubuk', in: C.D. Grijns and S.O. Robson (eds), *Cultural contact and textual interpretation*, pp. 204-18. Dordrecht/Cinnaminson: Foris. [KITLV, Verhandelingen 115.]

Massier, A.H.W.
1988   Onder slangen en kikkers; Een uitgave en interpretatie van handschrift 161 van de verzameling-Klinkert. [MA thesis Rijksuniversiteit Leiden, Vakgroep Talen en Culturen van Zuidoost-Azië en Oceanië.]

Matheson, V.
1985   'Kisah pelayaran ke Riau: journey to Riau, 1984', *Indonesia Circle* 36:3-22.
1991   (ed.) *Tuhfat al-Nafis; Sejarah Melayu-Islam.* Translated by Ahmad Fauzi Basri. Kuala Lumpur: Dewan Bahasa dan Pustaka.

McRoberts, R.W.
1984   'An examination of the fall of Melaka in 1511', *Journal of the Malaysian Branch of the Royal Asiatic Society* 57-1:26-39.

Meijer, H.K. (ed.)
1984   Syair Ikan Terubuk. [MA thesis Rijksuniversiteit Leiden.]

Milner, A.C.
1982   *Kerajaan; Malay political culture on the eve of colonial rule.* Tucson: University of Arizona Press.
1983   'Islam and the Muslim state', in: M.B. Hooker, *Islam in South-East Asia*, pp. 23-49. Leiden: Brill.

Muhammad Haji Salleh
1980   'Preliminary notes on the esthetics of the Malay pantun', *Tenggara* 11:45-53.
1981   *Sajak-sajak sejarah Melayu.* Kuala Lumpur: Dewan Bahasa dan Pustaka.

Muhammad Yusoff Hashim (ed.)
1980   *Syair Sultan Maulana; Suatu penelitian kritis tentang hasil pensejarahan Melayu tradisional.* Kuala Lumpur: Penerbit Universiti Malaya.
1992   *Hikayat Siak; Dirawikan oleh Tengku Said.* Kuala Lumpur: Dewan Bahasa dan Pustaka.

Mulyadi, S.W.R. (ed.)
1983   *Hikayat Indraputra; A Malay romance.* Dordrecht: Foris. [KITLV, Bibliotheca Indonesica 23.]

Netscher, E.
1870   *De Nederlanders in Djohor en Siak, 1602 tot 1865; Historische beschrijving.* Batavia: Bruining en Wijt. [Verhandelingen van het Bataviaasch Genootschap van Kunsten en Wetenschappen 35.]

Nieuwenhuyzen, F.N.
1858 'Het rijk Siak Sri Indrapoera', *Tijdschrift voor Indische Taal-, Land- en Volkenkunde (TBG)* 7:388-438.

Nik Maimunah binti Yahya and Zaharah Mohd. Khalid (eds)
1964 *Hikayat Panji Semirang dan Hikayat Ken Tambohan*. Kuala Lumpur: Dewan Bahasa dan Pustaka.

Norris, Ch.
1987 *Derrida*. London: Fontana Press.

Ong, W.J.
1977 *Interfaces of the word; Studies in the evolution of consciousness and culture*. Ithaca/London: Cornell University Press.
1982 *Orality and literacy; The technologizing of the word*. London/New York: Methuen.

Overbeck, H.O.
1922 'The Malay pantun', *Journal of the Straits Branch of the Royal Asiatic Society* 85:4-28.
1934 'Malay animal and flower shaers', *Journal of the Malayan Branch of the Royal Asiatic Society* 12-2:108-48.

Owen, S.
1986 *Remembrances; The experience of the past in classical Chinese literature*. Cambridge, Mass./London: Harvard University Press.

Panuti H.M. Sujiman
1982 *Adat raja-raja Melayu*. Jakarta: Penerbit Universitas Indonesia.

Penulis Lama
1964 'Kewajipan orang Melayu mengetahui bahasa Melayu', in: Zabedah Awang Ngah (ed.), *Antologi esei Melayu dalam tahun 1924-41*, pp. 61-3. Kuala Lumpur: Dewan Bahasa dan Pustaka.

Phillips, N.
1981 *Sijobang; Sung narrative poetry of West Sumatra*. Cambridge: Cambridge University Press.

Pigeaud, Th.
1938 *Javaans-Nederlands handwoordenboek*. Groningen/Batavia: Wolters.

Poerbatjaraka, R.Ng.
1940 *Pandji-verhalen onderling vergeleken*. Bandoeng: Nix. [Bibliotheca Javanica 9.]

Propp, V.
1968 *Morphology of the folktale*. Austin/London: University of Texas Press. [Translation from the Russian first edition of 1928.]

Raja Ali Haji ibn Ahmad
1982 *The precious Gift (Tuhfat al-Nafis)*. An annotated translation by Virginia Matheson and Barbara Watson Andaya. Kuala Lumpur: Oxford University Press.

Ras, J.J.
1968 *Hikajat Bandjar; A study in Malay historiography*. The Hague: Nijhoff. [Bibliotheca Indonesica 1.]

1976 'The historical development of the Javanese shadow theatre', *Review of Indonesian and Malaysian Affairs* 10-2:50-76.
1982 'The social function and cultural significance of the Javanese *wayang purwa* theatre', *Indonesia Circle* 29:19-32.
1992 *The shadow of the ivory tree; Language, literature and history in Nusantara* Leiden: Vakgroep Talen en Culturen van Zuidoost-Azië en Oceanië, Rijksuniversiteit. [Semaian 6.]

Rassers, W.H.
1922 *De Pandji-roman*. Antwerpen: De Vos-Van Kleef. [PhD thesis Rijksuniversiteit Leiden.]

Reid, A. and L. Castles (eds)
1975 *Pre-colonial state systems in Southeast Asia; The Malay peninsula, Sumatra, Bali-Lombok, South Celebes*. Kuala Lumpur: Perchetakan Mas. [Monographs of the Malaysian Branch of the Royal Asiatic Society 6.]

Rimmon-Kenan, S.
1983 *Narrative fiction; Contemporary poetics*. London/New York: Methuen.

Robson, S.O.
1969 (ed.) *Hikajat Andaken Penurat*. The Hague: Nijhoff. [KITLV, Bibliotheca Indonesica 2.]
1971 (ed.) *Wangbang Wideya; A Javanese Panji romance*. The Hague: Nijhoff. [KITLV, Bibliotheca Indonesica 6.]
1992 'Java in Malay literature; Overbeck's ideas on Malayo-Javanese literature', in: V.J.H. Houben, H.M.J. Maier and W. van der Molen (eds), *Looking in odd mirrors; The Java Sea*, pp. 27-42. Leiden: Vakgroep Talen en Culturen van Zuidoost-Azië en Oceanië, Rijksuniversiteit. [Semaian 5.]

Ronkel, Ph.S. van
1895 *De roman van Amir Hamza*. Leiden: Brill.
1909 *Catalogus der Maleische handschriften in het Museum van het Bataviaasch Genootschap van Kunsten en Wetenschappen*. Batavia: Albrecht, 's Hage: Nijhoff. [Verhandelingen van het Bataviaasch Genootschap van Kunsten en Wetenschappen 57.]
1921 *Supplement-catalogus der Maleische en Minangkabausche handschriften in de Leidsche Universiteits-Bibliotheek*. Leiden: Brill.

Roolvink, R.
1967 'The variant versions of the Malay Annals', *Bijdragen tot de Taal-, Land- en Volkenkunde* 123:301-24.
1987 Review of Russell Jones (ed.), *Hikayat Sultan Ibrahim ibn Adham* (Lanham, 1985), *Bijdragen tot de Taal-, Land- en Volkenkunde* 143:591-4.

Roorda van Eysinga, P.P.
1838 *Radin Mantri, eene romance naar een Indisch handschrift van Ali Mustathier*. Breda: Broese.
1847 'Abdoel Moeloek, koning van Barbarije', *Tijdschrift voor Neêrlands Indië* 9-4:285-526.

Rorty, R.
1982 *Consequences of pragmatism; Essays 1972-1980*. Brighton: Harvester Press.

Rubinstein, R.
1988   *Beyond the realm of the senses; The Balinese ritual of kakawin composition* [PhD thesis University of Sydney.]

Ryding, W.W.
1971   *Structure in medieval narrative*. The Hague/Paris: Mouton.

Sahlins, M.
1983   'Other times, other customs; The anthropology of history', *American Anthropologist* 85:517-44.

Salmon, C.
1981   *Literature in Malay by the Chinese of Indonesia; A provisional annotated bibliography*. Paris: Maison des Sciences de l'Homme.

Schadee, W.H.M.
1918-19   *Geschiedenis van Sumatra's Oostkust*. Amsterdam: Oostkust van Sumatra-Instituut. 2 vols.

Schimmel, A.
1975   *Mystical dimensions of Islam*. Chapel Hill: University of North Carolina Press.
1980   *The triumphal sun; A study of the works of Jalaloddin Rumi*. London/The Hague: East-West Publications. [First edition 1978.]

Schulte Nordholt, H.
1992   'Origin, descent and destruction; Text and context in Balinese representations of the past', *Indonesia* 54:27-58.

Seltmann, F.
1987   *Die Kalang; Eine Volksgruppe auf Java und ihre Stamm-Mythe; Ein Beitrag zur Kulturgeschichte Javas*. Stuttgart: Steiner.

Shellabear, W.G. (ed.)
1982   *Sejarah Melayu*. Petaling Jaya: Fajar Bakti. [Reprint.]

Sidney, Ph.
1971   *A defence of poetry*. Edited and with an introduction and notes by J.A. van Dorsten. London: Oxford University Press. [First published 1595.]

Siegel, J.
1969   *The rope of God*. Berkeley/Los Angeles: University of California Press.
1979   *Shadow and sound; The historical thought of a Sumatran people*. Chicago: University of Chicago Press.

Siti Hawa Saleh
1970   (ed.) *Hikayat Merong Mahawangsa*. Kuala Lumpur/Singapura: University of Malaya Press.
1986   (ed.) *Hikayat Gul Bakawali*. Petaling Jaya: Fajar Bakti.
1993   'Pengajian teks Melayu tradisional; Penilaian semula penelitian dan interpretasi', *Dewan Sastera* (disember):52-5.

Situmorang, T.A. and A. Teeuw (eds)
1952   *Sedjarah Melaju menurut terbitan Abdullah*. Djakarta: Pembangunan.

Skeat, W.W.
1900   *Malay magic, being an introduction to the folklore and popular religion of the Malay peninsula*. London: Macmillan.

Skinner, C. (ed.)
1963   Sja'ir Perang Mengkasar (The rhymed chronicle of the Macassar War) by Entji' Amin. 's-Gravenhage: Nijhoff. [KITLV, Verhandelingen 40.]
1982   Ahmad Rijaluddin's Hikayat Perintah Negeri Benggala. The Hague: Nijhoff. [KITLV, Bibliotheca Indonesica 22.]
1985   The battle for Junk Ceylon; The Syair Sultan Maulana. Dordrecht/ Cinnaminson: Foris. [KITLV, Bibliotheca Indonesia 25.]

Stapel, F.W.
1922   Het Bongaais verdrag. [PhD thesis Rijksuniversiteit Leiden.]
1936   Cornelis Janszoon Speelman. 's-Gravenhage: Nijhoff. [Reprinted from Bijdragen tot de Taal-, Land- en Volkenkunde 94:1-221.]

Striedter, J.
1971   (ed.) Russischer Formalismus; Texte zur allgemeinen Literaturtheorie und zur Theorie der Prosa. München: Fink.
1976   'Einleitung', in: F. Vodicka, Die Struktur der literarischen Entwicklung. München: Fink.

Sulastin Sutrisno
1986   'Studi sastra Melayu di Indonesia', in: C.M.S. Hellwig and S.O. Robson, A man of Indonesian letters; Essays in honour of Professor A. Teeuw, pp. 116-31. Dordrecht/Cinnaminson: Foris. [KITLV, Verhandelingen 121.]

Sweeney, A.
1972   The Ramayana and the Malay shadow-play. Kuala Lumpur: Penerbit Universiti Kebangsaan Malaysia.
1980   Authors and audiences in traditional Malay literature. Berkeley: University of California, Center for South and Southeast Asian Studies.
1987   A full hearing; Orality and literacy in the Malay world. Berkeley: University of California Press.

Teeuw, A.
1946   Het Bhomakāwya; Een Oudjavaans gedicht. Groningen: Wolters.
1952   Taal en versbouw; Rede uitgesproken bij de aanvaarding van het ambt van gewoon hoogleraar in de vergelijkende en algemene taalwetenschap aan de Rijksuniversiteit te Utrecht op 19 mei 1952. Amsterdam: Djambatan.
1966   Shair Ken Tambuhan. Kuala Lumpur: Oxford University Press.
1992   'A recently published Malay courtpoem', Bijdragen tot de Taal-, Land- en Volkenkunde 148:129-34.

Tenas Effendy
1989   'Sedikit catatan tentang "Syair Perang Siak" ', in: D.J. Goudie, Syair Perang Siak; A court poem presenting the state policy of a Minangkabau Malay royal family in exile, pp. 257-68. Kuala Lumpur: Malaysian Branch of the Royal Asiatic Society.

Thomas, P.L.
1979   'Syair and pantun prosody', Indonesia 27:51-63.
1980   'Long and short pantun lines', Review of Indonesian and Malaysian Affairs 14-1:23-39.
1984   'The Malay pantun; A problem of redundancy', Indonesia Circle 33:15-22.

1986 'Rasa, genealogy, and disappearing characters in Malay fiction', *Review of Indonesian and Malaysian Affairs* 20-1:38-49.

Todorov, Tz.
1984 *Mikhail Bakhtin; The dialogical principle.* Translated by Wlad Godzich. Manchester: Manchester University Press.

Tol, R.
1990 *Een haan in oorlog; Toloqna Arung Labuaja; Een twintigste-eeuws Buginees heldendicht van de hand van I Mallaq Daéng Mabéla Arung Manajéng.* Dordrecht/Providence: Foris. [KITLV, Verhandelingen 141.]

Tomashevsky, B.
1965 'Thematics', in: L.T. Lemon and M.J. Reis (eds), *Russian formalist criticism; Four essays*, pp. 61-95. Lincoln: University of Nebraska Press.

Tsuchiya Kenji
1987 *Democracy and leadership; The rise of the Taman Siswa movement in Indonesia.* Translated by Peter Hawkes. Honolulu: University of Hawaii Press.

Tuti Munawar (ed.)
1978 *Syair Bidasari.* Jakarta: Departemen Pendidikan dan Kebudayaan.

Tuuk, H.N. van der
1875 'Geschiedenis der Pandawa's naar een Maleisch handschrift der Royal Asiatic Society, No. 2 in Fol.', *Tijdschrift voor Indische Taal-, Land- en Volkenkunde (TBG)* 21:1-90.

Umar Yunus
1984 *Sejarah Melayu; Menemukan diri kembali.* Petaling Jaya: Fajar Bakti.

Vance, E.
1979 'Roland and the poetics of memory', in: J.V. Harari (ed.), *Textual strategies; Perspectives in post-structuralist criticism*, pp. 374-403. Ithaca, N.Y.: Cornell University Press.

Vickers, A.H.
1986 *The desiring prince; A study of the Kidung Malat as text.* [PhD thesis University of Sydney.]

Vinaver, E.
1971 *The rise of romance.* Oxford: Clarendon Press.

Voorhoeve, P.
1968 'The origin of the Malay sja'ir', *Bijdragen tot de Taal-, Land- en Volkenkunde* 124:277-8.

Watson, C.W.
1971 'Some preliminary remarks on the antecedents of modern Indonesian literature', *Bijdragen tot de Taal-, Land- en Volkenkunde* 127:417-33.

White, H.V.
1978 *Tropics of discourse; Essays in cultural criticism.* Baltimore/London: Johns Hopkins University Press.
1980 'The value of narrativity in the representation of reality', *Critical Inquiry* 7-1:5-27.

Wilkinson, R.J.
1906 *Malay beliefs.* London: Luzac, Leiden: Brill.

1907   *Papers on Malay subjects; Malay literature part 1 (romance, history, poetry)*. Kuala Lumpur: Government of Federated Malay States.
1913   'The poetry of the Malays', in: *Noctes orientales; Being a selection of essays read before the Straits Philosophical Society between the years 1899 and 1910*, pp. 86-97. Singapore: Kelly and Walsh.
1943   *A Malay-English dictionary (romanised)*. 2 vols. Tokyo: Daitoa Syuppan Kabusiki Kaisya. [Reprint.]

Winstedt, R.O.
1977   *A history of classical Malay literature*. Kuala Lumpur: Oxford University Press. [Reprint.]

Wittig, S.
1978   *Stylistic and narrative structures in the Middle English romances*. Austin/London: University of Texas Press.

Woelders, M.O.
1975   *Het sultanaat Palembang 1811-1825*. 's-Gravenhage: Nijhoff. [KITLV, Verhandelingen 72.]

Yusoff Iskandar and Abdul Rahman Kaeh
1978   *Sejarah Melayu (Edisi Shellabear); Suatu perbicaraan kritis dari pelbagai bidang*. Kuala Lumpur: Heinemann.

Zainal Abidin Bakar (ed.)
1983   *Kumpulan pantun Melayu*. Kuala Lumpur: Dewan Bahasa dan Pustaka.

Zoetmulder, P.J.
1974   *Kalangwan; A survey of Old Javanese literature*. The Hague: Nijhoff. [KITLV, Translation Series 16.]
1982   *Old Javanese-English Dictionary*. 's-Gravenhage: Nijhoff. 2 vols.

Index

'Abd al-Karim al-Jili 81
Abdullah ibn Abdulkadir al-Munsyi
   10-2, 240-1, 247
Abdul Rahman Kaeh 164
Abhandlungen über die Fabel 224-5
actantial scheme 195-7
Adat Raja-Raja Melayu 91
akal 69, 77, 90, 140, 147, 171-2, 179,
   182, 220, 225, 228-9, 235, 240-1
al-lawh al-mahfuz *see* Safely Preserved
   Tablet
allegory 9-12, 87, 151-2, 188, 191, 201,
   208-12, 215, 225-6, 241, 249, 251
Alfonso d'Albuquerque 23-4
alienation 8, 174, 176, 180, 189, 192-3,
   see also anak jamu, exile, fakir, gharib,
   musafir
alterity 1-2, 23, 123-5
Amin, Enci' 71, 101, 106, 112
amnesia 174, 176, 181, 189, 192, *see
   also* forgetfulness
amplification 4-5, 8-10, 19, 30, 45, 47,
   84, 91, 110, 112, 116-7, 120, 193-4,
   249, *see also* memanjangkan,
   proliferation of the signifier
anak jamu 72
Angreni-motif 163-6, 196-7
author, implied – 241, 244-5, 248-50
authority 1-2, 6, 10, 56, 58-60, 76, 78-
   80, 83-4, 86-7, 92, 127, 153, 241,
   244, 248-9
authorship 4-5, 10, 54, 58-60, 63, 65-
   77, 80, 83-93, 149, 224, 242, 244,
   247-51
Aziz Nasafi 81
Ayub (Job) 75, 85, 151

badan 66, 78, 85 *see also* lafaz

Bangsawan theatre 29
Barthes, R. 34, 105, 118
Bayezid 83
beauty 4, 11, 19, 28, 30-1, 46-8, 52, 54-
   61, 66-8, 87, 90, 92, 113, 156, 167,
   171, 176-7, 179, 183, 188, 195-7,
   219-20, 229, 231, 235, 239-41, 250
Beethoven, Ludwig van 155
Blagden, O. 199
Bloch, R.H. 136, 193
Book
   – of the Devil 10, 89, 235-6, 250
   – of Geomancy 55
   – of God's Writing 7-8, 132-3, 247-8,
      see also Koran, Safly Preserved
      Tablet
   – of Hindu-Javanese Mythology 133,
      183-90
   – of the Malay *Kerajaan* Order 6-9,
      55, 62, 86, 91, 132, 140, 142, 156,
      168, 181-2, 192-3
   – of Memory 55, 80, 85-6, 182,
   – of the Universe 55, 80-1, 85, 182
   – of the Writings by Holy Men and
      Inspired Theologians 55, 80, 85-7
Boon, J.A. 191
bujangga 53, 57-9, *see also* wisdom
Bukhari al-Jauhari 87-8
Bustan ul-Katibin 11
Bustan us-Salatin 11, 87

carnival 8, 193
cautionary tale 144, 152, 155
Chinese, peranakan 218-9, 223, 237
Chronicle 114
Collingwood, R.G. 122
comedy 5-7, 131-7, 142-4, 147, 152
commemoration 4-9, 54-5, 62, , 76-8,

82, 89-91, 127-59, 180, 182, 187, 192-3, 195, *see also* copying, imitation, mengadakan, mengingat, remembrance, repetition, representation, return
copying 4-5, 55, 80, 85-6, 88, 90, 92-3, 199, 224
copyright 250
Culler, J. 97-8, 224

dagang
   narratorial role of – 4, 6-10, 53-5, 60, 64-77, 80, 84-5, 90, 92, 107, 150-1, 153, *see also* fakir, gharib, musafir
   narratorial role of – 4, 8, 10, 53-64, 62-5, 76-7, 80, 84, 89-90, 92, 176, *see also* bujangga, paramakawi, yang empunya cerita
Dalang, Allah 242
dalil 87
Defence of Poetry 22-3
Derrida, J. 80
desire 4-5, 7-8, 10, 56-8, 61-2, 69, 74, 77, 85, 90-1, 127, 132, 140, 155-6, 166-70, 173, 177, 179, 191-2, 206, 214, 222, 234-9, *see also* hawa nafsu
Dharmaja, Mpu 185
dialogue 2-3, 42, 62, 156, 192-4
dirge 154
disguise 163-4, 166, , 181, 190
divination 147
Divine Comedy 8, 75, 149-52
dominanta 38, 99, 102, 109, 124
drama 137-42, 149, 165-6, 180, 190-2
dream 167-70, 178, 180, 185
Duggan, J. 43
Dul Muluk theatre 66
dying injunction 140

elegy 7, 156
encyclopaedia of tradition 5, 21, 55, 78, *see also* totalizing mode of cognition
epic
   heroic – 5, 9, 97-126, 128, 131-2, 135-9, 144, 161, 183, 197-8, 202-8, 212, 231

literary – 108
exemplariness 15, 19, 21-2, 27-8, 30, 32-3, 67, 76-7, 86-7, 108, 123-4, 135, 224, 232, 236, 241
exile 7-8, 64-7, 69-73, 75, 77-8, 84-5, 128-31, 138-9, 142-6, 150-1, 156, 161, 171, 173, 175-6, 181, 183, 192-3, 195, 198, 210, 215, 239, 242

fable 9-10, 20-1, 65, 215, 224-6, 240-1
Fairy Queen 89
fakir 53-4, 65-6, 70-1, 74-5, 84, 90, 92, 107, 130, 151, 153-4, 219, 240-2
Fariduddin 'al-'Attar 71
fiction, subservient – 10, 55, 86, 89
fictionality 4-5, 9-10, 55, 63-4, 86-93, 243-51
forgetfulness 4-6, 8, 11-2, 30-1, 54-5, 62-4, 76-7, 79, 83-5, 88-92, 127, 132, 136-42, 145, 149, 150, 156-7, 174, 179-81, 192-3, 220, 222, 224-5, 228, 239-41, *see also* exile, mengada-ada, opacity
formula 4, 18-9, 43, 78, 109, 169
formulaic devices 1, 4, 35-6, 43-8, 135, 180, 192, 202
formulaic expression 4, 30, 43, 109
Fantosme, Jordan of 114
Foucault, M. 125
Frye, N. 108, 123, 132, 143-4, 168, 174

garden, the literary work as – 10-2, 220, 228-30, 233-4, 236, 239-40
Gardner, H. 155
Geguritan Pakang Raras 196-8
Gellrich, J.M. 79-80
genealogical chronicle 7, 128, 133-9
genre 3, 21, 98-102, 108-10, 123-5, 128, 131-2, 161, 166, 174, 195-8, 204-5, 209, 217, 227-8, *see also* heroic epic, genealogical chronicle, romance
gharib 53-4, 65-6, 70-1, 107
Gospels 88
Goudie, D.J. 130-1
Gulshan-i Raz 81

hadith 70, 248
Hamzah Fansuri 72-3, 83, 242

Harun Mat Piah 164
Havelock, E.A. 19, 21
hawa nafsu 140, 225, 228-9, 235-6, 239
Hazeu, G.A.J. 64
Heins, E. 48
helper (penolong) 202-6, 213, 221-2, 227-9
Hempfer, K.W. 99
Hikayat
 — *Andaken Penurat* 55-7, 60, 62-3, 165, 231, 234, 236
 — *Amir Hamzah* 25, 27
 — *Berma Shahdan* 235
 — *Bidasari* 220-1
 — *Cekel Wanengpati* 57-9, 62-3, 165, 175, 197, 219, 231-2
 — *Dewa Asmara* 184
 — *Dewa Asmara Jaya* 164, 233
 — *Dewa Mandu* 59-60, 109-10
 — *Dewa Mengindra* 232
 — *Galuh Digantung* 233
 — *Gul Bakawali* 11
 — *Indera Bangsawan* 243
 — *Indra Nata* 233
 — *Indraputra* 20, 88-9, 234
 — *Iskandar Zulkarnain* 238
 — *Kuda Semirang Sira Panji* 56
 — *Kuda Semirang Sira Panji Pandai Rupa* 233
 — *Kuraisy* 233
 — *Maharaja Boma* 90
 — *Merong Mahawangsa* 89, 236, 238
 — *Merpati Emas* 221
 — *Merpati Emas dan Merpati Perak* 221
 — *Misa Taman Jayeng Kusuma* 63, 110, 197, 229-30, 232, 234-5, 237-8
 — *Muhammad Hanafiyyah* 25-7, 238
 — *Pandawa Lima* 110, 189, 231, 233-4
 — *Panja Tanderan* 10-12, 239-41
 — *Panji Kuda Semirang* 56-7, 162
 — *Raden Cekel* 219
 — *Raja Bermadewa* 219
 — *Raja Muda* 21
 — *Raja Pandawa* 219
 — *Sang Boma* 184, 189
 — *Sang Bima* 133
 — *Seri Rama* 33, 88-90, 182
 — *Si Burung Pingai* 82
 — *Siak* see *Sejarah Melayu* of the Royal House of Siak
 — *Sultan Ibrahim ibn Adham* 71-2, 74, 150
 — *Sultan Taburat* 218-21
 — *Syah Mardan* 75
hikayat-style, origin of the — 110
historiography as fiction-making 122-3
Hollander, J.J. de 165
Hooykaas, C. 100

Idea of the Book, the 4-5, 54-5, 79-83, 85
identity 8, 165-6, 171, 173-84, 192-3, 195-6, 198
illusion 4-5, 7-9, 61-4, 77, 88-91, 152, 174, 176-82, 189, 193
imitation 5, 21, 30, 55, 80, 86, 101, 182, 241, 251
impropriety 4-7, 9-10, 91, 108-9, 135-42, 146, 148, 153, 167-9, 172, 180, 193, 203-8, 228-9, 235, 241-50, *see also* memanjangkan, signifier and signified in disjunction
influence 101
interpretation 4-5, 7-8, 10-1, 54, 78, 80, 83-4, 91-2, 97-8, 137, 151-2, 156-7, 173, 176-81, 191, 193, 199, 201-2, 204, 214, 224
intertextuality 33, 35-6, 56-64, 70-5, 81-3, 97, 103-4, 107-9, 114-5, 118-123, 128, 132-5, 140-5, 149-51, 169, 173-5, 182-90, 199-215, 217, 224-40, 242-3, 245-8
irony 5, 241-50
 dramatic — 173

Jauss, H.R. 3, 19, 36
Jones, R. 34
justice
 poetic — 6, 9, 119-22, 136, 181
 retributive — 127, 139, 144, 149, 156

kakawin 57-8, 61, 110, 183

Kakawin Arjunawiwaha 63-4, 183-4, 187
Kakawin Bharatayuddha 110
Kakawin Bhomakavya 90, 184
Kakawin Hariwangsa 189
Kakawin Kresnayana 185-9
Kakawin Smaradahana 185, 187
Kanwa, Mpu 183
karma 188, 191
Kemas Fakhruddin al-Palimbani 74
Kern, R.A. 64
kidung 57, 62, 166, 186, 195
Kidung
 – *Malat* 186
 – *Wangbang Wideya* 62, 166, 186, 195-6
Kitab
 – *al Insan al-Kamil* 81
 – *Mukhtasar* 74
Klinkert, H.C. 200-1
Koran 18-9, 55, 75, 80-2, 86-7, 92, 236, 245, 247-8
Kristeva, J. 97

lafaz (signifier) 78, 84
law 4-5, 7-8, 108-9, 127, 132-4, 140, 142-4, 146, 149, 152-3, 155-7, 166-74, 188, 191-2, 202-4, 207, 212, 225, 228, 235, 242, 247-9, *see also* karma
Liaw Yock Fang 100
literacy 4, 17-9, 54, 56, 78-80, 251
literary competence 35, 52, 97-8
logocentrism 5, 78
Lord, A.B. 43
Lotman, Y. 36, 105
lying 4, 55, 86-9, 107-8, 113-4, 119, 142, 244-6, *see also* mengada-ada, signifier and signified in disjunction
lyric 193-4, 198

makna (signified) 78, 83-4
magician 58-61, 63-4, 88, 90
Mahmud ash-Shabistari 81
Malayness 15
marriage
 arranged – 166-7, 169-70, 192
 – by consensus 169-70, 187, 192
mediation 7-9, 155-6, 161, 190-3
Meijer, H.K. 199

memanjangkan 4-5, 10, 57, 65, 71, 84-5, 90-1, 135, 176, 180, 193, 249, *see also* amplification, proliferation of the signifier
mematutkan 4-6, 8, 55, 59, 84-5, 90-1, 135
memorability 135
mengada-ada 4-5, 8-9, 63-4, 79-80, 88, 113-4, 119-20, 134, 136, 156, 178, 181, 183, 193, *see also* illusion
mengadakan 4-6, 8, 79, 88, 11-3, 115-7, 132, 136, 156, 181, 183, 193, *see also* representation
mengenangkan 4-5, 7-8, 77, 83-5, 153-4, 180, *see also* forgetfulness
mengingat 4-5, 7-8, 65, 77, 83-5, 132, 153-4, 159
Milner, A.C. 55, 115, 125
mimesis 4-5, 8, 55, 76, 91, 135, 181-2, 195-6, 226-7
mirror 5, 55, 70, 79-80, 84-5, 87
 – of the heart 82-3
misreading 179
monologue 5-6, 8, 156, 193, 241
Muhammad Bakir vii, 9, 217-9, 226-7, 241
Muhammad Haji Salleh 24
Muhammad, Tengku 131, 141, 157
musafir 53, 65, 70-1

Nafron Hasyim 48
narratee 219, 241, 249
narration 3-4, 53-94, 152-7, 218-9, 241-50
narrative 20-1
narrator
 – as distinct from oral storyteller and writer 53
 – as fictional construct
 omniscient – 244
 unreliable – 10, 241-9
Nasihat al-Muluk 87
Norris, Ch. 80
Nuruddin al-Raniri 88

oath, heroic – 6, 9, 101, 109-16, 119, 124, 131-2, 202-3, 205-9, 213
omina 148, 182

Ong, W.J. 19, 241
opacity 7-8, 10, 78-9, 83, 85, 137-8, 145, 156, 180, 192
opposition, archisemic – 105, 228-9, 235
oral-aural
 – communication 1-2, 18-9, 35, 54, 76-9, 218, 241, 243-4, 246-7, 251
 – features in Malay manuscripts 18-9
orality 4, 18, 54, 56, 76-80, 241, 243
origin 4, 6, 8, 10, 55, 75-7, 80, 83, 85-6, 88-9, 92, 101, 132-5, 182-3, 193, 196, 246-7
originality 36, 251
Orlando Furioso 165
Overbeck, H. 1-2, 42, 62, 200-1, 217, 226, 229, 237, 250
Owen, S. 149

Pancatantra 240
pantun 21-2, 42, 73, 203, 222-4, 226, 229, 233, 236-7, 250
Panuluh, Mpu 189
parable 240
paramakawi 53, 57-8, 60
parody 5, 9-10, 91, 204-6, 211-2, 227, 229-37, 241, 250
Parry, M. 43
pengarang 10, 219, 244, 248-50
Piers Plowman 75
pilgrimage 75-6
plot 5-8, 122-3, 132, 142, 144, 149, 152, 157, 161-6, 174, 182-3, 189-90, 195-8, 202, 204, *see also* comedy, drama, romance, tragedy
Poerbatjaraka, R.Ng. 162-4
poetics of
 – dalangship in Javanese oral tradition 58-60, 77, 79
 – dalangship in the Wayang Siam 58, 79
 – Old Javanese literature 54, 60-1, 81-3, 86, 90
 – Rasa in Sanskrit literature 61-2
 – Sufi literature 54, 81-4
 – traditional Malay literature 53-93
prayer 134, 147, 157
print culture 1-2, 218

profitable (berfaedah, berguna, bermanfaat) 3-4, 15, 19-20, 22-3, 27-9, 32-3, 54, 65, 69-75, 77, 83-4, 86-7, 92, 127, 156-7, 159, 193, 200, 236, 240-1, 246
Propp, V. 164, 195
propriety 4-6, 8, 16, 18, 21, 33, 55, 79-80, 83-4, 90-1, 108-9, 135, 138-9, 141-4, 148-9, 153, 166, 169-70, 180, 192-3, 202-3, 207, 228-9, 235, *see also* signifier and signified in conjunction, mematutkan
proverb 224-6

quest-motif 60-1, 75, 81, 83, 174

Ras, J.J. 164, 190-1
Rassers, W.H. 191
reading 2-3, 33-5, 44, 56, 68-9, 80-4, 87, 97-8, 105, 122, 129, 149-52, 155, 166-7, 173, 176-80, 192-3, 201-2, 208, 214, 219-21, 227, 235-41
reality effect 33-4, 118
reception 3, 15-35, *see also* profitable, soothing
recall 4-6, 8, 76, 78, 82-3, 90, 132, 134, 182, 193, 198
referentiality 15, 22, 24, 33-4, 56, 68-9, 103, 105, 108, 117-23, 129-31, 157-8, 208-15, 218-9, 226-7, 229, 232, 235
remembrance 4, 6, 8, 54-5, 61-2, 64, 69-75, 83-5, 127, 131-9, 142, 146, 150, 181-2, 189, 213, 220, 222, 225, 228-9, 235, 239-40
repetition 4-5, 19, 21, 30, 35, 43-4, 52, 55, 78, 92, 101, 109-10, 133-5, 180, 182-3, 187, 193, 241
representation 3-6, 8-9, 11, 35-49, 55, 78, 88, 91, 132-3, 136, 147, 180, 182, 192-3, *see also* copying, imitation, mimesis, recall, repetition
reputation (aib, fitnah, nama, malu) 108-9, 111, 113-5, 118-9, 121, 132-6, 141-3, 207, 222
return 7-8, 55, 61-2, 69-73, 75-7, 80-3, 173-4, 181-2, 189, 192, 195-6, 198, 220, 239-40

rhetoricity 15, 18, 21-3, 28, 33, 56, 69-70, 104-5, 108, 117-23, 127, 157-9, 229, 235
rhyme-formula 42
Rimmon-Kenan, S. 20, 241
Robson, S.O. 56, 162-6, 196
romance 3-5, 8-9, 29, 53, 55-8, 62-3, 75, 89, 100, 109, 123, 143-5, 161-98, 202-8, 212, 227, 229-39, 243-4, 250
ronggeng 224, 236
Rorty, R. 122

Sair
  – *Buah-Buahan* vii, 9-10, 202-5, 217-51
  – *Kembang Merabat* 221
  – *Nasihat* 221
  – *Rinum Sari* 220-1
  – *Sang Kupu-Kupu dengan Kembang dan Belalang* 218, 227
satire 9, 211-2, 215, 226, 235
Schulte Nordholt, H 125
Sejarah Melayu 3, 21-8, 134-5, 141, 200-1, 203, 207, 209, 246-7
  – of the Royal House of Siak 141, 209-12
Serat al-Mustakim 88-9
Seafarer 75
Sifat
  – *ul-Muluk* 87
  – *us-Salatin* 87
signification 5, 8-9, 54, 80, 173, 191-2
signifier
  – -errant 8, 161, 179-81, 192-3, 196
  proliferation of the – 8-9, 11, 92-4, 205
  – and signified in conjunction 5-9, 79, 109, 133-5, 181, 192, 205, see also mematutkan
  – and signified in disjunction 5-10, 79, 113-4, 119, 134-5, 141, 145, 180-1, 193, 203, 205, 207-8, 237-9, 241-50, see also memanjangkan, proliferation of the signifier
Sidney, Ph. 22-3
Sijobang 89
Skinner, C. 98, 203-6, 108, 118, 120-1
Song of Roland 114-5

soothing (menghiburkan, melipurkan lara) 3-4, 11, 15, 19-20, 22-3, 27-33, 53-4, 57-8, 61-2, 66, 71, 77, 84, 127, 152, 156-7, 159, 168, 193-4, 200, 220, 223-4, 228, 230, 233, 236-41, 246
Spenser, E. 89
status, reduction in social – 174, 195
Stempel, W.D. 99
story 131-52, 218-9, 214, 247
Suprabaduta, wayang purwa lakon– 186
Sweeney, A. 18
syair
  animal and flower – 201-4, 226, 227-9
  sung performance of – 4, 48-52, 159
  prosody of the – 4-5, 32-42
Syair
  – *Abdul Muluk* 66
  – *Bidasari* 52, 165, 231, 234
  – *Bunga Air Mawar* 202, 227
  – *Burung* 92-3
  – *Burung Pungguk* 202, 227
  – *Dagang* 73, 247
  – *Ikan Terubuk* 9, 199-215, 226-7
  – *Ken Tambuhan* 3-4, 8-9, 21, 29-52, 63, 77, 145, 161-98, 229-34
  – *Kerajaan Bima* 109, 242
  – *Kumbang dan Melati* 202, 227
  – *Lampung Karam* 65
  – *Mambang Jauhari* 235
  – *Negeri Mekah dan Medina* 65-6
  – *Nuri* 20-1, 215, 227
  – *Nyamuk dan Lalat* 65-227
  – *Pelanduk Jenaka* 226
  – *Perahu* 73
  – *Perahu*, Rencong version 82
  – *Perang Mengkasar* 5-6, 85, 97-125, 202-3
  – *Perang Menteng* 100-1, 202
  – *Perang Siak* 6-8, 48, 101-2, 127-59, 161, 202, 211-2, 248
  – *Puteri Akal* 233
  – *Raja Siak* 102, 127
  – *Raja Tedung dan Raja Katak* 215
  – *Siti Zubaidah* 66-70, 77-8, 85, 89
  – *Sultan Maulana* 84, 101-2, 108,

Index 273

Taj us-Salatin 70-1, 87, 152
Tablet, Safely Preserved – 78, 80-1, 247-8
– Unggas 226
203, 244-5
Tasso, Torquato 165
taxonomy 21, 100, 164, 201
Teeuw, A. 165
Tomashevsky, B. 20
topical scheme 43-4
– for the dagang-narrator 64-5, 69, 73, 76
– for the dalang-narrator 57-8, 76
Torah 88
totalizing mode of cognition 78-80
tragedy 5, 7-8, 143, 152, 155-7
– of divine nemesis 7, 146-50
revenge – 7, 141-5, 149
tragicomedy 212
Triguna, Mpu 185
truth 4-5, 7-8, 10-1, 55, 60-4, 76-80, 82, 84-6, 89-92, 243-4, 246-7
Tuhfat al-Nafis 135, 140, 150
Tun Seri Lanang 23
Turoldus 114
Tuuk, H.N. van der 66
twin-souls (jodoh) 187-90, 192, 237, 248
Tynyanov, Y. 38, 98-9
type-scene 4, 9, 29, 43-8, 109, 111-22, 124, 132, 145, 185-6, 202-8, 212, 231

Umar Junus 213

Undang-Undang Melaka 21

Vance, E. 76-7, 135, 156
variation within identity 4, 21, 35-52, 120-1, 202

wayang 30, 53, 56, 58-60, 63-4, 77, 79, 89, 186, 231, 246
– stories 4, 53, 101, 109, 132, 218, 231-2
Wayang
– Arjuna 218
– Pandu 218
Wayfarer 75
White, H.V. 122-3, 127
Wilkinson, R.J. 52, 201
Winstedt, R.O. 165, 199-201
wisdom (arif, bijaksana) 4, 55, 57-60, 65-6, 69, 76-80, 83-4, 90, 136, 182-3, 240, see also akal, commemoration, remembrance
Woelders, M.O. 101
writing 18, 44, 55-6, 65, 76, 78-81, 83-7, 89-92, 97-8, 122-3, 131-3, 147, 149, 182, 201, 218, 224, 241, 247-50

yang empunya cerita 53, 57, 59, 90

Zainuddin Mahbub, Datuk 91
Zoetmulder, P.J. 60-1, 63-4
Zubdat al-Haqaiq 81-2

I2048UKWH00008B/425
UKHW041952304426
Pitfield, Milton Keynes, MK11 3LW, UK
Ingram Content Group UK Ltd.
www.ingramcontent.com/pod-product-compliance